Legends of the Kings of Akkade

MESOPOTAMIAN CIVILIZATIONS

General Editor
Jerrold S. Cooper, *Johns Hopkins University*

Editorial Board

Walter Farber, *University of Chicago*
Jean-Pierre Grégoire, *C.N.R.S.*
Piotr Michalowski, *University of Michigan*
Simo Parpola, *University of Helsinki*
Marvin Powell, *Northern Illinois University*
Jack Sasson, *University of North Carolina*
Piotr Steinkeller, *Harvard University*
Marten Stol, *Free University of Amsterdam*
Irene Winter, *Harvard University*

1. *The Lamentation over the Destruction of Sumer and Ur*
   Piotr Michalowski
2. *Schlaf, Kindchen, Schlaf! Mesopotamische Baby-Beschwörungen und -Rituale*
   Walter Farber
3. *Adoption in Old Babylonian Nippur and the Archive of Mannum-mešu-liṣṣur*
   Elizabeth C. Stone and David I. Owen
4. *Third-Millennium Legal and Administrative Texts in the Iraq Museum, Baghdad*
   Piotr Steinkeller and J. N. Postgate
5. *House Most High: The Temples of Ancient Mesopotamia*
   A. R. George
6. *Textes culinaires Mésopotamiens / Mesopotamian Culinary Texts*
   Jean Bottéro
7. *Legends of the Kings of Akkade: The Texts*
   Joan Goodnick Westenholz

Legends of the Kings of Akkade

The Texts

Joan Goodnick Westenholz

Eisenbrauns
Winona Lake, Indiana
1997

Paperback reprint, 2014
ISBN 978-1-57506-311-9

Library of Congress Cataloging-in-Publication Data

Westenholz, Joan Goodnick, 1943–
Legends of the kings of Akkade : the texts / Joan Goodnick Westenholz.
p. cm. — (Mesopotamian civilizations ; 7)
Includes bibliographical references and index.
ISBN 0-931464-85-4 (cloth : alk. paper)
1. Assyro-Babylonian literature. 2. Legends—Iraq—Babylonia.
3. Babylonia—Kings and rulers. I. Title. II. Series.
PJ3725.W47 1996
892′.1—dc21 96-45516
CIP

The paper used in this publication meets the minimum requirements of the American National Standard for Information Sciences—Permanence of Paper for Printed Library Materials, ANSI Z39.48-1984. ♾™

Table of Contents

Acknowledgments vii
Note on Transliteration ix
Concordance of Museum Numbers xi
Concordance of Publication Numbers xi
Abbreviations xii

Chapter 1. Introduction 1
Definition of the Corpus 3
Recovery of the Texts and the History of Scholarship 6
Terminology 16
Poetic Discourse, Orthography, and Grammar 24

Part A: Sargon

Chapter 2. The Sargon "Autobiographies" 33
Text 1. Old Babylonian Fragment: "I, Sargon" 34
Text 2. "The Wisdom of Sargon": The "Birth Legend" of Sargon 36

Chapter 3. Sargon's Rise to Power: Sargon, Ur-Zababa, and Lugalzagesi 51
Text 5. Sumerian-Akkadian Bilingual Exercise Text 52

Chapter 4. *Res Gestae Sargonis* 57
Text 6. "Sargon, the Conquering Hero" 59
Text 7. "Sargon in Foreign Lands" 78
Fragments 92
Text 8. "Sargon, the Lion" 94
Text 9. "King of Battle" 102
Text 9B. Amarna Recension 102
Text 9C. Amarna Fragment 132
Text 9D. Assur Fragment 134
Text 9E. Nineveh Recension 136

Chapter 5. The Sargon Letters 141
Text 10. Nippur Letter 143
Text 11. Ur Letter 148

Part B: Naram-Sin

Chapter 6. Naram-Sin and the Lord of Apišal 173
Text 12. "Naram-Sin and the Lord of Apišal" 173

Chapter 7. Erra and Naram-Sin 189
Text 13. "Erra and Naram-Sin" 189

Chapter 8. Elegy on the Death of Naram-Sin 203
Text 14. "Elegy on the Death of Naram-Sin" 203

Chapter 9. The Great Revolt against Naram-Sin 221
Text 15. The Old Akkadian Exercise 223
Text 16. The Old Babylonian Excerpt Versions 230
Text 16A. Mari Version 231
Text 16B. Geneva Version 238
Text 17. "Gula-AN and the Seventeen Kings against Naram-Sin" 246
Text 19. "The Tenth Battle" 258

Chapter 10. "Naram-Sin and the Enemy Hordes": The "Cuthean Legend" of Naram-Sin 263
Text 20. The Old Babylonian Edition 267
Text 21. The Middle Babylonian Recension 280
Text 22. The Standard Babylonian Recension 294
Introduction 294
Composite Text and Translation 300
Manuscripts and Score 332

Indexes 369
Index of Personal Names 369
Index of Divine Names 370
Index of Geographical and Topographical Names 371
Index of Literary Texts 372
Index of Words Discussed 373
General Index 375

Plates 377

Acknowledgments

The project of an investigative study of Mesopotamian Heroic Epics was conceived in 1984 at the University of Chicago and was begun in 1985–86 with the support of a fellowship from the National Endowment for the Humanities, an agency of the federal government of the United States. The primary goal of this project is to provide a complete annotated edition of all epics of the Akkadian kings. This volume contains the edition of all Akkadian compositions related to the founder of the Akkadian Empire, Sargon of Akkade, and his grandson, Naram-Sin.

The following friends and colleagues have assisted this project by providing advice, collations, tablets, and comments: J. Black, J. Cooper, S. Franke, J.-J. Glassner, S. Izre'el, W. G. Lambert, W. Mayer, A. Rainey, E. Reiner, M. Sigrist, W. Sommerfeld, and N. Veldhuis. Two must be singled out for special thanks. Alan Millard not only informed me of a tablet but also generously supplied me with his copy of the text for publication. Daniel Arnaud was most magnanimous in providing his field photographs and copies of an unpublished text, also for publication. A special word of thanks is also due to Claus Wilcke, who provided his collations at the last minute.

I wish to offer my thanks to the following people and institutions for giving me access to the tablets in their collections: Béatrice André-Salvini, Conservateur des inscriptions of the Département des Antiquités Orientales of the Musée du Louvre; Dominique Charpin and Jean-Marie Durand of the Mission Archéologique de Mari; William W. Hallo, Curator of the Babylonian Collection in the Sterling Memorial Library at Yale University; Åke Sjöberg, Curator of the Tablet Collections in the University Museum, Pennsylvania; Raci Temizel, Director of the Museum of Anatolian Civilizations, Anakara; and Christopher Walker, Assistant Keeper of the Department of Western Asiatic Antiquities of the British Museum. For permission to publish photographs of material from their collections, I would like to thank the Ashmolean Museum, the Trustees of the British Museum; Couvent Saint-Étienne; Musée du Louvre; Staatliche Museen zu Berlin Preußischer Kulturbesitz, Vorderasiatisches Museum; The University Museum (of the University of Pennsylvania); and the Yale Babylonian Collection.

The burden of reading the manuscript was shared by Jerry Cooper and Aage Westenholz. To both of them I owe a debt of gratitude for their solicitude, comments, and suggestions. I hope that they understand my very sincere appreciation of what each has done to bring this volume into being. Aage Westenholz has also provided advice, interest, and untiring help throughout the many years of preparation of this book; it is impossible to footnote each of his numerous contributions. I would also like to take this opportunity to offer my thanks to Lindsey Taylor-Guthartz not only for her superb English editing and proofreading of the manuscript in all its stages but also for her continual help and assistance. I would also like to acknowledge the help that I received from Dalit Weinblatt, who assisted with the graphics necessary to complete the cuneiform copies.

This book has undergone many stages of preparation and various persons have helped me during this period. I am particularly beholden to Phylis Naiman for all she did to bring *Legends of the Kings of Akkade* to book form. To Paul Frandsen and the members of the Carsten Niebuhr Institute at the University of Copenhagen I would like to give full credit for their support and efforts on my behalf. The typesetting of the first edition of the book was made possible thanks to a grant from the Institute.

Finally, I would like to express my appreciation to Jim Eisenbraun of Eisenbrauns for accepting my volume in his series and for adapting it, as well as to Beverly Butrin Fields for her stylistic improvements.

This book was written in various stages, the last stage being in 1993, when it was submitted for publication. Consequently, only the most pertinent references could be added at that time. Two major works that could not be incorporated at the last minute were B. Foster, *Before the Muses* (Bethesda, Md., 1993) and D. Frayne, *Old Akkadian and Gutian Periods (2334–2113 BC)* (Royal Inscriptions of Mesopotamia, Early Periods, vol. 2; Toronto, 1993). While acknowledging my immense debt to my colleagues and friends for their help, I must naturally point out that all responsibility for the interpretations offered in this book and for any errors rests with me alone.

Joan Goodnick Westenholz
Jerusalem, 1996

Note on Transliteration

The numbering and marking of homophones is according to R. Borger, *Assyrisch-babylonische Zeichenliste*, 4th ed. with supplement (AOAT 33/33A; Kevelaer: Butzon & Bercker / Neukirchen-Vluyn: Neukirchener Verlag, 1988).

The following symbols are employed in the transliteration:

[ ]	completely lost
⌜ ⌝	partially lost
⟨ ⟩	omitted by scribe
⟨⟨ ⟩⟩	pleonastically written by scribe
/	alternate reading
//	indented continuation of previous line
:	new line of verse indicated in copy by two "Winkelhaken"
,	beginning of new line of text
!	emended sign
X	illegible sign
x	lost sign
. . .	lost sign(s), number uncertain
[( )]	reconstruction uncertain
/ /	phonemic transcription
*	collations by the author
†	collations by Jeremy Black
+	collations by Brian Lewis
#	collations by Anson Rainey
f	collations by Aage Westenholz

Various writings of the name of the goddess Ištar occur in the literature: ^{d}INANNA, (^{d})U+DAR, ^{d}*Iš-tar.* The second poses the problem of its phonetic realization in the transliteration and translation. This writing originally reflected a syllabic spelling *aš-dar* = ^{c}Aštar, the Old Akkadian pronunciation of the goddess's name. In Ur III and later, this developed into Eštar and from that, irregularly, into Ištar, as early as Old Babylonian. In the latter period, the writing U.DAR was surely taken as a logogram (see discussion by W. G. Lambert, *MARI* 4 [1985] 536), probably even as a single sign, as it certainly was later (Ea II lines 292–94; MSL 14 259; and Aa II/6 iv A 26′–27′, B 2′ff.; MSL 14 296; see A. R.

George, *Iraq* 47 [1995] 222–23 on the later development of the ligature). There is no other evidence for the values of $eš_{18}/iš_8$ or $eš_4/iš_4$ for the Old Akkadian sign written variously as a horizontal, an oblique, or a vertical wedge (personal communication, A. Westenholz; see also M. Krebernik, *ZA* 81 [1991] 135–36). Consequently, I have decided to write U.DAR in the transliteration of the Old Babylonian texts and to translate this logogram as Ištar, since the writers of the legends have not attempted to archaize the script in any other manner.

In general, personal names in the main body of the text and in the translation have been normalized, such as the Old Akkadian kings: Sargon for Śarru-kēn, Maništušu for Maniśtūśu, Naram-Sin for Narām-Sîn/Suyin, as well as the Amorite names, such as Ašduni-erim for Ašdūni-yarīm.

Concordance of Museum Numbers

Museum No.	*Text No.*
A 1252	16A
AO 6702	6
Ash. 1924,2085	22
Bo 1202/z	21A
BM 17215	20B
BM 47449	2
BM 79987	17
BM 120003	13
BM 139965	12
Cairo 48396	9B
CBS 15217	10
IM 52684a+	7
IM 85544	11
K.2021B	22
K.3401+Sm. 2118	2
K.4470	2
K.5418a	22
K.5640	22
K.7249	2
K.8582	22
K.13228	9E
K.13328	22
L.74.225	14
MAH 10829	16
MLC 641	1
MLC 1364	20A
Sm. 2118	2
St. Étienne 150	8B
S.U. 51/67a+	22
TA 1931, 729	15
UM 29-13-688	8A
VAT 7832a	19
VAT 10290	9D
VAT 17166	5
81-2-4, 219	22

Concordance of Publication Numbers

Publication No.	*Text No.*
AfO 13 46ff.	12
AfO 20 16ff.	9E
BiOr 30 357ff.	13
BRM 4 4	1
CT 13 39-41	22
CT 13 42	2
CT 13 43a	2
CT 13 43b	2
CT 13 44	22
CT 46 46	2
EA 359	9B
EA 375	9C
JCS 11 83ff.	20A
JCS 31 229	8A
JCS 33 191ff.	20B
KAV 138	9D
KBo 19 98	21A
MAD 1 172	15
OECT 9 103	22
RA 70 103ff.	16A, 16B, 17
STT 1 30	22
TCL 16 73	3
Thompson, *Gilgamesh*, pl. 34	22
TIM 9 48	7
UET 7 73	11
VAS 12 193	9B
VAS 17 42	19
VAS 24 75	5

Abbreviations

All abbreviations used are those of the *Assyrian Dictionary of the Oriental Institute of the University of Chicago* (Chicago: Oriental Institute, 1956–) and the *Pennsylvania Sumerian Dictionary* (Philadelphia: The University Museum, 1984–), with the following exceptions and additions:

aK — Ignace Jay Gelb and Burkhart Kienast, *Die altakkadischen Königsinschriften des dritten Jahrtausends v. Chr.* (FAOS 7; Stuttgart: Steiner, 1990).

BBVO — Berliner Beiträge zum Vorderen Orient (Berlin: Dietrich Reimer).

CRRAI — Compte rendu de la Rencontre assyriologique internationale.

CTH — Emmanuel Laroche, *Catalogue des Textes Hittites* (Paris: Klincksieck, 1971).

EAE — *Enūma Anu Enlil*, incipit of astrological omen series.

Glassner, *La Chute d'Akkadé* — Jean-Jacques Glassner, *La Chute d'Akkadé: L'événement et sa mémoire* (BBVO 5; Berlin: Reimer, 1986).

Glassner, "Récit" — Jean-Jacques Glassner, "Le Récit autobiographique de Sargon," *RA* 82 (1988) 1–11.

Glassner, "Sargon" — Jean-Jacques Glassner, "Sargon «Roi du Combat»," *RA* 79 (1985) 115–26.

Grayson, RIMA 1 — Albert Kirk Grayson, *Assyrian Rulers of the Third and Second Millennium* BC *(to 1155* BC*)* (The Royal Inscriptions of Mesopotamia, Assyrian Periods 1; Toronto: University of Toronto Press, 1987).

Hecker, *Epik* — Karl Hecker, *Untersuchungen zur akkadischen Epik* (AOAT Sonderreihe 8; Kevelaer: Butzon & Bercker, 1974).

Labat, *Les Religions* — René Labat, *Les Religions du Proche-Orient asiatique* (Paris: Fayard et Denoël, 1970).

Lewis, *Sargon Legend* — Brian Lewis, *The Sargon Legend: A Study of the Akkadian Text and the Tale of the Hero Who Was Exposed at Birth* (ASOR Dissertation Series 4; Cambridge, Mass.: American Schools of Oriental Research, 1980).

Longman, *Autobiography* [1983] Tremper Longman III, *Fictional Akkadian Royal Autobiography: A Generic and Comparative Study.* Ph.D. diss., Yale University, 1983.

Longman, *Autobiography* [1991] Tremper Longman III, *Fictional Akkadian Autobiography: A Generic and Comparative Study* (Winona Lake, Ind.: Eisenbrauns, 1991).

RGTC Répertoire Géographique des Textes Cunéiformes (Beihefte zum Tübinger Atlas des vorderen Orients; Wiesbaden: Reichert, 1974–).

Roberts, *Earliest Semitic Pantheon* J. J. M. Roberts, *The Earliest Semitic Pantheon: A Study of the Semitic Deities Attested in Mesopotamia before Ur III* (Baltimore: Johns Hopkins University Press, 1972).

RSém *Revue Sémitique d'Épigraphie et d'Histoire Ancienne* (Paris).

Sb Sigla of objects in the Louvre excavated in Susa not included in the AO series.

SEb *Studi Eblaiti.* Missione archeologica italiana in Siria, Istituto di Studi del Vicino Oriente, Rome.

Chapter 1

Introduction

In the third millennium B.C.E. a dynasty arose in the hitherto insignificant town of Akkade which, within a few decades, came to exercise not only hegemony over Mesopotamia but also great influence over much of the Near East. It conducted military campaigns over an area stretching from Syria to Iran, and commercial ties linked it to the highlands of Anatolia to the north, the Mediterranean to the west, and the Indus Valley to the east.

The dynasty of Akkade (ca. 2310–2160 B.C.E.)[1] had a decisive impact on the development of the culture and language of Mesopotamia. This was the formative period of Akkadian society, which can in some ways be compared to the Greek and Teutonic heroic ages. For two and one-half millennia, the duration of Mesopotamian history, the Akkadian kings represented the ideal monarchy. Their statues stood in the sanctuaries of the great urban centers, and sacrifices were brought before them.[2] Pilgrimages to Akkade were made by kings as

[1] Traditionally dated at 2334–2154 B.C.E. but more recently dated at 2310–2160 B.C.E., based on a reevaluation of the lengths of the individual reigns of Sargon and Naram-Sin; see B. R. Foster, *Umma in the Sargonic Period* (Memoirs of the Connecticut Academy of Arts and Sciences 20; Hamden, Conn., 1982) 152–56. For a recent reassessment of all opinions on the subject, see J. Boese, "Zur absoluten Chronologie der Akkad-Zeit," *WZKM* 74 (1982) 33–55.

[2] Note the references collected in H. Hirsch, "Die Inschriften der Könige von Agade" (*AfO* 20 [1963] 5, 16, 24), concerning offerings to deified Sargon, Maništušu, and Naram-Sin in Ur III. For the existence of statues of Sargonic kings in Old Babylonian Ur, see D. Loding, "Old Babylonian Texts from Ur," *JCS* 28 (1976) no. 11 ii 7. In Old Babylonian Nippur, there were apparently many statues standing in the Ekur; note the following references: (1) the colophon on the Sammeltafel CBS 13972 (= PBS 5 34 + 15 41) left edge: [. . . S]ar-ru-GI Rí-mu-uš ⸢Ma-an-iš⸣-[tu-s]u šà É-kur-⸢ra⸣ a-na-me-a-bi '[inscriptions] of Sargon, Rimuš, and Maništušu as many as were in the Ekur', for which now see *aK* 139ff.; (2) the colophon on N 3539 vii (P. Michalowski, "New Sources concerning the Reign of Naram-Sin," *JCS* 32 [1980] 239): mu-sar-ra ti-x-bi-ni Rí-mu-uš-kam murub$_4$?? kisal??-ka al-gar šà kisal É-kur-ra 'inscriptions . . . of Rimuš set up in the courtyard(?), in the courtyard of the Ekur'; (3) the subscripts to individual

diverse as Šamši-Adad I of Assyria (1813–1781 B.C.E.)[3] and Nabonidus, the last Babylonian king (555–539 B.C.E.).[4] The titulary of the Assyrian kings, two of whom even bore the name of Sargon, imitated the Sargonic titulary, expressing conscious Assyrian emulation of the world dominion of the Sargonic empire.[5] The late Babylonians concerned themselves with discovering the archeological remains of the Sargonic period.[6]

The most impressive legacy of the dynasty of Akkade was the widespread and popular legends of its kings. Their deeds stirred the imagination of all the surrounding cultures, inspiring legends that were handed down not only in Akkadian but also in Sumerian and Hittite. The accomplishments of the Akkadian dynasty were told and retold throughout the generations and were magnified and embellished with each retelling. This saga and its heroes soon became the subject of a tradition of folklore, then of literature, beginning directly after the events themselves. Folktale motifs such as that of the exposed child were added,[7] and at the same time, the stories were constantly simplified and edited.

---

sections mu-sar-ra alan-na 'inscription of his statue' (*aK* 165: "Sargon C 2" Kolophone A and Bm; p. 178: "Sargon C 6" V11:35; p. 186: "Sargon C 12" Kolophon). In Old Babylonian Mari, note the *kispu* offerings to the *lamassātu*-statues of Sargon and Naram-Sin; see M. Birot, "Fragment de rituel de Mari relatif au *kispum*," *Death in Mesopotamia* (CRRAI 26; Copenhagen, 1980) 139–50. Middle Babylonian evidence comes from the statues and stelae taken as booty by Šutruk-Naḫḫunte from Babylonian cities to Susa. Two of the statues of Maništūsu are inscribed as coming from Akkade (Sb 47 + Sb 9099; see P. Amiet, *L'Art d'Agadé* [Paris, 1976] no. 13) and from Ešnunna (Sb 49; see ibid., no. 11). Neo-Babylonian evidence of offerings to the statues of Sargon and Naram-Sin comes from royal inscriptions (W. G. Lambert, "A New Source for the Reign of Nabonidus," *AfO* 22 [1968–69] 1ff.), as well as from administrative texts (see 8 texts listed in D. Kennedy, "Realia," *RA* 63 [1969] 79, to which can be added CT 55 469:13, CT 56 442:23, CT 57 256:4; [I would like to thank Matt Stolper for these references]). Neo-Assyrian evidence speaks of statues of Sargon and Naram-Sin; see W. H. P. Römer, "Einige Bemerkungen zum dämonischen Gotte ^{d}Kūbu(m)," *Symbolae Böhl* (Leiden, 1973) 310–19, ND 4394.

3 For the pilgrimage of Šamši-Adad I, see ARM 1 36:5; for the pilgrimage of his son, Yasmaḫ-Adad, see ARM 5 34:5.

4 Royal inscriptions of Nabonidus that deal with his excavation of the Eulmaš in Akkade are Nabonid Zylinder III 4 and Nabonid Tafel-Fragment VI 1 according to numbering of P.-R. Berger, *Die neubabylonischen Königsinschriften* (AOAT 4/1; Neukirchen-Vluyn/Kevelaer, 1973).

5 For example, the titulary of Šamši-Adad in A.4509 (D. Charpin, "Inscriptions votives d'époque assyrienne," *MARI* 3 [1984] 44–45): lugal kalag-ga lugal A-ga-dè^{ki}. For a discussion of his titulary, see ibid., 49–50. To be added to his titles is lugal kiš found in AO 4628; see Grayson, RIMA 1, 60. For a discussion of Šamši-Adad's patterning his aspirations to world dominion on the dynasty of Akkad, see M. Birot, "Fragment de rituel de Mari," 145–49.

6 G. Goossens, "Les Recherches historiques a l'époque néo-babylonienne," *RA* 42 (1948) 149–59.

7 This is a simplistic evaluation of the development. Relationships between folklore analogues and legends embedded in literary versions are not obvious; see L. Dégh, "Processes of Legend Formation," *IV International Congress for Folk-Narrative Research in Athens (1.9–6.9 1964)* (ed. G. Megas; 1965) 77–87; J. Krzyzanowski, "Legend in Literature and Folklore," *Fabula* 9 (1967) 111–17; A. Renoir, "Oral Theme and Written

The feats and deeds of the entire dynasty were telescoped and assigned to the two most prominent of its five members—Sargon, the founder of the empire (ca. 2310–2273 B.C.E.), and his grandson and third successor, Naram-Sin (ca. 2246–2190 B.C.E.).[8]

The present volume offers an annotated edition of all the known legends of the Akkadian kings. It contains transliterations and translations of the texts, as well as philological commentaries. Each text is discussed in terms of its findspot, its external appearance, its orthography, and its language, and an attempt is made to describe its stylistic peculiarities.

A future volume is planned that will contain a literary-critical evaluation of all the legendary compositions as a whole, including a structural analysis of their content and form, an investigation of their historical background, and an interpretation of their purpose and the needs they fulfilled. The purpose of the volume will be to explain the raison d'être of these works and to develop a definition of legendary literature based on criteria inherent in the literary form, historical content, and cultural values of the texts themselves.

Definition of the Corpus

The corpus consists of all the scattered texts dealing with the heroic deeds of the kings of Akkade. Some of these works concentrate on the glories of the age, others on its catastrophic end. The selection of texts in this volume has thus been made on the basis of content rather than form, function, or language, ignoring current attempts at genre categorization. Actual inscriptions of the kings of Akkade (or copies of them) are excluded, as are historiographic documents such as the Sumerian King List, various chronicles, and omens.[9]

Texts," *Neuphilologische Mitteilungen* 77 (1976) 337–46. For comparisons between folktales and legends, see M. Lüthi, "Aspects of the *Märchen* and the Legend," *Folklore Genres* (ed. D. Ben-Amos; Austin, 1976) 17–33. For a convenient survey of hero pattern studies in which the schemes of von Hahn, Rank, Raglan, Campbell, and Propp are outlined and compared, see A. Taylor, "The Biographical Pattern in Traditional Narrative," *Journal of the Folklore Institute* 1 (1964) 114–29. Another approach is that of Dutch folklorist J. de Vries, *Heroic Song and Heroic Legend* (London, 1963) 210–26.

[8] See note 1. As far as we know, the deeds of Maništušu were known down to Neo-Babylonian times, but he himself was never a legendary figure. Evidence of familiarity with his existence is provided by the learned Neo-Babylonian forgery of the cruciform monument, of which there has now been found in Sippar a new text that begins: *a-na-ku Man-nu-iš-tu-us-su* DUMU LUGAL.GI.NA (F. N. H. Al-Rawi and A. R. George, "Tablets from the Sippar Library, III: Two Royal Counterfeits," *Iraq* 56 [1994] 139–48).

[9] For the Sumerian King List, see T. Jacobsen, *The Sumerian King List* (AS 11; Chicago, 1939). For the most recent edition of the chronicles, see Grayson, *Chronicles*. Unfortunately, the omens concerning the Sargonic kings are scattered among various publications: L. W. King, *Chronicles concerning Early Babylonian Kings* (London, 1907) 2.25–45; F. Thureau-Dangin, "Humbaba," *RA* 22 (1925) 23–26; E. Weidner, "Historisches Material in der babylonischen Omina-Literatur," *MAOG* 4 (1928–29) 230–34; J. Nougayrol,

Throughout this volume, the texts of the corpus are referred to by numbers assigned to them as follows:

Part A: Sargon

The Sargon "Autobiographies"

(**1**) BRM 4 4 (OB Akkadian). "I, Sargon." See pp. 34–35.

(**2**) CT 13 42, 43a, and 43b; CT 46 46 (SB Akkadian). This text is generally known as the "Sargon Birth Legend." See pp. 36–49.

Sargon's Rise to Power

(**3**) TCL 16 73 (OB Sumerian). Edited by J. Cooper and W. Heimpel in "The Sumerian Sargon Legend," *JAOS* 103 (1983) 67–82. Not included in the present volume.[10]

(**4**) 3N-T296 (OB Sumerian). Edited by J. Cooper and W. Heimpel, ibid. Not included in the present volume.

(**5**) VAS 24 75 (OB/MB Sumerian-Akkadian bilingual). See pp. 52–55.

Res Gestae Sargonis

(**6**) J. Nougayrol, "Un Chef d'oeuvre inédit de la littérature babylonienne," *RA* 45 (1951) 169–83 (OB Akkadian). "Sargon, the Conquering Hero." See pp. 59–77.

(**7**) TIM 9 48 (OB Akkadian). "Sargon in Foreign Lands." See pp. 78–93.

(**8**) "Sargon, the Lion"

(**8A**) M. Ellis, "Akkadian Literary Texts and Fragments in the University Museum," *JCS* 31 (1979) 229, no. 9 (OB/MB Akkadian). See pp. 94–101.

(**8B**) St. Étienne 150, unpublished (OB/MB Akkadian). See pp. 94–101.

(**9**) "King of Battle"

(**9A**) KBo 3 9, 10; 12 1; 13 46; 22 6; KUB 48 98 (Late Hittite, Empire period); cf. H. G. Güterbock, "Ein neues Bruchstück der Sargon-Erzählung 'König der Schlacht,'" *MDOG* 101 (1969) 14–26. The number of copies as well as compositions represented by these six fragments is uncertain. Not included in the present volume.

(**9B**) EA 359 (MB peripheral Akkadian). See pp. 102–31.

"Note sur la place des 'présages historiques' dans l'extispicine babylonienne," *École Pratique des Hautes Études, 5e* section, *Annuaire* (1944–45) 1–41; A. Goetze, "Historical Allusions in Old Babylonian Omen Texts," *JCS* 1 (1947) 253–65; J. Nougayrol; "Textes Religieux (II)," *RA* 66 (1972) 143–45; E. Reiner, "New Light on Some Historical Omens," *Anatolian Studies Presented to H. G. Güterbock* (ed. K. Bittel et al.; Istanbul, 1974) 257–61; U. Jeyes, *Old Babylonian Extispicy* (Istanbul/Leiden, 1989) no. 14 rev. 27′, no. 19:8. Moreover, there exist omina concerning these kings that are still unpublished.

[10] This text as well as nos. 4, 9A, and 23 are not included in this volume due to limitations of space and the fact that they have received competent treatment recently. Texts **18** and **21B** are not included because of the author's lack of competence in Hittite.

(**9C**) EA 375 (MB peripheral Akkadian). See pp. 132–33.
(**9D**) KAV 138 (SB Akkadian). See pp. 134–35.
(**9E**) W. G. Lambert, "A New Fragment of the King of Battle," *AfO* 20 (1963) 161–62 (SB Akkadian). See pp. 136–39.

The Sargon Letters

(**10**) CBS 15217, unpublished (OB Akkadian). See pp. 143–47.
(**11**) UET 7 73 (OB Akkadian). See pp. 148–69.

Part B: Naram-Sin

(**12**) H. G. Güterbock, "Bruchstück eines altbabylonischen Naram-Sin-Epos," *AfO* 13 (1939–40) 46–49 (OB Akkadian). "Naram-Sin and the Lord of Apišal." See pp. 173–87.
(**13**) W. G. Lambert, "Studies in Nergal," *BiOr* 30 (1973) 357–63 (OB Akkadian). "Erra and Naram-Sin." See pp. 189–201.
(**14**) L74.225, unpublished (OB Akkadian). "Elegy on the Death of Naram-Sin." See pp. 203–20.

The Great Revolt against Naram-Sin

(**15**) MAD 1 172 (Old Akkadian). See pp. 223–29.
(**16A**) A 1252; cf. A. K. Grayson and E. Sollberger, "L'Insurrection générale contre Narām-Suen," *RA* 70 (1976) 103–28 (OB Akkadian). See pp. 231–37.
(**16B**) MAH 10829; cf. ibid. (OB Akkadian). See pp. 238–45.
(**17**) BM 79987; cf. ibid. (OB Akkadian). See pp. 246–57.
(**18**) KBo 3 13 (Middle Hittite[?]). Cf. CTH 311 A. Not included in the present volume.
(**19**) VAS 17 42 (OB Akkadian). See pp. 258–61.

Naram-Sin and the Enemy Hordes

(**20A**) J. J. Finkelstein, "The So-Called Old Babylonian Kutha Legend," *JCS* 11 (1957) 83–88 (OB Akkadian). See pp. 267–78.
(**20B**) C. B. F. Walker, "The Second Tablet of *ṭupšenna pitema*: An Old Babylonian Naram-Sin Legend," *JCS* 33 (1981) 191–95 (OB Akkadian). See pp. 278–79.
(**21A**) KBo 19 98 (MB peripheral Akkadian, period of Hittite Middle Kingdom). See pp. 280–93.
(**21B**) (1) KBo 3 18 + 19; (2) KBo 3 16 + KUB 31 1 + Bo 1309; (3) KBo 3 17; (4) KBo 3 20; (5) KBo 22 85 (Middle Hittite[?]). Cf. CTH 311 B. Not included in the present volume.
(**22**) O. Gurney, "The Cuthean Legend of Naram-Sin," *AnSt* 5 (1955) 93–113 (SB Akkadian). See pp. 294–368.

The Downfall of Akkade

(**23**) J. Cooper, *The Curse of Agade* (Baltimore: Johns Hopkins University Press, 1983); cf. also P. Attinger, "Remarques à propos de la 'Malédiction d'Accad,'" *RA* 78 (1984) 99–121 (OB Sumerian). Not included in the present volume.

In form, these texts display great diversity. They vary from panegyric poetry to narrative poetry and prose, with monologues and dialogues more prevalent than third-person narratives. Some texts seem to be early attempts at writing down oral legends, while others are the finished products of a long literary development; some are crude writing exercises, while others are elegant library exemplars.

In content, the texts are equally varied, a fact that has occasioned much discussion of genre definition (see further pp. 16–21). Some point out a moral or theological lesson to be learned from the fates of the exceptional men they celebrate.

This corpus is fragmentary and limited by the accidents of discovery and cannot necessarily be assumed to be representative. New discoveries could well invalidate assertions made on the basis of the present assemblage of texts.

In the presentation of the texts, the term *edition* refers to the earliest known appearance of a particular legend in written form. The term *version* refers to different contemporary versions of the same text, while *recension* refers to a later reworking of a particular legend known from earlier written texts.

Recovery of the Texts and the History of Scholarship

The history of the discovery, decipherment, transliteration, and translation of this corpus mirrors that of the development of Assyriology.[11]

The first publications and attempts to understand the "Sargon Birth Legend" (text **2**) belong to the dawn of cuneiform studies in the third quarter of the nineteenth century. In 1870 pioneer Assyriologist George Smith identified a "Tablet of Sargina I, King of Agane" and offered a translation and treatment of the text in 1872. By the end of third quarter of the century, there were five different translations of the text.[12] These translations reflected contemporary scholars' inexperience with the cuneiform script, bewilderment with the Akkadian language, and ignorance of Mesopotamian history and culture. These factors made decipherment of new texts an exploration of unfamiliar territory, a terra incognita.

1870

H. C. Rawlinson and G. Smith, *The Cuneiform Inscriptions of Western Asia*, vol. 3. London: Bowler. Pl. 4, no. 7. K.3401 (text **2**: "Sargon Birth Legend"). *Copy.*

[11] The following is not an exhaustive inventory of every copy, transliteration, and translation of the texts in the corpus over the past 120 years but just an annotated catalogue of the major contributions.

[12] For a discussion of the detailed history of the publication of the texts, see Lewis, *Sargon Legend*, 3–7, as well as Glassner, "Récit."

1872

G. Smith, "Early History of Babylonia." *Transactions of the Society of Biblical Archaeology* 1. Pp. 46–47 (text **2**: "Sargon Birth Legend"). *Translation.*

H. F. Talbot, "A Fragment of Ancient Assyrian Mythology." *Transactions of the Society of Biblical Archaeology* 1. Pp. 271–80 (text **2**: "Sargon Birth Legend"). *Copy, transcription, and translation of col. i 1–12.*

The last quarter of the nineteenth century saw the publication of the "Sargon Birth Legend" in every anthology of historical and/or literary texts from Assyria and Babylonia. In addition, another composition came to light, though the royal protagonist who was the subject of the composition continued to be unknown for almost a century: the so-called "Cuthean Legend" (text **22**). Again, it was George Smith who made the first translation of this piece: "a legend of creation stated to be copied from a tablet at Cutha" (1876: 102). It was for some years known as the Cuthean Legend of the Creation, which was understood as having been "put in the mouth of the god Nergal, who was supposed to be waging war against the brood of Tiamat; and it was assumed that Nergal took the place of Marduk in accordance with local tradition at Cuthah" (King 1902: 140 n. 1). In his catalogue of the cuneiform tablets of the British Museum, drawn up in 1891, Carl Bezold listed the "Cuthean Legend" as "a mythological legend concerning the deeds and fortunes of an ancient Babylonian(?) king, his religious ceremonies and an oracle communicated to him in the city of Cuthah by means of an inscription" (1891: 715). He added a footnote concerning the king: "perhaps that king who is supposed to have escaped the Deluge." This discovery stimulated others to publish similar tales. In 1898 Vincent Scheil published the Old Babylonian version of the "Cuthean Legend" (text **20A**) as a text of King Tukulti bêl niši, and Heinrich Zimmern related it to the Standard Babylonian pieces (text **22**). Ultimately, it was Peter Jensen who recognized not only that K.8582 was another piece of the "Cuthean Legend" but also that 81-2-4, 219 might be related (Jensen 1900: 553). For the next half century, the former text was ignored or attached to the "Gilgameš Epic," while the latter was treated as a separate legend of Naram-Sin (see below).

1876

G. Smith, *The Chaldean Account of Genesis, Containing the Description of the Creation, the Fall of Man, the Deluge, the Tower of Babel, the Times of the Patriarchs, and Nimrod; Babylonian Fables, and the Legends of the Gods; from the Cuneiform Inscriptions.* London: Sampson, Low, Marston, Searle, and Rivington. Pp. 102–6, K.5418a and K.5640 (text **22**: SB "Cuthean Legend"). *Translation.*

1887

S. A. Smith, *Miscellaneous Assyrian Texts of the British Museum.* Leipzig: Edward Pfeiffer. Pls. 6–7. K.5640 (text **22**: SB "Cuthean Legend"). *Copy and notes.*

1891

C. Bezold, *Catalogue of the Cuneiform Tablets in the Kuyunjik Collection*, vol. 2. London: Harrison and Sons. P. 715, K.5418a (text **22**: SB "Cuthean Legend"). *Copy of lines 149–63.*

P. Haupt, *Das babylonische Nimrodepos.* Leipzig: Hinrichs. P. 78, no. 42 K.8582 (text **22**: SB "Cuthean Legend"). *Copy.*

1892

H. Winckler, "Legende Sargons von Agane." *Historische Texte altbabylonischer Herrscher.* KB 3. Berlin: Reuther & Reichard. Pp. 100–103 (text **2**: "Sargon Birth Legend"). *Transliteration and translation.*

1894

H. Winckler, *Sammlung von Keilschrifttexten, vol. 2: Texte verschiedenen Inhalts.* Leipzig: Edward Pfeiffer. Pls. 70–71. K.5418a (text **22**: SB "Cuthean Legend"). *Copy.*

1896

T. G. Pinches, "Assyriological Gleanings." *PSBA* 18. P. 257, BM 47449 (text **2**: NB "Sargon Birth Legend." *Copy, transliteration, and translation.*

1898

V. Scheil, "Le Roi Tukulti bêl niši." *RT* 20. Pp. 65ff., MLC 1364 (text **20A**: OB "Cuthean Legend"). *NA copy, transliteration, and translation of one col.*

H. Zimmern, "'König Tukulti bêl niši' und die 'kuthäische Schöpfungslegende'." *ZA* 12. Pp. 317–30, K.5418a and K.5640 (text **22**: SB "Cuthean Legend"). *Transliteration and translation; relates it to Old Babylonian.*

A. Boissier, "Notes d'Assyriologie," *RSém* 6. Pp. 357ff., 81-2-4, 219 (text **22**: SB "Cuthean Legend"). *Transcription.*

1900

P. Jensen, *Assyrisch-babylonische Mythen und Epen.* KB 6/1. Berlin: Reuther & Reichard. Pp. 290–301 and 548–58, K.5418a, K.5640, K.8582, and MLC 1364 (texts **20A**, **22**: SB and OB "Cuthean Legends"). *Transliteration, translation, and extensive notes.*

The first quarter of the twentieth century witnessed the publication of new copies and transliterations of the "Sargon Birth Legend" and the "Cuthean Legend." In 1901 Leonard King published the definitive copies of legends of early kings: "Legend of an Ancient King of Cuthah," K.5418a and K.5640; "Legend of Sargon, King of Agade," K.3401 + S. 2118, K.4470, BM 47449; and "Legend of Naram-Sin, the Son of Sargon," 81-2-4, 219. In 1907 he published his treatment of the "Sargon Birth Legend." In the following decades, the "Sargon Birth Legend" received much attention in comparative studies with other literary traditions.[13] A fragment containing the story of Sargon's birth and rise to power in the Sumerian language (text **3**) was found in excavations at Warka and was published in 1916.

A most exciting discovery was made in the German excavations at Tell el-Amarna in 1913, where a tablet recounting the "King of Battle Epic" (text **9B**) was found. It was immediately treated by Otto Schroeder, who published very clear photographs, a translation, and a copy one year later. He assumed that the text contained an account of the campaign of an Egyptian king called 'the warlord' (*šar tamḫāri*) against the Syrian town of Bor-Anath. Other translations established Sargon as the protagonist, and in 1922 Ernst Weidner presented the definitive study of the composition in his monograph. In 1920 Schroeder identified an Assyrian edition of the "King of Battle Epic" among the texts excavated at Aššur (text **9D**).

German excavations at the Hittite capital of Hattuša (modern Boghazköy in Turkey) unearthed pieces of the Hittite versions of legends about both Sargon and Naram-Sin: "King of Battle" (text **9A**), the "Revolt of the 17 Kings against Naram-Sin" (text **18**) and the Hittite version of the "Cuthean Legend" (text **21B**). Various fragments were published in 1918 and 1923.

From the nineteenth-century excavations at Nippur, fragments of historical inscriptions of Sargon and Naram-Sin that were to turn into the first pieces of the Sumerian version of the "Downfall of Akkade" (text **23**) were published in 1922.

In 1919 Alfred Boissier edited a tablet giving an account of the revolt against Naram-Sin (text **16B**). The last piece to be published in this productive period was furnished by Albert Clay; it was the Old Babylonian fragment apparently containing the beginning of a Sargon autobiography (text **1**: "I, Sargon"). Thus, by 1925 the major compositions were known, and the first period of publication ended.

1901

L. W. King, *Cuneiform Texts from Babylonian Tablets in the British Museum*, vol. 13. London: British Museum. Nos. 39–40 K.5418a; 41 K.5640; 42 K.3401 + Sm 2118; 43 K.4470, BM 47449; 44 81-2-4, 219 (texts **2**, **22**: "Sargon Birth Legend," "SB Cuthean Legend"). *Copy.*

1902

L. W. King, *The Seven Tablets of Creation*. London: Luzac. Vol. I, 140–55, Text VI. The "Cuthean Legend of the Creation" K.4418a and K.5640 (text **22**). *Transliteration and translation.*

[13] The Sargon tale was first used in the studies of the French folklorists, e.g., E. Cosquin, "Le Lait de la Mère et le Coffre Flottant," *Revue des Questions Historiques* 83 (1908) 353–425; I. Lévi, "Le Lait de la Mère et le Coffre Flottant," *Revue des Études Juives* 59 (1910) 1–13. Its application to psychoanalytic interpretations of cultural phenomena can be found in O. Rank, *The Myth of the Birth of the Hero and Other Writings* (ed. P. Freund; New York, 1959 [first appeared 1909]). For further references, see Lewis, *Sargon Legend*, 4ff., 149; Glassner, "Récit," 2–3.

1907

L. W. King, *Chronicles Concerning Early Babylonian Kings, Including Records of the Early History of the Kassites and the Country of the Sea, vol. 2: Texts and Translations*. London: Luzac. Pp. 87ff. "The Legend of Sargon, King of Agade" (text **2**). *Cuneiform type-print, transliteration, translation, and notes.*

O. Weber, *Die Literatur der Babylonier und Assyrer*. Leipzig: Hinrichs. Pp. 202–5, "Cuthean Legend"; 206–7, "Sargon Birth Legend" (texts **22**, **2**). *Translation and notes.*

1914

O. Schroeder, "Die beiden neuen Tafeln." *MDOG* 55 (1914) 39–45, EA 359 (text **9B**: "King of Battle"). *Photo, transliteration, and translation.*

1915

O. Schroeder, *Die Tontafeln von El-Amarna*, vol. 2. Vorderasiatische Schriftdenkmäler der königlichen Museen zu Berlin 12. Leipzig: Hinrichs. No. 193 EA 359 (text **9B**: "King of Battle"). *Copy.*

1916

V. Scheil, "Nouveaux renseignements sur Šarrukin d'après un texte sumérien." *RA* 13 (1916) 175–79, AO 7673 (text **3**: "Sargon's Rise to Power"). *Copy, transliteration, translation, and introduction.*

1918, 1923

H. H. Figulla, *Keilschrifttexte aus Boghazköi*, vol. 3. WVDOG 30. Leipzig: Hinrichs. Nos. 9, 10, 16, 17, 18, 19, 20 (texts **9A**, **18**, **21B**: Hittite "King of Battle" fragments, Hittite "Revolt of the 17 Kings," Hittite "Cuthean Legend" fragments). *Copy.*

1919

A. Boissier, "Inscription de Narâm-Sin." *RA* 16. Pp. 157–64, MAH 10829 (text **16B**: "The Great Revolt against Naram-Sin"). *Copy, transliteration, and translation.*

1920

O. Schroeder, *Keilschrifttexte aus Assur verschiedenen Inhalts*. Leipzig: Hinrichs. No. 138, VAT 10230 (text **9D**: "King of Battle"). *Copy.*

1922

E. Weidner, *Zug Sargons von Akkad nach Kleinasier*. BoSt 6. Leipzig: Hinrichs. EA 359, VAT 10290 (text **9B**: "King of Battle"). *Transliteration, translation, and treatment.*

E. Forrer, *Die Boghazköi-Texte in Umschrift*, WVDOG 42. Leipzig: Hinrichs. Nos. 1–5 (texts **9A**, **18**, **21B**: Hittite "King of Battle" fragments, Hittite

"Revolt of the 17 Kings," Hittite "Cuthean Legend" fragments). *Transliteration, translation, and treatment.*

A. Clay, *Epics, Hymns, Omens, and Other Texts.* BRM 4. New Haven: Yale University Press. No. 4, MLC 641 (text **1**: "I, Sargon"). *Copy.*

L. Legrain, *Historical Fragments.* PBS 13. Philadelphia: University Museum. Nos. 15, 43, 47 (text **23**: "Curse of Agade"). *Copy.*

The quarter century from 1925 to 1950 saw few publications of new texts, but the earlier discoveries motivated the only scholar capable of treating the Akkadian, Sumerian, and Hittite material: Hans Güterbock. He published his epoch-making contribution to the study of all the legendary texts in two parts in 1934 and 1938. Later, he found among Pinches' copies another text of Naram-Sin, "Naram-Sin and the Lord of Apišal" (text **12**), which he published in 1939–40.

Between the two world wars, several excavations were undertaken in the Near East and many tablets were discovered, though there was a considerable time lapse between discovery and publication. In 1931 an Old Akkadian literary tablet concerning Naram-Sin (text **15**) was found, and it was finally published in 1961. During the fifth campaign at Mari in 1937, a text concerning Naram-Sin (text **16A**) was discovered, but its publication was delayed until 1976. In one of the campaigns at Ur undertaken during the 1920s and 1930s, the Sargon letter was recovered, but the copy did not appear until 1974.

1934

H. G. Güterbock, "Die historische Tradition und ihre literarische Gestaltung bei Babyloniern und Hethitern bis 1200." *ZA* 42. Pp. 1–91.

1938

H. G. Güterbock, "Die historische Tradition und ihre literarische Gestaltung bei Babyloniern und Hethitern bis 1200." *ZA* 44. Pp. 45–145.

1939–40

H. G. Güterbock, "Bruchstück eines altbabylonischen Naram-Sin Epos." *AfO* 13. Pp. 46–49 (text **12**).

The second half of the twentieth century ushered in a second period of publication of many related texts and fragments containing historical legends of the Akkadian kings. Excavations undertaken at sites in Iraq and Turkey resulted in the discovery of new tablets. From Sultantepe in Turkey came the key text of the "Cuthean Legend" that confirmed its attribution to Naram-Sin. Oliver Gurney then edited all of the known texts and presented a unified text. Consequently, Jacob Finkelstein was enabled to republish the Old Babylonian version of the "Cuthean Legend" with a new copy of the whole text, both obverse and reverse. Excavations were resumed at Boghazköy and new Hittite fragments were found. In 1967 an Akkadian text concerning Naram-Sin was discovered there. The text, inscribed on a prism, was published by Heinrich

Otten in 1970 (text **21A**). Additional Akkadian and Sumerian texts were discovered in the heartland of Mesopotamia. From Tell Harmal in Iraq came an Akkadian Sargon text (text **7**), and more recently, at Larsa, the French excavated a prism with a text extolling Naram-Sin (text **14**). During the third season at Nippur, a tablet containing a Sumerian version of the Sargon legend was unearthed (text **4**). Other tablets were uncovered in museum collections. In the Louvre, Jean Nougayrol found a complete Sargon text (text **6**). The British Museum was and is a constant source of additional texts. In 1963 Wilfred G. Lambert found a Kuyunjik version of the "King of Battle" (text **9D**), in 1965 a fragment of the "Sargon Birth Legend" (text **2**), and in 1973 a text concerning Naram-Sin and Erra (text **13**). In 1976 Kirk Grayson and Edmond Sollberger published a tablet from the British Museum, BM 79987 (text **17**: "The Great Revolt against Naram-Sin"), together with a Mari text (text **16A**: "The Great Revolt against Naram-Sin"), and analyzed them in relation to the Boissier text published in 1919. In 1981 Christopher Walker located a fragment of a second tablet of the Old Babylonian version of the "Cuthean Legend" in the British Museum (text **20B**). In addition, Lambert identified two small fragments of the "Cuthean Legend" in the Kuyunjik collection of the British Museum and told me of their existence. In the Vorderasiatisches Museum in Berlin, two fragments were also discovered by Jan van Dijk. He published one as VAS 17 no. 42, an Old Babylonian exercise concerning Naram-Sin (text **19**: "The Great Revolt against Naram-Sin") and the second as VAS 24 no. 75, a bilingual exercise related to the "Sumerian Sargon Legend" (text **5**: "Sargon's Rise to Power"). In the University Museum of the University of Pennsylvania, Maria Ellis found another historical legend. On the basis of a parallel text found by Alan Millard in the collection of St. Etienne in Jerusalem and made available by him for publication here, this text can now be identified as a text about Sargon (text **8**: "Sargon, the Lion"). In addition to Gurney's primary edition of the "Cuthean Legend," three major reeditions of earlier known texts were completed: Anson Rainey's editions of the Amarna text of the "King of Battle," Brian Lewis's edition of the "Sargon Birth Legend," and Jerry Cooper's edition of "The Curse of Agade." During this period, fictive letters of Sargon were first found and placed beside the narratives as other vehicles for the transmission of legendary stories. In 1974 Oliver Gurney published such a letter from Ur (text **10**), and Stephen Lieberman located another from Nippur in the collection of the University Museum (text **11**).

1951

J. Nougayrol, "Un Chef-d'oeuvre inédit de la littérature babylonienne." *RA* 45. Pp. 169–83, AO 6702 (text **6**: "Sargon, the Conquering Hero"). *Copy, transliteration, and translation.*

1955

O. Gurney, "The Cuthean Legend of Naram-Sin." *AnSt* 5. Pp. 93–113, S.U. 51/67a+ (text **22**). *Transliteration, translation, and treatment.*

1957

J. J. A. van Dijk, "Textes du Musée de Baghdad." *Sumer* 13. P. 66, pls. 16–19 IM 52684+. Republished in *Cuneiform Texts of Varying Content,* Texts in the Iraq Museum 9. Leiden: Brill, 1976. No. 48 (text **7**: "Sargon in Foreign Lands"). *Copy.*

J. J. Finkelstein, "The So-Called Old Babylonian Kutha Legend." *JCS* 11. Pp. 83–88, MLC 1364 (text **20A**: "Cuthean Legend"). *Old Babylonian copy, transliteration, translation, and treatment.*

J. J. Finkelstein and O. Gurney, *The Sultantepe Tablets,* vol. 1. London: British Institute of Archaeology at Ankara. Nos. 30–31 S.U. 51/67a+ (text **22**: "Cuthean Legend"). *Copy.*

1961

I. J. Gelb, *Sargonic Texts from the Diyala Region.* Materials for the Assyrian Dictionary 1. 2d ed. Chicago: University of Chicago Press. No. 172 TA 1931–729 (text **15**: "The Great Revolt against Naram-Sin"). *Transliteration.*

1963

W. G. Lambert, "A New Fragment of the King of Battle." *AfO* 20. Pp. 161–62, K.13228 (text **9E**: "King of Battle"). *Copy, transliteration, and translation.*

H. Otten, *Texte aus Stadtplanquadrat L/18,* vol. 1. KBo 12. WVDOG 77. Berlin: Gebr. Mann. No. 1 Bo 110/t (text **9A**: Hittite "King of Battle"). *Copy.*

1965

W. G. Lambert, *Cuneiform Texts from Babylonian Tablets in the British Museum,* vol. 46. London: British Museum. No. 46 K.7249 (text **2**: "Sargon Birth Legend"). *Copy.*

1967

H. Otten, *Texte aus Stadtplanquadrat L/18,* vol. 2. KBo 13. WVDOG 78. Berlin: Gebr. Mann. No. 46 Bo 624/u (text **9A**: Hittite "King of Battle"). *Copy.*

1969

H. G. Güterbock, "Ein neues Bruchstück der Sargon-Erzählung 'König der Schlacht.'" *MDOG* 101. Pp. 14–26, Bo 68/28. Later republished in KBo 22 (text **9A**: Hittite "King of Battle"). *Photo, transliteration, translation, and treatment.*

1970

H. Otten, *Aus dem Bezirk des grossen Tempels.* KBo 19. WVDOG 84. Berlin: Gebr. Mann. No. 98 Bo 1202/z (text **21A**: "Cuthean Legend"). *Copy.*

A. Rainey, *El Amarna Tablets 359-379.* AOAT 8. Kevelaer: Butzon & Bercker / Neukirchen-Vluyn: Neukirchener Verlag. Pp. 6–11, EA 359 (text **9B**: "King of Battle"). *Transliteration, translation, and references.*

1971

J. J. A. van Dijk, *Nicht kanonische Beschwörungen und sonstige literarische Texte.* Vorderasiatische Schriftdenkmäler der Staatlichen Museen zu Berlin 17. Berlin: Akademie. No. 42 VAT 7832a (text **19**: "The Great Revolt against Naram-Sin"). *Copy.*

1973

W. G. Lambert, "Studies in Nergal." *BiOr* 30. Pp. 357–63, BM 120003 (text **13**: "Erra and Naram-Sin"). *Copy, transliteration, translation, and treatment.*

1974

O. R. Gurney, *Middle Babylonian Legal Documents, and Other Texts.* UET 7. London: British Museum. No. 73 (text **10**: "Sargon Ur Letter"). *Copy.*

H. Otten and C. Rüster, "Textanschlüsse von Boğazköy-Tafeln (21–30)." ZA 63. Pp. 86–87, no. 24. Bo 1309 (text **21B**: Hittite "Cuthean Legend"). *Transliteration.*

H. Otten and C. Rüster, *Aus dem Bezirk des grossen Tempels.* KBo 22. WVDOG 90. Berlin: Gebr. Mann. No. 85 Bo 69/699 (text **21B**: Hittite "Cuthean Legend"). *Copy.*

1974–77

A. Westenholz, "Old Akkadian School Texts." *AfO* 25. Pp. 97, TA 1931-729 (text **15**: "The Great Revolt against Naram-Sin"). *Copy.*

1976

A. K. Grayson and E. Sollberger, "L'Insurrection générale contre Narām-Suen." *RA* 70. Pp. 103–28, A.1252, MAH 10829, BM 79987 (texts **16A**, **16B**, **17**: "The Great Revolt against Naram-Sin"). *Copies, transliterations, translations, and treatments.*

1977

H. Berman and H. Klengel, *Texte des hattischen Kreises und verschiedenen Inhalts.* Keilschrifturkunden aus Boghazköi 48. Berlin: Akademie. No. 98 Bo 3715 (text **9A**: Hittite "King of Battle"). *Copy.*

1978–79

T. Jacobsen, "Ipḫur-Kīshi and His Times." *AfO* 26. Pp. 1–14, TA 1931-729 (text **15**: "The Great Revolt against Naram-Sin"). *Transliteration, translation, and treatment in relation to 1976, Grayson and Sollberger.*

1979

M. de Jong Ellis, "Akkadian Literary Texts and Fragments." *JCS* 31. P. 229, no. 9 UM 29-13-688 (text **8A**: "Sargon, the Lion"). *Copy.*

1980

B. Lewis, *The Sargon Legend.* American Schools of Oriental Research Dissertation Series 4. Cambridge, Mass.: American Schools of Oriental Research, K.3401+, K.4470, K.7249, BM 47449 (text **2**). *Photos, transliteration, translation, and treatment.*

1981

C. B. F. Walker, "The Second Tablet of *ṭupšenna pitema*: An Old Babylonian Naram-Sin Legend." *JCS* 33. Pp. 191–95, BM 17215 (text **20B**: "Cuthean Legend"). *Copy, transliteration, translation, and treatment.*

1983

J. S. Cooper and W. Heimpel, "The Sumerian Sargon Legend." *JAOS* 103. Pp. 67–82, 3N-T296 (text **4**: "Sargon's Rise to Power"). *Copy, transliteration, translation, and notes of Sumerian text from Nippur.*

J. S. Cooper, *The Curse of Agade.* Baltimore. Johns Hopkins University Press (text **23**: "The Downfall of Akkade"). *Photos, transliteration, translation, and treatment.*

1987

J. J. A. van Dijk, *Literarische Texte aus Babylon.* Vorderasiatische Schriftdenkmäler der Staatlichen Museen zu Berlin 24. Berlin: Akademie. No. 75 VAT 17166 (text **5**: "Sargon's Rise to Power"). *Copy.*

1989

O. R. Gurney, *Literary and Miscellaneous Texts in the Ashmolean Museum.* OECT 9. Oxford: Clarendon. No. 103 Ash. 1924.2085 rev. (text **22**: "Cuthean Legend"). *Copy.*

Unpublished texts in this edition

St. Etienne 150 (text **8B**: "Sargon, the Lion").
CBS 15217 (text **11**: "Sargon Nippur Letter").
L.74.225 (text **14**: "Elegy on the Death of Naram-Sin").
K.2021B (text **22**: "Cuthean Legend").
K.13328 (text **22**: "Cuthean Legend").

The above survey includes all texts known to me. It is hoped that there will be more discoveries and publications of these fragmentary texts in the coming years. In this book, reference will be made to the most recent copy and treatment of each text, and when relevant, earlier editions will be indicated in the notes.

Terminology

In discussions of the corpus of the legends of the kings of Akkade, the concept of genre has attained a central position.[14] A discussion of genre may serve as a framework for research, within which problems may be formulated, and as a methodological goal in order to propose solutions.[15] In the following pages, I survey the terms for literary genres that have been suggested for characterizing the various texts, and I evaluate their usefulness for further research and analysis before offering an alternative classification.

Assyriologists began to classify the known texts in the early twentieth century, despite the scarcity of texts capable of supporting any meaningful analysis and the difficulty of categorizing fragmentary texts. An ad hoc approach developed that tended to affix arbitrary labels based on the characteristics of individual texts and then to fit texts deciphered or discovered post hoc into the already existing categories. The main influences on these labels were the perspectives and expectations of scholars trained in biblical studies, and thus biblical classification and classical typologies were employed. Consequently there was an emphasis on mythology, especially concerning creation, the fall of man, and the flood. Thus, a few of our texts were labeled "mythological texts" by Smith[16] and "mythological legends" by Bezold (see above, p. 7).

At present there are two main approaches to classifying the texts in the corpus of this book. These approaches could be termed the historiographic and the literary. Both approaches base their analysis on a mixture of content and form, though, as would be expected, the emphasis is on form in the literary approach and on content in the historiographic approach. Moreover, the historiographic approach attempts to explain the function of the literary texts in a wider context, while the literary approach ignores the contextual problems and sociological factors.

The development of the historiographic approach has been complex. In the early years few distinctions were made between different types of historical writings, and the legends were thus treated as historical texts. Note that Winckler had included the "Sargon Birth Legend" (text **2**) in his *Historische Texte altbabylonischer Herrscher* (1892). The first attempt to separate the historical-literary texts from other historical writings was made by Hans Güterbock in his fundamental work "Die historische Tradition und ihre literarische Gestaltung bei Babyloniern und Hethitern bis 1200" (1934). In this work he introduced the term *narû*-literature as a *Literaturgattung* to characterize compositions in the form of a royal inscription and often purporting to be inscribed on a stone monu-

[14] For example, see Longman, *Autobiography* [1991] 3–49.

[15] Note the discussion of the application of generic analysis and its usefulness as a hermeneutical tool in relation to Mesopotamian literature by H. Vanstiphout, "Some Thoughts on Genre in Mesopotamian Literature," *Keilschriftliche Literaturen: Ausgewählte Vorträge der XXXII. Rencontre Assyriologique Internationale* (ed. K. Hecker and W. Sommerfeld; Berlin, 1986) 1–11.

[16] G. Smith, *The Chaldean Account of Genesis* (London, 1876) 4.

ment (a *narû*).[17] The texts that he admitted to this category are of two types, according to content and form. The first group comprises the traditions concerning the kings of Akkade, among which he included only the "Sargon Birth Legend" (text **2**) and the "Naram-Sin Legend" (81-2-4, 219 = CT 13 44, which we now know is part of text **22**). Because of stylistic similarities, he added the "Cuthean Legend," despite its mythological content. He also listed the Boissier text of the "Great Revolt against Naram-Sin" (text **16B**) because of its content similarities, though with reservations due to its lack of a closing benediction. He characterized the typical events chronicled by these texts as the rise and fall of empires and the protagonists as *Typen des Heils- und Unheilsherrschers.*[18] The second group of texts consists of later traditions that contain less historical reality and more eschatological ideas, the Šulgi and Marduk "autobiographies" and the prophecies, Texts A and C. All of these were considered by Güterbock as canonical literary texts, distinguished from noncanonical texts, such as *šar tamḫāri* (text **9B**), for example.[19] He described the latter as an adventure novel (*Abenteuer-Roman*) that was divorced from its historical background and set in the world of fable. Consequently, he did not consider it a piece of *narû*-literature.

In 1964, Grayson and Lambert reevaluated the term *narû*-literature in their study of prophecies, a text group that Güterbock had considered the second group of this category. They divided the two groups into separate literary genres: the first group they called *poetic autobiographies* and the second group, "prophecies." They defined *poetic autobiographies* as "poetic narratives of historical events told in the first person by a king."[20]

Kirk Grayson continued to investigate historiographic texts and attempted another classification of all such texts. In 1975, forty years after the appearance of Güterbock's monumental work and the publication of many additional texts, Grayson reevaluated the texts again. In his *Babylonian Historical-Literary Texts*, Grayson introduced the "historical-literary category," under which he subsumed three genres: prophecy, historical epic, and "pseudo-autobiographies."[21] The features that unite them are that "they belong to various refined literary forms and their content is concerned mainly with historical or natural events rather than with mythological or supernatural occurrences."[22] Of the three genres, only the last two are related to the corpus of texts in this volume. The Akkadian "historical epics" are "poetic narratives concerned with the activities of kings. In contrast to other Akkadian epics the events described are essentially historical rather than mythological."[23] Under this rubric, he included

[17] Güterbock, "Die Historische Tradition," 19.

[18] Ibid., 20.

[19] Ibid., 21.

[20] A. K. Grayson and W. G. Lambert, "Akkadian Prophecies," *JCS* 18 (1964) 8.

[21] A. K. Grayson, *Babylonian Historical-Literary Texts* (Toronto, 1975) 7. Note that he maintains this classification system in his article "Histories and Historians of the Ancient Near East: Assyria and Babylonia," *Orientalia* 49 (1980) 182–87.

[22] Grayson, *Babylonian Historical-Literary Texts*, 5.

[23] Ibid., 7.

poetic narratives about Sargon ("King of Battle Epic," text **9**) and about Naram-Sin ("Naram-Sin and the Lord of Apišal," text **12**).[24] The "pseudo-autobiographies" are defined as "first person narrations by kings of their experiences. The phenomena described are historical, legendary, and occasionally supernatural."[25] In this group, he included the "Sargon Birth Legends" and the "Cuthean Legend."[26]

In her review of Akkadian literature in 1978, Erica Reiner used two terms: *autobiography* (in the classical sense of *res gestae*), describing those texts written in the first-person narrative mode ("Sargon Birth Legend"), and *narû*-literature, including poetic narratives of historical events concerned with a famous king of the past, which have a moral message to future kings as a conclusion ("Cuthean Legend" and Sargon legends).[27]

The class of texts that Erica Reiner termed autobiography included that of Idrimi. Jack Sasson in his study of Idrimi likewise placed that king's inscription among memorials written to remember the activities of a past leader, cast in the first-person narrative mode, a category that he termed *simulated autobiographies.*[28]

In his study of the letter of Gilgameš, F. R. Kraus posited another genre, *fiktiver Brief einer literarischen Sagenfigur*, parallel to *narû*-literature, which he defined as *fiktive Königsinschrift.* One of the distinguishing features of these two genres is their characters: a *Sagenfigur* in the former and *historische alter Könige oder selbst Götter* in the latter. For this reason, Kraus excluded the Sargon letters from the first category on the grounds that Sargon was a historical king, but included the Sargonic legends in the second. In order to comprehend the rationale underlying these texts, Kraus suggested taking the texts at face value first and then understanding the intentional form employed by the authors.[29]

Consequently, the term *narû* as a literary genre has been variously defined. Most recently, the nine points listed by Lewis in *The Sargon Legend* have been taken as a starting point for discussion.[30] They are:

1. The texts concern the figure of a great king and record either significant events or unusual experiences during his rule;
2. They are pseudepigraphical and purport to be genuine royal inscriptions;

[24] Ibid., 42.

[25] Ibid., 7.

[26] Ibid., 8.

[27] E. Reiner, "Die akkadische Literatur," *Altorientalische Literaturen* (Neues Handbuch der Literaturwissenschaft; Wiesbaden, 1978) 176ff.

[28] J. M. Sasson, "On Idrimi and Šarruwa, the Scribe," *In Honor of Ernest R. Lacheman on His Seventy-Fifth Birthday, April 29, 1981* (ed. M. A. Morrison and D. I. Owen; Studies on the Civilization and Culture of Nuzi and the Hurrians 1; Winona Lake, Ind., 1981) 311.

[29] F. R. Kraus, "Der Brief des Gilgameš," *AnSt* 30 (1980) 115.

[30] Lewis, *Sargon Legend*, 87–88. See also Sasson, "On Idrimi," 312–13; H. Galter, "Probleme historisch-lehrhafter Dichtung in Mesopotamien," *Keilschriftliche Literaturen: Ausgewählte Vorträge der XXXII. Rencontre Assyriologique Internationale* (ed. K. Hecker and W. Sommerfeld; Berlin, 1986) 72–73.

3. They are written in the first person in the style of an autobiography;
4. Following the pattern of the royal inscription, they are constructed with a prologue, narrative, and epilogue;
5. The prologue begins with a self-presentation and may include information concerning the king's origin or the cause of the predicament he faces in the narrative section;
6. The narrative is devoted to a specific episode in the life of the king;
7. The narrative contains a message for future kings expressed in the form of a blessing, oracle, or curse;
8. The texts are didactic in nature; there is a moral to be learned from the personal experiences of the king that can be acquired by reading his "stela";
9. They are written in a poetic or semipoetic narrative style.

Through a process of arbitrary selection of fifteen texts, Tremper Longman created a genre of "fictional Akkadian royal autobiography" with the following features: (1) fictionality, (2) Akkadian language, (3) royal narrator, (4) autobiographical style, and (5) prose style.[31] Most of these features are debatable. With regard to his second point, it may be noted that choice of language is irrelevant for a genre definition. Three of Longman's features might be equated with points outlined by Lewis: (1) fictionality might be equated with Lewis's (2) pseudepigraphy; (3) royal narrator with Lewis's (1) texts of a great king; and (4) autobiographical style with Lewis's (3) autobiography. Since the common assumption of a poetic or semipoetic narrative style (Lewis's no. 9) exists, Longman's fifth point is controversial and must be proved.

The last person to review this subject was Hannes D. Galter. He concluded that:

> Die Existenz einer homogenen Gattung akkadischer autobiographisch-lehrhafter Literaturwerke für den Gesamtzeitraum mesopotamischer Literaturgeschichte nicht zu belegen ist. Ab der altbabylonischen Zeit wechseln autobiographische Dichtungen über bedeutende Herrscher mit thematisch gleichen Kompositionen in der dritten Person. Eine didaktische Funktion lässt sich bis jetzt für keinen der frühen Texte nachweisen.[32]

As Galter pointed out, if the literary application of the term *narû* or pseudo-autobiography is limited to a false poetic royal inscription written in the first person with didactic intent, it hardly applies in its entirety to a single text in the corpus. Further, writing in the first person is considered a distinctive feature of Sumerian praise poems (i.e., royal hymns)[33] and thus may not be

[31] Longman, *Autobiography* [1983] 479–99. In his book, *Autobiography* [1991] 199–212, Longman reduces these characteristic traits by one; he removes the criterion of "royal" in his genre classification.

[32] Galter, "Probleme," 78.

[33] J. A. Black, review of Klein, *Three Šulgi Hymns*, in *AfO* 29/30 (1983–84) 110–12. He thinks that the use of the first person preserves the immediacy of contact between the poet and his subject (given the possibility of performance before the king's statue in the cult).

meant to mimic royal inscriptions. As for its didactic character, didacticism is a characteristic of many works of Akkadian literature.[34] If neither the use of the first person nor a didactic nature uniquely characterizes our corpus, we have come full circle to a stage before Güterbock's work and must begin again.

The literary approach attempts to organize the literature of Babylonia and Assyria into typological groupings such as myths and epics, hymns and prayers, incantations and wisdom literature. The "Cuthean Legend" was included among the myths and epics in the first collection of such texts to be published, that of Peter Jensen, *Assyrisch-babylonische Mythen und Epen* (1900). In this approach, structure and style are very important.[35] Distinctions are based on either the classical typologies of epic and lyric or the narrative modes of myth and epic. The term *epic* is used in two ways—which I have termed the maximal and the minimal[36]—in Assyriological studies, and both subsume various texts of my corpus. The maximal school of thought is exemplified by Karl Hecker, who in his *Untersuchungen zur akkadischen Epik* (1974) listed as his epic 10 "Sargon—bzw. *šar-tamḫāri*-Epos," which is my texts **6**, **7**, **9**, and the World Map (CT 22 48); and as his epic 11 "Naram-Sin Epos," which is my "Naram-Sin and the Lord of Apišal" (text **12**).[37]

Jean Nougayrol, who tends to use a minimalist definition of the term *epic*, stated in his search for an Akkadian heroic epic: "Nous *devrions*, tout d'abord, avoir une épopée sur Sargon d'Agadé. Toutes les conditions requises se trouvent réunies: moment historique et stature du personnage, péripéties dramatiques et 'merveilleux.'"[38] He then discussed the appropriateness of text **9** ("King of Battle Epic") and text **6**. Noting the admonitory conclusion of text **6** placed in the speech of Sargon, he related it to the genre of *narû*-literature (in which he included the "Sargon Birth Legend"), and that in turn to "Gilgameš." He further investigated the "fonds héroïque" in the life and legends of Naram-Sin, in particular the "Cuthean Legend" (text **22**). Thus, Nougayrol was occupied with the hero and with the literary forms in which the hero appeared. He examined the figures of Sargon and Naram-Sin in all the texts in which they appeared. His approach was the nearest to the approach taken in forming the present corpus.

In the latest survey of Akkadian literature (1987), Wolfgang Röllig has three subdivisions under which he could have put our texts: §4.1.2 Epen ("die

[34] Note the application of the genre *Lehrgedicht* to cuneiform literature: *Lehrepos* was introduced by B. Landsberger, "Die Eigenbegrifflichkeit der babylonischen Welt," *Islamica* 2/3 (1926–27) 370; re-ed. and trans. in *The Conceptual Autonomy of the Babylonian World* (Monographs on the Ancient Near East 1/4 [1976] 13), and was accepted by Assyriologists. See discussion by J. S. Cooper, *The Return of Ninurta to Nippur* (AnOr 52; Rome, 1978) 5. Note in addition its application to the "Poem of Erra" by L. Cagni, *The Poem of Erra* (Sources from the Ancient Near East 1/3; Malibu, 1977) 71–72.

[35] E. Reiner, "Akkadische Literatur," 151–59.

[36] J. G. Westenholz, "Heroes of Akkad," *JAOS* 103 (1983) 327.

[37] K. Hecker, *Untersuchungen zur akkadischen Epik* (AOATS 8; Kevelaer, 1974) 36–37.

[38] J. Nougayrol, "L'Épopée babylonienne," *La poesia epica e la sua formazione* (Rome, 1970) 855.

'Gattung' der historischen Epen"), where he listed none of our texts; §4.1.3 *narû*-Literatur ("Erzählgattung ... historische Episoden als Thema, ... berühmte Könige als Helden, ... im Stile der Weisheitsliteratur moralische Folgerungen"), where he listed: the "King of Battle Epic" (text **9**) and "Sargon the Conqueror" (texts **6–7**); and §4.1.4 Pseudo-autobiographische Texte "Von der *narû*-Literatur wahrscheinlich zu trennen sind eine Anzahl von Texten, die den Hauptakteur in der 1. Person Sg. einführen; sie haben teilweise legendären, teilweise historischen Inhalt ... und ... lehrhafte Zwecke"), where he listed: (a) "Birth Legend of Sargon of Akkade" (text **2**); (b) "Sargon Text from the Old Babylonian Period" (text **1**); (c) "Revolt against Naram-Sin" (texts **16–17**); (d) Narām-Sin-Text, "King of Kutha" (texts **20**, **22**)."[39] Röllig's categories do not agree with any of the preceding, thus reflecting the present divisive state of classification in Assyriology.

Since there is no agreement within Assyriological studies, it would appear logical to begin by examining native classifications. Before setting out his schema, Grayson considered native classification systems used for archival purposes and mentioned the modern and ancient conceptions of genre.[40] However, inquiry into native classifications is usually the prerogative of the Sumerologists, since they possess written texts with colophons, subscripts, and rubrics.[41] The Akkadian texts were named by the ancient scribes and serialized but were never classified as were the Sumerian compositions. None of the texts in our corpus has a native classification, so we must define our own analytic framework within which to view them.

At this point, I would propose the following alternative schema in which to study this specific corpus, due to the deficiencies and unsuitability of the historiographic and literary approaches outlined above. As we have seen, the former places too much emphasis on the historical component and the latter on poetic structure. In this study, the point of view of folk literature, which includes all types of narratives, both oral and written, will be used. In this view, which also considers the oral tales, all narratives are seen to have an unlimited number of variants; they may be shaped into fictitious, credible, revered, or ridiculed treatments. In general, folklorists divide folk narratives into three categories commonly designated myth, legend, and fairytale. Recently Alan Dundes summed up the present understanding of *legend*: "Since the days of the Grimm brothers in the early nineteenth century, there has been general agreement among scholars as to generic distinctions between myth, folktale, and legend....

[39] W. Röllig, "Literatur: §4 Überblick über die akkadische Literatur," *RlA* 7 (1987) 52–53.

[40] Grayson, *Babylonian Historical-Literary Texts*, 5.

[41] See C. Wilcke ("Formale Gesichtspunkte in der sumerischen Literatur," *Sumerological Studies Jacobsen*, 205–316), who compares the native classifications with the classical lyric and epic; J. Krecher ("Sumerische Literatur der Fara-Zeit: Die UD.GAL.NUN-Texte [I]," *BiOr* 35 [1978] 155–60), who compares the native classifications with *Mythos* and *Epos*. The latest review of the opinions is that of D. O. Edzard, "Literatur," *RlA* 7 (1987) 35–36.

By and large, Bascom's definitions of myth, folktale, and legend are shared by most folklorists."[42] Bascom defined *legend* as "prose narratives which, like myths, are regarded as true by the narrator and his audience, but they are set in a period considerably less remote, when the world was much as it is today. Legends are more often secular than sacred, and their principal characters are human. They tell of migrations, wars and victories, deeds of past heroes, chiefs and kings, and succession in ruling dynasties." [43]

The term *legend* is not a scholarly innovation, since many of these texts have been so designated since their first publication, and the word *legend* has continued to appear in their nomenclature. As a classification, it was used by Otto Weber in 1907 in his volume on the literature of the Babylonians and Assyrians. Under the category of historical texts, he listed historical legends, historical inscriptions, and historiographic texts. All the known texts of our corpus plus the "Siege of Uruk" text were classified as *legends*. His schema was a diachronic one based on the Bible: (a) stories of cosmogony encapsulated in mythic texts; (b) antediluvian kings, with whom "betreten wir bereits den Boden der historischen Legende"; (c) postdiluvian kings ("geschichtliche Legende"), "in allen diesen Texten das legendarische Element schlechthin überwiegt und das im Hintergrund stehende geschichtliche Ereignis fast ganz verflüchtigt ist"; and (d) historical kings of "unglaublichen Geschichten." [44]

Two aspects of folk legends that recur in scholars' discussions are their historical features (the "belief factor") and their didactic nature, the identical two problems that have concerned Assyriologists, as described above. The rela-

[42] A. Dundes (ed.), *Sacred Narrative: Readings in the Theory of Myth* (Berkeley, 1984) 5.

[43] W. Bascom, "The Forms of Folklore: Prose Narratives," *Journal of American Folklore* 78 (1965) 3–20; reprinted in *Sacred Narrative*, 9. Note that there is no agreed technical definition, in contrast to a general definition, of *legend*, despite two international congresses in 1962–63 with that goal in mind: "*International Society for Folk-Narrative Research*" *in Antwerp (6.–8. Sept. 1962): Bericht und Referat* (Antwerp, 1963); for some of the discussions at Budapest in 1963, see C.-H. Tillhagen, "Was ist eine Sage? Eine Definition und ein Vorschlag für ein europäisches Sagensystem," *Acta Ethnographica* 13 (1964) 9–17; W. D. Hand, "Status of European and American Legend Study," *Current Anthropology* 6 (1965) 439–46. In 1963, after meetings of the International Society for Folk-Narrative Research at Antwerp in 1962 and at Budapest in 1963, a special committee of legend experts drew up the following tentative system of classification: (1) etiological and eschatological legends, (2) historical legends and legends of the history of civilization, (3) supernatural beings and forces / mythic legends, (4) religious legends / myths of gods and heroes. Such a four-part classification upsets the commonly accepted tripartite division of folk narratives into myth, legend, and folktale. Note the typology of L. Dégh, "Folk Narrative" (*Folklore and Folklife* [ed. R. M. Dorson; Chicago, 1972] 53–83), who divides narrative genres into tale genres, legend genres, and true-experience stories. This classification seems to obscure rather than to clarify. The most negative assessment of the situation is given by R. A. Georges, "The General Concept of Legend: Some Assumptions to be Reexamined and Reassessed," *American Folk Legend: A Symposium* (ed. W. D. Hand: Publications of the UCLA Center for the Study of Comparative Folklore and Mythology 2; Berkeley, 1971) 1–19.

[44] O. Weber, *Die Literatur der Babylonier und Assyrer* (Leipzig, 1907) 200, 207.

tion of legend to history is closer than that of fiction to fact; the legend may not contain objective truth, but it is accepted as true in its cultural context. This belief in its historicity is an essential element of legend.[45] Likewise, the didactic aims of the legend are also clear: "The reason for telling a legend is basically not to entertain but to educate people, to inform them about an important fact, to arm them against danger within their own cultural environment." [46]

Linda Dégh has stated: "Scrutinizing the form of the legend, one . . . feels the legend has only content and no fixed form at all." [47] The content of the legend is the story, which recounts the events, actions, and happenings, and the existents, the characters, and the settings. It may be transposed from one medium to another, for example from a novel to the stage or screen, without losing its essential properties. Likewise, it can be transposed from one genre to another (e.g., from epic to parody). In the following pages, each legend is preceded by an outline of the story elements.

There are two obstacles to compiling story elements. The first obstacle is the fragmentary nature of the texts; in every single case we have less than the complete composition. Second, the texts are highly laconic; whereas normally the audience of a narrative can fill in the interstices with knowledge acquired through ordinary life experiences, we are not able to supply the causal inferences and the logical connections of the events. Whereas the ancient Assyrians or Babylonians recognized the substance from which the story elements were derived and understood the cultural code, modern scholars are ignorant of that code as well as of the interplay of the cultural code with literary and artistic codes.

The story of the legend is fixed or realized in the written text. The discourse or expression of the story in its written form can be analyzed on two levels: (1) the structure of the narrative, which concerns the order and selection of the story elements, the time of the story in relation to the time of the recounting, the source or authority for the story: narrative voice, the real author, the implied author, the narrator, the real audience, the implied audience, the person in the story to whom the narrator is speaking, and so forth; and (2) the manifestation in a specific medium: song, poetry, or prose.[48] It is essential to remember that all Akkadian written texts were realizable orally: they could all be performed. In the following chapters, the introduction to each text will

[45] On the subject of legends and belief, see L. Dégh and A. Vázsonyi, "Legend and Belief," *Folklore Genres* (ed. D. Ben-Amos; Austin, 1976) 93–123; L. Röhrich, *Märchen und Wirklichkeit* (2d ed.; Wiesbaden: Steiner, 1964); H. Jason, "Concerning the 'Historical' and the 'Local' Legend and Their Relatives," *Toward New Perspectives in Folklore* (ed. A. Paredes and R. Bauman; Austin, 1972) 134–44.

[46] L. Dégh, "Folk Narratives," 73.

[47] Ibid.; see also Hand, "Status of European and American Legend Study," 441.

[48] The ideas expressed in this and the above paragraphs are based in general on the French structuralist school of thought (see J. Culler, *Structuralist Poetics* [London, 1975]) and in particular on the developments of S. Chatman (*Story and Discourse* [Ithaca, 1978]; N. Goodman, S. Chatman, and B. Herrnstein Smith, *On Narrative* [ed. W. J. T. Mitchell; Chicago, 1981]).

describe the discourse, the form of expression of the narrative transmission, and the literary medium. For example, the surface discourse can express time distinctions through a whole set of grammatical elements, durative and punctual, stative and iterative.[49] In these legends, as in most narratives, the story is set in past time, which is expressed by the use of the preterite.

Certain technical terms are used in the body of this book. *Narrative statement* and *to state narratively* are phrases employed for any expression of a narrative element viewed independently of its literary medium. *Narrative mode* is the mode of the discourse. *Story time* refers to the period during which the story took place and *discourse time* to the time within which the narrative statement occurred. In most of our texts, discourse time is shorter than story time, with narrative statements summarizing a group of events. Likewise, we can speak of *story space* and *discourse space*. *Reading (out)* is the process of decoding from the surface or manifestation level through to deep narrative structures.

Thus, we have an analytical framework offering a powerful key to unlock the puzzles in these difficult legendary texts. In particular, we can speak of the story or legend of Sargon's expedition to the northwest and the various discourses in which specific events from that campaign are realized. Likewise, we can speak of the stories or legends embedded in the discourse of letters or of hymns. Here, we shall attempt to describe the discourse features that combine into various patterns, rather than forcing the texts into categories or fixed genres that may fit only some of the features of the texts as they stand.[50]

Poetic Discourse, Orthography, and Grammar

In this volume, the focus is on the analysis of the surface expression of each individual text. The primary goals are to determine the origin of tablets of unrecorded provenance, to establish their orthographic conventions, and to identify the literary tradition within which they stand. Unfortunately, such an attempt is hampered by the embryonic state of our present knowledge, especially of Old Babylonian dialects. Likewise, we are largely unfamiliar with local orthographic traditions. Since the pioneering work of Goetze,[51] there have only been phonological or morphological descriptions of separate archives as part of text publications.

Poetic Diction

Our study adopts as one of its major concerns that of defining poetic diction. The problem is essentially whether and to what extent poetic expression differs from that of prose. Since the age of classical Greece, it has been recog-

[49] Chatman, *Story and Discourse*, 79.

[50] Ibid., 166.

[51] A. Goetze, "The Akkadian Dialects of the Old-Babylonian Mathematical Texts," *Mathematical Cuneiform Texts* (ed. O. Neugebauer and A. Sachs; AOS 29; New Haven, Conn., 1945) 146–47; idem, "The Sibilants of Old Babylonian," *RA* 52 (1958) 137–49.

nized that the poetic arts are distinguished by their techniques: rhythm, language, and harmony. Furthermore, even Aristotle himself realized they are a means of expressing content and that the content is the deciding factor in the definition of poetry. Speaking of the fact that the poetic arts are distinguished by their means, he wrote:

> The means with them as a whole are rhythm, language, and harmony—used, however, either singly or in certain combinations. A combination of harmony and rhythm alone is the means in flute playing and lyre playing.... Rhythm alone, without harmony, is the means in the dancer's imitations;... There is further an art which imitates by language alone, without harmony, in prose or in verse, and if in verse, either in some one or in a plurality of metres. This form of imitation is to this day without a name. We have no common name for a mime of Sophron or Xenarchus and a Socratic Conversation; and we should still be without one even if the imitation in the two instances were in trimeters or elegiacs or some other kind of verse—though it is the way with people to tack on "poet" to the name of a metre, and talk of elegiac poets and epic poets, thinking that they call them poets not by reason of the imitative nature of their work, but indiscriminately by reason of the metre they write in. Even if a theory of medicine or physical philosophy be put forth in a metrical form, it is usual to describe the writer in this way; Homer and Empedocles, however, have really nothing in common apart from their metre; so that, if the one is to be called a poet, the other should be termed a physicist rather than a poet.[52]

He describes the characteristics of the language of poetry in the following words:

> The perfection of Diction is for it to be at once clear and not mean. The clearest indeed is that made up of the ordinary words for things, but it is mean, as is shown by the poetry of Cleophon and Sthenelus. On the other hand, the diction becomes distinguished and non-prosaic by the use of unfamiliar terms, i.e., strange words, metaphors, lengthened forms, and everything that deviates from the ordinary modes of speech.... A certain admixture, accordingly, of unfamiliar terms is necessary. These, the strange words, the metaphor, the ornamental equivalent, etc., will save the language from seeming mean and prosaic, while the ordinary words in it will secure requisite clearness.[53]

Nevertheless, from the time of Aristotle, the poetic arts have been defined by their rhythmic techniques, such as the regularity of metrical pattern. Whether such an overt definition can be claimed for earlier periods is a moot point, since no Babylonian thinker has left us his musings on the poetic arts.

The modern scholar is thus forced to make his own personal assessment of the characteristics of Akkadian poetic language. Von Soden even claimed that there was a special "dialect" in use for poetry.[54] But, as has been pointed out

[52] Aristotle, "*Poetics*" (trans. I. Bywater; The Pocket Aristotle; New York, 1958) 342–43.

[53] Ibid., 370.

[54] See W. von Soden, "Der hymnisch-epische Dialekt des Akkadischen," *ZA* 40 (1931) 163–227 (Part 1); *ZA* 41 (1933) 90–183 (Part 2); and more recently B. Groneberg, *Untersuchungen zum hymnisch-epischen Dialekt der altbabylonischen literarischen Texte* (Ph.D. diss., Münster, 1972); idem, *Syntax, Morphologie und Stil der jungbabylonischen "hymnischen" Literatur* (FAOS 14; Stuttgart, 1987).

repeatedly afterwards, this "dialect" is not a dialect at all but a literary style loaded with archaisms, inverted word order, often trochaic verse ends, shortened pronominal suffixes, use of rare words—all in agreement with Aristotle. However, the scribes differed considerably in the extent to which they made use of this literary style. Some, like the composer of the Old Babylonian "Gilgameš" tablets, hardly use any features of this style, while others, like the writer of the "Agušaya Hymn," write in such a complex literary style that it is barely intelligible to us. Most of the texts in this volume seem to fall somewhere between these two extremes, though in general terms the "Elegy on the Death of Naram-Sin" (text **14**) is closer to "Agušaya," and the Old Babylonian fragment of the "Cuthean Legend" (text **20A**) is closer to "Gilgameš." The latest assessment of Akkadian literature states:

> Sprachlich und stilistisch ist die akkadische Literatur durchaus nicht einheitlich. Mythen, Epen und andere erzählende Literatur können in einer schlichten Diktion abgefasst sein, die der Umgangssprache sehr nahe gestanden haben muss. Die altbab. Dichtung—ohne Königsinschriften, Epen und Mythen—benutzt eine Kunstsprache, die gegenüber nicht-literarischen Texten durch poetisch überhöhte Wortwahl und grammatische Besonderheiten gekennzeichnet ist, die zumindest z. T. archaisierende Tendenzen aufweist.[55]

For the present limited investigation, the rhetorical features that would normally be assigned to poetic diction are described in relation to each individual text. In addition, the phonological and syntactical artifices that act together in structuring the Akkadian verse are indicated.

Phonology

The subject of sound in Akkadian poetry has received little attention. The exploitation of the sound patterns of the vowels and consonants can be either qualitative or quantitative.

Qualitative changes result in the poetic features of alliteration, assonance, and rhyme. Although rhyme is rarely found, alliteration and assonance both appear to be poetic devices commonly employed in Akkadian poetry. Examples of alliteration might be *iḫillā ḫāḫilātum* in text **6**:20; *kišši* . . . *kiššati* . . . *kiššūti* in text **9B**:17–18; *lušārik elik lušarpiš* in text **13**:28. An instance of assonance of vowels *i-u* might be *libbum išdum tībum* in text **6**:4. A tendency to reduplicative phonetic patterns is seen in the common use of homoeoteleuton, the use of similar case endings and other morphological features in proximity, within a single line as well as at the end of two or more lines in succession: for example, the series of duals in text **13**:49 and the series of first-person accusative *-anni* in text **2**:5–12.

The quantitative differences of pitch, stress, and duration are harder to assess from written evidence alone. In Akkadian literature, much depends on the analysis of the so-called plene writings.

[55] Röllig, "Literatur," 48.

On the assumption that the epic texts were meant to be performed[56] and on the analogy of many other languages (modern Arabic, for instance),[57] we can expect the requirements of the melody to have changed words considerably, lengthening short vowels, shifting the stress, adding extra syllables, and so on. An example of the last is *kilal kilalal . . . qarnam qarnaʾam* "two by two . . . horn by horn" (text **12** obv. col. ii 6–7). Unlike later Akkadian, Old Babylonian orthography was not so rigid that such prosodic features could not be revealed in the written text, though the individual scribes varied in the extent to which they did so. A case in point is the short forms of *ana* and *ina* (e.g., *i-na ki-ma // ik-ki-ma* **8** rev. 11′).

Morphology

The morphological differences between the surface structure of the literary texts and the nonliterary texts are obvious. It is interesting to compare the archaisms of poetic diction to the archaisms of contemporary royal inscriptions. Some features are common to both, such as the extensive use of the terminative and locative adverbial postpositions *-iš* and *-um* endings, and status constructus forms ending in *-u*. Others are found in the royal inscriptions only, such as *in* written for *ina*, uncontracted vowels, antiquated orthography (use of *ù* and *bí*, for instance), Sargonic Old Akkadian Š-forms of verbs primae *w*, and so forth. With these latter features, the royal authors clearly tried to link themselves with the illustrious kings of the Dynasty of Akkade, while the archaisms of the poetic diction serve the same purpose as literary archaisms anywhere: to give the text an aura of solemnity and dignity deemed suitable to the contents. The use of "Bible English" in modern times is essentially the same phenomenon.

Syntax

The normal prose declarative sentence order, subject-object-verb, may undergo poetic transformations. Chiasm and ring composition influence the order of the words in a set of verses. Any verbal or nominal phrase may be placed at the beginning of the verse for emphasis. These poetic transformations of declarative sentences occur in varying measure in the texts in the corpus.

Semantics

Whether one approaches semantics from the semiological and linguistic point of view and speaks of signs, signification, signified, and signifier, or from the side of the literary critic and speak of puns and metaphors, it is incumbent upon the investigator of poetic diction to analyze "figures of speech" (words and expressions used in ways that are out of the ordinary) and "figures of thought"

[56] The word *zamāru* appears often in the concluding section of epic works. I hope to publish an article concerning this topic in the near future.

[57] Cf. E. Littmann, *Neuarabische Volkspoesie* (Berlin, 1902) 12.

(words and expressions used in different senses from those that properly belong to them). An example of the former might be *urram qablam Akkade ušarra [i]sinnum ša muti inneppuš* "Tomorrow, Akkade will commence battle. A festival of warriors/death will be celebrated" (text **6**:18–19). The latter are represented by the various metaphors with which these texts are replete, for instance, the ascription of names of domesticated animals to the warriors of Sargon (see further p. 58).

Prosody and Metrical Schemes

Of all the aspects of poetic diction, the features of prosody and metrics are the most difficult to evaluate on the basis of written texts, with no living tradition concerning the rhythm of speech. Traditionally this analysis involved "the study of 'accent' (Latin *accentus, adcantus* = Greek *prosoidia*), of phonetic properties . . . of syllables and words as relevant to the measure (Greek *metron*) of rhythm especially in verse, and of meters and the forms of verse generally."[58] One attempt at analyzing Akkadian prosody and metrics has recently been made by von Soden.[59] He provides a rhythmic structure for Akkadian verse based on the counting of syllables and the disposition of stresses. However, this attempt suffers from arbitrary word forms and inconsistent stress patterns and must therefore be judged unconvincing. Karl Hecker devised an approach to understanding Akkadian metrics that has, unfortunately, been neglected; his approach was based on tropes, or figures of speech, together with free rhythm composed of a fixed number of accented stresses plus variable unstressed syllables.[60] Despite an infinite amount of ingenuity and labor, biblical scholars have yet failed to establish a metrical scheme for ancient Hebrew.[61] Therefore, it seems likely that in the field of Akkadian poetics people have also been looking for metric patterns where there are none: for regular, recurrent, and predictable rhythmic patterns, whether they be syllabic, accentual, accentual-syllabic, or quantitative.

Poetic Structure

The basic structural unit is the single line of verse, or stich, as indicated in the textual manuscripts, with the exceptions of texts **7** and **9B**. The stich may or may not be divisible into parts. The line units can be combined into larger units of verse; most frequent is the couplet or distich, followed by the tercet, the qua-

[58] J. C. La Drière, "Prosody," *Princeton Encyclopedia of Poetry and Poetics* (ed. A. Preminger; Princeton, 1974) 699.

[59] W. von Soden, "Untersuchungen zur babylonischen Metrik," *ZA* 71 (1981) 161–204 (Part 1); *ZA* 74 (1984) 213–34 (Part 2).

[60] Hecker, *Epik*, 101–60.

[61] For a review of the ancient Hebrew, see M. O'Connor, *Hebrew Verse Structure* (Winona Lake, Ind., 1980) 55–67; and for a review of previous opinions on the subject, see ibid., 29–54.

train, and the stanza. Nevertheless, as in most narrative poetry, most of the texts in this corpus are stichic and not stanzaic, thus achieving an effect of linear development in which the narrative line itself provides the essential structure. However, a few texts seem to have stanzaic structure, such as texts **7** and **14**.

The most common devices employed in Akkadian verse for arranging lines into larger units of poetry are: (1) repetition of a sound, syllable, word, or phrase, including anaphora (from Greek 'a carrying up or back'), the repetition of the same word or words at the beginning of several successive sentences or sentence members; (2) homoeoteleuton (from Greek 'similarity of endings'), the use of similar case endings and other morphological features in proximity, within a single line, as well as at the end of two or more lines in succession; (3) parallelism,[62] repetition of the same grammatical pattern, reinforced by the recurrence of actual words and phrases, but whose semantic substance may be synonymous, antithetical, or supplemental.

[62] Parallelism is the central principle of biblical verse. It was rediscovered by Bishop Robert Lowth, who called it *parallelismus membrorum*; see J. Kugel, *The Idea of Biblical Poetry: Parallelism and Its History* (New Haven, 1981). For the most recent structural analysis of parallelism, see A. Berlin, *The Dynamics of Biblical Parallelism* (Bloomington, 1985).

Part A

Sargon

Chapter 2

The Sargon "Autobiographies"

The narrative mode that characterizes the following two texts is that of "autobiography," first-person narration by an overt narrator, Sargon, who relates his exploits for the edification of his implied audience, his people. Thus Sargon is at the same time the protagonist and the narrator, whose perceptual and conceptual points of view alone are conveyed. The perceptual point of view is that of an older man, grown wiser from his experiences. The discourse time is at the end of Sargon's life, and the story time is prior to the discourse time, with a retrospective order of events and existents.[1]

The following two texts are grouped together in this section because of their surface discourse similarities, but their actual story content is not evident. The first is merely a fragment of a composition of unknown content, and the second is a composition in which the autobiography functions as a prologue to a wisdom text.

[1] My use of the word *existents* is based on a literary approach of Seymour Chatman that first interested me some years ago. His diagram on p. 26 of *Story and Discourse* encapsulates his approach. The *existents* are the characters and settings that, together with the events, make up the form of the content (as opposed to the expression or discourse) of the narrative.

1
Old Babylonian Fragment: "I, Sargon"

Introduction

This Old Babylonian piece contains the first nine lines of a first-person narrative. All that remains of the text is the list of epithets that recalls Ištar's love for Sargon and his wanderings to the corners of the world. The content of the story (if there was any) is lost.

Transcription

1. *a-na-ku ša-ru-ki-in*
2. *na-ra-am* ^{d}INANNA
3. *mu-ta*$^{!}$*-li-ik*
4. *ki-ib-ra-a-at*
5. *er-bi-ti-in*
6. [x]-*mi* ⸢*ša*⸣-*ru-ru* ⸢^{d}⸣[UTU]
7. [x *l*]*i-lim/ši pa*/SI[PA(?)]
8. [x] ta la [x x]
9. [x x] a i [x x]

    (break)

Philological and Textual Notes

2. The epithet *narām* + DN appears for the first time as a royal epithet a few centuries after Sargon, in the inscriptions of Šu-Sin (Seux, *Épithètes*, 189–97).

3. The verb *atalluku* 'to walk about' (CAD A/1 324a; AHw 233a) appears in royal epithets (Seux, *Épithètes*, 37–40). Our reference is translated there "qui a parcouru les quatre contrées" (p. 37).

This composition is preserved on the upper third of a single-column Old Babylonian tablet. The tablet has been baked since Clay's copy was made and has lost a few bits in the process.

It is written in a classical OB ductus. Graphic peculiarities are seen in the extra wedges in IK, TA, and PA. Very little can be said concerning the language of such a small fragment. There are two archaic features: no duplication of double consonants and the presence of nunation (*erbettin*, line 5).

Manuscript

Unknown Provenance
MLC 641 = BRM 4 4 (see photograph, p. 379).

Translation

1. I, Sargon,
2. beloved of Ištar,
3. who roamed

4.–5. through all the four quarters,

6. .... radiance of the sun,

7.–9. (too fragmentary for translation)

4.–5. On the meaning of the term *kibrāt erbettin*, see J.-J. Glassner, "La Division quinaire de la terre," *Akkadica* 40 (1984) 17–34.

6. There exists another reference to *šarūru šamši* 'radiance of the sun', also with an apparently incorrect *-u* Auslaut on the word *šarūru* in the status constructus as the direct object of the sentence: *mati mītum līmuram ša-ru-ru* dUTU-*ši* 'when may the dead see sunlight?' Gilg. M i 15 (OB). A land *ša šarūrša iktumu* among Sargon's goals is found in text **7** ii 18.

2
"The Wisdom of Sargon": The "Birth Legend" of Sargon

Introduction

Knowledge of this composition is limited to the extant fragments of the first two columns. Column i contains a prologue incorporating the narrative story of Sargon as related retrospectively by Sargon. The events include his birth, his youth, and his elevation to kingship; and the actions include his heroic feats. He concludes the story with a challenge to any future king to emulate his extraordinary achievements. The surface level of the discourse in this section contains the introductory formula ('Any king who will arise after me') found in the concluding curse and blessing section of royal inscriptions, but clearly it is quite different from the curses and blessings that otherwise follow the formula.[2] The same substance of a challenge concluding Sargon's declaration of his military achievements is found in text **6**:120ff.: *Šarru-kīn ummatam unaḫḫad agan[a š]arrum ša iša[nna]nanni ša anāku attall[a]k[u] šū littallak* 'Sargon instructs the troops, "Lo, the king who desires to equal me, let him go where I have gone!"'

Column ii poses many problems, since it contains no narrative but a series of rhetorical questions. These questions are also addressed to an implied audience. The seemingly obvious message to be read out of the text is a commentary on the futility of all human effort. The relationship of this section to the story of Sargon is unfortunately not clear. It could contain his reflections at the end of his life. On the other hand, it may describe a tragic cataclysm at the end of his reign. Though most unlikely, it is also possible that col. ii contains an unrelated composition, traditionally copied on the same tablet as the "Sargon Autobiography."[3]

In general, for the latest treatment of this composition, see B. Lewis, *The Sargon Legend*.[4] This work contains a detailed discussion of manuscript transmission, the composition, its sources and development, and the character of the text. In lieu of repeating the statements contained in earlier publications, references to the pertinent passages will be given in the philological and textual notes.

[2] Similarly, B. Lewis, *The Sargon Legend: A Study of the Akkadian Text* (American Schools of Oriental Research Dissertation Series 4; Cambridge, Mass., 1980) 94 and 116 n. 24; pace Longman, *Autobiography* [1991] 55–57.

[3] See the latest discussion of this possibility, in Longman, *Autobiography* [1991] 58–59.

[4] See Lewis, *The Sargon Legend*. See also my review in *JNES* 43 (1984) 73–79.

General Observations

On the basis of the present state of the tablets, it is impossible to substantiate the copies of King in CT 13. In particular, the brittle right edge of col. i of K.3401+ has flaked off a bit more and lines 5–8 of BM 47449 are unreadable. In the following pages, the transliteration reflects the present state of the tablets. The four extant tablets probably represent three manuscripts, since as W. G. Lambert has observed, text C (K.7249) appears to be the reverse of text A (K.3401+).[5]

Circumstances of Discovery

Accessioned as part of the Kuyunjik collection, the first three fragments presumably came either from Layard's rummaging in Sennacherib's palace (southwest) and its library in the southern part of the mound in 1849–51 or Rassam's ransacking of the north palace of Aššurbanipal, his other royal library and adjacent libraries in 1852–54. In the palace of Sennacherib at Kuyunjik in 1874, George Smith discovered Sm. 2118 and joined it to K.3401.[6] The Neo-Babylonian tablet is registered as coming from Dailem (Dilbat) in a shipment from Daud Thomas in 1881, who worked at this site under the direction of Rassam.[7]

Poetics

This composition has a very clear poetic structure. The basic line is an indivisible line of verse that alternates with verses divisible into two measures of varied length. These lines of verse combine to form a stanza consisting of seven lines: one single line and two sets of three verses (1, 2–4, 5–7, 8, 9–11, 12–14, 15, 16–18, 19–21, 22, etc.). The sets are unified by homoeoteleuton and parallelism. The language emphasizes the truth element in the story by use of the morphological form for "asseveration," the fientic precative (GAG §81–82). This form is found in lines 9ff. relating to Sargon's rescue from the waters of the deep and his rise to political dominance in southern Mesopotamia. Likewise, in the section of rhetorical questions meant to be applicable to any time and place, the verb form used is the reiterative Gtn form.

[5] Lambert, *apud* Lewis, *The Sargon Legend*, 11, 73, and 92.

[6] G. Smith, *Assyrian Discoveries: An Account of Explorations and Discoveries on the Site of Nineveh during 1873 and 1874* (London, 1875) 98, 224.

[7] J. Reade, "Rassam's Babylonian Collection: The Excavations and the Archives," in E. Leighty, *Catalogue of the Babylonian Tablets in the British Museum, vol. VI: Tablets from Sippar. I* (London, 1986) xxxii.

Manuscripts

Neo-Assyrian: Nineveh

A K.3401 + Sm. 2118 = CT 13 42 (see photograph, p. 380).
B K.4470 = CT 13 43a (see photograph, p. 379).
C K.7249 = CT 46 46 (see photograph, p. 380).

Transcription

1.	A:1	LUGAL.GI.NA LUGAL *dan-nu* LUGAL *A-kà-dè*.KI *a-na-ku*
	B i 1	LUGAL.G[I.NA] ⸢LUGAL⸣ *dan-nu* LUGAL *A-kà-*[. . .]
	D rev. iii 1–2	LUGAL.DU LUGAL.KALAG; LUGAL *A-kà-dè*.KI
2.	A:2	*um-mi e-ni-tum a-bi ul i-di*
	B i 2	*um-m*[*i*] *e-ni-tum a-bi ul i-*⸢*di*⸣
	D rev. iii 3–4	AMA *e-ni-tum*; AD *la i-ši*
3.	A:2	: ŠEŠ.AD-*ja i-ra-mi šá-da-a*
	B i 3	ŠEŠ.AD-*ja i-ra-mi šá-da-a*
	D rev. iii 5–6	[. . .] ⸢x⸣; [. . .]
4.	A:3	*a-li* URU.A-*zu-pi-ra-a-ni šá i-na a-ḫi* ÍD.UD.KIB.NUN.KI *šak-nu*
	B i 4	*a-li* URU.A-*zu-pi-ra-nu šá i-na a-ḫi* [ÍD].UD.KIB.NUN.KI *šak-n*[*u*]
	D rev. iii 7–9	[. . .]; [. . .]; *šak-*[*nu*]

Philological and Textual Notes

1. For a detailed discussion of the writing LUGAL KALAG, see Lewis, *The Sargon Legend*, 32–35, and for the latest treatment of the development of the epithet *dannum* and *šarrum dannum*/LUGAL.KALAG.GA, see W. W. Hallo, "Royal Titles from the Mesopotamian Periphery," *AnSt* 30 (1980) 189–95. Note also the use of the epithet in relation to the Hurrian kings of Simurrum: E. Sollberger, "Two New Seal-Inscriptions," *AnSt* 30 (1980) 63–65.

2. For the term *ēnetu*, see Lewis, *The Sargon Legend*, 37–42; Lewis states that "the identification of *ēnetu* as a singular form of *ēntu* (pl. *ēnētu*) has been accepted by many authorities" and equates it with Sumerian NIN.DINGIR and EN. Since this is not the place to discuss the role and function of the holders of these titles, suffice it to say for the present that the situation regarding the various cults in different localities is extremely complex.

Neo-Babylonian: Dilbat
D BM 47449 (81-11-3, 154) = CT 13 43b (see photograph, p. 381).

Translation

1. Sargon, the mighty king, king of Akkade, am I.

2. My mother was an en-priestess(?), my father I never knew.

3. My father's brother inhabits the highlands.

4. My city is Azupirānu, which lies on the bank of the Euphrates.

---

3. For inhabitants of the mountains, highlanders, as an ethnic designation during the Old Akkadian period, see P. Steinkeller, "The Old Akkadian Term for 'Easterner,'" *RA* 74 (1980) 1–9. For fratriarchal kinship structures in Mesopotamia, see I. J. Gelb, "Household and Family in Early Mesopotamia," *State and Temple Economy in the Ancient Near East* [OLA 5; Leuven, 1979] 77–79), as well as C. Wilcke, "Familiengründung im alten Babylonien," *Geschlechtsreife und Legitimation zur Zeugung* (Munich, 1986) 219–22, who emphasizes the importance of the father's brother.

4. As has already been noted, no such city has been located, but its meaning, "a specific *azupīru*-like spice and medicinal plant," is well known. Note, however, the logogram Ú.ḪUR.SAG would mean 'Mountain Plant' in Sumerian, which may be related to Sargon's supposed origins in the highlands. This herb was also used as a potion to produce abortions, which may lend a double entendre to this so-called place-name.

5.	A:4	i-ra-an-ni um-mu e-ni-tum i-na pu-uz-ri ú-lid-an-ni
	B i 5	i-ra-an-ni um-mi e-ni-tum i-na pu-[uz]-ri ú-lid-an-ni
	D rev. iii 9–12	[. . .]; AMA e-⸢ni⸣-tum; ina pu-uz-zu; ú-lid-da-an-ni
6.	A:5	iš-kun-an-ni i-na qup-[p]i šá šu-ri i-na ÉSIR KÁ-ja ip-ḫi
	B i 6	iš-kun-an-ni i-na qup-pi šá šu-ú-[x] i-na ÉSIR KÁ-ja ip-ḫi
	D rev. iii 13–16	iš-ku-na-an-ni; ina qu-up-pu; šá šu-ú-šú ina ÉSIR; KÁ-ja ip-ḫi
7.	A:6	id-dan-ni a-n[a Í]D šá la e-li-e-[a]
	B i 7	id-dan^{an}-ni a-na ÍD šá la e-li-e-⸢a⸣
	D	(end of excerpt)
8.	A:7	iš-šá-an-ni ÍD a-na U[GU ^{l}A]q-qí LÚ.A.BAL ú-bil-a[n-ni]
	B i 8	[. . .].BAL ú-bi-la-an-[ni]
9.	A:8	^{l}Aq-qí LÚ.A.BAL i-na ṭí-i[b da]-⸢li⸣-[e-šú l]u ú-še-la-an-n[i]
	B i 9	[^{l}]Aq-qí LÚ.A.BAL i-na ṭí-ib ⸢x⸣ [. . . l]u-u ú-še-la-an-*⸢x⸣
10.	A:9	^{l}Aq-qí LÚ.A.BAL a-na ma-ru-ti-⸢šú⸣ [l]u ú-rab-⸢ban⸣-[. . .]
	B i 10	[^{l}]Aq-qí LÚ.A.BAL a-na ma-r[u . . .] ú-rab-ba-ni-$^{+}$ma
11.	A:10	^{l}Aq-qí LÚ.A.BAL a-na LÚ.NU.KIRI$_{6}$-ti-šú lu-u [i]š-kun-[. . .]
	B i 11	[^{l}]Aq-qí LÚ.A.BAL a-na LÚ.NU.KI[RI$_{6}$ x x x x] iš-kun-an-ni
12.	A:11	[. . .] LÚ.NU.KIRI$_{6}$-ti-iá ^{d}Iš-tar lu-u i-ra-man-n[i-ma]
	B i 12	⸢i⸣-na LÚ.NU.KIRI$_{6}$-ti-iá ^{d}I[š-tar . . .]-ra-man-ni-ma
13.	A:12	[x+]4$^{?}$ MU.MEŠ LUGAL-ú-ta lu-u e-pu-[uš]
	B i 13	[x+]4 MU.MEŠ LUGAL-ú[. . . u]š
14.	A:13	[ÙKU].MEŠ SAG.GI$_{6}$.GA lu-u a-be-el lu-u áš-[. . .]
	B i 14	[ÙKU].MEŠ ṣal-mat SAG.DU lu-u a-b[e-el . . .]
15.	A:14	[šá-di]-e KAL.MEŠ ina ak-kul-la-te šá URUDU.ḪI.A lu-u up-[ta-aṣ-ṣi-id]
	B i 15	[KUR-di]-i KAL.MEŠ ina ak-kul-la-[. . .]

---

13. The number of years of Sargon's reign is much debated; thus, no conjecture is offered for this text. Note that the figure for Sargon's reign in the Tell Leilan recension of the Sumerian King List is 54 (C.-A. Vincente, ZA 85 [1995] 242 iii 23; and see discussion on p. 263).

15.–19. These lines could make geographical sense if one assumes that Sargon proceeded first eastwards across the Zagros, perhaps to the area of Kerman, then southwards to the Indian Ocean and took in Dilmun in the Persian

5. She conceived me, my en-priestess mother, in concealment she gave me birth,

6. She set me in a wicker basket, with bitumen she made my opening watertight,

7. She cast me down into the river from which I could not ascend.

8. The river bore me, to Aqqi the water-drawer it brought me.

9. Aqqi the water-drawer, when lowering his bucket, did lift me up,

10. Aqqi the water-drawer did raise me as his adopted son,

11. Aqqi the water-drawer did set me to his gardening.

12. While I was (still) a gardener, Ištar did grow fond of me,

13. And so for [. . .] years I did reign as king,

14. The black-headed people, I did rule and govern.

15. With copper pickaxes, I did cut my way through the (most) difficult mountains.

Gulf on his way home. On the other hand, they could represent categories of heroic activities.

15. Rather than *ár*-[*ḫi*?-*iṣ*?] (suggested by Lewis, *The Sargon Legend*, 62), we might read *up*-[*ta-aṣ-ṣi-id*] 'I cut through'. *Puṣṣudu* is often used in connection with pickaxes, e.g., *ḫuršānīšunu ina akkullāt erî lupeṣṣid* (Weidner Tn. 27 No. 16:44; cf. ibid., 32 No. 18:7).

16.	A:15	[*lu-u*] *e-til-li šá-di-i e-lu-t*[*i*...]
	B i 16	[...]-*li* KUR-*di-i* [...]
17.	A:16	[*lu-u*] *at-ta-tab-lak-ka-ta šá-di-i šap-l*[*u-ti*]
	B i 17	[... *l*]*ak-ka-ta* [...]
18.	A:17	[*ma*]-*ti ti-amti lu-ú al-ma-a* [...]
	B i 18	[...] *al-*⌜*ma-a* 3-*šú*⌝
19.	A:17	: NI.TUK.KI *lu-u ik-*[...]
	B i 18	: NI.TU[K ...]
20.	A:18	[*a-n*]*a* BÀD AN.KI GAL-*i* [...] *lu-u* [...]
	B i 19	[...].KI GAL-*i* [...]
21.	A:19	[*ab*(?)]-*ni lu ú-nak-kir-ma* [...]
	B ii 20	[...]-*nak-kir-ma* [...]

16.–17. The translation assumes that the pair *elûti-šaplūti* refers to the topographical features of the landscape; but it might just as well be taken in the geographical sense of "northern-southern." In the latter case, it would be a calque on the "upper and lower seas" of the Old Akkadian period.

18. On the writing *ti*-GEMÉ, a Standard Babylonian literary orthography for *tiʾāmtum*, written *ti-a-am-tum* in Old Akkadian, see RGTC 1 203ff.; AHw 1353. As to the nomen regens at the beginning of the sentence, the following compounds existed in Old Akkadian during the period of the greatest expansion of Mesopotamian presence in the Indian Ocean: *pūti tiāmtim* (*aK* 164: Text A VO6:12–13; Text B VO6:18–19 "Sargon C 2") and *abarti tiāmtim šapiltim* (*aK* 221:32–34 "Maništūšu C 1"). Unfortunately, the vertical wedge in line 29 leaves us no choice but to read [*m*]*āti tiāmti* 'the sea land', an anachronism. Although in the "Chronicles of Early Kings," Sargon is said to have crossed the sea in the east, according to the NA omen collection (King Chron. 3:24), he crossed the sea in the west (*ma-a-ti* A.AB.BA) (see the discussion by Grayson, *Chronicles*, 235–36, sub Sargon).

19. On the location of Dilmun, see the articles in D. Potts (ed.), *Dilmun: New Studies in the Archaeology and Early History of Bahrain* (BBVO 2; Berlin, 1983) and the review of T. Howard-Carter, "Dilmun: At Sea or Not at Sea" (*JCS* 39 [1987] 54–115), as well as S. H. A. Al Khalifa (ed.), *Bahrain through the Ages: The Archaeology* (London, 1986).

20. There are three possible interpretations of the graphemes BÀD.AN.KI GAL-*i*:

(1) The accepted interpretation is Greater Dêr, equating it with Dêr or Dîr (Akkadian for Sumerian BÀD.KI, BÀD.A.KI, BÀD.AN.KI), known from the Pre-

16. I did ascend all the high mountains,

17. I did traverse all the foothills,

18. The sealands, I did sail around three times.

19. Dilmun did submit to me (?) . . .

20. The Great Wall of Heaven and Earth(?), I did ascend.

21. [(Its very) st]ones(?), I did remove [. . .]

Sargonic Period onwards (see RGTC 1 22, RGTC 2 22, RGTC 3 33). Apparently variant writings of the city Dêr appear in 2 out of the 4 year-dates of Šulgi, which mention the city Dêr as follows: (a) mu [B]À[D G]A[L A]N [K]I ki-a ba-gar 'the year in which Dêr(?) was restored', year-date 5 (for latest evidence see C. Wilcke, "Neue Quellen aus Isin zur Geschichte der Ur-III-Zeit," *Or* 54 [1985] 300); (b) mu dKA.DI BÀD.GAL.AN.KI é-a ba-dù 'the year in which the temple of Ištaran of Dêr(?) was built', year-date 11; (c) [mu BÀ]D.AN.KI ba-ḫul 'the year in which Dêr was destroyed', year-date 21a; (d) [mu-ú]s-sa BÀD.AN.KI ba-ḫul 'the year after Dêr was destroyed', year-date 22. It is known that more than one location was designated as BÀD.AN.KI, and the one on the periphery of the Mesopotamian core was probably the goal of Šulgi's expedition in his 21st/22d year. On the other hand, there is no tradition connecting Sargon of Akkade with a city of Dêr except in the "Sargon Geography" (*AfO* 25, 55:17). Furthermore, there is no such entity as Greater Dêr, as the Akkadian must be read.

(2) "The Great Wall of Heaven and Earth": The combination bad-gal 'great wall' is a common designation of the walls of various fortified cities, as well as a symbol of divine or royal protection (see PSD s.v. bàd). It could be the proper name of the walls of Dilmun or of another locality. Since this verse refers to an extraordinary feat of Sargon beyond those mentioned in the preceding lines, it could refer to some hitherto unknown cosmic term for the ends of the earth.

(3) Another possibility is the equation BÀD.AN.KI = *kālû* 'dike' (see PSD B 45).

21. As pointed out by Lewis (*The Sargon Legend*, 65), the reading [*ka*]-*zal-lu* is problematic, because there is insufficient room for KA in the break. The

22.	A:20	[*man*]-*nu* LUGAL **š*[*á*] *i-la-a* EGIR-*ja*
23.	A:20	: [x MU.MEŠ LUGAL-*ú-ta li-pu-uš*]
24.	A:21	[UK]Ù.MEŠ SAG.GI$_6$.GA *li*-[*be-el*]
25.	A:22	[KUR].MEŠ KAL.MEŠ *ina ak-kul-la*-[. . .]
26.	A:23	[*l*]*i-te-tel-li* KUR.MEŠ AN.TA.MEŠ
27.	A:23	: [. . .]
28.	A:24	[*m*]*a-ti ti-amti lil-ma-a* 3-*šú*
29.	A:24	: [. . .]
30.	A:25	[. . .] BÀD AN.KI GAL-*i li-li-ma*
31.	A:25	: [. . .]
32.	A:26	[. . .] *ul-tu* URU-*iá* A-*kà*-[. . .]
33.	A:27	[. . .] *ki-ma mul-mu*-[. . .]

(gap of ca. 15 lines)

49.	B ii 1	⸢x-x⸣ [. . .]
50.	B ii 2	*ù šu*-⸢*ru*⸣ [. . .]
	C:1	[. . .] x [. . .]
51.	B ii 3	*ir-tap-pu-ud* ⸢U$_8$⸣? [. . .]
	C:2	[. . . *i-n*]*a* EDIN *am-me-ni la* [. . .]
52.	B ii 4	*ù* MAŠ.DÀ *is-ra*[*t* . . .]
	C:3	[. . .]*is-rat šá-a-ri lu-li-ma* [. . .]

---

proper writing should in any case contain a determinative, either the Old Akkadian KI or the traditional first-millennium KUR. Moreover, just as there is no reason to read Dêr in the preceding line, there is no reason to read Kazallu in this one. It may be more feasible to read [*lum*]-*ni lu ú-nak-kir* 'I banished evil' (see CAD N/1 *nakāru* 8e 'to expel evil'). Nevertheless, all the narrative state-

22. Whatever king will arise after me,

23. [Let him exercise kingship for x years]!

24. Let him rule the black-headed people!

25. Let him cut his way through the (most) difficult mountains with copper pickaxes!

26. Let him ascend all the high mountains!

27. [Let him traverse all the foothills]!

28. Let him circumnavigate the sealands three times!

29. [Let Dilmun submit to him (?)]!

30. Let him ascend to the Great Wall of Heaven and Earth(?)!

31. [Let him remove (its) stones . . .]!

32. . . . . from my city Akkade. . . .

33. . . . . like arrows(?) . . .

(break)

49. . . .

50. And the steer . . .

51. The ewe ran about in the steppe, why not. . . . ?

52. And the gazelle driven by the wind, the stag. . . . by. . . .

---

ments concern deeds of action, and this line should accord. The suggestion [*ab*(?)]-*ni* given in the transliteration and translation is very tentative.

51. For the phrase *ṣēra rapādu*, see D. O. Edzard, "Kleine Beiträge zum Gilgames-Epos," *Or* 54 (1985) 47.

53.	B ii 5	*iṣ-ṣu-ru qa-du-*[. . .]
	C:4	[x-x]-*ru qa-du-ú šá iš-ta-su* [. . .]
54.	B ii 6	*ina ši-tas-si-šú* [. . .]
	C:5	[x-x-x]-*si-šú mi-na-a il-qí*
55.	B ii 7	*il-lik šá-a-ru* [. . .]
	C:5	: *il-lik* [. . .]
56.	B ii 8	*ir-tap-pu-ud* ANŠE.[EDIN.NA . . .]
	C:6	[x-x-*p*]*u-ud sír-ra-mu a-a-*⸢*ka*⸣ [. . .]
57.	B ii 9	*il-lak šá-a-r*[*u* . . .]
	C:7	[x]-*lak* IM *ina* A.RI.[A . . .]
58.	B ii 10	*ir-tap-pu-ud* ANŠE.[. . .]
	C:8	[x-x-(x)-*u*]*d* ANŠE.EDIN.NA *i-biṭ ina* EDIN
59.	B ii 11	*i-šá-ʾ-ú* [. . .]
	C:8	: *i-šá-*[. . .]
60.	B ii 12	*šá*(?) *pa-ri-i la-si-*[*me* . . .]
	C:9	[. . . -*r*]*i-e la-si-me a-a-*⸢*ka*⸣ [. . .]
61.	B ii 13	*ul i-šet* UR.[. . .]
	C:10	[. . .]-*šet* UR.BAR.RA *da-mi* [. . .]
62.	B ii 14	UR.MAḪ *a-ki-lu* [. . .]
	C:11	[. . .] *a-ki-lu da-mi* [. . .]
63.	C:12	[*la-ba*]-*tum ta-bi-ik da-mi* [. . .]
64.	B ii 15	[*ù*] x-*šú la-pit* [. . .]
	C:13	[. . .]-*šu la-pit da-mi* [. . .]

53. The *qadû* bird is used as a symbol in descriptions of destroyed cities; see J. G. Westenholz, "Review," *JNES* 43: 76–77. The *qadû* bird of Ea is described as shrieking "lament" (KAR 125:9); cf. W. G. Lambert, "The Sultantepe Tablets IX: The Bird Call Text," *AnSt* 20 (1970) 111–17; also Bauer Asb. 78 K.7673:18 (Asb. epic?).

58. Because these verses draw a picture of the futility of incessant action, the verb *ebēṭu* 'to have spasms' seems preferable to *biātu* 'to stay overnight'.

61. The verb is *šêtu* 'leave over', i.e., 'to spare'.

53. The screech owl which kept crying out. . . .

54. For all its crying, what did it achieve?

55. The wind blew. . . .

56. The onager constantly running about, where is. . . . ?

57. The wind blows in the steppe. . . .

58. The onager constantly runs about, he twitches in the steppeland.

59. They run. . . .

60. Of the swift mule, where . . . ?

61. The wolf did not spare, the blood. . . .

62. The lion, the devourer of blood,. . . .

63. The lioness, the spiller of blood,. . . .

64. Its cub, the smearer of blood,. . . .

62.–64. For the suggestion that the series lion-lioness-cub be read here, see Glassner, "Récit," 9. However, in line 63 we should expect *tābikat.* For a metaphorical picture of a lion drinking (rather than eating) the blood of enemies, see UR.MA[*Ḫ annium*] *šāti* [*d*]*ami na*[*kri*] '(the name of) this lion is: Drinker of the Blood of the Enemies (of Šamši-Adad by the command of the goddess Ištar)' (Charpin, *MARI* 3 [1984] 46:9–11 [copy of inscription of Šamši-Adad I]). As pointed out by Charpin, the only reference in the CAD to an *ākil dami* 'devourer of blood' is to the demons (CT 16 14 iv 34); but note *nēši ākili* 'devouring lions' in Borger Esarh. 109 iv 7.

65.	B ii 16	[*ir-tap-p*]*u-ud ina* [. . .]
	C:14	[x-x-*p*]*u-ud ina di-in* ^{d}*Šamaš a-*[. . .]
66.	B ii 17	[. . .] *a* [. . .]
	C:15	[*il-lik*(?)] *šá-a-ru* É.LÚ.M[EŠ(?)]
67.	B ii 18	[. . .] DINGIR [. . .]
	C:16	[. . .] pa *di-ʾa-ti* É.DINGIR.[. . .]
68.	B ii 19	[. . .] *a-na*(?) [. . .]
	C:17	[. . .]*-lak na-mu-ta*
69.	B ii 20	[. . .] x [. . .]
	C:18	: DUMU [. . .]
70.	B ii 21	[. . .] x [. . .]

65. It is constantly roaming by the decree of Šamaš, where is . . . ?

66. The wind. . . . , human habitations. . . .

67. . . . . concerns for the temples. . . .

68. . . . . will turn into wasteland . . .

69. . . . .

70. . . . .

Chapter 3

Sargon's Rise to Power: Sargon, Ur-Zababa, and Lugalzagesi

The story of Sargon's relationship with Ur-Zababa, king of Kiš, and his usurpation of power are embedded in three discourses: texts **3**, **4**, and **5**. The first two are unilingual Sumerian texts; text **3** is a fragment of the lower left-hand corner of a two-column tablet (TRS 73:AO 7673); text **4** is a single-column tablet with Akkadian glosses (3N T296); and text **5** is a bilingual exercise on a school tablet (VAS 24 75: VAT 17166). It is interesting to note that the first two were written in the centers of Sumerian culture, Uruk and Nippur, while the third was copied in the center of Babylonian culture, Babylon.

These compositions contain the events of Sargon's early childhood and life in the court of Ur-Zababa of Kiš. There is also emphasis on the existents, the setting, and the characters: a description of the prosperity of Kiš under the reign of Ur-Zababa, until the ominous advent of Sargon, of whom it is foretold that he will be the cause of its downfall. The story follows Sargon as he escapes the machinations of Ur-Zababa.

[N.B.: Texts **3** and **4** do not appear here; see p. 4 above for publication information.]

5
Sumerian-Akkadian Bilingual Exercise Text

Introduction

The following exercise contains three enigmatic lines relating Sargon's departure from the palace of Ur-Zababa and his tarrying at a canal. It is probably the continuation of the story line of the 3N T296 text. The discourse in which it is embedded is an excerpt from either a literary text concerning Sargon or a chronicle concerning early kings. For a bilingual version of the Weidner chronicle, see I. Finkel, "Bilingual Chronicle Fragments."[1] Further, the

[1] I. Finkel, "Bilingual Chronicle Fragments," *JCS* 32 (1980) 72ff.

Transcription

1. šar-rum-GI é-gal Ur-^{d}Za-ba$_{4}$-ba$_{4}$ íb-ta-è
   MIN *iš-tu e-kal* MIN *ú-ṣa-am-ma*
2. pa$_{5}$-sar-ra-ta mu-un-na-an-te-na-ra
   a-na pa-lag mu-ša-ri-e iṭ-ṭe$_{4}$-ḫi

Philological and Textual Notes

1. The first line of this text is almost identical to the line written on the left edge of text **4**: ^{l}šar-ru-um-ki-in é-gal ^{d}Ur-^{d}Za-ba$_{4}$-ba$_{4}$ im-ma-da-ra-ab-è. The differences between the two texts are: (1) the personal determinative on the name of Sargon; (2) the spelling of the name Sargon: text **4** šar-ru-um-ki-in (found also in an Old Babylonian economic text from Ur, *JCS* 28 [1976] 242, no. 11 ii 7, and text **10** [Sargon Letter]), and text **5** šar-rum-GI (found nowhere else); (3) the divine determinative on the name of Ur-Zababa; and (4) the prefix chain of the verb.

In contrast to the copy, the photograph of 3N T296, text **4**, shows the line clearly written towards the top of the tablet; its first sign is on the level between lines 1 and 2. In the edition of the 3N T296 text, this line was inserted as line 38a on the reverse, with no reason given for placing it there. There are three possible explanations for its appearance on the left edge: (1) an incipit containing the name of the series (e.g., N1454+; A. Berlin, *Enmerkar and Ensuḫkešdanna*, 61, comment to line 1, which has an incipit on the left edge), but

name of Sargon appears in a bilingual fragment, which may represent a similar type of text.[2]

This text is written on an oblong Old Babylonian school tablet. According to the paleography, it is late Old Babylonian or early Middle Babylonian. It was found by the Deutsche Orient-Gesellschaft in their excavations of Babylon before World War I, in the same area as the Old Babylonian tablets published in VAS 22, in the areas "Ischin aswad" and "Merkes." The exact findspot of the text is unknown.

Manuscripts

Babylon
VAT 17166 = VAS 24 75 (see photograph, p. 382).

[2] See D. J. Wiseman, "The Nimrud Tablets," *Iraq* 15 (1953) 153, ND 3474:5. I would like to thank M. Civil for this information.

Translation

1. Sargon left the palace of Ur-Zababa, and

2. Having neared the canal of the garden,

---

note that in such cases they are usually introduced by gi_4-ba; (2) a forgotten line that the scribe wanted to insert at the beginning of the composition (evidence for the latter explanation might be found in the evident attempt at erasure of the first line of the composition on the tablet, judging from the photograph); for a general discussion of such insertions of forgotten lines, see W. W. Hallo, "Haplographic Marginalia," *Finkelstein Mem. Vol.*, 101–3; (3) the line is the continuation of the end of the composition, the last line of the composition, or the first line (catch-line) of the next composition. The third possibility seems the most likely.

2. Sumerian: The subordination of the clause in this line is marked by nominalization followed by the case marker -ra. It is obviously not the dative case marker of animate nouns and must be related to the ablative infix -ra-, which alternates with the ablative infix -ta-. Note that in the next line, which is a particularizing verse, the clause is marked with the case marker -ta. On the other hand, it may be the construction Verb + a + ri, in which -ra appears in place of -ri,

3\. šar-rum-GI pa_5-sar-ra-ta ì-dúr-ru-na-ta
MIN *i-na* MIN [*it-ta-á*]*š*!-*ba-ma*

4\. 14 / PAD

---

but this is only found in Emesal Laments (M.-L. Thomsen, *The Sumerian Language* [Copenhagen, 1984] §492).

In reference to the canal of the garden, see mú-sar-ra pa_5-sikil-la GIŠ.SAR-ke_4 é-tu_5-a šu-mu-un-dù: *ina musarê palag kirî elli bīt rimki ēpušm*[*a*] 'in the garden, at the canal of the pure orchard, he built a *bīt rimki*' (STT 200:58).

The noun is marked by the "ablative-instrumental" -ta, postposition with locative meaning. For the locative use of the ablative, see M.-L. Thomsen, *The Sumerian Language*, §212 and the references cited there.

Akkadian: Note the use of the perfect tense to denote pluperfect aspect.

3. Sargon, having reclined by the canal of the garden,

---

4. ?

---

3. Sumerian: The subordination of the clause in this line is marked by nominalization followed by the ablative case marker -ta. The same construction is exhibited by 3N T296 (*JAOS* 103, 79 n. 2), which has a predilection for subordinating clauses with nominalization and following ablative case marker.

According to normative Sumerian, durun is plural of tuš (Thomsen, *The Sumerian Language*, §270), but there is no plurality of either subject or object. However, for dúr as sing. *marû* in pre-Ur III Sumerian, see P. Steinkeller, "Notes on Sumerian Plural Verbs," *Or* 48 (1979) 55 n. 6.

Akkadian: Most of the signs of the verb at the end of the sentence are lost. The reading [*it-ta-á*]š!-*ba-ma* is provisional: no sign except the -*ma* is certain.

Chapter 4

Res Gestae Sargonis

The story elements within the narrative statement of the following discourses comprise various events. Among the actions are the military expeditions to the northwestern territories of the Akkadian Empire and the bringing of booty to the land of Akkade. The most striking happening is the darkening of the sun.

Among the existents are a great number of characters: Sargon; his vizier; the *sukkallu*; later the *sukkallu* of the merchants; the merchants; the champion of the army; the *ašaredu*; the warriors; and Nur-Dagan king of Purušḫanda, the enemy.

In all these texts, Sargon appears as *primus inter pares*, a military commander seeking the advice and assistance of his subordinates before he hazards them and himself upon unknown paths of glory. Aside from these literary texts, a similar portrayal of the relationship between Sargon and his warriors appears in the omen literature. See, for instance, *amūt Šarrukīn ša ina* UR.SAG.MEŠ-*šú* KUR ŠÚ-*tú bēlu* (variant: UR.SAG.ME TUK-*ma* ŠÚ[-*tú bēlu*]) 'omen of Sargon, who with his warriors ruled the totality of the land'[1] and [UR.SA]G.KALAG.MEŠ *izzizzūniššumma êkiam i nillik iqbûšu* 'the mighty warriors stood around him and they said to him, "Where shall we go?" '[2]

If Sargon is clearly the protagonist of the narrative, the identity of his antagonist is uncertain. In text **6**, Sargon leads an expedition to the land of *Uta-rapaštim* (for the possible etymology of this difficult name, see comment to **6**:58). Texts **7** and **8** do not indicate the name of the antagonist of Sargon. In texts **9A–E** appear the following variants: ^{1}*Nu-ur-da-ga-*[*an*] (**9A**, KBo 13 46 x + i 8); ^{1}*Nu-úr-da-aḫ-ḫi* (**9A**, KBo 22 6 i 21); ^{1}*Nu-ur-dag-gal* (**9B** rev. passim); ^{1}ZALAG-^{d}*Da-gan* (**9D** 3, 9). Nougayrol relates the names Uta-rapaštim of text **6**

[1] K.2065:6 and dupls., see E. Reiner, *Anatolian Studies Presented to H. G. Güterbock*, 259.

[2] King Chron. 32 §viii 29, Ass. omen coll.

and Nur-Dagal/n to an unattested original *UD.DAGAL, the former being a translation and the latter being a poor rendition.[3] The later Akkadian tradition preserved in "The Babylonian Map of the World" or "Mappa Mundi" (CT 22 48 obv. 10′) reads: [. . .]$^{\ulcorner d \urcorner}$*Ut-napištim*(ZI)^{tim} *Šarru-kīn*(LUGAL.DU) *u Nūr*(ZALAG)-^{d}[*D*]*a-gan* LUGAL *Bur-š*[*a-ḫ*]*a-an-*[*da*]. Thus, there was no memory of any similarity between the first and third names by the first millennium. If Nougayrol is mistaken and the land of Uta-rapaštim is not related to Nur-Dagan, then it is possible that the name Uta-rapaštim refers to the land and not its ruler. Some confirmation of such an assumption can be found in text **7**, in which *me-ri-sú*! *rapaštam* appears in the description of the land (ii 13).

The characterization of the warriors is unique: they are depicted as domesticated animals, strong bulls (**6**:44), great oxen (**7** i 17′), and steers (**9B** obv. 1(?), 20).

The setting is painted in some detail, giving a description of the costume of the soldiers as well as a description of the fruitfulness of the faraway land.

Embedded in the deep structure of the narrative are binary oppositions between warfare : peace, action : non-action, light : darkness.

The surface discourse has an omnipresent covert narrator, but there is minimal narrator mediation since the deep binary oppositions are realized in the discourse as dialogue. These texts are unified by their use of dialogue, between the reluctant hero or soldiers and the eager king or merchants.

Certain specific words and idioms occur in these discourses. The most significant is the title of Sargon, *šar tamḫāri*, a title which is an epithet of the gods Nergal and Ninurta, the gods of warfare,[4] as well as Rib-Addi's designation for the pharaoh of Egypt.[5]

This saga tradition is considered the "Sargon Epos," according to Hecker's analysis and is treated by Glassner.[6]

[3] Nougayrol, "Chef d'oeuvre," 174.
[4] Tallqvist, *Götterepitheta*, 237.
[5] Seux, *Épithètes*, 319–30.
[6] Hecker, *Epik*, 36; Glassner, "Sargon."

6
"Sargon, the Conquering Hero"

Introduction

This composition concerns the values of valor and heroism more than any other text in the corpus. The terms *qurādūtum* and *qurdum* resound in the dialogue, and the text dwells in loving detail on the description of the armor of the soldiers.

The narrative is set at the court of Sargon. The story begins in the middle of a crucial situation, an event known to the ancient audience but not to the modern scholar. The reason that the composition opens in medias res could be that it is part of a larger work and thus forms only a second or third tablet in a series. The narrative segments are:

a. Sargon's address to his warriors in praise of heroism (lines 1–9);
b. Response of the champion of the army, the *ašaredu*, advising the king to let his words influence his actions (lines 10–16);
c. Narrator describes the situation and the positive reaction of the audience, the king and the army (lines 17–29);
d. Lecture by a courtier relating the glory to be achieved by the champion of the army, the *ašaredu*, in feats of arms (lines 30–39);
e. Narrative concerning the expedition to the faraway land of Uta-rapaštim, in which is related the description of the armor worn by the warriors, the darkening of the sun, the conquest of the land of Simurrum, and lastly the meting out of justice (lines 40–91);
f. Speech by one of the king's servants(?) (lines 92–93);
g. Transitional narrative line (lines 94–95);
h. Concluding oration of Sargon, listing his conquests and giving his challenge to future kings (lines 96–123).

The discourse contains a surface structure identical to that of text **7** in certain blocks. The parallel texts are:

6 30–52 parallels **7** iii 2′–11′
6 57–64 parallels **7** iv 9′–13′(?)
6 65–71 parallels **7** iii 13′–16′

However, although the surface discourse is identical, the deeper semantics seems to be different.

General Observations

The text is recorded on a two-column Old Babylonian tablet, written in a practiced hand, characterized by the use of both archaic and standard Old

Babylonian signs, unevenness of line spacing, unevenness in the clarity of the signs, unevenness in the depth of the signs, and erratic spacing. Note also the lack of a column divider, also found in text **14**.

Orthography and Language

There are a few graphic idiosyncracies displayed by this scribe, such as ligature RA×AM, as well as a specific shape of TI. The text is written in a syllabic script with few logograms (É.GAL, KASKAL.GÍD) appearing in the text. The few CVC signs include the common CVm series: TUM, TAM, TIM, KUM, LUM, LAM, NAM, RUM, plus GÀR with the syllabic value *kàr* (line 13) and QÀR (line 17).

The contrast of the graphemic pair BI:PI (line 16, *bi-ir-ki-ka*; line 15, *pi-ka*) expresses in writing the voiced/voiceless distinction which is characteristic of the southern tradition of orthography. The rest of the syllabary is normal southern Old Babylonian. There are no Q-signs in the text. Also in the southern tradition is the rendering of postulated affricated */ts/[7]: initially written with Z-signs (ZA [line 56, *sà-aḫ-pu*], ZI [lines 34–35, *sí-in-na-as-sú*]); intervocalically rendered as a single consonant by S-signs (line 22, *i-si-in-nam*) and as double consonant by Z-signs (line 72, *iz-zu-uḫ*). Furthermore, the southern Old Babylonian development of the nasalization of double-voiced stops is seen in line 70: *ma-an-da-at* = 7 iii 15′ *ma-da-at*. In addition, from either poetic constraints or regular linguistic process of assimilation, the */ana/* in line 6 assimilated to the following /k/: *ak-ku-nu-ši-im*. On the basis of these southern orthographic traits, one can conclude that the manuscript was written in southern Babylonia. The same conclusion was reached by Glassner.[8] There are a few doubtful contradictions, but the lack of clarity of the writing makes definite statements difficult.

[7] For this interpretation, see A. Faber, "Akkadian Evidence for Proto-Semitic Affricates," *JCS* 37 (1985) 101–7. Reference courtesy of A. Westenholz.

[8] Glassner, "Sargon," 116.

Transcription

Column i

1. [*at-tu*]*-nu-ma tu-ta-ak-ki-la-ni-in-ni*
2. [*aš-šu*]*m Ḫa-ar-mi-na-ri-ka*

Philological and Textual Notes

In these notes, the original publication of the text (J. Nougayrol, "Un Chef-d'œuvre inédit de la littérature babylonienne," *RA* 45 [1951] 169–83) will be referred to as "Noug.," and von Soden's collations ("Zu einigen altbabylonischen Dichtungen, 3. Zu der altbabylonischen Sargon-Sage *RA* 45, 169ff.," *Or* 26 [1957] 319–20) will be referred to as vS. In addition, the emendations were checked when I collated the tablet.

Morphologically, this text has a predilection for constructing adverbs with vocalic endings alone: *-a* (GAG §150) and *-ī* (GAG §113k). Mimation is used pretty consistently throughout this text.

Poetics

The short stich is the basic component of the poetic structure. These components are held together by various stylistic devices of parallelism (e.g., lines 20–21) and repetition (e.g., verbs *šutarruḫu* and *maḫāru* in lines 28–35). The use of the couplet is frequent (e.g., lines 15–16), and there are several examples of alliteration (e.g., *iḫillā ḫāḫilātum*, line 20) and assonance (e.g., *libbum išdum tībum*, line 4). In addition, there are hymno-epic morphological archaisms, such as the third plural determinative pronoun *šūt.*

Manuscript

Tablet AO 6702 arrived in the Louvre in 1914 as part of an acquisition of tablets and objects from the Parisian dealer Géjou. It has no apparent relationship with other tablets in this lot. In general see the original publication of the text by J. Nougayrol, "Un Chef-d'œuvre inédit de la littérature babylonienne," *RA* 45 (1951) 169–83 and also von Soden's collations: "Zu einigen altbabylonischen Dichtungen, 3. Zu der altbabylonischen Sargon-Sage *RA* 45, 169ff.," *Or* 26 (1957) 319–20. Nougayrol's line numbering of half-line continuations is maintained in the following edition in order to be consistent with past citations of this text; however, the scribe did not treat them as separate lines.

Unknown Provenance
AO 6702 = J. Nougayrol, "Chef-d'oeuvre," 169–80 (see photographs, pp. 382–83).

Translation

Column i

1. "[Yo]u were the ones who encouraged me.
2. "[Con]cerning Harminarika,

---

1. For this reading, see vS 320.

2. This line is difficult. Since Sargon is addressing his audience in second-person plural, von Soden's suggested reading for this line, [*aš-šu*]*m ḫa-ar-mi na-ri-ka* 'des Buhlen, deines Musikers', has not been accepted. Note that this reading still appears in the Ntrg. to AHw (1559b) with meaning "unkl." In its place, I would prefer two plural imperatives, but there are no verbs that fit

3. [*t*]*a-ap-ta-a uz-ni-i-a*
4. [*l*]*i-ib-bu-um iš-du-um ti-bu-um qú-ra-du-tum*
5. [*š*]*u-ta-tu-ku-nu-ši-im pa-na iš-tu ul-la*
6. [?] *ak-ku-nu-ši-im qú-ur-du-um*
7. [*ša a-t*]*a-wu-ú nu-ḫu-uš-ni qú-la*
8. [x-x]-*a šu-qá-a šu-di-a šu-ur-ḫ*[*a*]
9. [x]-⸢x⸣-*šu na pa lu ú* DI-*ḫi-a ṣa-ab*-[x]
10. ⸢*i-na-an-na*⸣?-*a-ma a-ša-re-du-um is-sà-a*[*k-k*]*a-ar*
11. *te-er pa-ag-ru-uk šu-ku-ut-ta-ka*
12. // *t*[*i-i*]*l-li-ka*
13. *wu-di at-*[*t*]*a ša ṭe-*⸢*mi*⸣ *ka-ši-id-ka na-kàr*
14. // (x)-x-x-x-*ul*-x
15. *pi-ka li-ib-ba-ka li-wa-ḫi-ir*
16. *ù li-ib-ba-ka li-wa-ḫi-ir bi-ir-ki-ka*
17. *an-na mi-it-ḫu-ru-um-ma ša qàr-ra-di*
18. *ur-ra-am qá-ab-lam ak-ka-di ú-ša-ar-ra*
19. [*i*]-*si-nu-um ša mu-ti in-ni-pu-uš*

---

grammatically. The present reading as a geographical name is a very tentative suggestion.

3–4. The readings of these lines are in accordance with von Soden's suggestions. Note that *taptâ* is a contracted form of *tapteā*, the expected Old Babylonian form.

5. The form of the verb *šutātû* is Št of *atû* stative plural. The verb *šutātû* 'to meet one another, especially in battle' occurs also in line 54 and in **7** i 18′. However, the four abstract nominatives of line 4 are the subject of the verb, which must be understood as meaning to 'meet, converge' in someone or for someone, an unattested usage of this verb.

8. This is a line of four imperatives, just as line 4 was a line of four nouns. Moreover, they all begin with the letter *š*, thus achieving obvious alliteration. Unfortunately, only two verbs are clearly preserved, and they could be a D-stem *šaqû* and an Š-stem *idû* (*šūdû*). Another possibility for the third verb was suggested by Walter Sommerfeld: *nadû* Š 'Cause (the enemy) to fling down (their weapons)'. The last verb in the line is probably *šarāḫu*.

9. This line makes little sense. The sequence DI-*ḫi-a* seems to continue the plural imperatives of the previous line. On the other hand, the beginning of the preserved section seems to have a verb in the subjunctive, as in line 7. Another possible interpretation is to remove this line from the end of the speech of Sargon and place it in the narrative transition. Evidence for this

3. "[y]ou have informed me.
4. "[Co]urage, strength, vigor, heroism—
5. "[th]ey have always found you (in battle) since times past.
6. "Valor is fitting for you.
7. "Take heed of our well-being [whereof I sp]oke!
8. "[. .] . ! stand tall! proclaim! be pro[ud]!
9. "that . . . approach! seize!"
10. Now(?), the champion speaks,
11–12. "Restore to your body your jewelry, your festive garb!

13–14. "Certainly, you are endowed with *ṭēmu*, your attacker is the enemy of . . .
15. "Let your mouth command your mind,
16. "and let your mind command your legs!"
17. Here, then, is the clashing of heroes.
18. Tomorrow, Akkade will commence battle.
19. A festival of men at arms will be celebrated.

---

might be found in the pronoun *-šu*. A tentative reading might be: [*pu-ḫu*]*-ur-šu na-la*(?) *ú-ṭe-ḫi-a ṣa-ab-*[*šu*] 'his "assembly" was . . . it summoned his army'.

11. The verb can only be a D imperative of *târu* 'wende zurück' (vS 320). The object of the verb is clearly *šukuttum*, and the form *pagruk* must be a terminative adverbial. The festive garb may refer to the festival of battle that is impending.

13. The reading *ša ṭe-*⌜*mi*⌝ 'der mit Verstand' was suggested by Walter Sommerfeld. Having *ṭēmu* was a most important human quality, the divine spark that animated mortal clay.

14. The rare word *šurḫullu*(*m*), read here by AHw 1283, does not fit the traces of the signs.

18. The identity of the subject and object of this line has been interpreted as follows: 'tomorrow Akkadi (subject) will resume (*utarra*) the battle (object)'. In this edition, the verb *utarra* 'resume' has been dropped in favor of *ušarra* 'begin' (AHw *šurrû*), since it fits the contents better. This verse forms the second line of a couplet and seems to be a particularizing verse. It specifies the time (tomorrow) and the place (Akkade).

19. The image of a battle as a festival also appears in the "Tukulti-Ninurta Epic," as well as in several other texts, all of which are heroic poetry: "Agushaya," "Erra," "Lugal-e." The ambiguity of the word *mu-ti* (*mūtu* 'death' versus *mutu* 'warrior') seems intentional. The speaker thus conveys battle as the test of manhood, as well as the fight to the death.

20. *i-ḫ*[*i-i*]*l-la ḫa-ḫi-la-tum*
21. *ur-ta-am-ma-ka da-ma a-li-ta-an*
22. *a-iš* ⸢*i*⸣*-si-in-nam i-na-aṭ-ṭa-lu ú-šu-ur-ru*
23. *uš-ša-ab ta-*x[-x]*-ú-um a-ḫa-am-ma*
24. *ù na-ḫi-iš a-wi-lum ša ur-ra-am in-nam-ra*
25. // *i-na ša-pa-ri-im*
26. *pi-šu e-te-el a-na a-pa-*[*a*]*l* [*ša*]*r-ri*
27. *ú-ul i-šu ge-ri-i i-na um-ma-an ša*[*r-ri*]
28. [*i-n*]*a li-ib-bi* [*ki-i*]*ṣ-ri*
29. [*ú*]*-ul šu-ta-ar-*[*r*]*u-uḫ*
30. *ki-ma ur-ra-am tu-uš-ta-ra-ḫu*
31. // *i-na qé-re-eb* É.GAL*-li*
32. *ta-ak-li-ma-tim li-im-ḫu-u*[*r*]
33. // *šu-kal-l*[*um*]
34. *ka-ak-ki na-ki-ri mu-ḫu-ur sí-*in-*
35. //*-na-as-sú*
36. *a-ta-aḫ-da-kum-ma šar-rum a-li-li*
37. // *li-še-di-kum.*

20–21. These lines are read in accordance with vS. This couplet conveys the life and death struggle of women in labor as either a metaphor for battle or as a contrast to it. Cf. *kî qarrādi muttaḫḫiṣ ina damēša ṣallat* 'she (the woman in childbirth) lies in her own blood like a fighting warrior' (*Iraq* 31, 31:40). The grammatical form of *ālittān* is dual, perhaps metaphorically depicting a battle between two champions.

22. For the reading *i-na-aṭ-ṭa-lu*!?, see vS, and for *ušurru* 'companion, comrade', see AHw 1443b. The sound play on the word *ušarra* (l.18) found in verse final position has influenced the normal syntactical order of the present verse.

29. For the reading, see vS.

33. Despite his suggestion in *Orientalia* (*sú-un-ka*), von Soden reads this line as *šukkall*[*um*] in AHw 1263 (*šu*!*-kal-l*[*um*!]).

34–35. Nougayrol had suggested reading the end of the line as: *ze-ru-ni* // *na-as-sú* 'Notre adversaire, broie-le!' while the CAD N/2 32b lists this reference as uncertain under the adj. *nassu* in predicative use, which indicates a possible reading such as 'our enemies are wretched'. However, the word 'enemy' in Old Babylonian has the uncontracted form *zāʾiru*. Therefore, I rejected the reading and suggested another based on collation of the tablet.

20. The women in labor are in travail,
21. two women giving birth are drenched in blood.
22. Where are the comrades observing the festival?
23. The . . . dwells apart.
24–25. But prosperous the man who was seen on the morrow in a position of command.
26. His voice was noble in responding to the king.
27. He did not have opponents in the army of the king.
28. In the midst of the regiments,
29. he was not thirsting for glory.
30–31. "When you are singled out for praise tomorrow in the palace,

32–33. "let the vizier take instructions (from you),

34–35. "But (you) face the weapon of the enemies, his lance!

36–37. "I have paid careful attention to you so that the king as 'my warrior' might acclaim you.

---

36. The verb at the beginning of the line is *naʾādu* with dative suffix, meaning 'to pay attention to, to be concerned about someone or something'.

There has been some confusion in the treatment of the word *a-li-li.* This rises from two words: (1) *alālum* 'an exclamation of joy', 'song', in relation to agricultural celebrations (CAD *alāla, alāli, elilu* ["Sum. lw."], *elēlu*), from which is derived the denominative verb *alālu* B (= AHw *alālu* III denom. of *alālu* I). This word is related to Sumerian a-la-la/u (PSD a-la-la [an exclamation; a work cry], a-la-lu [a song or an exclamation], a-lu-lu [an exclamation]); see M. Civil, "The Song of the Plowing Oxen," *Kramer AV*, 83–95; A. Livingstone, "A Fragment of a Work Song," ZA 70 (1981) 55–57; and (2) *ālilu* 'brave one, warrior', epithet of gods and kings. The relationship between these two lexemes may be etymological, the latter having a participial form and originally meaning: 'He who sings or shouts Hallelujah', perhaps describing a warrior going into battle singing a battle hymn. On the basis of morphology, the form *a-li-li* appears to belong under (2). Nonetheless, CAD puts our reference under *alāla* (328a) and translates 'may the king honor you with *public acclamation*' and links it with "Agušaya" *išātu ul tamḫat a-li-li* '(Ištar) fire (which) nobody can hold, (I exclaim) "Hurrah!"' VAS 10 214 iii 9 and 13. The latter reference is now read by B. Groneberg: *i-ša-ṭú-ú-ul ta-am-ḫa-at a-te-li* 'Sie missachtet (?), packt

Column ii

38. *ṣa-lam-ka li-iš-zi-iz i-*[*n*]*a ma-ḫa-a*[*r*]
39. // [*ṣ*]*a-al-mi-šu*
40. *e-ru-is-sú-un ṣa-li-lum ú-ḫa-li-iq*
41. *n*[*a-a*]*ḫ-du a-lam ú-ša-al-li-im a-na be-li-*[*šu*?]
42. *ú-bi-il-ma qá-as-sú um-ma-nam*
43. // *ú-ta-ab-bi-i*[*b*]
44. *mi-ri da-an-nu-tim a-li-li uš-*[*ta-li-ik*]
45. 40 *li-mi mi-it-*[*l*]*u tu-*[*qú-um-tam*]
46. *šu-ut i-na-li-im* 3-*šu qú-*[*ra-du-tim*]
47. *šu-ut ta-aq-*[*ri-ba-tim*(?)]
48. *i-ra-at ḫu-ra-aṣ ḫa-pi-*[*ru*]
49. [*i-n*]*a ka-ar ḫa-ši-im-ma*
50. *šu-ut pa-ar-zi-il-li*

---

nicht die . . .' (*RA* 75 [1981] 109 and see note to line on p. 120). The reading *a-li-li* is an emendation of this line. Furthermore, there is another hapax in "Agušaya" that has been related to *ālilu*: *a-li-wi-tim* (*RA* 15 [1918] 174ff. i 23). The latter line is translated 'she makes many c-cries for battle' by B. Foster, who relates it to the *a-li-li* of our composition as 'cry of triumph' and describes the "Agušaya" passage as containing a misformed plural and the Sargon passage as containing an indeclinable form ("Ea and Ṣaltu," *Finkelstein Mem. Vol.*, 83 n. 31). Note that in her treatment of "Agušaya," B. Groneberg hesitates to give any interpretation to this passage (*RA* 75 [1981] 132). Thus, our reference would be an exceptional formation. Consequently, it seems more logical to use the most common understanding of the form *a-li-li* as an accusative of the noun *ālilu* with a first-person possessive suffix: 'my warrior'.

40–41. This couplet seems to be a proverbial saying. It is not preserved in text **7**. The direct object is the noun *erûtu* plus a plural suffix. Despite von Soden's emendation *e-ru-ús*!*-sú-un*, the tablet has a clear *e-ru-*IS*-sú-un*. This broken writing is of a very common type; see B. Groneberg, "Zu den 'Gebrochenen Schreibungen,'" *JCS* 32 (1980) 151–67. The plural pronoun can only be taken to refer to an impersonal collective.

42. Although the phrase *qātam abālu* 'to lay hands on' is usually used in connection with a sacred or taboo object, in these texts it means 'to initiate activity'. Cf. *qātī ana dâki ul ūbilšunūti* 'I did not lift my hand to kill them', **22**:148.

43. The verb is understood as D perfect of *ebēbu* 'to make clean, purify', perhaps related to the ceremony of *tēbibtu*. In Mari, this ceremony was an act of purification accompanying census-taking; see J. Sasson, "The Calendar and Festivals of Mari during the Reign of Zimri-Lim," *Studies Jones*, 125. Neverthe-

Column ii

38–39. "that he might erect your statue in front of his own statue."

40. (As it is said,) the drowsy destroyed their wakefulness,
41. (but) the vigilant saved the city for his lord.

42–43. He took control and the army he purified/mustered.

44. The strong bulls, the warriors he put into action.
45. 40,000 were they, filled with battle.
46. Those from the city, threefold heroic,
47. those of the escort,
48. adorned with a gold breastplate,
49. from the marketplace of Ḫaššum.
50. The ironclad,

---

less, we know that the army underwent a purification ceremony before battle; see J. van Dijk, "Un Rituel de purification des armes et de l'armée: Essai de traduction de YBC 4184," *Symbolae Böhl*, 107–17.

44. Both the readings *mi-ri-it an-nu-tim* 'die Weide dieser' suggested by vS, as well as CAD's 'musical instrument' have been rejected. Since the signs ID and DA are not clearly distinguished in this text, the second word might be *dannūtim*. Thus, the signs *mi-ri* must form a plural oblique noun. Possibly, the word *mīru* 'stud bull' could be meant, although *mīru* is never used figuratively (except in Sumerian); cf. *alpū rabûtu* in **7** i 17′–18′.

48. Note that the word *ḫurāṣu* is in status absolutus.

49. For the reading, see vS, and for the location of the port-of-trade Ḫaššum, see the latest summary in V. Davidović, "Trade Routes between Northern Syria and Central Anatolia in the Middle of the III Millennium B.C.," *ASJ* 11 (1989) 4 and the references listed there. A further reference to Haššum in the Old Babylonian period is found in a letter of a traveling merchant AbB 12 51:13.

50. On iron in the Old Babylonian period, see H. Limet, "Documents relatifs au fer à Mari," *MARI* 3 (1984) 191–96, J. D. Muhly, "The Bronze Age Setting," in *The Coming of the Age of Iron* (ed. T. A. Wertime and J. D. Muhly; New Haven, 1980) 25–67. One of the earliest examples of the use of iron for something more than pins and beads is the famous iron sword from Tomb K at Alaca Höyük. This tradition of early ironworking in Anatolia can be seen in the many objects listed in J. Waldbaum, *From Bronze to Iron* (Göteborg, 1978) 19–20. In the texts of the Old Assyrian period are found the words *amūtum* and *aši*ʾ*um*, both of which have been identified as some sort of iron, as well as *šadwānum*,

51. *na-šu re-eš na-ap-lu-ḫa-tim*
52. *na-al-ba-aš šu-ut ki-ti-i ša-ad-du-*[*tim*]
53. *em-qá-am bi-ir-ki-***im*
54. *šu-ta-tu-ú qú-ur-da-am*
55. *šu-ut ki-ma ka-ak-ka-bi*
56. *ú-ga-ri sà-aḫ-pu*
57. *it-ta-aḫ-ba-at šar-rum-ki-in*
58. *a-na ma-tim ša ú-ta-ra-pa-áš-tim*

---

identified as hematite. On the other hand, there are several Old Babylonian references to objects of iron that use the word *parzillum* (AHw 83–84, as well as references above). The designation 'those of iron' in this composition could refer to soldiers carrying swords or other weapons of iron but could not be a metaphor for hardihood and fortitude in battle, since such an interpretation would be anachronistic. The wrought form of iron known in this period was not very strong. Another possibility is that the delineation of the warriors in these lines designates ethnic groups. For possible Sumerian literary references to iron, cf. Hallo, "Lugalbanda Excavated," *JAOS* 103 (1983) 173, lines 344–45, 354–55, and note on p. 178.

51. The word *na-ap-zu/lu-ḫa-tim* is a hapax. The AHw offers *napluḪatim* unkl., and the CAD N/1 306 **napluḫtu* mng. uncert. The latter proposes the following translation of this line: 'who pays attention to the *n*'s'. Although it sounds like *naḫlaptu* 'outer garment', one must resort to metathesis to explain the word thus. If one reads the third sign as *-lu-*, one arrives at the root p-l-ḫ, meaning 'fear', which is the base of *apluḫtu* 'armor' and of *puluḫtu* 'fear'. Note the use of *puluḫtu*, pl. *pulḫātu* in the following quotations: *pulḫāti ušalbišma* 'she (Tiamat) clothed (the terrible ušumgallus) in fear' En. el. III 27; *naḫlapta apluḫti pulḫāti halipma* '(Marduk) enveloped in an armored garment of fear' En. el. IV 57; *šūt pulḫāti ṣaʾinu* 'those who are decorated with fear' En. el. IV 115. A nominal form *napluḫtu* would be the feminine of the verbal adjective N-stem of *palāḫu*, similar to *nāmurtu* from *amāru*. This hapax is most probably a conflation of *naḫlaptu* and *apluḫtu*. A similar alternation of nominal forms *apras*(+) and *napras*(+) can be found in the lexemes *antalû* and *namtalû*.

52. The word *nalbaš* 'a fine cloak' has no syntactic connection to the rest of the sentence. Formally, it is in status constructus or absolutus. Perhaps the surface form is the result of auditory haplography for *nalbašu šūt kitî*. Both expressions, *nalbaš* and *šūt kitî*, relate to actual professional classes; cf. gada-lá = ŠÚ-*lu*, šà-gada-lá = *labiš kitê*, šà-túg-TÚG-lá = MIN *nalbaši* Lu IV 98–100. Furthermore, there is the designation *šūt* GADA in **11**:87. The word *šaddûtum* may be related to *šaddûʾa*, meaning 'easterner(< highlander)' (see P. Steinkeller, "The Old Akkadian Term for 'Easterner,'" *RA* 74 [1980] 1–9) or to the Old Assyrian customs (*šaddûʾatum*) and Old Babylonian tax collections (*šadduttum*). Note

51. Raising (their) frightful head;
52. the linen-cloaked dressed in mountain-gear,
53. swift of knee,
54. finding each other in heroism.
55. Those (warriors) like the stars (in the sky),
56. covered the plain.
57. Sargon had (barely) ventured into
58. the land of Uta-rapaštim,

---

that von Soden emends the last word in the line: *il*!-*la*!-*ab*!-[*šu*] and translates 'mit der Bekleidung derer von Leinen bekleideten sie sich'. This attractive reading finds support in **7** iii 10′: ⌜*ki il-la-ab*⌝-*šu* ⟨*šu*⟩-†*nu ki-ta-a-ti-im*. Unfortunately, the reading of this line is absolutely certain (collated).

53. For the latest discussion of the grammatical construction of an adjective with the ending -*a*(*m*) preceding a substantive in the genitive, see E. Reiner, "*DAMQAM-ĪNIM* Revisited" (*StOr* 55 [1984] 177–82), where our example is listed as *emqam birkīn* (p. 179). This reading is based on von Soden's reading of the photograph -*i*[*n*] (*JNES* 19 [1960] 164). Although it is tempting to read here a dual form, the traces of the last sign in this line seem to be -*im* and there are traces of an erased -*im* directly after -*ki*- as well. Note that this line does not agree in person with the preceding and following lines, in that it is in the singular while all others are in plural.

57–64. Sargon's experience of the sun's darkening is found throughout the historiographic texts: J. Nougayrol, "Notes sur la place des présages historiques dans l'extispicine babylonienne," *École pratique des hautes études, section des sciences religieuses, Annuaire* (1944–45) nos. 54 (Marḫaši), 55, 62, 66; A. Goetze, "Historical Allusions in Old Babylonian Omen Texts," *JCS* 1 (1950), nos. 11, 12; King Chron. no. 3:19–21. Other occurrences of the darkening of the daylight are found in "Lugal-e" and "Anzu." As clearly stated in the omen texts, the responsibility for such feats is Ištar's. Cf. eden-da[gal]-sig-ga u_4-zalag kukkú an-bir_4(NE) mul-SIG_7-šè mu-un-dù-x 'in the wide (and) low steppe she darkens the bright daylight, turns midday light into darkness' (In-nin-šà-gur_4-ra Hymn to Inanna, line 49, repeated in lines 177, 210).

57. For the various meanings of *ḫabātu*, see F. R. Kraus, "Akkadische Wörter und Ausdrücke, IX: ḫabātum," *RA* 69 (1975) 31ff. Our example pertains to the group CAD *ḫabātu* D = AHw *ḫabātu* III. It basically means physical movement and is defined in the lexical tradition as *ḫabātu ša alāki*, *ḫabātu ša šalāli* in Antagal A 114; see also Goetze, *JCS* 1 (1950) 257.

58. In the name *Ú-ta-ra-pa-áš-tim* appears the only occurrence of ÁŠ for the syllable /aš/ in this text. Does this indicate a traditional spelling of a proper name? The name could either be personal or geographic. As a personal name, it has been emended to coincide with the name of the survivor of the flood:

59. *tu-ša ge-ri-ma qí-iš-tum ig-re-e-šu*
60. *iš-ku-un ik-li-tam*
61. *a-na nu-úr ša-ma-i*
62. *id-ḫi-im ša-am-šu-um*
63. *ka-ak-ka-⟨⟨ak-ka⟩⟩-bu ú-ṣú-ú*
64. // *a-na na-ak-ri-im*
65. *ša-ak-nu du-ru ša na-ak-ri a-na* *9 **ti-*ši-šu-nu*
66. *a-wi-lam al-pa-am ù i*(wr. over er. ME)*-mi-ra-am*
67. *mi-i*[*t-ḫa-r*]*i-*[*i*]*š ik-*[*mi*]
68. *i-n*[*a* u_4*-mi-šu-*]*ma ši-mu-ur-r*[*a-am ik-mi*]
69. [*ma-an-d*]*a-at ak-ka-di ša iš-ti-i*!*-šu*
70. [*ù*] *ma-an-da-at ak-ka-di li-ta-at* x x
71. *a-lam ut-te-er a-na ti-li ù kàr-mi*

Uta-napištim. However, there does not seem to be any necessity to make such an emendation. It would be appropriate for Gilgameš to search for him who has found life and for Sargon to search for him who has found the wide (land). Nonetheless, neither *napištim* nor *rapaštim* are in the accusative case and thus cannot grammatically be direct objects. Furthermore, *rapaštim* is an adjective without an antecedent, which is exceptional, but not a noun. Morphologically, the surface form most resembles an adjective followed by a noun in the genitive similar to *emqam birkim* of line 53. There happens to be a homophonous noun *rapaštum* 'pelvis, lumbar region (of a human), hind leg, thigh (of an animal)'; cf. AHw 955a. Such an interpretation based on the morphology was offered by von Soden: "Als unklar genannt werden müssen hier noch die beiden aB Namen *Ú-ta-ra-pa-áš-tim* '? des (Hüft-)Beckens' und *Ú-ta-na-iš-tim* '? der Kehle (? der Lebens?)' (Gilg. M iv 6.13; Gilg. Nin dafür ᵐ*Ut*-ZI; *KAR* 27 Vs.! 2.4 = *BWL* 95 2.4 ᵐ*Ut-na-pu-u*[*š-te*]). Vielleicht steht hier das mir unverständliche Element *uta-* für noch älteres **utam*, das allerdings als Adjektiv eine etwas merkwürdige Form hätte" (von Soden, "Status Rectus-Formen vor dem Genitiv im Akkadischen," *JNES* 19 [1960] 165a.) In the dictionary he lists but does not assign any semantic value to the first element of the personal name, as found only in these two contexts; see **utum* AHw 1445a. However, we might compare the Old Akkadian feminine personal names beginning with *Tūtaʾ-*, which are definitely forms of the verb *watûm* 'to find'.

In relation to geographic terms, the adjective *rapaštum* appears in connection with land masses; cf. text **7** ii 13–14. Moreover, there existed the land known as Utûm, in which the city Šušarra was located; see RGTC 3 252.

59. The adverb *tuša* is the shortened form of *tušā*(*ma*) and is used to denote irrealis or potentialis.

59. (When) as if he were hostile, the forest waged war against him.
60. It set darkness
61. in place of the light of the heavens.
62. The sun dimmed,
63–64. the stars sallied forth against the enemy.

65. Securely founded were the strongholds of the enemies, all nine of them,
66. (but every) man, ox, and sheep,
67. to[geth]er he cap[tured].
68. On [that day], he [captured] Simurrum,
69. [the trib]ute(??) of Akkade, in his possession,
70. [and] the tribute(??) of Akkade, (from) victories over . . .
71. He turned the city into a ruin heap.

---

65. Although the copy has the signs *a-na ri-gi-im-šu-nu*, this ungrammatical phrase has been emended in accordance with **7** iii 13′–15′ *a-a[l na-ak]-ri-im a-na ti-ši-šu a-wi-la-am al-pa-am bu-la-a[m] ù i-me-ra-am ik-mi* 'the city of the enemy nine times men, cattle, goats, and sheep he took captive'. In the second text, it is not clear whether the "nine times" belongs to the first sentence or the second sentence. For the paradigmatic usage of number nine, see pp. 236–37. Note that the conquests listed at the end of this composition are also nine in number.

68–70. These difficult lines seem to be an interruption, interposed between lines that describe the defeat of an unnamed enemy, the surrender of the strongholds in our text and the city itself in text **7**, the despoiling of the city, in lines 65–67, and the demolishing of the city in lines 71ff. This interlude contains a reference to the conquest of Simur(r)um, the gateway to the Hurrian territory, whose exact location is unknown; see Hallo, "Simurrum and the Hurrian Frontier," *RHA* 36 (1978) 71–83. This event is alluded to in this flashback. A possible interpretation based on the writing of *ši-mu-*RI*-a-am* (text **7** iii 15′) is 'at that time (during the same battle) he (Sargon) captured the Simurrian and the tribute of Akkade which was with him (the Simurrian) he (Sargon) led away to Akkade'. The historical conquest of Simur(r)rum is claimed by Sargon in his year-dates: mu Sar-um-GI Si-mur-um^{ki} ⸢i⸣-gen-⸢na-a⸣; see A. Westenholz OSP 1 115 #7.

71. In historiographic tradition, this sentence commonly describes the destruction of Kazallu by Sargon: "Chronicles of Early Kings," line 9 (Grayson, *Chronicles*, no. 20) and Neo-Assyrian and Neo-Babylonian omen collections (King Chron. no. 3:33–34 and no. 4:1–4). It also occurs in broken context in text **20A** i 2.

72. 50 KASKAL.GÍD-*e ki-di* É.GAL *is-sú-*[*uḫ*]
73. [x]-*mi-id ú-ul iḫ-mu-ṭa-am*
74. [*ka-ṣa*]*-ṣú-um ik-ṣú-uṣ*.

Column iii

75. 50 *a-la-ni t*[*u*]*-uq-ma*!?*-tum* [. . .]
76. *i-na mu-uḫ-ḫu-u*[*m*] *ra-ti* [. . .]
77. x-*ru-ut* 10+x+2(??) x [. . .]
78. [x-x]-*tum šu-uḫ-zu ù* DAM(?).GÀR(?) [. . .]
79. *t*[*u*-x-x] *ḫu-ra-am* [x x] tum [. . .]
80. [. . . *ú-*]*ši-ir-da-am* x[. . .]
81. [. . .] *a-na* ú(?) [(x)] te [. . .]
82. [. . .]ma [x] ma za x [. . .]
83. [. . .]x-[x]-*am pa-*[. . .]
84. [. . .] an [. . .]
85. [. . .] *tu u*[*l* . . .]
86. [. . .] ša x x [x]-ri
87. [. . .] *a-na* [. . .] *ri-mi-im*
88. [. . .] si bi
89. [. . .] ⌜*ša*⌝ *ri it-ta-ad-di-in*
90. [. . .] *ri pi id di/ki*
91. [. . .] ⌜*it*⌝*-ta-ad-di-in*
92. [. . .] *i*[*l-l*]*i-ku*
93. [. . .] *be-lí*
94. [. . .] *i-na pa-ra-ki-šu*

---

72. This sentence may also reflect the passages in the historiographic tradition concerning the stationing of his court officials at five double hours; see "Chronicles of Early Kings," line 7; Omen Collections no. 3 rev. 5–9, no. 4 rev. 1–7. The reading of vS is: 'x Doppelstunden das Gebiet des Palastes (*e-qé-el*! *ekallim*) riss er aus (?) (*is-sú-*[*uḫ*?])'. However, since the word for a region outside a city or the open country is *kīdu*, there is no need to emend the present text. Therefore, we read 'fifty double miles (50 KASKAL.GÍD-*e*) belonging to the outskirts (*ki-di* from *kīdû*) of the palace he depopulated (*nasāḫu*)'.

73–74. In accordance with von Soden's suggestion (AHw 453b *kasāsu*) for line 74, B. Foster (*RA* 77 [1983] 190) offers the following reading of lines 73–74:

> ⌜*eṣ*⌝*-me-et ú-ul iḫ-mu-ṭa-am*
> [*ku-ru-si*]*-su-um ik-su-us*

72. Fifty double miles about the outskirts of the palace he depopulated.
73. . . . he did not hurry.
74. He let loose all his fury.

Column iii

75. Fifty cities the fighting [laid waste].
76. . . .
77. . . .
78. The . . . s were . . . . and the . . .
79. . . .
80. . . . he released / he made him follow . . .
81–86. (too fragmentary for translation)

87. . . . for . . . mercy,
88. . . .
89. . . . he was wont to give.
90. . . .
91. . . . he was wont to give.
92. . . . they went.
93. . . . my lord."
94–95. [Sargon sat] . . . on his throne.

> the bones which he [Sargon] did not burn up
> the rat gnawed on

There is not enough space for the [*ku-ru-si*] at the beginning of line 74, and although *kurusissu* is indeed a rodent, it is one that feeds on flax, *šamaššammū*. Moreover, such a translation is unlikely, especially with the ventive ending; note that vS himself proposes to translate *ul iḫmuṭam* as 'er beeilte sich nicht'. Line 74 is here understood as a paranomastic infinitival construction from *g/kaṣāṣu* 'to rage (against the enemy)'.

80. Von Soden suggested *še/irṭu* 'eine (abgerissene?) Binde' in AHw 1219a, which forms part of the bow equipment in Old Akkadian texts.

94. For the topos of Sargon sitting on his throne and giving a speech, cf. **9B** rev. 10ff. and 14ff.

95.
96. [. . .] ma [. . .] *a-na-ku*
97. [x x *l*]*a-ka* [. . .] *š*[*a*]*r-rum*
98. [. . .]al si x *e-ni-ir-ma*
99. [. . .]-*ḫa-ar ra-šu-ú-ma ap-pu-ul*[x-x]-*la-a-šu*
100. [. . .] *e-ni-ir-ma*
101. [. . . *i-n*]*a p*[*a*]-*ni-šu ši-im-tam*
102. [*a*]-*mu-ur-ra*-[*am e-n*]*i-ir-ma*
103. ⸢x x x x x⸣ [. . . *ma-ḫa-a*]*r* ^{d}[x] *aq*-[*q*]*í*
104. *su-bir*$_4$ ⸢*i*⸣-[*na kališu*] *e-ni-ir-ma*
105. [. . .]-*aš-tam l*[*i-i*]*b-ša-am ù li*-[x x]-*tam aš*-[*lu-ul*(?)]
106. *nam*-[x] ⸢x x x⸣-*am e-ni-ir-m*[*a*]
107. *e* ⸢*zé*⸣(?) [x] ⸢*ni*⸣-*šu* ⸢*i-na*⸣ *a-mi-im-ma e*-⸢x⸣-[. . .]
108. [. . .] x x [. . .]
109. *k*[*a-a*]*r-k*[*a*]-*mi-i*[*š*!] *e-ni-ir-ma*
110. [. . .] ⸢x x x⸣ [*aš-k*]*u-na-aš-šu di-ir-ri-t*[*am*]
111. [. . .]-*ki-a e-ni-ir-ma*
112. [. . . ki/d]i-ir-x [. . .]x *ut-ta-na*[. . .]
113. [. . . *e-ni-ir*]-*ma*.

Column iv

114. [*iṣ-ṣí*-]*šu ab*-[*tu*]-*uq si*!?-*pi-it*-[*ta*]*m aš-ku*-[*u*]*n*
115. [. . .]-*za-am*^{KI}? *e-ni-ir-ma*
116. [*aš-ku*]-*un ga*-[. . .]-*nu-ma*
117. [*i-ša*]-*tam ad-di*
118. [*i*]*š-tu ak-sú-šu-nu-ti zu*-[x]-⸢x⸣ *ši-ru-šu-nu*
119. *a-na ma*-[*ḫa*]-*ar* [*ì-lí*]-*šu ši-it*!-[*ru-ku*(?)]-*ma*

98–117. These fragmentary lines consist of couplets describing the destruction of nine cities or countries and an accompanying act of Sargon. Most of Nougayrol's tentative readings have been kept here. Although the names of the first two countries are broken, the next two are large territorial designations: Amurru, the western territories, and Subartu, the northern territories. The remainder of the geographical terms are merely guesses, of which Carchemiš (Noug. p. 176, note to line 109) has no relationship to Sargonic traditions and is not mentioned in Old Akkadian documents, whereas NaGURzam (Noug. p. 176, note to line 115; RGTC 1 126) is a hapax found only in the Old Akkadian period.

96. "[Truly, the mighty king(?), king of battle(?)] am I.
97. "[No (other)] king [has yet gone where I have(?)].
98. "[The country of . . .] I conquered, and
99. "[the . . .] which he owned I tore down, . . .
100. "[The country of . . .] I conquered, and
101. "[I pronounced] (its) fate before it.
102. "(The country of) Amurru I conquered, and
103. "the . . . . [. . . before DN] I offered.
104. "(All of) Subartu I conquered, and
105. " . . . . , clothing, . . . , I pl[undered].
106. "[The country of . . .] I conquered, and
107. "the people abandoned (it?), in a raft I . . .
108. " . . . .
109. "(The country of) ⸢Carchemiš⸣ I conquered, and
110. "[. . .] I placed on him the halter.
111. "[The country of . . .] I conquered, and
112. "I . . .
113. "[The country of . . .] I conquered, and

Column iv

114. "its [trees] I felled, lamentation I instituted.
115. "[The city(?) of . . .]zam I conquered, and
116. "I placed(?). . . . , and
117. "I set afire.
118. "After I had bound them, . . . they themselves (lit. their own flesh)
119. "before his (sic, Sargon's) god, they dedicated," and

---

114. The Sargonic kings commemorated their felling of cedars in year-dates and royal inscriptions: [*in* 1 MU . . . *ù* su_4*-ma*?] *in* [KUR *La-a*]*b-na-an* [GIŠ]. EREN *ib-du-kam* '[the year when Naram-Sin . . . and personally(?)] felled cedars in Mount Lebanon'; A. Westenholz OSP 2 16 iv 1–8 and GIŠ.EREN *in A-ma-nim ša ba-qí-iš* É.^{d}INANNA *ib-tu-qú* 'they cut down cedar in the Amanus mountains for an extension of the temple of Inanna' (D. R. Frayne, *ARRIM* 2 [1984] 24) 54–58.

120. *šar-ru-ki-*[*i*]*n um-ma-tam ú-na-ḫ*[*a*]*-ad*
121. *a-ga-n*[*a š*]*ar-rum ša i-ša-a*[*n-na*]*-na-an-ni*
122. *ša a-na-ku at-ta-al-l*[*a*]*-k*[*u*]
123. *šu-ú li-it-ta-la-ak*

120. Sargon instructs the troops:
121. "Lo, the king who wants to equal me,
122. "where I have gone,
123. "let him also go!"

7
"Sargon in Foreign Lands"

Introduction

Because of its fragmentary nature, it is difficult to define the narrative statement. There is a covert third-person narrator. The definable story segments are:

1. A section in which the narrator extols Sargon's desire for victory, his greatest achievement, and his pious thanksgiving (col. i 7′–15′);
2. A dialogue between Sargon and his "heroes," in which Sargon appeals to the troops to support his design to attack the country of Mardaman (a Hurrian dominion that straddled the northern road through the Tur Abdin to Diyarbekir) and the agreement of the troops (col. i 15′–19′);
3. Dialogue between unknown people concerning a land that is not Amurru (Subartu ?), possibly trying to dissuade Sargon from his plan of conquest, or a speech by a king of the foreign land offering submission and tribute to Sargon (col. ii);
4. Speech of a courtier to a reluctant soldier, a description of the armor of the warriors and the conquest by Sargon of an enemy city (col. iii);
5. Dialogue between Sargon and his heroes concerning mercy, a description of the passage through the forest in darkness and the safe return journey (col. iv).

The characters in the narrative are similar to those of text **6**, with one exception. Unlike the previous story, the divine dimension appears: the goddess Ištar in her persona of Irnina is given a role that is difficult to determine. As Irnina she is literally the personification of victory, "Victoria."[9] Moreover, Irnina is a prominent goddess in the traditions about the Akkadian kings: (1) in our text Sargon is called *migir Irnina*; (2) in text **12**, Irnina accompanies Naram-Sin as his companion; (3) the Akkadian translation of the title in-nin šà-gur$_4$-ra, written by Enḫeduanna, daughter of Sargon, is: *Irnina rabītam libbi*. Furthermore, the cedar forest, the goal of Sargon's expedition, is associated with Irnina: in the SB "Gilgameš Epic" Tablet V 6, the cedar forest where Humbaba was wont to walk is described as KUR-*ú* GIŠ.ERIN *mūšab ili parak Irnini* 'the mountain of cedar trees, seat of the gods, throne (dais) of Irnina'.[10] Furthermore, Ištar speaks to King Naram-Sin of her desire for victory, *irnittišša*, in text **13**:13.

[9] Jacobsen, *PAPS* 107 (1963) 476 n. 6. In general, see I. J. Gelb, *JNES* 19 (1960) 78–79; Tallqvist, *Götterepitheta*, 329.

[10] See B. Landsberger, *RA* 62 (1968) 113 n. 52.

General Observations
(based on collations by J. Black)

The tablet consists of the following pieces (see reassembled pieces on diagram, p. 384):

(1) One large fragment, IM 52684 A + B, + 52305 (= TIM IX 48 main piece), with parts of four columns. There is a part of the left-hand edge of the tablet at col. i 13′–18′; in col. ii 15′–16′ there is a genuine physical join (part of the KA in 16′ is on the right-hand piece).[11] This joined piece is the right-hand edge of the tablet, thus leaving no doubt that it is a two-column tablet, of which approximately the upper half of the obverse remains. The obverse and reverse are in separate pieces and the back-to-back join is extremely uncertain; they cannot be glued together (they simply do not fit). Nevertheless, the join is correct, as can be seen in col. iii 14′ *bu-la-am ù i-me-ra-am.* Although there is no direct join here between the fragment of the right edge and the central piece of the reverse, the color and spacing fit exactly. Consequently, the BI in col. iv 4′ must be very close to the left edge of the tablet with room for perhaps one sign, and col. iv 19′ might be only a few lines from the end of the tablet.

(2) Two additional fragments published separately by van Dijk (TIM IX pl. xxxix 'fragm.[?]' + pl. xxxvii 'fragm.') and joined by J. A. Black. This fragment probably belongs where the one on pl. xxxvii was placed by van Dijk, that is, above the main preserved portion of col. ii. The color of the tablet, marks of burning (on obverse only), and the general shape of the fragment suggest that the rejoined fragments may belong close to the joined right edge of col. ii.

(3) Van Dijk's fragments 1, 2, 3, 4. Of these four, fragment 4 is probably from the upper edge of the obverse (i.e., col. i or col. ii), while the other three are black with burning, like most of the obverse, and so are to be fitted in somewhere in cols. i and ii.

(4) Three additional fragments not drawn by van Dijk, drawn by J. A. Black. One (A) is probably from the upper edge of the obverse, and the other two fragments (B and C) are from the lower edge of the reverse, though their position is uncertain.

Circumstances of Discovery

This is one of the few texts in this book that was found in controlled excavations, but the results of the third expedition to Tell Harmal were never published. Prof. van Dijk first published his copy of the present text in *Sumer* 13 (pls. 16–19) and later republished it in TIM IX 48.

Orthography and Language

On the whole, the paleography is plagued by the scribe's curious sign forms and some real blunders. There are some obvious cases of omitted signs

[11] Cf. van Dijk, *Sumer* 13 (1957) 66.

that must be emended in, and there are less obvious cases where the emendation may be questionable.

The linguistic features of this text may be described as follows: the opposition of voiced/voiceless in the labials may be rendered in the writing (BI:PI as well as BA:PA). Examples are: *il-bi-in* i 14′; *li-še-pi-ka* iii 6′; *i-ta-aḫ-ba-at* iv 9′; *pa-ga-ar-ka* ii 16. Moreover, PI renders /wa/ as consistent with normal Old Babylonian usage. For velar + /a/, there are three signs in use: KA, GA, and QA (*ka-ki-šu* i 13′; *pa-ga-ar-ka* ii 16; *qa-su* i 12′) but only two, KI and GI, for the velar + /i/ (*tu-ki-il* ii 16; *te-gi-ri* ii 17; *qí* [KI]*-ir-bi-ti-im* iv 9′) and likewise for velar + /u/, KU and *GU.[12] The use of the ḪI sign for /ṭa/ is found in ii 7 and known in other texts from the Diyala area.[13] In marking the postulated affricated */ts/, there is some evidence that points to initial affricate written with Z-signs (ZI in ZI-*n*[*a-su*] iii 5′) and intervocalic /s/ written with S-signs, since both SA (*mu*-SA-*ri-ra-ti-ka* iv 8) and SU (*pa*-SU-*tu* i 18) occur. Likewise, the combination of dental with the suffix of the third person results in *SA, *SI, and SU (cf. *qa-su* in i 12), known from Ešnunna from the time of the Laws.[14] One grapheme found only in the Diyala is the AB = /is/, which is used systematically in the text (e.g., *ìs-qú-ur* i 14′, 15′). There are also some cases of CVC signs: ŠUM,

[12] The one instance of KUM is uncertain; see line ii 10.

[13] F. Reschid, *Archive des Nūršamaš und andere Darlehensurkunden aus der altbabylonischen Zeit* (Ph.D. diss., Heidelberg, 1965) 35; R. M. Whiting, *Old Babylonian Letters from Tell Asmar* (AS 22; Chicago, 1987) 6, 125 #229.

[14] A. Goetze, *The Laws of Eshnunna* (AASOR 31; New Haven, 1956) 9ff.; idem, "The Sibilants of Old Babylonian," *RA* 52 (1958) 144.

Transcription

Column i

1′. [. . .] x ba x x [. . .]
2′. [. . .]-*tim bi-ru* ku? [. . .]
3′. [. . .]-*šu ša-ru*(?)-[*ki*?-*in*? . . .]
4′. [. . .] *ni* [. . .]
5′. [. . .] *ṣa-ba-t*[*am* x x]-*ṣa-am li-x*-[. . .]
6′. [. . .] *ù šu pi ki i*[x (x)] *šu a-pa-an qí*-[*ša-at* . . .]

Philological and Textual Notes

i 6′. The last extant signs, *a pa an ki*, can comprise only two types of lexemes: either a geographical term with the determinative KI (cf. Appān in Old Babylonian, RGTC 3 19, though no determinative is found otherwise in this text) or a shortened form of *ana* + *pān* 'to the fore of' (cf. AHw 820b *pānu sub* 8) 'Zugangsseite eines Landes'. If the latter suggestion is followed, then the next

MAR, NAM. The expression of double consonants by the writing system is inconsistent (*um-ma-an-šu* i 11′; *ka-ki-šu* i 13′), even in the writing of the same word (*ap-pa-šu* i 13′; *a-pa-šu* i 15′). Moreover, there are few determinatives or logograms in this text. It is written in a completely syllabic script.

The morphology of the text is consistent with its Old Babylonian date. The mimation is used correctly in the text although there are no other early traits. In addition, there are various examples of the accusative morpheme occurring as an accusative of relationship; see col. ii 17 and col. iv 9–10, where on the basis of text **6**, the nominative forms are expected. There is very little use of plene writings to render phonetic or phonemic length or prosodic features.

Poetics

The poetic diction is found in this text in shortened prepositions, inverted syntax, and certain lexical items, such as *išti.* In addition, chiastic repetition of lines and regular repetition of lines apparently only occur in col. i, which may be the refrain of a song. Note that the verse lines do not match the line division of the text.

Manuscripts

Šaduppûm (Tell Harmal)

IM 52684A + 52684B + 52305 (coll. J. A. Black) = J. J. A. van Dijk, *Sumer* 13 (1957) pls. 16–19 = *TIM* IX 48.

Translation

Column i

1′–6′. (too fragmentary for translation)

---

word begins with *ki-* and *qišat erēnim* is a possible restoration. There are various foreign territories beginning with *ki-*, the most famous of which is Kimaš, but its location north of the Jebel Ḥamrīn does not seem to fit the story; see RGTC 1 89, RGTC 2 100–101, RGTC 3 139.

7′. [. . .] ⸢x⸣ DI-*ni-im a-di* U.D[A]R *i-ka-ša-du ir-*[*ni-ta-šu-ma?*]
8′. [*Ša-ru-ki-in ú-še*]-*pu im-ma-ti-im a-di Ir-ni-na i-ka-š*[*a-du* x (x)]

9′. [x x x Š]*a-ru-ki-in ú-še-pu im-ma-ti-im mu-te-*[*ir?* . . .]
10′. [*ša iš*]-*ti-šu ši-in-ši-ri-it i-bi-ir zu-bi*(-)*im*(-)*mar-m*[*a* x x (x)]

11′. [x *Ḫa*]-*ma-na-am uš-te-ti-iq uš-te-ti-iq um-ma-an-šu Ḫa-*⸢*ma-na-am*⸣
12′. [*qí-š*]*a-at e-ri-ni-im ik-šu-ud qa-su bi-ri ik-*[*ki?*]-*li-šu ḫa-ni-iš*
13′. *iš-ku-un ka-ki-šu i-ta-qí ni-qí-šu il-bi-in ap-pa-*(er.)-*šu*
14′. *te-li-*†*ša-am ìs-qú-ur e-lu-ti-im i-ta-qí ni-qí-šu il-bi-in*
15′. *a-pa-šu-ma te-li-*†*ša-am ìs-qú-ur i-sa-qa-ra-*⟨*am*⟩ *me-gi-ir Ir-ni-na*

---

i 7′–8′. Syntactically, these lines are composed of two subordinate clauses dependent on the subjunction *adi.* The verb in the second clause written *ú-še-b/pu* could be understood as: *wašābu* 'to dwell', G preterite subjunctive *ūšibu*; *šâbu* 'to make tremble', D preterite subjunctive *ušibbu*; *šapû* 'to make silent', D preterite subjunctive *ušeppû*; *šapû* 'to make noise', D preterite subjunctive *ušeppû*; *šebû* 'to be sated', D present/preterite subjunctive *ušebbû*; *ešēbu* 'to make prosperous', D (MA only); and *šūpû* 'to proclaim', Š preterite subjunctive *ušeppû.* However, the verb in the first clause is the third-person singular present of *kašādu.* Consequently, the second should also be the same morphological form. The best grammatical and logical sense is to associate this verb with *šêpu*, derived from *šēpu* 'foot' and attested only in the infinitive G in lexical texts as a synonym of *etēqu.* While the meaning is suitable, the D-form and the poor attestation of the root are not. On the other hand, the subject of the second clause is Sargon, while the subject or object of the first clause could be Ištar (the reading of the sign is uncertain), Irnina, or Sargon. In addition, there is a play on the words *irnittam kašādu* 'to triumph over an enemy, to attain one's desire'.

i 9′. The apparent participial epithet at the end of the line could refer to Sargon, Irnina, Sargon's entourage, or even to the land. There are many possibilities for an epithet beginning with *mu-te*: the verbs *ṭepû*, *ṭeḫû*, and *târu* are all possible. The most common is, of course, *mutīr gimilli* 'avenger'. Note the epithet of Irnina in the "In-nin-šà-gur$_4$-ra Hymn": *mu-te-el-le-tum ša e-nu-na-ki* 'proudest among the Anunna gods' (line 1).

i 10′. Separating this line of text into its proper verse division is difficult. There is only room for two signs at the beginning of the line. Walter Sommerfeld suggests [x *iš*]-*ti-šu* for the first word. If the pronominal referent is Sargon, then the subject could be Irnina or his warriors. The numeral *šinšeret* is the cardinal number in status absolutus feminine. It could therefore be the predicate of the preceding clause, the object of *i-bi-ir* (if understood as the verb

7′. . . . . As long as Ištar will gain vic[tories for him],
8′. [Sargon will let his voice re]sound in the land. As long as Irnina will attain victories for him [. . .],
9′. [. . . Sa]rgon will let his voice resound in the land. The . . .
10′. [who are wi]th him are twelve, the crossing of the Zubi (canal or mountain) he will see(??) and [. . .]
11′. He made (them) cross the Amanus; he made his troops cross the Amanus.
12′. He reached the cedar forest. Amidst its din(?) he bowed down, (and)
13′. readied his weapons. He offered a sacrifice, made obeisance,
14′. spoke distinctly. He offered his pure sacrifices, made
15′. obeisance, spoke distinctly. He speaks, the favored one of Irnina,

---

ebēru), or preceding the genitive chain *ibir zubi*(*m*). If it is the predicate, the subject must be the warriors who are said to be twelve in number. The identification of the *zubi* is either a canal (RGTC 1 227 sub RÉC 107; RGTC 2 296; RGTC 3 316 sub ⁱ⁷ZUBI) or a mythical mountain. The latter occurs twice in the Lugalbanda tales as a source for weapons and in "Enmerkar and the Lord of Aratta" as a location on the route to Aratta; see S. Cohen, *Enmerkar and the Lord of Aratta* (Ph.D. diss., University of Pennsylvania, 1973) 49. Another factor to be considered is that the Hittite version of the story contains an account of the crossing of the river Aranzaḫ (= Euphrates [?]) and sacrifices performed by Sargon before that crossing; cf. KBo 22 6 i 16′–20′; see Güterbock, *MDOG* 101 (1969) 19, 22, and 25.

i 12′. Because of the orthographic system employed in this text, in which the labials are distinguished for voice, it is impossible to accept B. Groneberg's excellent suggestion (*JAOS* 98 [1978] 522) to read here *pí-ri-ik* [*pa*]-*li-šu* 'the border of his realm'. We are left with the signs *bi ri ik* [x] *li šu*. The word *bi-ri-ik* from *birku* 'knee' is a possibility; cf. *emqam birkim* **6**:53. However, the best solution is to interpret these two words as *biri* (prep.) followed by a noun plus possessive +*šu*. A similar phrase is found in text **17** ii 18: *ina Hawannim* KUR GIŠ.EREN *bi-ri-š*[*u* . . .]. The verb *ḫaniš* is treated, according to the suggestion of B. Groneberg, as a writing of the verb *kaniš*. In addition to the references from OAkk. and NA that she mentions, there is another from Harmal: *kīma pāniššu ḫa-an-šu* 'since he made obeisance before him', IM 54005:19; see van Dijk, *AfO* 23 (1970) 66. Another suggested reading for this line is: *bi-ri-iq i-li-šu Ha-ni-iš* (D. O. Edzard and W. G. Lambert, "Haniš, Šullat und," *RlA* 4, 108). However, note the writing *ì-lí* in iii 8′.

i 14′. The lexeme *têlišam* is to be analyzed as containing the root *têlu* 'to enunciate' and the adverbial ending -*išam*. It modifies the manner in which Sargon is speaking (*saqāru*); cf. AHw 1345.

16′. *qa-ra-du-ja ma-ta-am ša Ma-al-da-ma-an e-ge-ri mi-im-ma*

17′. *ša ta-qa-bi-⟨a⟩-ni-im lu-pu-uš qa-ra-du-šu ap-lu-ni-šu al-pu*

18′. *ra-bu-tu* ⌜x x⌝ *šu-ta-tu-ut ti-ti-ni-im-ma pa-su-tu šu-ta-tu-ut*

19′. [. . .] ⌜x x *da*⌝*-am la-ma ap-lu*

20′. [. . .]*-am ba*{er.}*-al*

21′. [. . . *-t*]*a lu tu*

22′. [. . .] ⌜*du*⌝

Column ii

1. (frg. 4 + 1′) [. . .]*-am lu-uš-pu-ḫa*-x[. . .]x
2. (2′) [. . .] *-bi-*[.]
3. (frg. ? + 3′) [. . *li*]*-ik-mi ka-li ta* x [. . .] x
4. (frg. 1′ + 4′) [. . .]*-am li-di* ⌜x-x-*ši*⌝*-ta-šu* [. . .]*šu*
5. (frg. 2′ + 5′) [(*ṣābum*) *a-*]*li-ik-tu-um šu-a-t*[*u . . . ša-ar t*]*a-am-ḫa-ri-im*
6. (frg. 3′ + 6′) [. . .] *in-bu er-ṣé-ti-im* x[. . . †*t*]*a-*†*na/šu-nu*
7. (frg. 4′ + 7′) [. .] *lu-uš-mu-ṭà-am lu-ra-*⌜x⌝-[. . .] *šu-qa-ti-šu-nu*
8. (frg. 5′ + 8′) [*ina š*]*u-pa-li na-aḫ-li li-im-*[*qu-ut*(?). . .] *an-ni-a-am*

---

i 16′. For the country of Mardaman, cf. RGTC 1 118 sub Maridaban; RGTC 2 118; RGTC 3 160 sub Mardaman; as well as Hallo, "Simurrum and the Hurrian Frontier," *RHA* 36 (1978 = CRRAI 24) 74. On the location of Mardaman, which lies somewhere in the Upper Tigris region of Northern Mesopotamia, see most recently D. O. Edzard, "Mardaman," *RlA* 7 (1989) 357–58 and K. Kessler, *Untersuchungen zur historischen Topographie Nordmesopotamiens* (TAVO Supplement Series B/26; Wiesbaden, 1980) 64 and notes. In his year-date, Naram-Sin is credited with the subjugation of *Maridabān* (*aK* 51 D-9, "Narāmsîn 3") and in the legendary texts it also appears among the territories that rebelled against Naram-Sin; see **16B** line 34. Note that in **9B** it is not the country of Mardaman but the city of Kaniš(?) that Sargon desires to conquer. Cf. Sargon's speech to his soldiers in **9B**:5–6.

i 17′. Since a form *ta-qa-bi-ni-im* (*taqabbinim*) does not exist, I emend it to *ta-qa-bi-⟨a⟩-ni-im* (*taqabbiānim*). The next-to-last sign is nearer to the sign AL than to the sign GAB, a most unlikely syllabic value in this text. Therefore, the last word is probably to be read *al-pu*. It is possible that this word could be taken from *elēpu* 'to send forth to battle' in the stative third-person plural. However, the most reasonable suggestion is to understand *alpū rabûtum* 'the mighty oxen' as an epithet of the soldiers. Note the term *mīrī dannūtim* 'the strong bulls' in reference to the soldiers in **6**:44. The dropping of the mimation on the plural adjective is inexplicable but found also in *pa-su-tu*, line 18′, but not in *e-lu-ti-im*, lines 14′–15.

i 18′. The form of *šutātût* is Št of *atû* adjective plural in status constructus with the following noun. Under his entry *šutātû*, von Soden reads the next

16′. "My heroes, the country of Mardaman I want to fight. Anything
17′. that you say to me, I will do." His heroes answered him, the great oxen,
18′. who had met (in battle) with the Didnu-nomads, the exterminators(??), who had met (in battle) with
19′ff. (too fragmentary for translation)

Column ii

1. ". . . . Let me scatter . . . "
2. . . . [. . . .]
3. ". . . . let him capture all the. . . .
4. ". . . let him cast down his. . . . , his . . .
5. "that detachment of foot [soldiers]. . . . O King of Battle!"
6. "(But?) . . . the fruit of the earth. . . . their/they
7. ". . . . Let me tear up, Let me . . . [. . .] their heights.
8. ". . . [into the d]efiles of the ravines, let him fa[ll]. This. . . .

---

word as *sissinnim* (1291b) 'date spadix', but the signs are clearly to be read *ti-ti-ni-im*. A possible interpretation of this noun is to see in it a reference to the Didnu nomads; cf. RGTC 1 157 sub Tid(a)num and RGTC 2 30 sub Didnum. Moreover, there is a hymn to king Gungunum of Larsa, TIM IX 41, where mention is made of *di-id-ni* (lines 3–4, 9, 20), which may also refer to the Didnu nomads. Note also the writing *Ti-ni-ti-ni-im* (var. Šu-Sin year-date 5), Hallo, *BiOr* 16 (1959) 236a. I owe this proposal to a suggestion of M. Stol.

The next word is also understood as an adjective plural from the root *pasāsu* 'to eradicate, exterminate' which should have the passive meaning of 'exterminated'.

ii 6. Fruits are also mentioned in **9B** in connection with the road to Purušḫanda and its products: the apple and the fig (obv. 29), as well as the apple, the fig, the medlar, and the vine (rev. 24).

ii 7–8. These two lines describe Sargon's wish to ascend to the heights of the foreign land and to have his enemy(?) groveling in the depths of its valleys, using the parallelism: *šūqu* // *šuplu*. It is interesting to note that these words are elongated but still form a rhymed pair by forming the first noun in the plural *šūqātu* and the second noun in its elongated variant *šupālu*. An alternative interpretation is to separate the sentences and understand line 7 in conjunction with line 6 and to read *šūqātu* as 'their abundance'.

ii 8. If the word written *na-aḫ-li-li-im* is from *naḫalu* (*naḫlu*) 'wadi, gorge, ravine', then it is spelled with reduplicated *-li-*, another mistake of the less-than-careful scribe, or the last two signs *li-im* begin a new word. Cf. *damīšina šupālū*

9. (frg. 6′ + 9′) [. . ṣ]*í-nu a-ga-lu e-ri-qú-um* ⌜x⌝ [x] ⌜*i*⌝*-sa-qa-ar-šum*
10. (frg. 7′ + 10′) [. . .] DINGIR-*šu* DINGIR ⟨*šu*⟩?-*a-tu ṣí-nu-šu* [*ú-u*]*l ṣí-*⟨*nu*⟩ *ra-qu*(wr. KUM)-*ti*
11. (frg. 8′ + 11′) *ù* ⌜†*su*(?)-x-x-x⌝ [. . .] *ša-ap-ra-am* [(x x) *ú*]-*ul ma-tu-um*
12. (frg. 9′ + 12′) *ú-ul ma-tu-um ša* MAR.⌜TU⌝ [*i-n*]*a ki-di* [(*irtanappudu*)] ⌜*nu*⌝*-ul-la-*[*nu*]
13. (13′) *me-ri-sú*!(wr. †MA) *ra-pa-aš-tam wi-il-di-ša li-*[*x x*]*-ma*
14. (14′) *i-šu* †*ma-li-ni e-zu-ub i-ša-ru-ti-im ra-pa-*[x †*u*]*l-*†*la-*†*ni*
15. (15′) *šu* ⌜x x⌝ *ra-ni-im šu-bi-iš be-li ú-ma-na-am ṣa-*[*b*]*a-am*
16. (16′) *tu-ki-il* [*du*]*-ra-am ú-ṣú*(wr. IŠ)*-ur-ma ù pa-ga-ar-ka šu-li-im*
17. (17′) *te-gi-ri be-li pu-ta-am* 1 KASKAL *bi-ri ši-id-d*[*a*!*-am* (x)]

18. (18′) *ma-ta-am ša ša-ru-ur-ša ik-tu-*[*mu . . .*]
19. (19′) *aš-ta-li li-im-da* ⌜†*ša*?⌝ [. . .]

---

u naḫall[*ū umtallû*] 'the depressions and the wadis were [filled] with their blood', **17** ii 24.

ii 9. The first broken sign ends in ŠE, from which we could construct several possible restorations. First, if we just read ŠE.NU, it could be a variant writing of ŠE.IN.NU = *inninnu*, a type of barley. Second, the first sign could be read ZI, yielding a reading [*z*]*i-nu*, which can be many words, of which *ṣēnū* 'flock of sheep' is one and *zinnu* 'rain' is another; cf. *ZI-nu-šu* in the next line. Note also in the "World Map" (CT 22 48 rev. 13′) in the description of the fifth *nagû*: [. . .] *zi-nu-šú* '. . . its frond/rain'; see W. Horowitz, "The Babylonian Map of the World," *Iraq* 50 (1988) 163.

ii 10. The graphemes *an šu an* could perhaps be a clumsy attempt at writing Anšan, but this seems improbable in connection with the other geographical locations in this text. The emendation to the end of this line is tentative, but no better reading can be yielded by the graphemes. Note, however, that the plural adjective should be in the nominative in agreement with the noun, though it is apparently in the genitive, and it is missing the mimation as well.

ii 13. According to collation, the first word reads *me-ri-*†*ma*. This reading is difficult; it is possibly the same word as *mīru* 'young bull'; cf. **6**:44 *mīrī dannūtim* 'strong bulls', referring to the soldiers. On the other hand, it could be *mērû* 'pregnancy', yielding two superficially parallel phrases: [*k*]*ulla*[*t*] *mērîma* : *rapaštam wildīša*. Unfortunately, these phrases are enigmatic, as well as orthographically difficult and grammatically unaccountable. Consequently, some emendation must be made. First, Glassner ("Sargon," 116 and n. 17) reads Na-wa-al^{ki} as an otherwise unattested form of Nawar/Namar. Orthographically, the signs do not exactly fit (not *na*, *wa*, or *al*!) but the /l/ in place of the /r/, we

9. ". . . . flocks, asses, wagon. . . . " He says to him,
10. ". . . . his god, that god, his flocks are not scrawny flocks(??),

11. "and . . . the envoy . . . is not the country.
12. "It is not the country of Amurru, in (whose) outskirts evils(?) [prowl?].

13. "As for his widespread pasture, [let it raise?] its offspring, and
14. "it has as much as we except for righteousness. . . . . is our. . . .
15. ". . . . My lord, conscript people! The army
16. "make trustworthy! Guard the fort and keep yourself safe!
17. "My lord, will you fight? With respect to the front side, it is one double-mile long and with respect to the flank side it is. . . .
18. "With respect to the land whose splendor cove[red . . . I have entered it(?)].
19. "I have shot. Learn. . . .

---

already have in the place-name of Maldaman in col. i 16′. Unfortunately, it leaves *me ri ma ra* at the beginning of the line, which yields little sense. On the other hand, a slight emendation of the *ma* to *sú*! would yield the form *me-ri-sú* from *merītu* + *šu* 'his pasture', a feminine noun in agreement with the feminine adjective *rapaštam*. 'His' must refer to the enemy. This phrase is syntactically an accusative of relationship. The second half of the line contains a plural oblique object *wildī* + possessive *ša* 'her', possibly referring to the land, as well as a verb in the precative.

ii 15–16. These lines contain a statement of pacifism very similar to that of the SB "Cuthean Legend," *dūrānika tukkil* 'make secure your strongholds', line 160; *qarrādūtīka uṣur pūtka šullim* 'safeguard your warriors, take heed of your person', line 165.

ii 17. This line may contain a description of the eventual battlelines. A battlefield can be described in the same terms as an agricultural field, with *pūtu* and *šiddu*; cf. *ana šiddi u pūti . . . ana nakri azīq* 'on flank and front I pressed upon the enemy', OIP 2 45:76 (Senn.). Note, however, that *pūtam* and *šiddam* are in the accusative case and must represent the accusative of relationship; cf. col. iv 10′.

ii 18. Note that Glassner ("Sargon," 123) takes the possessive suffix of the noun to refer not back to the land but to Ištar, whose awesomeness covers the land.

ii 19. For the reading here of *aštalû* 'singer', see AHw Ntrg. 1545. The form is not the expected status absolutus or the status rectus in the nominative found in the vocative slot. Because of these grammatical difficulties, I have preferred to read here a verb in the perfect, first-person singular.

20. (20′) *ra*-AB-ZA *e-lu-ti-im ša* [...]
21. (21′) *ú-ru-um-ti i-na-ri* [...]
22. (22′) [*iš-me-m*]*a an-ni-a-am qa-ba-šu ma*-[...]
23. (23′) [...] *ma ni* [...]

Column iii

(break)
2′. *ki*-[*ma*(?) ...]
3′. *ki-ma* [(*ur-ra-am*) ...]
4′. ⌈*ša na-ak*⌉-*ri-i*[*m* (*kakkīšu*) ...]
5′. *mu-ḫu-ur sí-n*[*a-as-sú* ...]
6′. *li-še-pi-ka ṣa-la-a*[*m* ...]
7′. ⌈*ú-bi-il ša-šu-ma ú-ma*⌉-[*na-am* ...]
8′. *a-li ì-lí-šu uš-ta-li-ik* [...]
9′. *ša* 6 *li-me a-ša-la-aṭ na*-†*ku-u*[*r* ...]
10′. ⌈*ki il-la-ab*⌉-⟨*šu*⟩ *šu*-†*nu ki-ta-a-ti-im* [...] x
11′. *ga*/*ša* [x (x)] *ša-at ri*-⌈*èš*⌉ x *tu* [...*ša-at*] *pa-ar-zi-li-im*
12′. *ša*-†⌈*šu*?-x-x⌉ *šu-nu ú-ra*-[... *k*]*a*? *šu ma-ti*

---

ii 20. The first word, *ra*-AB/P-ZA, can be taken from the verb *rapāsu* 'to beat, thrash, to thresh' or *rabāṣu* 'to hover, lie down, lie in wait', and in either case it is a feminine stative plural. On the other hand, *ellūtim* from *ellu* 'pure ones' or less likely, *elûtim* from 'high, upper ones', is a masculine plural oblique adjective and, thus, probably the beginning of the next verse. Another interpretation of this line was offered by von Soden, "Status Rectus-Formen vor dem Genitiv im Akkadischen" (*JNES* 19 [1960] 164b), where he presented these words as a single phrase: *rabṣa elûtim* 'kauerend auf hohen (Bergen? Bäumen?)', as an adjective preceding a substantive in the genitive. The dropping of the mimation on the adjective would be surprising in this text, and the second word is an adjective, not a substantive. Further, as Erica Reiner has pointed out ("*DAMQAM-ĪNIM* Revisited," *StOr* 55 [1984] 181), this phrase would be one of two that do not have an inalienable possession as the second term. For these reasons, the phrase is divided into two separate clauses.

ii 21. *Uruttu*, *uruntu* is the name of the Euphrates associated with Subartu, probably the Upper Euphrates; cf. AHw 1437.

iii 2′. For an alternative restoration, *ki*-[*iṣ-ri*], see Glassner, "Sargon," 121 n. 40.

iii 7′. The signs are ⌈*ú-bi-il ša-šu-ma ú-ma*⌉-[*na-am* ...], but it could be emended to read ⌈*ú-bi-il-ma*! ŠU-*ma* (or: *su*!)⌉, reading of ŠU for *qātam*, based on

20. "are lying in wait. The holy (ones)....
21. "My Euphrates, among rivers(?) / in the stela...."
22. [He heard] this his speech ...
23. (too fragmentary for translation)

Column iii

(break)

2′. ....

3′. "When tomorrow [you make your resplendent appearance ...],

4′. "and the enemy's [weapons ...]

5′. "face his [lance(s)(?) ...]

6′. "May he (the king) make you appear. A statue [....]"

7′. "I brought to him and [....ed the p]eople.

8′. "Wherever he leads his gods [....]

9′. "Of six thousand, I will take control of the property of [...]"

10′. As they were clad in linen, [....]

11′. [...], who [bore a ....] countenance, [bearing] iron (weapons)

12′. [...]. They [....]. As soon as(?) it

---

the parallel text *ūbilma qāssu ummānam utabbi[b]* in **6**:42. Such a reading seems unlikely in this text; see the syllabic spelling *qa-su* in i 12′. Note that the signs are not very clear, since there is a crack through this line.

iii 8′. It is possible to read *a-li-ì-lí-šu uš-ta-li-ik* 'he put his warriors into action', in accord with the parallel *a-li-li uš-[ta-li-ik]* in **6**:44. However, such a plene writing would be highly unusual in this text. We must assume that although the surface discourses of both texts have similar-sounding words, they hide dissimilar semantic structures. A possible emendation to adjust the equilibrium between the two texts could be *a-li-⟨li⟩ ì-lí-šu uš-ta-li-ik* 'he put the warriors of his god into action'.

iii 9′. The suggested reading of *na-ku-u[r]* is taken as an otherwise unattested variant of *namkūru* 'property'. The sense of the line would then be: 'I will seize the spoils'. The "six thousand" might be the number of conquered enemy towns from which the booty would be taken, and we might restore *na-ku-u[r-šu-nu]*.

iii 10′. The sign NU appears to have been squeezed in later by the scribe, who had forgotten to write *šu-nu* 'they'. The sense of this line may be: 'Sargon's warriors were clad in linen (i.e., they were rich already), but after the campaigns, they will be wearing gold and purple'.

13′. *a-na* ⟨*ša*⟩*-ar ta-am-ḫa-ri-im ša-ak-nam a-a*[*l na-ak*]*-ri-im*
14′. *a-na ti-ši-šu a-wi-la-am al-pa-am bu-la-a*[*m*] *ù i-me-ra-am*
15′. *ik-mi i-nu-mi-šu-ma ši-mu-ri-a-am* [*ik*]*-mi-i ma-da-at*
16′. *a-ka-di ša iš-ti-šu it-*[*ru*] *a-ka-di* [x x] ⸢*ta/du*⸣ *lu-mi a-la-am*
17′. [. . .] x *lu-li-im*
18′. [. . .] ⸢*am*?⸣ *uš-te-ri-iš*

Column iv

(break)
1′. (traces)
2′. [. . .] *x im lu* [. . .]
3′. [. . .]*-ti-im* ⸢*qa-ra*⸣*-*[*d*]*u i-pa-lu-ni-šu* ⸢x x x x⸣
4′. [*i*]*-bi* u_4*-*⟨*ma*⟩*-am Ša-ru-*[*ki-in*] *bi-li pa-di ḫu-li ìs-su*

5′. [. . .] *x pa-di ḫu-*⸢*li*!⸣ *tu-li im-ta-aš-ḫu i-bi*
6′. [. . .] *šu ḫu bi* [x] *ra ur-ra-am al zi-i-ni-šu*
7′. [. . .]*-um ša-*⸢*di*⸣*-im lu-ra-ma-am a-na wa-ar-ki-šu*
8′. [. . .]*ka mu-sa-ri-ra-ti-ka ta-ḫa-zu-um da-an*
9′. [. . .] x *ba i-ta-aḫ-ba-at a-na qí-ir-bi-ti//-im*
10′. [. . .] *qí-iš-ta-am ig-ri-e-šu//-un*
11′. [. . .]*-pi-im da-im ša-am-ša//-am*
12′. [. . .] *gu* [x (x)] x *na-ki-ri-šu ik-mi*

---

iv 2′. This line is restored on the basis of col. i 16′–17′.

iv 4′. The beginning of the line is puzzling: [x (x)] *bi ud am.* Therefore, the text is emended u_4-⟨*ma*⟩*-am* 'today', since it seems to contrast with the word *urram* in line 6′. Likewise, the word [*i*]*-bi* is restored according to *i-bi* in the following line.

The writing *bi-li* for *bēlī* 'my lord' instead of *be-li* (ii 15, 17) is exceptional, and the reading therefore is tentative (cf. p. 206 i 9). The signs could be parsed to read *li-pa-di-ḫu,* but it would be a unique D form of the verb *padû* 'to redeem, to spare'. The sparing of enemies is a theme known from these Sargonic tales. In his royal inscriptions, Sargon is noted for his mercilessness: *mammana pānīšu ula ubbal* 'he does not give pardon to anyone', ***aK*** 182:14–17 "Sargon C 8"; ***aK*** 186:17–20 "Sargon C 12." Nevertheless, in AHw Ntrg. 1581, von Soden reads this word as a noun, *pa-di-ḫu* = *paddiʾu* 'Unglücklicher?' and relates it to the one known instance in Gilg. X v 35 where it occurs in a parallel passage to *mēlula.* The sentence reads: *jāši pa-ad-di-ʾu išammaṭ* '. . . is separated from me'.

13′. was placed at the disposal of the King of Battle. The city of the enemy,
14′. nine times, (and every) man, cattle, goat and sheep
15′. he took captive. At that time he captured the Simurrian and the tribute
16′. of Akkade which was with him he led away (to?) Akkade. . . . the city
17′–18′. (too fragmentary for translation)

Column iv

(break)

1′–2′. (too fragmentary for translation)
3′. [. . .] the warriors answer him [. . .],
4′. "Command, today, Sargon, my lord, the loosening of the neckrings," they cried.
5′. "[. . .] the loosening of neckrings, the . . . they have plundered, Command (it)!
6′. ". . . . . tomorrow, the city of his ornaments
7′. ". . . . of the mountain(?), let me release after him
8′. "your [. . . .], your. . . . " The battle was hard.
9′. [. . . . . . .] . . . He had (barely) penetrated into the interior,
10′. [and traversed] the forest, (when) it opposed them.
11′. [. . . .]. . It darkened with respect to the sun.
12′. [. . . .]. . . . .his enemies he captured.

---

iv 8′. The parsing of the signs *mu sa ri ra ti ka* is difficult. The word *musarriru* is given as 'meaning unknown', in CAD S 175 under *sarāru* D 'to contest', in contexts concerning battle and army units. The stumbling block in any interpretation is the identity of a second-person singular *-ka* in the present context.

iv 10′. Cf. *tuša gerîma qištum igrēšu* in **6**:59. Note the difference in the cases between the nominative in text **6** and the accusative in this text. Thus, in the translation I attempted to divide the sentences differently, but it could also be treated as an accusative of relation, like *šamšam* in the next line. In addition, the object in text **6** is third-masculine singular, obviously referring to Sargon, while in text **7**, the object is third-masculine plural, perhaps referring to Sargon's troops.

iv 11′. Cf. *ana nūr šamāʾi idʾim šamšum* in **6**:61–62. Note again the difference in the cases between the two texts. The [. . .]-*pi-im* might be read as *ina ūmim erpim* 'in the dark day'.

13′. [. . .] *zi-im* x[. . .] x-*bi te*//-*er*
14′. [. . .]-*di-šu-nu bi-ri a*[x x (x)] *ḫu*
15′. [. . . *a-na*] *pa-ni-šu ki er-bi ru*-[x]-x *id-di*
16′. [. . . *a-na ka-ar*(?)] A-*ka-di šu/ú-še-ir ru*?-*ba*-[*am*?]-*ma*
17′. [. . .] *ba i ru*? [x] *ig-ri*
18′. [. . .] *it-ta-qí*
19′. [. . .] *i-qa-an-ni*
(break)

Fragments:

Fragment 1, obverse

1′. [. . .] x [. . .]
2′. [. . .] x *ba* [. . .]
3′. [. . .]-*um* [. . .]

Fragment 2, obverse

1′. [. . .] *ut/ta-ta-ab* [. . .]
2′. [. . .] *az* [. . .]
3′. [. . .] *lu-um/ab* [. . .]
4′. [. . .] x *am-ma* [. .]
5′. [. . .] an [. . .]

Fragment 3, obverse

1′. [. . .] *di/ki*(?) *li*(?) [. . .]
2′. [. . .] *qa* (?) [. . .]

Fragment 4 = obv. col. ii 1

Fragment pl. xxxvii = obv. col. ii 4–12

Fragment (?) pl. xxxix = obv. col. ii 3 (join with above fragment)

---

iv 19′. For the verb *qanû* 'to keep(?)', cf. CAD Q. s.v.

13′. . . . .
14′. their. . . . omens. . . . .
15′. before him like . . . -locusts . . . he abandoned
16′. [to the quay of] Akkade, he. . . . and

Fragment A (not drawn by van Dijk; courtesy J. A. Black), upper edge of tablet, obv. (i.e., col. i or ii)

1. [. . .] *šu*? *tu/li* [. . .] *me*? *ni*? [. . .]

Fragment B (not drawn by van Dijk; courtesy J. A. Black), from lower edge

[. . .] *tu ma aḫ ḫu/ri* [. . .]

Fragment C (not drawn by van Dijk; courtesy J. A. Black), from lower edge

(traces of three signs follow double ruling)
17′. . . . . he fought.
18′. . . . . he sacrificed.
19′. . . . . he kept.
(a few lines to the end of the tablet)

Fragments are untranslated.

8
"Sargon, the Lion"

Introduction

Although extant in two manuscripts, the fragmentary nature of this composition precludes definitive statements about its narrative structure. The story elements are not clear. The actions involve a battle in the environs of Elam and the cedar forest in the east(?). As to the existents, it is again the character of Sargon that attracts notice. In this text he is presented as a terrifying conqueror endowed with an awesome aura, whose essence is epitomized as a lion. Note that this characterization appears later in relation to Naram-Sin in **12** v 2, *ki-ma ni-e-ši-im-mi na-ḫi-ri-im ta-ba-aš-ši* 'You become like a raging lion', and 18, *bé-li at-ta-a-ma lu-ú la-bu* 'My Lord, verily you are a lion'.

In addition, there is an unnamed opponent who perhaps surrounds himself with a guard of seven champions and an army of thousands. His name could have been lost accidentally in the gaps of the text rather than purposely omitted.

The discourse mode of this composition varies between monologue, dialogue, and narrative. It begins with a section, extant only in **8A**, which seems to contain a hymn of praise to Sargon. After a gap, there is a dialogue (or a quotation within a monologue) between Sargon and an unknown person. A series of rhetorical questions comprises the first seven extant lines of the reverse. The speech is reminiscent of the declaration of submission that Nur-Dagan, lord of Purušḫanda, makes to Sargon in **9B** rev. 19–23, as well as the wisdom section of text **2**, the "Sargon Birth Legend." Following the dialogue, and physically divided from it by a double line, **8B** has a narrative section concerning the unnamed enemies.

Of these two texts, one comes from the nineteenth-century excavations at Nippur, probably the fourth expedition, in which little was recorded concerning findspots. The second comes from the collection of Père V. Scheil, through whose hands text **20A** also passed before it became part of the Morgan Library Collection. The former has been published in copy and the latter is unpublished.[15] I would like to thank Alan Millard for bringing the latter tablet to my attention and permitting me to include his copy in my publication.

[15] It is listed in the catalogue of cuneiform tablets in the possession of the Saint Étienne monastery in Jerusalem; see M. Sigrist and A. R. Millard, "Catalogue des tablettes cunéiformes du Couvent Saint-Étienne," *RB* 92 (1985) 576, no. 150, "Texte littéraire babylonien ancien; non identifié."

General Observations

The Nippur manuscript is written on the first and last columns of a tablet that originally had at least four columns. The St. Étienne manuscript is on a single-column tablet. The latter may be an excerpt tablet, since it has a double-line divider on the reverse, perhaps indicating the beginning of another literary excerpt.

Orthography and Language

On the basis of paleography, orthography, and vocabulary, both these texts may be assigned to either the late Old Babylonian or the early Middle Babylonian period. There are no obvious MB developments, such as the *š* to *l* before dentals or the nasalization of the dental in intervocalic position. Mimation is occasional, especially in manuscript **8A**, as in late Old Babylonian. There is more use of CVC signs than in any previous Old Babylonian text: KIŠ (**8A** obv. 3′, 7′), TAB (rev. 3′, both texts), KAB (**8B** rev. 19′), ŠAR (**8A** obv. 6′, 8′), as well as MAR and NAM. Moreover, LIM (**8B** rev. 16′) and LUM (**8B** rev. 6′) appear in positions other than final. Further, TIM occurs with the value /ti/ (**8B** rev. 6′). On the other hand, there is one case of double consonants not expressed in the writing: *li-ba-aš* (**8B** rev. 15′).

While the plene writing *ú-ul* is typical Old Babylonian, the writing of diphthong *aj* as *a-a* (**8A** rev. 2′; **8B** rev. 17′) is characteristic of Middle Babylonian; see J. Aro, *Studien zur mittelbabylonischen Grammatik* (StOr 20; Helsinki, 1955) 34. Furthermore, primae *w-* has dropped (wa > a): *a-ru-ú* (**8B** rev. 17′).

There are certain rare lexemes and idioms peculiar to this text. There is frequent use of interjections: (1) *gana* (obv. 5′, 9′, rev. 4′), which is known from Old Babylonian letters and literary texts, as well as some Standard Babylonian literary texts; (2) *mā* (rev. 4′, 6′), found mainly in third- and early second-millennium texts. The prepositional phrase *ina kīma* (rev. 11′) is unique to this text and is only known from the idiom *ina kī(ma) inanna.*

Poetics

The first column contains a hymn of praise with two stanzas composed of two couplets each. This poetic structure also appears in the first column of text **7**. However the closest in structure with repetitive couplets in a hymn is the second column of text **14**.

There seems to be little use of hymno-epic morphological elements, with perhaps the exception of the shortened pronominal possessive suffix found on *li-ba-aš* (**8B** rev. 15′) and *bu-nu-uš* (rev. 16′), as well as the terminative adverbial postposition in *-iš* (*paniš* rev. 13′). On the other hand, there is the clear case in rev. 11′ of one scribe's revealing the actual sound pattern in his copy of the composition and of the other scribe's setting down a conservative morphophonemic writing: *ik-ki-ma* // *i-na ki-ma.*

Manuscripts

A **8A**
Nippur
UM 29-13-688 = M. de Jong Ellis, *JCS* 31 (1979) 229, no. 9 (see photographs, p. 385).

Transcription

Obverse
Side "a" Tablet A

(break)
1′. // [x]-*ir*-[. . .]
2′. [*i-n*]*a e-ni k*[*a-li-šu-nu*(?) . . .]
3′. // *ša kiš-š*[*a!-tim* . . .]
4′. ⸢*ta*⸣-*ma-li šu*-[. . .]
5′. // *ga-na l*[*u* . . .]
6′. *i-na šar-ri ka*-[*li-šu-nu*(?) . . .]
7′. // *šu-ut kiš-š*[*a-tim* . . .]
8′. *ta-ma-li šar-ru*-[*tam* . . .]
9′. // *ga-na lu*-[. . .]
10′. *ip-te* ^{d}GÌR ⸢X⸣[. . .]
11′. // *i*-[*di-in*? . . .]
12′. *i-na* GIŠ.ḪUR *ṣir*!-[. . .]
13′. // x x [. . .]
14′. *ip-te* ^{d}GÌR X *m*[*a*? . . .]
15′. // *i-di*-[*in*? . . .]

Philological and Textual Notes

Obverse

3′, 7′. Note the difference between the writing of the phrases: *ša kiššatim*, *šūt kiššatim*. The first is correct and the second archaizing.

10′, 14′. The writing ^{d}GÌR represents ^{d}Šákkan, protector of wild animals such as the lion, envisaged here as the incarnation of Sargon, and the son of Šamaš, mentioned in rev. 14′. Commonly it is Nergal who opens the paths, as in

B **8B**
Unknown Provenance
St. Étienne 150 (see photographs and copy, pp. 386–87).
dimensions:
length: 6.5 cm.
width: from 3.5 to 4.5 cm.
thickness at widest point: 2.5 cm.

Translation

Obverse

(break)
1′. . . .
2′–3′. "[Am]ong a[ll] en-priests [. . .] of the wor[ld . . .]

4′–5′. "You fulfilled the [priesthood(?)], indeed, verily [you are . . .]

6′–7′. "Among al[l] kings [. . .] of the wor[ld. . . .]

8′–9′. "You fulfilled the kingsh[ip. .], indeed, verily [you are. . . .]

10′–11′. "Shakkan opened . . [. . .] he ga[ve(?) . . .]

12′–13′. "In the exalted des[ign . .]. .[. . .]

14′–15′. "Shakkan opened . . . [. . .] he gav[e(?) . . .]

UET 1 275 i 12–16 (= *aK* 255:12–16 "Narāmsîn C 5"): ᵈKIŠ.UNU.GAL *ba-da-an* ᵈ*Na-ra-am-*ᵈEN.ZU *da-núm ip-te-ma*. For the close association of Nergal/Erra and Naram-Sin, see texts **13** and **22**. The unreadable sign after GÌR could be either part of the divine name or the object of the verb *petû*. An unusual spelling of Nergal's name would be unexpected at this period. A word such as *padānu*, *ḫarrānu* would be expected, but the sign is not KASKAL or GÍR. The *m*[*a*? . . .] might be the beginning of a ṬU and thus *ṭūdu* might be possible. For

16′. ŠÀ UR.MAḪ *na-ad-r*[*i* . . .]

17′. // [. .i]m(?) *lu*/*ib šu ša* [. . .]

18′. ⸢*li*⸣-[. . .]

(break—perhaps one line to end of column)

Reverse

(break)

1′.	A rev. 0	⸢x⸣-[. . .]
	B 1′	⸢x⸣ [(x)] ⸢x x⸣ [. . .]
2′.	A "b" 1′	// *ma*-[. . .]
	B 2′	[. . .] ⸢*ma-an*⸣-*na-šu š*[*a* . . .]
3′.	A "b" 2′–3′	*a-a-ú-um tab-b*[*a*(?) . . .]// *ú-ki-il um-ma*-[*nam*? . . .]
	B 3′	*a-i-ú-um tap-pu-šu* [. . .]
4′.	A "b" 4′	*ma na-aḫ-ra-rum ga-n*[*a* . . .]
	B 4′	*na-aḫ-ra-ru ga!-na*-[. . .]
5′.	A "b" 5′–6′	*be-el mar-ṣa-tim li-i*[*d* . . .]// *pa-ag*-[*ra-am*?? . . .]
	B 5′	*be-el mar-ṣa-tì li*-⸢*id-di*(?) *x*⸣-[(x)]
6′.	A "b" 7′	*ú-ul aš-šum-ma ša*-[. . .]
	B 6′	*ú-ul aš-šum-ma-a ša-lum-ma-tì-šu* [(x)]
7′.	A "b" 8′	*ri-ig-mi-šu ša*-[. . .]
	B 7′	*ù ri-ig-mi-šu ša-gi-mi-im* [(x)]
8′.	A "b" 9′	// *ú-ul i*-⟨*ṭe-eḫ*⟩-*ḫi a-di ma*-[*aḫ-ri-šu*]
	B 8′	*ú-ul i-ṭe*$_4$*-eḫ-ḫi ma-am-ma-a*[*n* (x)]
9′.	A "b" 10′–11′	*ù a-na-ku šar-ru*-[. . .] // UR.MAḪ-*ku-nu na-ad*-[*ru* . . .]
	B 9′	*a-na-ku šar-ru-gi-in ne-iš-ki*(sic)-*nu* ⸢*na-ad*⸣-*ru*

---

the opening of roads in the legends of Naram-Sin, cf. **12** i 3′: *a-ta-al-ka-am-ma li-pe-ti-a-nim* // *ṭù-da-at ša-du-ú-i ta-ab-ra-at* // *UN-ni*; and **13**:11: *ip-pa-ti-a-ma z*[*u*? *x x x*]-*ú šu-ṣi-a-ku*-[*um*].

Reverse

3′. Compare the lines from the other compositions of the "King of Battle": [*ajû*] LUGAL ⟨ŠÚ⟩ *ú-ša-an-na-an*, **9B** rev. 21′; *ajû* MAN *kiš-šá-a-t*[*e* . . .], **9D**:6′.

4′. The particle *mā* is known from OAkk. onwards. In the early texts, this interjection frequently expresses doubt and disbelief (CAD M/1 *mā* 1). Its omission in the second manuscript does not seemingly change the sense.

5′. The phrase *bēl marṣātim* is a hapax. There exist two instances of EN NÍG.GÍG in SB omen texts (SB Alu, Physiogn.); the term can equal *bēl marušti*

16′–17′. "Heart of a raging lion [. .] . . .

18′. "Let him [. . . .]"
(break)

Reverse

(break)

2′. "[. . .] who is he who [. . .]?

3′. "Which friend of his maintained the ar[my]?

4′. "What? a helper? indeed, [. . .]

5′. "Let the man of misfortune abandon his corpse/himself(?)!

6′. "Was it not because of his frightening radiance,

7′. "and his bellowing roar

8′. "that no one dared to approach [him]?"

9′. "I, Sargon, am your raging lion [. . .].

---

and seems to mean 'enemy' in the context of the apodosis. The plural form *marṣātum* is not found in a genitival construction with *bēlum*. On the other hand, it is used in reference to hardships and experiences of a heroic protagonist; cf. Gilg. I 26. Thus, the nominal compound could mean 'man of experience' or 'man who has experienced adversities'.

6′. Sargon's radiance is termed *šalummatu* in "Chronicles of Early Kings," line 2, as well as in the NA omen collection (King Chron. no. 3:23). For another reference to *šalummatu* in Old Babylonian, cf. [*kīma*] UR.MAḪ-*im* *š*[*a*]-*l*[*um-m*]*a-tum li-ik-l*[*a*?]-*ka* (ZA 75 [1985] 202:83, love incantation). For the expression of *šalummat nēši* in the corpus, see **21A** b 10 and **22**:94.

7′. Roaring is commonly applied to lions and gods, especially Adad the storm-god. Note that manuscript B adds a coordinating conjunction *ù* between noun phrases.

10′.	A "b" 12′–13′	*ma-am-ma-an ú-ul i-⟨ṭe-eḫ⟩-ḫ[i]* // *a-na* ú?-tu?-*ti-ja* [. . .]
	B 10′	*ma-am-ma-an ú-ul i-ṭe*$_4$*-ḫi a-na ki-iṣ-ṣe-ja*
11′.	A "b" 14′	*i-na ki-ma mi-it-ḫu-ri-i[m . . .]*
	B 11′	*ik-ki-ma mi-it-ḫu-ri-im-ma*
12′.	2 "b" 15′	// *šu-mi zu-uk-ra-[am]*
	B (edge) 12′	*šu-mi zu-uk-ra-[am]*
13′.	A "b" 16′–17′	*ú-ul i-pa-ar-ri-k[u]* // *[pa]-ni-iš* NIM.KI *i-*[. . .]
	B 13′	*ú-ul i-pa-ar-ri-ku pa-ni-iš* GIŠ.⸢EREN⸣?
14′.	A (end of side "b")	
	B (rev.) 14′	*ù at-ta mi-ta-ḫa-ar* ᵈ*Šamaš-ma*
15′.	B 15′	*ni-im-ri ga-ṣi*(!?)*-ṣú li-ba-aš uz-za*
16′.	B 16′	*bu-i lim-nam bu-nu-uš la* ⸢x⸣*-ḫu-*⸢x⸣*-ma*

17′.	B 17′	*za-a-a-ru mu-du-ú a-ru-ú a-na-an-ta*
18′.	B 18′	7 KALAG.MEŠ *a-ša-ri-du-šu*
19′.	B 19′	*li-mi ša ú-ut-ta-ku kab-ta-as-sú*
20′.	B 20′	[*š*]*it-pa da-pí-nu qú-ra-du-um*
21′.	B 21′	*id-di*-x[. . .]

(break)

left side of tablet B (from bottom upward):

še(!?)*-na-ti-šu ki i*? *dar*/**si*? *di* [. . .]

11′. Cf. *anna mitḫurumma ša qarrādi*, 6:17.

14′. The verb is a Gtn Imperative of *maḫāru* ('to pray to a deity again and again', CAD M/1, p. 67). Compare the appeal to judgment of Šamaš in **2** ii 17, as well as in **6**:10. In general, cf. the prayer to Šamaš in Tn.-Epic col. II. The following two lines apparently refer to Šamaš, and certain phrases echo the passages relating to Gilgameš's expedition to the Cedar Forest; see J. Tigay, *The Evolution of the Gilgamesh Epic* (Philadelphia, 1982) 76–81.

15′. There seems to be a wordplay on *nimru* 'panther' as well as 'light', an apt pun for the description of Šamaš. For *uzzum* 'attack of rage', epitomized as an assault of various wild animals in incantations, see R. Whiting, "An Old Babylonian Incantation from Tell Asmar" (ZA 75 [1985] 179–87), and the parallel section in C. Wilcke, "Liebesbeschwörungen aus Isin," ZA 75 (1985) 188ff., IB 1554, lines 78ff.

10′. "No one will approach my sanctuary(?).

11′. "When there is combat,

12′. "invoke my name!

13′. "They will not block (my way) before the Cedar (Forest)/Elam.

14′. "As for you, beseech Šamaš!

15′. "My gnashing panther, his heart is (filled with) fury.
16′. "(But) seeking the evil one, he will not countenance
(or: seek the evil one, his countenance is not. . . .)."

17′. Enemies, experts, leaders of battle,
18′. seven strongmen are his champions,
19′. thousands are they whom he bends to his will.
20′. Bellowed the fierce warrior,
21′. . . .
(break)
left side of tablet B (from bottom upwards):
his teeth are like. . . .

16′. Cf. *mimma lemnu ša tazirru uḫallaq ina māti* '(until) he removes from the country everything evil which you (Šamaš) hate', Gilg. III ii 18; *Huwawa šanū būnūšu* 'Huwawa's appearance is strange', Gilg. Y v 12.

17′. Cf. "Agušaya," VAS 10 214 i 11: *itnarru ananātim* 'she always leads battles'.

18′. Seven awful wardens guarded the cedars in the Cedar Forest: *aššum šullu[m erēnim] pulḫiātim* 7 ⌜x⌝ [x x x {x}], Gilg. Y iv 1–2 (OB); cf. NA Tablet II v 5; NB Tablet *JNES* 11 rev. 11–12. In the Sumerian tale of Gilgameš and Huwawa, Utu presents Gilgameš with seven monstrous warriors to guide him ("Gilgameš and Huwawa" A 34–44, see D. O. Edzard, ZA 80 [1990] 165ff., ZA 81 [1991] 165ff.).

20′. Note that the adjective normally applied to Huwawa is *dāpinu*.

9
"King of Battle"

This narrative concerning the exploits of Sargon incorporates the story of Sargon's campaign against the Anatolian city of Purušḫanda to aid his merchants. The tale is recorded in Hittite, of which six fragments are preserved (**9A**), and in Akkadian, of which four(?) manuscripts exist. The Akkadian manuscripts are: **9B** from el-Amarna, a recension of tablet I; the remaining manuscripts—**9C**, **9D**, and **9E**—are fragments. Of these fragments, the Aššur fragment, **9D**, is another exemplar of the same recension as the Amarna tablet. The Nineveh fragment, **9E**, comes from another recension and thus is labeled the Nineveh recension. The last piece, **9C**, the Amarna fragment, is too small to allow any positive identification. The story elements and the discourse structure are discussed in relation to each individual text.

The Hittite fragments seem to be free adaptations of the same legendary material, with certain pieces echoing the Akkadian phrases[16] and others (e.g., duplicates KBo 12 1 and 22 6) apparently farther removed from any Akkadian forerunners.

Merchants are not usually the stuff of which epics are made, but they were essential to the Old Akkadian trade network. Merchants are mentioned in royal inscriptions: for example, the merchants of Subartu (*aK* 253:93–94 "Narāmsîn C 4"), and there exists a Hittite text in epic style about merchants (H. Hoffner, *JCS* 22 [1968] 34–45).

9B
Amarna Recension

Introduction

The story elements that compose the narrative statement are expanded in this edition when compared with the three previous compositions. The list of characters has grown. Appearing for the first time in this composition are: the Akkadian merchants residing in Purušḫanda; the *sukkallu* of the merchants; and Nur-Daggal, king of Purušḫanda, the tyrant and oppressor of the merchants. Nur-Daggal makes his first appearance in this text as king of Purušḫanda; the actual title is not found in any Akkadian text in our corpus but occurs in the Hittite recension, KBo 22 6 i 21, [l]*Nu-úr-da-aḫ-ḫi* LUGAL KUR URU.*Pu-ru-uš-ḫa-*

[16] P. Meriggi, "Die hethitischen Fragments vom *šar tamḫâri*," *Gedenkschrift für W. Brandenstein* (Innsbrucker Beiträge zur Kulturwissenschaft 14; Innsbruck, 1968) 259–67.

an-da, and in the Late Babylonian text pertaining to the "Map of the World," CT 22 48:10′, ZALAG-^{d}*Da-gan* LUGAL *Bur-š*[*a-ḫ*]*a-an-*[*da*]. The Hittite writing reflects a dictation mistake of the reader, who read aloud the GAN as ḪÉ, and who must have had before him the normal writing of the proper noun Nur-Dagan (compare with ^{1}ZALAG-^{d}*Da-gan*, **9D**:3, 9).

Divine help comes from another quarter in this text: Zababa makes his appearance as the divine partner of Sargon and Enlil as the patron of Nur-Daggal. However, they are both mentioned in passing and do not take any active role in the story. In the Hittite version, **9A**, Enlil actively misleads Nur-Daḫḫi by revealing himself in a dream and describing the powers of the divine weapons that the king possesses.

The backdrop is now the highlands of Anatolia and its most important city in the third millennium B.C.E., Purušḫanda. Kaniš, also known to have been a bustling metropolis in the third millennium, is mentioned in passing.[17] The events are fully described: the merchants residing in Purušḫanda persuade Sargon to come to their aid, despite the warnings of his soldiers that the way is long and hazardous. Sargon makes a surprise attack on Nur-Daggal, the king of Purušḫanda, who humbly submits and acknowledges the might of Sargon. Everyone lives happily in the country for three years before thinking of returning to the homeland.

The story segments are as follows:

a. Sargon's speech to his warriors indicating his desire for war (lines 1–7);
b. the warnings of the warriors that the road to Purušḫanda is long and hazardous (lines 8–12);
c. the persuasive plea of the merchants from Purušḫanda (lines 13–21);
d. some contretemps between the merchants and the warriors (lines 22–23);
e. Sargon's repeated declarations of intention and requests for detailed information (lines 23–25);
f. the repetition of the warnings of the warriors (lines 26–27);
g. the description given by the merchants of a land abundant with timber, minerals, and exotic fruits (lines 28–35);
h. break of some 70(?) lines;
i. Nur-Daggal, king of Purušḫanda, speaks with his warriors about their security (lines rev. 3–7);
j. the attack of Sargon (lines rev. 8–9);
k. Sargon enthroned before the city gate (lines rev. 10–18);
l. submission of Nur-Daggal (lines rev. 19–23);
m. speech of Sargon's warriors, seeking to leave the city (lines rev. 24–27);

[17] See my forthcoming article, "Relations between Mesopotamia and Anatolia in the Age of the Sargonic Kings," *XXXIV Uluslararsi Assiriyuloji Kongresi* (Istanbul, 1987).

n. withdrawal of Sargon from Purušḫanda after three years (lines rev. 27–28).

As stated in the introduction to this chapter, there is an omnipresent, covert narrator, but the narration is minimal, limited to certain introductory formulas. The deep binary oppositions are realized in the discourse mode of dialogue.

Circumstances of Discovery

This tablet was found in controlled excavations on the 15th of December, 1913, by the Deutsche Orient-Gesellschaft, in an alley next to a wall of the court of house O.47,2, at Tell el-Amarna.[18] Unfortunately, it was found in isolation from any other object or tablet and could have been thrown out hastily by some ancient refugee from Akhetaten. The tablet was immediately treated upon discovery by O. Schroeder, who tried to relate the hero of the tale to the Pharaoh of Egypt. Besides giving a translation and very clear photographs, he described the tablet in detail. He recognized immediately that the ductus of the tablet seemed to reflect the "Hittite" ductus but mentioned that the reverse had traces of red Egyptian ink.[19]

Although the tablet was copied and published by O. Schroeder in VAS and thus given a VAT number, it was never actually accessioned by the Vorderasiatisches Museum zu Berlin. It remained in Egypt, where it was housed in the Cairo Museum; there it was first given the number 48396. It now has the siglum of the Cairo Museum, SR, and the number 12223.

General Observations

The tablet consists of a single column, only the upper half of which is preserved. The left side of the obverse was water-damaged according to the excavator, but the remains of the edge can be seen on the reverse.[20] It is thus possible to reconstruct how much is missing at the edge of the tablet.

There are many obstacles to a clear understanding of the text. First, there are the graphic inconsistencies, extra consonants and/or syllables, morphological problems, and poetic syntax. Second, the line division of the text does not correspond to the verse division, making it difficult to tell where one sentence begins and another ends in cases of inverted syntax. Likewise, one cannot rely on the paragraph division to indicate the end or beginning of speeches. Third,

[18] L. Borchardt, "Ausgrabungen in Tell el-Amarna 1913/1914," *MDOG* 55 (1914) 34–36; L. Borchardt and H. Ricke, *Die Wohnhäuser in Tell el-Amarna* (WVDOG 91; Berlin, 1980) 72–73.

[19] O. Schroeder, "Die beiden neuen Tafeln," *MDOG* 55 (1914) 39–45. It is not clear whether he is referring to dots that separate words, as in EA 356–57. If so, it says nothing about the origin of the tablet, though much about its use.

[20] Borchardt, *MDOG* 55, 35.

there is the fragmentary nature of the text; only the upper half of the tablet is extant. Fourth, the scribe was extremely careless and omitted signs and even whole phrases. As Güterbock succinctly states, this is "ein ausserordentlich schlechter Text."[21]

The external features of the tablet, its shape and divisions, as well as the internal features (see below) indicate that this tablet was actually written in the Hittite tradition.

Orthography and Language

This composition is not written in any of the standard dialects of Akkadian, such as Old Babylonian or Standard Babylonian, but in one of the western peripheral dialects. In general, it seems to reflect features of the Syro-Anatolian dialects of Akkadian. As early as 1922, Weidner suggested that *šar tamḫāri* had Hittite affinities.[22] According to Gary Beckman (private communication), there is a good chance that this composition was inscribed at Ḫattuša during the late Middle Hittite period (late fifteenth or early fourteenth century).

For a detailed analysis of the paleography of this text, see Sabina Franke, *Das Bild der Könige von Akkad.*[23] She compares the sign forms with those of the Hittite and concludes that the graphic characteristics of this text resemble those of the Hittite texts of Arnuwanda I. However, Akkadian texts from Boghazköy are known to be written in a different ductus from that of contemporary Hittite texts.[24] Edzard likens *šar tamḫāri* in particular to the Gilgameš text from Boghazköy. Furthermore, particular to this text are the confusion of Ú and LU, as well as QA and DU.

As expected, this text shares many orthographical peculiarities with other texts written in western peripheral dialects.[25] Concerning the labials, the sign BI is used to render /bi/ and /pi/, and the sign PI is used to render /wa, wi, wu/.

[21] Güterbock, *ZA* 42, 86–87.

[22] Weidner, *Der Zug Sargons* (BoSt 6) 61 n. 4; see also D. O. Edzard, "Amarna: Die literarischen Texten," *Proceedings of the Ninth World Congress of Jewish Studies, vol. 8: Panel Sessions—Bible Studies and Ancient Near East* (Jerusalem, 1988) 27–33.

[23] S. Franke, *Das Bild der Könige von Akkad in ihren Selbstzeugnissen und der Überlieferung* (Ph.D. diss., University of Hamburg, 1989) 199ff.

[24] G. Beckman, "Mesopotamians and Mesopotamian Learning at Ḫattuša," *JCS* 35 (1983) 99 n. 11.

[25] At present, the dialects of Ḫattuša, Ugarit, Amurru, Carchemiš, and Mitanni have been described adequately, but others still require study, particularly those of Alalakh, Egypt, and Emar; see J. Durham, *Studies in Boğazköy Akkadian* (Ph.D. diss., Harvard University, 1976); J. Huehnergard, *The Akkadian of Ugarit* (HSS 34; Atlanta, 1989; see his bibliography for earlier publications); S. Izre'el, *Amurru Akkadian: A Linguistic Study* (HSS 40; Atlanta, 1991). See also G. Jucquois, *Phonétique comparée des dialectes moyen-babyloniens du nord et de l'ouest* (Louvain, 1966). Jucquois labels the orthography of the Akkadian texts written in Egypt, Hattuša, and Mitanni as "syllabaire akkado-hittite." As described by F. M. Th. Böhl (*Die Sprache der Amarnabriefe*, [LSS 2; Leipzig, 1909]) and later by R. Labat (*L'Akkadien de Boghaz-Köi* [Paris, 1932]), these texts have many unusual signs, as well as inconsistencies in the writing system.

Despite the confusion in other texts, our text seems to distinguish between /pa/ and /ba/.[26] As for the dentals, TA, DA, and TAM are employed to render /ta/, but only TI to render both /ti/ and /di/[27] and DU to render both /tu/ and /du/. As Labat suggests, the sign chosen is dependent on the vowel and not the consonant: Dental + i = TI and Dental + u = DU; but there is a confusion with Dental + a (Labat, pp. 25ff.). With the velars we have a similar picture: GA and KAM render /ka/; KI renders /ki/ and /gi/ and GI renders /qi/;[28] while KU renders /ku/ and */gu/. Thus, Velar + i = KI, Velar + u = KU, and Velar + a = GA. The initial /qa/ is written with the QA sign (rev. 22, 29). Peculiar to this text seems to be the system of rendering a plene /u/: syllables beginning with *u* are usually written with the U sign, and syllables with medial or final *u* are usually written with the Ú sign (*u-ur-ḫ̮é*, obv. 12; but *mi-lu-ú*, rev. 4′). Last, as expected in Boghazköy Akkadian (Durham, §24o), the sign ZÉ is used for the sequence /ṣe/ (*ṣi-it*, obv. 15).

Other peculiarities of the writing system include the tendency to double consonants in intervocalic position.[29] The doubling is especially common in the first syllable of a word. Not only are nouns such as the personal name Nur-Daggal written with geminating consonant, but also nominal formations such as *ammatu* and verbal formations such as *ukkannišu* and *unnammišu* (see Durham, §29e). Likewise, phonetic indicators are known from Boghazköy Akkadian (Durham, §23), as well as Ugaritic Akkadian (Huehnergard, 91), of which we have one example: *nu-uš-*^{ša}*šab*. Also known from northwestern peripheral Akkadian (Huehnergard, 276–77; Durham, §50b) are the Assyrian long consonants in place of long vowels: *-uttu* for *-ūtu* (cf. rev line 6′).

Phonologically speaking, noun forms that would have mimation in OB are written without it in this text. The late OB/MB sound change of *š* to *l* before a dental is evidenced in *ultēšebū* (rev. 15′). Note that although the preposition is normally written *ultu* (e.g., obv. 15), there seems to be an instance of the form *ištu* (rev. 8′). In addition, there is evidence of late second-millennium dialectal forms in which the vowel *-u-* appears for the expected vowel *-i-*, as in *burku* rather than *birku* in line 12.

Determinatives occur in this text in accordance with what is usual in Boghazköy Akkadian: (1) KUR and URU appear before the names of geographical locations. URU alone is the logogram for city (see Durham, §11b), but note earlier form URU.KI in rev. 26′; (2) LÚ appears before the names of occupations (see Durham, §11d). However, MEŠ, the plurality marker, apparently appears randomly; there do not seem to be any constraints on its appearance.

In morphology, final vowels neither follow normative Akkadian rules nor conventions of peripheral Akkadian. Certain extralinguistic factors affect the

[26] Böhl, p. 20; Labat, pp. 13–14; Huehnergard, p. 35; and Durham, §7b, §26a.

[27] There seems to be one exception in rev. 10′, in which dí (Borger #396/231) seems to occur, a syllabic writing not found in other peripheral dialects.

[28] The only exception is the spelling of the name of Sargon: LUGAL.GI-*en* (= *Šarru-kēn*).

[29] For graphic doubling, see Jucquois, 195ff.

grammatical forms. The social status of the speaker influences the use of the ventive suffix. Sargon speaks without ventive (*izzakar*), and everyone else speaks with ventive (*izzakara*) (toward Sargon !?). Likewise, Nur-Daggal speaks to his troops without ventive (*izzakar*). The plural morpheme on the verb can alternate with the same subject between *-ā* and *-ū* (cf. obv. 22 versus 23). The subjunctive with *-u* (obv. 19, 21, 22) and without *-u* occur (obv. 8, 26, 27, rev. 16). Note the Assyrian subjunctive *-ūni* in obv. line 30. In addition, there is the tendency found in Middle Akkadian dialects to employ the perfect form of the verb as the normal one for narrative (e.g., rev. lines 8–9, 15, 22, and passim). There seem to be certain examples of the incorrect use of case endings: nominative for accusative (cf. obv. 20[?], rev. 9′), accusative for nominative (cf. obv. 9, 21, 26), and genitive for nominative (rev. 6′) and for accusative (cf. obv. 2[?]). Such errors in case usage are known from Ḫattuša (Durham, §49e), as well as Ugarit (Huehnergard, 143–44). Likewise, there is the usage of case-vowels in bound forms of the noun, including status constructus; compare nominative [*iš*]*ātu utūni* (rev. 22′), accusative *ebera nāri* (rev. 20′), and genitive *ina alāki urḫi* (obv. 12). This phenomenon is known in Ugaritic Akkadian (Huehnergard, 149ff.).

Lexically, no West Semitisms are expected, since I am working under the assumption that this text was written in the Hittite tradition. Also known from northwestern peripheral Akkadian is the MA form of the preposition *adi, adu*. Another case of an Assyrian lexeme is the verb *namāšu* (rev. 27′), not used in MB, according to von Soden.[30] A case of homophony seems to be the writing of KASKAL-*ru* for *girru*, meaning 'fire' in rev. line 21′.

Poetics

This text was included by von Soden in his study of the hymno-epic dialect.[31] Its formal structure is bonded by inverted syntax in general and by its use of certain words and phrases in particular. For example, note the inverted genitive in lines 16 and rev. 10, as well as the words *ilka Zababa* at the beginning and conclusion of the speech of the merchants' spokesman. Furthermore, there is the use of certain sound patterns: *kiššī, kiššati, kiššūtu* (obv. 17–18) is one such set. The outstanding feature of the poetic structure is the abundant use of parallelism. Many lines contain several synonymous-parallel clauses, usually incremental in nature.

Manuscript

Akhetaten (Tell el-Amarna)

Cairo Museum 48396 = SR 12223 = VAT 10290 = VAS 12 193 = EA 359; see A. Rainey, *EA* (AOAT 8) 6ff. (coll. A. R. Rainey 10.01.81).

[30] Von Soden, *UF* 11, 750.
[31] Idem, ZA 40 (1931) 174.

Transcription

Obverse

1. [. . .]-*il* ^{d}U.DAR *a-*⟨*na*⟩ *šu-ri* URU.A[*k-kà-dì* . . .]
2. [. . . *mu-ba*]-*ú tam-ḫa-ri* LUGAL *qé-re-e*[*b* É.GAL-*lim* . . .]
3. [. . .] *i-qáb-bi qáb-la-*⟨*šu*⟩ LUGAL.G[I-*en* . . .]

Philological and Textual Notes

Many scholars have treated this text in detail. Among the most important treatments are: E. F. Weidner, *Der Zug Sargons von Akkad nach Kleinasien* (BoSt 6; 1922) 57–99; W. F. Albright, "The Epic of the King of Battle," *JSOR* 7 (1923) 1–20; P. Dhorme, "Les nouvelles tablettes d'El-Amarna," *RB* 33 (1924) 19–32; H. G. Güterbock, "Die historische Tradition und ihre literarische Gestaltung bei Babyloniern und Hethitern bis 1200," ZA 42 (1934) 86–91. In particular, see S. Franke, *Das Bild der Könige von Akkad*, 1989. Her work can only be cited briefly, since it appeared in the final stages of preparation of this manuscript. In the following commentary, references are made to the above authors and page numbers, rather than repeating the full bibliographical references. Not every suggestion made in the above studies is cited below, since the progress of Assyriology has made some of them obsolete.

Obverse

1. The beginning of the text has caused problems for many scholars. It has been repeatedly stated that the text opens *in medias res*. For a comparison with the Hittite version, which begins with Sargon waking from a dream in which Ištar told him to go on the campaign, see P. Meriggi, "Zu einigen Stellen hethitischer historischer Texte," *Festschrift Heinrich Otten* (Wiesbaden, 1973) 200. As Meriggi states, it is difficult to restore such an introduction in the lines here. Note that the Nineveh recension (text **9E**) reflects the Hittite story more closely. It is possible that the prayer to Ištar occurs in the break after the warriors and the merchants presented their arguments to Sargon and Sargon turns to Ištar for a divine decision.

The first lines seem to contain particularizing verses, in which epithets are later replaced by the name of the king. The first extant word seems to end in a clear [. . .]-*il*; it is most probably an epithet of Sargon in construct with Ištar; various possibilities suggest themselves: *ālil*, *dāgil*, *dālil*, *etel*, *tākil*. The third word, *a-šu-ri*, presents problems: (a) it cannot be the adjective 'Assyrian' (as suggested by Güterbock, 87 n. 1; Franke, 192) since it lacks not only the feminine *-ti*, but also the double *šš*, which is always written except in the OA period;

Translation

Obverse

1. [. . . (The hero of)] Ištar, to the steers of A[kkade . . .],
2. [. . . Seeker] of battles, the king in the mid[st of the palace . . .]
3. [. . . to his warriors(?)] he is speaking. Sargon [girds] his loins

---

(b) *asurrû* 'foundation, damp course' (as suggested by Albright, p. 7) would be unexpected, although the writing of /su/ with ŠU is consistent with Boghazköy Akkadian orthography (Durham, §25b); (c) it does not seem to refer to the god Aššur or to "eine zwittergestaltige Gottheit" (as suggested by Weidner, p. 70). Consequently, in accordance with the supposition that the first two lines contain epithets, it could be suggested that *a-šu-ri* is another epithet of Sargon, though it is difficult to surmise which epithet was intended. Possibilities are: *ašru* 'humble' or *ašāru* 'to muster, provide, organize', in a *parus* formation rather than a *pāris* formation. The latter appears as an epithet of kings; cf. Seux, *Epithètes*, 44–45. However, the final vowel *-i* in the status constructus should not be there in the nominative.

Güterbock (ZA 42, 87) suggests reading this line: [*šar tamḫārim ammata izzak*]*ar a-Ištar a-šuri* GN. However, in this text the prepositions are not shortened: there is no case of *a-* for *ana* or *i-* for *ina*. On the other hand, the preposition could have been written wrongly: the scribe could have omitted the ⟨*na*⟩. If such a surmise is correct, then we have a long introduction to the speech of Sargon to his warriors. Assuming the correctness of the supposition that *šu-ú-ru* in obv. 20 refers to the warriors as steers, then *šu-ri* could also refer to the warriors. For the characterization of the warriors in the Sargon texts as domesticated male animals, see p. 58.

2. The *-ú* at the beginning of the line limits the possibilities regarding the word in front of *tamḫāri*. One possibility is to read a participle *mubāʾʾû* from *buʾʾû*, which is found in line 6. The word *tamḫāri* is patently an oblique plural. I have restored *qereb ekalli* in place of *qereb Akkade* on the basis of lines 4 (⟨*qé-re-eb*⟩ É.GAL-*lim*) and 22 (*qé-re-eb* É.GAL-*lim*), as well as **6**:31 (*i-na qé-re-eb* É.GAL-*li*). In this line the scene is set inside the palace, where Sargon is speaking with his soldiers; in comes a representative of the merchants who are left standing outside the palace. For a different parsing of this line, *tamḫāri šarri qé-re-*[*eb* 'des Kampfes des Königs, der sich nähe[rt?', see Franke, 185, 192–93.

3. The phrase *qablam qabû* 'to speak war' occurs once in the corpus of Akkadian literature: *ana ḫulluq nišīja qabla aqbīma* 'How could I have ordered (such a) catastrophe to destroy my people?' (Gilg. XI 121, Enlil speaking).

4. [. . . (*ina*)] GIŠ.TUKUL-#⌜*šu*⌝ *ez-zi* ⟨*qé-re-eb*⟩ É.GAL-*lim* LUGAL.[GI-*en* KA×U-*šu* *e-ep-pu-ša*]
5. [*i-qáb-bi a-na* UR.SAG-*šu a-m*]*a-tá iz-za-kàr* UR.SAG-*ja* KUR.*Kà*-[*ni-iš*(?) . . .]
6. [. . . -*n*]*u ú-ba-a qáb-la uk-kà-an-ni-ša* [. . .]

---

7. [. . . *i*]*m-ma ud id ra a-ša-*⟨*ri*⟩*-id* LUGAL.G[I-*en* KA×U-*šu* *e-ep-pu-ša*]
8. [*i-qáb-bi iz-za-kà-ra be*(?)]*-li-iš pa-ra-ak-ki* KASKAL-*na be-lí š*[*a te-er-ri-i*]*š a-la-kam*

Despite the attractive translation of *iqabbi qabla* as 'he is speaking war', it seems to be a rare idiomatic expression. Noting the love of wordplay based on sound similarities (see *qabla buʾʾû* in line 6), I chose the homophonous *qabla* 'loins'. A phrase such as *qablam rakāsu* 'to gird' fits the context very nicely.

4. For the weapon of Sargon, cf. Izbu IX 61.

5. The last two words could be read KUR-*kà* 'your land', but this reading doesn't make much sense in the context. On the basis of the parallel passage in **7** i 16′, one expects Sargon to declare to his warriors which city would be the goal of his campaign. Another possibility is to relate these two words to ḪUR.SAG *ga-ap-šu* (lines 28, rev. 5, 17) with KUR replacing ḪUR.SAG, although kings do not usually battle mountains. At present, the GA is no longer extant on the tablet, having flaked off. Support for the reading *Kà-ni-iš* might be found in the next line in the use of the similar-sounding *ukkannišā*.

6. The form of the verb *kanāšu* with double *-kk-* here as well as in rev. 12 has been assumed to come from an incorrect ŠD *uškannišā*, but it is just an ordinary D form *ukannišā*, with duplication of the consonant in initial intervocalic position. For examples of incorrect doubling of *-kk-* and *-gg-*, see Huehnergard, 49. The verb *kanāšu* in D does not refer to an act of obeisance such as that described in **7** i 12′–15′ (Sargon's pious thanksgiving for having safely reached the Cedar Forest), but to the subjection of others, since the verb in the D must be transitive. This seems to be the act that causes Sargon's desire for war.

7. This line is very difficult, one-third of it is missing, and it is likely that the text should be emended. Neither Weidner nor Güterbock offers a translation of this line. Rainey has followed Albright's suggestion (p. 8 n. 11): [. . . *ḫi-i*]*m-ma-ta*$_5$ *it-ra-a ša-iṭ Šarru-k*[*è-en* . . .] '[. . . swe]epings he has brought! Despised is Sarg[on . .]'. Franke renders this line: *di*??*-i*]*m*?*-*?*ma-ta*$_5$ *it-ra-a ša* Á? *Šarru-k*[*é-en* 'mit Jammern holte er den der Seite? Sargons' (pp. 184–85, 195). It is also possible that the word *it-ra-a* may be related to the word *lu*(-)*ut-ra-a* in rev. 26′, both with similar objects: country/city.

Without emending the text, a tentative reading could have [. . .]-*im* as the end of a causative verb with two objects, *māta*(*m*) and *idra*, thus yielding 'May I cause the land to reveal saltpeter'. 'Saltpeter' probably refers to KNO_3, potassium nitrate, which is found in domestic structures such as house walls, where moisture from the ground can be drawn up by capillary action and then evapo-

4. [. . . (with)] his terrible weapon. ⟨In the midst of⟩ the palace, Sargon [opens his mouth]
5. [speaking to his warriors] he declares, "My warriors! (With) Ka[nish . . .]
6. "[. . .] I desire war. They have subjugated [. . .]."

---

7. [. . . .] . . . , the champion of Sar[gon opens his mouth]
8. [he speaks, saying to the lo]rd of thrones, "As to the road, O my lord, th[at you wis]h to travel—

---

rate. If the salts left behind by the evaporation are not washed away by rain, as in Mesopotamia, they can be seen as white hairy crystals. Such a description fits the context of *idru* (cf. CAD s.v.). It alternates with *idrānu* in formulas pronouncing curses on the fields, that they will become salinated. In the present context, Sargon could be pronouncing such a curse on the land of his enemy, threatening that he will make it infertile. The last three signs before Sargon, *a-ša*-ID, could then be another first-person verb from *šaḫāṭu* 'to jump, to attack'. However, the absence of the medial *-ḫ-* is unexpected in this text. Likewise, the word *mātu* is written KUR in this text in obv. 5, rev. 7′, 20′.

An interesting idea would be to emend *a-ša-id* to *a-ša-⟨re⟩-ed* and compare it to the *ašared* champion of the king, who speaks in **6**:10, delivering a very pacifistic speech; he could be performing the same role in this text. Then, *it-ra* could be from *arû* G Perf.(?) 'to lead' (Rainey, AOAT 8, 2d ed., 65), or *tarû* 'to take away' or *tarû* 'to raise'; *im-ma*-TAM could be adverbial or object, and the object or subject could be lost in the break. Thus, one arrives at the conjecture: 'as soon as he raised (?) . . . , Sargon's champion began to speak'.

8. The restoration of the introductory formula of direct speech only leaves room for at most two signs before *li-iš*. Thus, although there is insufficient room for *ana bēl kališ parakkī*, there is space for *bēliš parakkī*, assuming this is an unusual instance of the terminative adverbial *-iš*. It could also be a participle [x]-*li-iš*, or an adverb ending in *-liš*, such as *šapliš*, *eliš*, etc. As for a participle, there are few verbs where the last two radicals of the root are *lš*. They are *ḫalāšu* 'to scrape off (plaster)', *malāšu* 'to pluck out', *nalāšu* 'to bedew', *palāšu* 'to pierce', *šalāšu* 'to do for the third time'. At present, the signs after *be-* are no longer extant on the tablet, having flaked off. A similar epithet was applied to Sargon in the "Weidner Chronicle": *e-pu-uš gi-mir a-šib* BARÁ.(MEŠ); see F. N. H. Al-Rawi, "Tablets from the Sippar Library, I: The 'Weidner Chronicle'—A Supposititious Royal Letter concerning a Vision," *Iraq* 52 (1990) 6, line S 17. For a syntactic parallel, cf. *iliś ālīśunu*, Bāseṭkī Inscription of Narām-Sîn, *aK* 82:49 "Narāmsîn 1."

8–10. These lines duplicate lines 26–27, and both times they are the reply of the soldiers to Sargon:

8.	KASKAL-*na be-lí š[a te-er-ri-i]š a-la-kam*
26.	[KASKAL-*na*(?) *š*]*a te-er-ri-iš a-la-kà*

9. [*u-ur-ḫa-at šu-up-šu-qá-at a-l*]*a-ak-ta mar-ṣa-at* KASKAL-*an* URU.*Bur-ša-ḫa-an-da*

10. [*ša te-er-ri-iš a-la-kam*] KASKAL-*an ša a-da-mu-mu-uš ši-ip-pí-ir* ⟨7 KASKAL.GÍD⟩ *ni-nu*! *im-ma-ti*

---

9. [. . . . . *a-l*]*a-ak-ta mar-ṣa-at*
26. *u-ur-ḫa-at šu-up-šu-qá-at a-la-ak-ta mar-ṣa-at*

9. KASKAL-*an* URU.*Bur-ša-ḫa-an-da*
27. [URU.*Bur-ša-ḫa*]*-an-da*

10. [ ] KASKAL-*an ša a da mu mu uš*
27. *ša te-er-ri-iš a-la-kà* KASKAL-*an ša a da mu mu*
10. *ši ib bi ir* NI+BE/TIM *im-ma-ti*
27. *ši ib bi ir* 7 KASKAL.GÍD

Although the meaning of the first two lines is obvious, the grammar is not. The first nominal phrase headed by KASKAL-*na* seems to be an asyntactic anticipatory phrase, seemingly without any predicate. The word *urḫu* can be construed either as feminine or masculine in the singular and plural. Even though *u-ur-ḫa-at šu-up-šu-qá-at* has been translated as 'the road is difficult', it is worth pointing out that *urḫāt* can only be a feminine plural absolute (note that this text otherwise has masculine plural formations: *u-ur-ḫí* obv. 12, 14), and *šupšuqat* can only be singular. The correct grammatical congruence should be *urḫātu šupšuqā*. Consequently, it may be better to treat *urḫat supšuqat* as two statives in the fem. sg., the subject of which is the understood *ḫarrānu*. Thus, the only likely interpretation is *urḫu* < *warḫum* 'month', which is not found as a predicative. Furthermore, *alakta* seems to be in the accusative case instead of the nominative. If the form *alakta* is the accusative of relationship, it is a parallel construction to the previous clause, in which KASKAL-*na* is also in the accusative case instead of the nominative.

Whereas *ḫarrāna* and *alakta* are in the accusative case, the next two nouns heading nominal phrases *ḫarrān Purušḫanda* . . . *ḫarrān* . . . are not. They syntactically represent the two halves of a nominal sentence: 'the road to Purušḫanda . . . is the road . . .'. The surface forms of both are identical, although the former is in the construct state and the latter in a predicative state. The latter is most likely followed by a relative clause. Although the form *ḫarrānša* is possible, the possessive pronoun could not refer back to the land of Purušḫanda, because it is referred to in the masculine in lines 24–25, and lands are themselves masculine in this text; see rev. 20′. The interpretations of the signs in the relative clauses have been varied:

(a) *a-da-mu-mu-uš šippir* (for *šipir*) *ni-nu im-ma-ti* 'über den ich mich beklage, die Sendung wir jemals (. . . besetzen wir)' (Weidner, 63 and 71, note to line 10). A variant division of the verse is offered by Dhorme (p. 25 n. 2): '(route) dont je gémis c'est un voyage! Nous, autres, quand donc nous, (assierons-

9. "[it is a month-long, it is dangerous; as to tra]veling, it is arduous. The road to Purušḫanda
10. "[that you wish to travel—] the road of which I groan is a task of ⟨seven double-miles⟩ (?). When will we

---

nous sur un siège)?' The same interpretation of the word *damāmu* is offered by von Soden, AHw 155b s.v. *damāmu* 'jammern, klagen'.

(b) *atamu mušebbirtim immati* '(the road) of which I speak never lets (one) cross' (Albright, 8). Rainey's variant places the verse division before the word *immati*: '(the road) of which I speak is a very long one (lit. carries one far). When. . . . ' The version offered by Franke is: *atamu muššebbir* ⟨7 DANNA⟩ 'von dem ich spreche, führt ⟨sieben Doppelstunden⟩ hinüber'.

(c) *a-da-mu mu-(uš)-ši ib-bi-ir* 'der über die Abendröte hinausgeht' (Güterbock, 87 n. 4).

The relative *ša*-clause seems to be a verbal one with the subjunctive *-u* on the verb *a-da-mu* or *a-da-mu-mu* as in alternatives (a) and (b) above. If alternative (a) is correct, then the predicate is a noun *šippir* < *šipru*, a Babylonian form of the noun in status constructus with the doubling of the intervocalic *-p-*, and the regens could be ⟨7 KASKAL.GÍD⟩ from line 27; or it could be in status absolutus. The grapheme *-uš-* could render either a resumptive pronoun or a sandhi writing. If alternative (b) is correct, then the predicate consists of *mu-(uš)-ši-ip-pí-ir*, either an Š-participle of a verb whose root is *ebēru* or *epēru*; this could derive from *ebēru* A 'to cross (water)', *ebēru* B 'to paint the face', denominative from *eperu* 'dust, soil, etc.' or from *epēru* 'to provide', perhaps with some intentional pun or a D-participle of *šebēru* 'to shatter'. Note the negative connotations of a dusty road in "Erra": '(He who came water-borne will be forced to go back on) *ḫarrān turbaʾi* the dusty road!' (IIc 20). Again, it is in the status constructus or absolutus but not in gender agreement with the feminine subject *ḫarrānu*. I have chosen alternative (a) as the best solution.

The signs read *ni-nu! im-ma-ti* in the transliteration have caused problems. According to the collations of Rainey, the signs NI+BE were correctly copied by Schroeder. Although one of the signs listed by Schroeder in VAS 12 79 #47 s.v. TIM is identical with the NI+BE, the question arises whether this sign is our example and whether there are any other examples written in such an unusual way (cf. the sign forms in J. Friedrich, *Hethitisches Keilschrift-Lesebuch*, vol. 2, p. 11 #9; C. Rüster and E. Neu, *Hethitisches Zeichenlexikon*, Wiesbaden, 1989, 97, no. 14). Until we have evidence of other TIM-signs written in this way, we should try to work on the present traces: NI+BE. At present, it seems best to take Weidner's suggestion that *ninu* fits the traces best. Likewise, the verse division seems to be before *ninu*, in accordance with Dhorme's suggestion above. If the sign is TIM, then there would be a feminine ending for the participle in agreement with the noun *ḫarrānu*. Unfortunately, there is no TIM and no agreement between the noun and the participle. The use of *immati* in this line parallels its use in rev. 25′.

11. [. . . -š]*u nu-uš-*^{ša}*šab* GIŠ.GU.ZA *nu-šap-šaḫ sú-ur-ri-iš*

12. [. . . *i*]*q-ta-ta i-da-a-ni bur-kà-ni i-tá-an-ḫa i-na a-la-ki u-ur-ḫí*

---

13. [(*i-nu-mi-šu*) KA×U-*šu*] *e-ep-pu-ša i-qáb-bi iz-za-kà-ra* LÚ.SUKKAL *ša* DUMU.MEŠ LÚ.DAM.GÀR

14. [DINGIR-*kà* ^{d}*Za-ba*$_4$-*b*]*a*$_4$ *a-lik u-ur-ḫí mu-še-te-*⟨*še*⟩*-ru* KASKAL-*na ha-ja-aṭ ki-ib-ra-ti*

15. [. . . *be*(?)-*l*]*i-iš pa-ra-ak-ki ša ul-tù ṣi-it* ^{d}UTU *i-na ša-la-mi* ^{d}UTU-*ši*

16. [. . . *š*]*a* DUMU.MEŠ LÚ.DAM.GÀR ŠÀ-*šu-nu i-ra-a mar-ta bu-ul-lu-ul im-mé-ḫe-e*

17. [*i-na er*]-*ṣé*?-*ti mi-na i-na qé-re-eb* URU.*Ak-kà-dì ki-iš-ši li-il-qut*

18. [LUGAL.G]I-*en* LUGAL ŠÚ *šum-*⟨*šu*⟩ *ni-iz-kùr u-ur-ri-da-nu ni-ma-aḫ-ḫa-ra ki-iš-šu-ti ú-ul qar-ra-da-nu*

---

12. At the beginning of this line, Franke would restore the object of *nušapšaḫ* (pp. 185, 194). Note the correct dual formations on noun and verb.

13. The restoration of the broken beginning is conjectural. The context excludes Rainey's suggestion of Nur-Daggal. Following Güterbock (pp. 87–88), Glassner ("Sargon," 117 n. 23) suggests restoring the name of the merchants' spokesman. I would prefer an adverbial introductory word as the first word in the sentence.

14. All commentators assume that *mu-še-te-ru* is an erroneous writing for *muštēšir*(*u*) (see Güterbock, 88 n. 1, but note that he interprets it as an epithet of Sargon rather than Zababa).

16. Suggestions for the meaning of the verb *i-ra-a* are:

a. *arû* 'to cut twigs', meaning 'to break in two' (Dhorme, 26 n. 7; Güterbock, 88 n. 2). However, the dictionaries only list this verb in the D form.
b. *ḫarâ* (Hebrew) 'to kindle' (said of wrath) (Albright, 8 n. 16).
c. *arû* 'to lead' (Rainey, *EA*, Glossary, 1st ed., 9).
d. *arû* 'to vomit' (Rainey, *EA*, Glossary, 2d ed., 65). This interpretation is supported by the phrase in apposition, *marta bullul* 'filled with bile'. Franke (pp. 184–85, 194) parses the same words differently: 'Ihr Herz spuckt Galle (und) es/sie ist mit Sturm vermischt'.
e. *râ*ʾ*u* 'to be friends, cooperate', which suggest that the hearts of the merchants were united, that they were unanimous in their opinions, that they were presenting a united front.

Translators have left the last word in the line dangling. If a new sentence begins with IM *meḫê*, then the predicate would be at the beginning of the next line of text: [x x (x)] ⌜*zi*?⌝ *ti*. The sign IM could be read either logographically or

11. "[. . .] sit down on a chair? Will we rest even for a moment
12. "[when] our arms have no more strength, (and) our knees have become exhausted from walking the trails?"

---

13. [At that time] he opens [his mouth] and speaks, the spokesman of the merchants declares:
14. "[By your god, Zabab]a, who travels the roads, who proceeds on the way, who spies out the regions,
15. "[. . . for the lo]rd of thrones, from the rising of the sun to the setting of the sun,
16. "[. . .] the heart(s) of the merchants are vomiting, spattered with bile, disgorging
17. "[upon the ear]th(?). What can Kiši take from the midst of Akkade?
18. "We swore (loyalty) by the name [Sar]gon, king of the universe, so we went down (and now) we are facing violence and we are not (particularly) heroic.

---

syllabically. In the former case it could either be a determinative or could be read *šār* 'wind of' in status constructus, but note that *šāru* is written syllabically in line 25. The word *meḫê* appears to be in the genitive case, dependent on *šār*. It is probably not the object of the preposition *ina* > *im*-, since there are no other examples of shortened assimilated prepositions in this text. To avoid these problems, I suggest reading the signs as a verb *im-mé-he-e* from *mâʾu* 'to vomit'. Cf. *ḫe-pí-i-ma li-ib-ba-šu i-ma-aʾ ma-ar-ta-am* 'for his heart was broken and he was vomiting gall' (Lambert-Millard, *Atra-ḫasis*, 92, III ii 47). The phrase *martam mâʾu* is considered to be an epic formula by Hecker, *Epik*, 169. The writing with *ḫ* is probably directly related to a by-form *maḫû* 'to have stomach spasms' (cf. CAD M/1 116a; Labat TDP 134:34, 178:14). The stem vowel is harder to explain. The initial consonant is again doubled. Poetically, this solution of a third parallel phrase is similar to the lines containing three parallel phrases in the introduction to direct speech, as well as in lines 8–9 // 26–27, 14, rev. 4′–5′//17′–18′.

17–18. Sommerfeld suggests possibly reading the beginning of the line *u*]*l-ti-mi-na* from *lemēnu* D 'schlecht behandeln' as the predicate of the previous verse. That would mean the remainder of this verse would be read as a pathetic burst of surrender: 'Let Kiši destroy Akkade!'

As understood by Albright and Rainey, there seems to be a wordplay on the words *kišši* 'Kiši', the city, *kiššatu* 'totality', as well as *kiššūtu* 'power' in the next line. The city Kiš is normally written syllabically *Ki-ši*, in all cases reflecting a form Kīši (see T. Jacobsen, "Ipḫur-Kīshi and His Times," *AfO* 26 [1978–79] 1 n. 3). It could not be the gentilic, since the accusative form would be *Kiššiam* > *Kiššâ*. The doubling of the -*š*- again shows the gemination of a consonant in intervocalic position. Both Weidner (p. 71) and Güterbock (88 n. 3) prefer to read an ungrammatical *gi*$_5$-*mil-lim* in line 17 and similarly some garbled form

19. [*u-ud*]-*da-a u-ur-ḫí* LUGAL *ú/lu-mi-id* UR$_5$-⌈*ta*!⌉(wr. #BI) *ni-pa-lu* LUGAL *ša* ⟨⟨*ša*⟩⟩ *iz-za-za qáb-la-šu li-pu-la* LUGAL

20. [x-x-*ú*]*z*(?)-*zu-zu* GUŠKIN UR.SAG LUGAL.GI-*en li-id-dì-nu šu-ú-ru* KÙ.BABBAR

---

21. [*ki* KASKAL]-*ni ni-il-la-ak in-ni-pu-ša da-aṣ-ṣa-ti i-na ša ni-ḫu-ma* DINGIR-*kà* ^{d}*Za-ba$_4$-ba$_4$*

---

of the same word in line 18. Franke (pp. 184–85, 195) emends the text: URU.*ak-kà-dì*.KI *uš*!-*ši lilqut* 'Er soll im Inneren von Akkad die Fundamente weg-picken!' Dhorme (p. 26) sees in line 17 a curse placed on Akkade by the merchants. Another possible word could have been *kiššu* B 'strength, might', but there too we have the problem of the apparent genitive (or plural oblique) case of the object. A more probable candidate in the context of merchants and merchandise is *kiššu* 'piece of felt' (cf. P. Steinkeller, "Mattresses and Felt in Early Mesopotamia," *OA* 19 [1980] 89). On the other hand, note the antagonism of the city of Kish in the Sargonic traditions (see texts **15–16**).

For the syntactical structure, cf. Old Babylonian *mīnam libbum liqīp* 'What can one rely on?' (*Bagh. Mitt.* 2 57 ii 6–7).

18. The idiom *šumam zakārum* 'to swear an oath of allegiance' is paralleled by a similar idiom in **12** v 7: *lu-us-sà-qá-ar ni-iš-ka // lu-ut-ma* 'I will take an oath and swear upon your life'. Note the Amarnaic hybrid form *urridānu*. The correct form of the verb *warādu* in the D stative first-person plural would be *urrudānu*; however, the D form is found only once in Akkadian texts in an OB letter. There are instances in some Amarna letters from Palestine of a verb *arādu* 'to serve', derived from *ardu* 'slave' in an obvious calque on West Semitic *ᶜbd*, but, as stated above, West Semitisms would be unexpected, even though the meaning is appropriate.

19. The first word [. . .]-*da-a* should be in construct with the following noun *urḫi*, and there does seem to be a word *udû* (*udāʾu* AHw 1401b) 'Geräte, Utensilien für Zugtiere, Reisen, Handwerker usw.', which fits the context excellently. Since there seems to be space for two signs, the restoration [*u-ud*] follows the orthographic system of doubling the consonants in initial intervocalic position.

The verb after LUGAL could be understood as a D Imperative of *emēdu*, which takes *udû* as its object in certain examples, or of *lamādu* 'to inform', 'to charge somebody with an expense' (OA only). In his edition, Rainey emended the *ú* to *ri*!

The next word UR$_5$-⌈*ta*!⌉ is understood as the anaphoric pronoun *šuāti*. Albright (p. 8 n. 17) suggested 'his interest'. On the other hand, there is a difficulty with the verb *nippalu*, which is clearly subjunctive and might perhaps be dependent on the 'interest'; thus the verse could be understood as 'its interest which we shall pay'.

We now come to the last difficult section after the next LUGAL: *ša ša iz za za*, which seems to have a dittography of *ša*, unless part of a word like *ša-la-tu*

19. "[The neces]sities of the road, O King, impose, that which we shall pay, O King, but whoever will stand in his battle, the King will pay.
20. "[Let . . .] the warrior(s) of Sargon gold. Let the steers give (away?) silver.

---

21. "[How] shall we transact our [business] while treachery is being carried out in the place where your god Zababa rests?"

'booty' has been elided, in which case the meaning is something like 'the king who will divide the booty'.

20. The first sign in Schroeder's copy is [. . .]*uš*, which agrees with the photograph published in *MDOG* 55, despite Albright's statement (p. 8 n. 18), "Read [. . . *l*]*i-zu-zu ḫurāṣa qarrādu* (coll.)."

The parsing of the first signs is difficult: [x x *u*]*š zu zu*. The verb *zâzu* 'to divide' does not occur in the Š-stem, which is why most scholars have accepted Albright's statement. In light of the way in which the logogram GUŠKIN is supplied with phonetic indicators in line 28, it may function here as a determinative for *zūzu* 'a type of gold' (CAD s.v.). Another possibility is the reading of Güterbock (p. 88 n. 5), "[x-mal] 60 Halbsekel Gold," based on *zūzu* 'half-shekel'. If so, the first signs [x x *u*]*š* contain a verb in the singular, whose subject is probably Sargon. Nevertheless, the best solution is to assume that the verb is [x-x-*ú*]*z-zu-zu*, the object the gold, and the subject the warriors of Sargon. The reading of UŠ as *úz* could be expected on systematic grounds in Boghazköy Akkadian, although none occurs in that corpus according to Durham §25b.

The subject of the second verb could be the warriors or the unknown (*šu*)-*ú-ru*. The latter has been assumed to be an object of silver. It has been read *ūru*, but it is probably not a vulva, although bronze examples are known (L. Jakob-Rost and H. Freydank, "Eine altassyrische Votivinschrift," *AoF* 8 [1981] 325–27, pls. XXIII–XXV). Von Soden (AHw 1435a) gives the word *ūru* the meaning 'Stiel, Stange von Geräte'. On the other hand, it could be read *šūru* and related to the word *šu-*(*u*)*-ra* 'reed(?) staff', which appears in Farber, *Ištar und Dumuzi*, 211:4, as an ornament carried by a male figure. Weidner suggested (p. 72) that this word was an elliptical writing of *šawiru/semeru* : *šam-*⟨*mī*⟩*-ru* 'bracelets, coils' (used as money and presents). Cf. ḪAR.MEŠ KÙ.BABBAR (among booty taken from Urartu) TCL 3 360; also Winckler Sar. pl. 45 K.1671:36. Franke suggests reading: *kit*??*-ru* 'bevorzugter Anteil' (186–87, 195). No matter what the meaning of the word, grammatically it is in the nominative case and therefore may more rightly be construed as the subject of the clause rather than the object. In line with the use of animal imagery in texts **6**:44 (*mīrī dannūtim*) and **7** i 17′ (*alpū rabûtu*) to describe the warriors, the word *šu-ú-ru* might be *šūrū* 'bulls'.

21. Note the gemination of the consonant -*ṣṣ*- in the word *dāṣāti* 'treachery, dishonesty'. Although this word is in the oblique case, it is the subject of the verb *innippušā*. Franke (pp. 186–87, 195) emends: *ta*!*-ni-ti*!*-ma* 'zum Ruhme'.

22. [*i-i*]*p-pa-aḫ-ra* DUMU.MEŠ LÚ.DAM.GÀR *ir-ru-ba qé-re-eb* É.GAL-*lim ul-tù ir-ru-bu-ú*!(wr. #PA)
23. [DUMU.MEŠ] LÚ.DAM.GÀR *ú-ul im-ḫu-ru* UR.SAG.MEŠ LUGAL.GI-*en* KA×U-*šu e-ip-pu-ša i-qáb-bi*
24. [*iz-za-kàr*] LUGAL *tam-ḫa-ri* URU.*Bur-⟨ša⟩-ḫa-an-da ša du-bu-ba*! *lu-mu-ur ki-ri-it-ta-šu*
25. [*mi-iš*]-*šu ša-ar-šu a-i-ú* ḪUR.SAG-*šu mi-nu* (er.) *an-zu a-i-tù ki-i-li-il-tu*!-(er.)-*ma*
26. [(KASKAL-*na*) *š*]*a te-er-ri-iš a-la-kà u-ur-ḫa-at šu-*⌈*up*⌉-*šu-qá-at a-la-ak-ta mar-ṣa-at*
27. [URU.*Bur-ša-ḫa*]-*an-da ša te-er-ri-iš a-la-kà* KASKAL-*an ša a-da-mu-mu ši-ip-pí-ir* 7 KASKAL.GÍD

---

28. [x x x x] ⌈x⌉ ḪUR.SAG *ga-ap-šu ša ták-kà-sú* NA_4!.ZA.GÌN GUŠKIN-*ra-a-ṣú i-na* GAM-*šu*

---

23. It is not clear whether the merchants or the warriors are the subject of the verb *imḫurū*.

24. For the restoration [*izzakar*], see Dhorme (p. 27). Franke (pp. 186–87, 196) restores *ša du-bu-*[*ba-ku*] 'von der ich spreche'. The object of Sargon's desire is the *ki-ri-it-ta-šu* of Purušḫanda. The meaning of this word has been rendered:

a. Weidner (p. 72) and Güterbock (89 n. 1) derive it from *gerû* 'to be hostile' (cf. *girûtu* 'Feindschaft', AHw 291b).
b. Dhorme (p. 27), Rainey (*EA*, Glossary, 63), and Franke (pp. 186–87, 196) understand it as *gerru*, pl. *gerrētu* 'roads, routes'.
c. Albright (p. 9 n. 21) assumes an unknown word *qirittu* 'valor' (cf. **qarittu* CAD Q 132a).

Other possibilities might include:

d. *kirru*, *kīru* 'storage jars', EA pl. *kirrētu*.
e. *kirû* 'garden', pl. *kirâtu*, Mari pl. *kirêtu*.
f. *qerītu* 'banquet, festival'.

There does not seem to be sufficient evidence for any of these hypothetical readings, and the compilers of the dictionaries have refused to place this reference in their volumes. One could adduce the following reasons: (1) double consonants are usually written as such, especially in intervocalic position; even single consonants are written double, so a suggestion with double *-rr-* is suspect; (2) the writing of double *-t-* may indicate vocalic or consonantal length, so little can be proven on this basis; (3) the plural form in oblique should be *ki-ri-*

22. [. . .] The merchants were assembled, they enter the palace. After the merchants entered,
23. they did not confront the warriors. Sargon opens his mouth, he speaks,

24. the King of Battle [declares], "The fabled Purušḫanda, I would see its bravery(?).
25. "[What] is its direction? Which is its mountain? What Anzu-bird (lives there)? Which Kilili-demoness(!?)?
26. ["(You have said) 'As to the road that] you wish to travel—it is a month-long, it is dangerous; as to travelling, it is arduous.
27. ["Puruš]ḫanda where you wish to travel—the road of which I groan is a task of seven double-miles.'"

---

28. "[(But there is)] the Mighty Mountain whose boulders are lapis lazuli, (and) gold is in its circumference.

---

ti-šu and not *ki-ri-it-ta-šu.* In form, we seem to have a singular feminine noun of the formation *pirist,* which makes only suggestions (a) and (c) tenable.

25. Schroeder's copy does not support the traditional reading of this line: KASKAL-*an-sú a-i-tù ki-i li-il-*⌈*li-ik*⌉*-ma.* According to his copy, there are two erasures in this line: one is the KASKAL and the other the sign before *-ma* at the end of the line. The reading is not KASKAL-*an-sú* but (er.) *an zu.* Note that the former suggestion is not possible; it should be KASKAL-*an-šu.* The sign before the second erasure is either *-tu-* or *-šar-* but not *-li-*. A nominal form ending in *-tu* would be preferable, since *a-i-tù* (*ajjītu*) is obviously feminine. Following the copy, we have tried to interpret this line as referring to the enemy country as being inhabited by demons, traditional mountain dwellers who were the perennial aggressors against lowland Mesopotamia. The name of the demoness seems to be a hybrid of various beings, including *kilili,* the owl, an aspect of Ištar, perhaps in her guise as harlot (see T. Jacobsen, "Pictures and Pictorial Language," *Figurative Language in the Ancient Near East* [ed. M. Mindlin, M. J. Geller, and J. E. Wansbrough; London, 1987] 5–6); and *kuliltu* 'fish-woman' (one of the heroes slain by Ninurta), among others (see F. A. M. Wiggermann, *Mesopotamian Protective Spirits: The Ritual Texts* [Groningen, 1992] 182).

26–27. See comments to lines 8ff.

28. The logogram ḪUR.SAG renders *šadû* in texts from Ugarit, Boghazköy, and Amarna (AHw 1124 1e). As a term descriptive of mountains, *gapšu* is unknown outside this text (neither of the dictionaries recognize this word under *gapšu*). This phrase is repeated in rev. 5′ and 17′, and 'massive mountain(s)' seems correct despite the dictionaries. It could be a specific geographical term (cf. MDP 22 144:7), since the following description seems to refer to a

29. [x x x x G]IŠ.ḪAŠḪUR GIŠ.PÈŠ GIŠ.*ši-mi-iš-ša-lu*! GIŠ.*ur-zi-in-nu um-muq*! 7 ZU.AB *bi-ra-šu*

30. [x x x x (x)] *a-šar im-daḫ-ṣú-ni ur-du-ú ši-kar re-ši-šu* 7 KASKAL.GÍD GIŠ.*mu-ur-dì-in-nu*

31. [. . .] ⸢x⸣ *ḫu-*[*ul-la a*(?)]*-šar-ma gáb-bi-ša* 7 KASKAL.GÍD *iṣ-ṣú it-ta-du li-mi-it*

32. [. . . *z*]*i-iq-ti iṣ-ṣ*[*ú* x x (x)] *ṣú-up-pa* 7 KASKAL.GÍD *kà-lu-u*

33. [. . . *ṣ*]*ú-ú* [. . .] *šu lu-ú ṣú-up-pa*

34. [. . .] *zi-iz-za z*[*a* . . .]

35. [. . . (*naqba*)] *im-mu-ru*[. . .]

(break)

Reverse

(break)

1′. [. . .] *bu* [. . .]

2′. [. . . *s*]*u* ERÍN *e*[*n* . . .]

3′. [x (x) *ú*]-⸢*ul*⸣ ⸢*a*⸣(?) [. . .]-*ra* ^{1}*Nu-ur-d*[*ag-gal*] KA×U-*šu e-*⸢*ip-pu*⸣*-ša* ⸢*i-qáb-bi*⸣ [*a-na* UR.SAG-*šu*]

4′. [*a-m*]*a-tá iz-za-kàr a-dì-n*[*i* LUGAL.GI-*e*]*n la-a il-la-k*[*à-a*]*n-na-ši li-ik-la-aš-šu ki-ib-ru mi-lu-ú*

---

specific set of mountain(s) or mountain range. Note that both the noun ḪUR.SAG and the adjective *gapšu* seem to be in the singular. A possible fictional title of the mountain could be "Mighty Mountain." Schroeder's correction of the copied sign NA$_4$ can be found in VAS 12 95. For GAM = *šaplītu* 'unten', see Franke, 186–89, 226.

29. Schroeder's correction of the copied sign Ú to LU can be found in VAS 12 95. This confusion between Ú and LU is common in this text and in the Akkadian texts written in the Boghazköy tradition. The word *um-muq*! is understood as a hapax reflecting the root *ʿmq* (עמק). It could also be read GIŠ.X.X and refer to a type of tree. Despite various attempts to read the end of this line, it is impossible to read it any other way than as suggested above. Von Soden (AHw 1111b) reads the last five signs as one word, *ṣú*!*-um*!*-bi-ra-šu*, and relates it to an object made of jasper found in the inventory of gifts from Tušratta to Amenophis III.

30–31. Note that von Soden reads the last phrase as *ši-kar rēšī-šu* '(Hand-)Griff v Berg', AHw 1235b. For *murdinnu*, see *amurdinnu* 'bramble' in the dictionaries and for *ittadu*, see *eddetu* 'boxthorns' (Güterbock, 89 n. 5). For a similar image, cf. (my troops marched safely between tall trees, thorn bushes, [and] prickly vines on a) *ḫarrān eddeti* 'a road (full) of thorns' (Streck Asb. 71:85).

29. "[. . .] the apple tree, the fig tree, the boxwood, the *urzinnu*-wood are of a depth of seven abzu. Between it (in the mountain passes),
30. "[. . .] the place where the servants had fought each other. The bolt of its summit (the timber line?) is seven double-miles. The brambles
31. "[. . .] . . . all of it is seven double-miles. The trees, the mountain box-thorns, the region where
32. "[. . . .] the thorns(?) of the trees are 60 cubits long, is seven double-miles. The *kalû*-thorny plants

33–34. (too fragmentary for translation)

35. "[. . .] they saw [the depth(?) . . .]

(break)

Reverse

(break)

1′–2′. (too fragmentary for translation)

3′. "[. . .] not [. .]". Nur-d[aggal], opening his mouth and speaking [to his warriors]

4′. declares, "Up to now, [Sargon] has not come against us. May the bank, the flood (or: high ground) prevent him!

The words *murdinnu* and *eddetu* form a word-pair in Akkadian. The reading *ašar* . . . *ašarma* is very tentative. The sign seems to be ŠAR and not LI. Another tentative suggestion is to understand *urdu* as the Assyrian form of the word *ardu* 'servant, slave'.

32–33. The word *ṣú-up-pa* is understood as *ṣuppā*(*n*) (AHw 1112b '60 Ellen'), which is metrologically equivalent to 5 rods = 10 reeds = 60 cubits; see M. Powell, *RlA* 7 (1989) 464. It is also found in the description of the fifth *nagû* of the "World Map" (CT 22 48 rev. 12′): 1 UŠ.TA.ÀM *ṣu-ub-ban* [. . .] '660 cubits is its. . . . '

32. The word *kalû* is understood as *kalû* D (CAD K 95); it is known only from plant lists but fits the context here, since it is synonymous with *murdinnu* and *eddetu*.

Reverse

4′. If the last word is *mīlu* 'seasonal flooding of the rivers', note the lengthening of the final *-u* in *mīlu* for expressing an exclamatory sentence or for poetic lengthening. Another possibility is *mēlû* 'elevation, high ground'. In either

5′. [HUR.SA]G *ga-ap-šu li-pu-uš a-pu qí-il-tá* ⟨?⟩ *ḫu-bu-tá qal*$_4$*-la* ⟨*ki-i*(?)⟩ *ki-iṣ-ṣa-ri i-ta-wu-lu-ú*

6′. [UR].SAG-*šu ip-pa-lu-šu* ⟨*a-na*⟩ [1]*Nu-ur-dag-gal am-ma-tá iz-za-kà-ru-šu a-*⟨*i*⟩*-ú-ut-ti* LUGAL.MEŠ EGIR-*ku-tù*

7′. [*ù*] *pa-nu-ti a-i-ú* LUGAL *ša il-la-kà-ma im-mu-ra* KUR-*ta-a-ti-ni* [1]*Nu-ur-dag-gal am-ma-tá*

8′. [*i*]*š-tu* KA×U-*šu ú-ul ú-qá-at-ta*$_5$ LUGAL.GI-*en iḫ-ta-*(er.)*-pa-ra* URU-*šu* 2 GÁN KÁ NUN-*be úr*!*-tap-pí-iš*

---

case, it is a noun in apposition to *kibru*. Dhorme took it as construct, 'la hauteur de la montagne épaisse' (p. 29), but the construct form *mi-li* is found in line 9′.

5′. This line in Nur-dagan's speech is quoted by Sargon in line 18. The lines parallel each other as follows:

5′.	*li-pu-uš a-pu qí-il-tá*	*ḫu-bu-da qal*$_4$*-la*
18′.	*li-pu-šu a-pu qí-il-ta li-ša-pí-šu*	*ḫu-bu-da qal*$_4$*-la*
5′.	*ki-iṣ-ṣa-ri i-ta-wu-lu-ú*	
18′.	*ki-*#*iṣ-ṣa-ri*	

Both the sentences have two verbs and four nouns. If we accept the nominative suffix on the first noun, *apu*, it should be the subject of the sentence. Assuming the grammar to be correct, the first verb governs three objects in line 5′ and one object in line 18′. Note that the verbs in line 18′ have the addition of the dative suffix for emphasis 'against him (Sargon)'. The image of the forest's opposing Sargon appears in texts **6** and **7**: *tu-ša ge-ri-ma qí-iš-tum ig-re-e-šu* '(When) it seemed the forest itself had warred against him' (**6**:59); [. . .] *qí-iš-ta-am ig-ri-e-šu*//*-un* '[and traversed] the forest, (when) it opposed them' (**7** iv 10′).

The last two nouns, *ḫu-bu-da* and *qal*$_4$*-la*, are rare or unknown: *ḫubutu* AHw 352b 'Gehölz', CAD Ḫ 243b (mng. unkn.); and *qallu* II AHw 894b 'Wald', *qallu* B CAD Q 66 'forest' "EA foreign word(?)." For the first, a possible root could be *ᶜbh* (עבה), meaning 'to be thick' + *ūtu*. These two objects are governed by the verb *šūpû* in line 18′.

Finally, a fifth and last object appears in the sentence, if it is an object at all, and the second verb in line 5′. The word *kiṣru* refers to the structure of the mountains; they should intertwine so that Sargon cannot find a pass through them. The collation of line 18′ -#*iṣ*- in place of -MA- renders obsolete the various interpretations of *ki* MA *ṣa ri*.

As for previous interpretations, Albright, followed by Rainey, takes as the subject the mountain barrier, which is to produce the three objects, the cane-brake and the forests as well as *ḫu-bu-da*. Further, he takes the fourth noun *qalla* to be in construct with the noun *kiṣṣari*.

The verb *i-ta-wu-lu-ú* is a plural stative Gtn of *eʾēlu* 'to bind' < *jʾl*. It is emended by Franke (pp. 188–89, 197): *i-ša-pi-lu-ú* 'tief, niedrig sein'. The subject of the verb is not obvious, since *ki-iṣ-ṣa-ri* is in the oblique case, and it would make better sense to emend ⟨*kī*⟩.

5′. "Also, the Mighty [Mounta]in! May the reed thicket constitute forest, copse, and. . . . , becoming completely interlocked like knots!"

6′. His warriors answer him, ⟨to⟩ Nur-Daggal they declare, "Of which kings, later

7′. "[or] earlier, what king came and saw our lands?" Nur-Daggal,

8′. had not yet finished the(se) word(s) in his mouth, when Sargon undermined his city, broadened the Gate of the Princes, two *ikū* wide.

6′. The spelling and form of *a-ú-ut-ti* is problematic. One would expect the form *a-i-ú-ut-tù* (or: *a-i-ú-tù*) if nominative case; unfortunately the interrogative adjective is in the oblique masculine plural. Of the following two masculine plural adjectives, *arkûtu* is in the nominative, and *panûti* is in the oblique. Since two of the three adjectives are oblique, it makes better grammatical sense to assume that the third is in the incorrect case. It could possibly be a partitive genitive with a preceding ⟨*ša*⟩ omitted by mistake.

7′. Note the consecutio temporum *illakama immura* present tense conjoined to preterite(*īmur* > *immur* in accordance with the phonological rules of this northwestern peripheral Akkadian). When the verb *alāku* appears in hendiadys in standard Akkadian, which it frequently does, the two parts are necessarily in the same grammatical tense. This is not the case in peripheral Akkadian: *illakma* RN . . . *ana* RN_2 *išpuramma mā* 'Niqmandu then wrote a message to Šuppiluliuma as follows' (MRS 9 49 RS 17.340:9).

8′. The verb *iḫ/uḫ-ta*-(er.)-*pa-ra* has been variously interpreted:

a. For *ḫapāru* 'umgeben', see von Soden, AHw 321, where he cites our example as Bo., since he quotes BoSt 6. Cf. Franke (pp. 188–89, 197): *uḫ-ta-pi*!-*ra*. Note that the existence of this verb is doubtful; CAD divides the references under G sub *apāru* mng. 2 and the references under D sub *ḫepēru*.
b. For *ḫapāru*/*ḫepēru* 'to dig' (AHw 340a), see Güterbock, 89 n. 8; and Dhorme, 29 n. 3; as well as CAD *ḫepēru*.
c. From Hebrew *ḥāpar* and Arabic *iḥtábara* 'to spy out' (see Albright, 10 n. 33).
d. Jerry Cooper suggests *ḫapāru*/*ḫepēru* 'to collect, assemble' (CAD Ḫ 170 mng. 2; AHw 340a 'ausgraben') and translates 'when Sargon (and his army) were assembled at his city over an area of two acres (?). The prince's gate he cast down into a ditch' (*at*!-*tap-pí-iš*).

There are orthographic and grammatical problems with all these solutions. First, Rainey's collation of the third sign confirms Schroeder's copy, which seems to me to be an erased incorrect sign. Second, the form could be a G perfect (though seemingly with a ventive suffix, it should be *iḫtapra*), Gt preterite, Gtn preterite, or a Dt present tense. The expected form according to the consecutio temporum is perfect, perfect, preterite (*urtappiš* . . . *issalit* . . . *imḫaṣ*). The difficulty is that the vowel /a/ appears in place of the thematic vowel /e/. Third, the semantics of

9′. [*it-t*]*a-du-šu mi-li* BÀD-*šu is-sà-li-it-ma im-ḫaṣ kà-la ša* GEŠTIN *šu-pu-ú eṭ-lu-tù-šu*

10′. [LUGAL].GI-*en i-na pa-ni* KÁ.GAL *it-ta*-ḪI GIŠ.GU.ZA-*šu* LUGAL.GI-*en* KA×U-*šu e-ip-pu-ša*

11′. [*i-q*]*áb-bi a-na* UR.SAG-*šu a-ma-tá iz-za-kàr in-ga-na* ^{1}*Nu-ur-dag-gal mi-gi*$_5$*-ir* ^{d}*En-líl*

12′. [*li-id-d*]*ak-ki-šu li-ik-kà-ni-iš-šu-ma lu*(wr. Ú)-*mu-ur*

13′. [*up-pu-u*]*r a-gi*$_5$ *ták-kà-sú ša re-ši-iš-šu* GIŠ.GÌR.GUB(wr. #QA) NA$_4$.ZA.GÌN *ša šu-pá-la-aš-šu a-du* 55 LÚ.MEŠ.MAŠKIM

14′. [(LÚ.SUKKAL)] *ú-ši-ib pa-ni-šu ša ki-ma ša-a-šu i-na* GIŠ.GU.ZA GUŠKIN *aš-bu a-ši-ib* LUGAL *ki-ma* DINGIR-*lim*

15′. [*ma-a*]*n-nu* ⟨*ša*⟩ *ki-ma* LUGAL *il-lu-ú* ^{1}*Nu-ur-dag-gal ul-te-še-bu ma-ḫar* LUGAL.GI-*en* LUGAL.GI-*en* KA×U-*šu*

---

a Dt form in the present context is not clear. The most likely solution seems to be to ignore the vowel and to take the verb from *ḫepēru* G Perfect.

According to the collations of Weidner (p. 66 n. 5), the last signs on the line are: NUN-*be úr-tab-bi-iš*. Nevertheless, Rainey's collations confirm Schroeder's copy. The sign *úr* would be not unexpected, because it is known occasionally from Boghazköy Akkadian (see Durham, §21 and p. 323 n. 425). The first two signs are probably a rendering of *rubê* 'prince(s)'. The last four signs must be the verb *rapāšu*.

Although the measurement GÁN = *ikū* 'dike' is usually a unit of surface area in Mesopotamia proper, it occurs as a unit of measure for distances in upper Mesopotamia and certain cities in the periphery. In this case, the system is based on the length of the side of a square *ikū*, that is, 1 *ašlu* 'rope' = 20 GI/*qanû* 'reeds' = 120 *ammatu* 'cubits' (cf. M. Powell, "Masse und Gewichte," *RlA* 7 [1989–90] 472, 477).

9′. In the subordinate phrase, the subject is GEŠTIN, the verb is in the subjunctive *šu-pu-ú*, and the object *eṭlūtušu* 'his men' is incorrectly in the nominative case.

10′. Although Dhorme and Rainey read *iṭ-ṭa-ḫi* as a passive, with the throne as subject, in form it is a G Perfect of the intransitive verb *ṭeḫû* (no N form exists). Albright translates the G form correctly, 'Sargon . . . approached his throne' (p. 10), and Güterbock (p. 89) does likewise, identifying the possessive pronoun associated with the throne as Nur-Dagan's. Weidner translates the G form as though it were D: 'Sargon . . . nähert sich seinem Throne' (p. 67). Franke (pp. 188–89, 197) suggests reading *it-ta-dí* as a G Perfect of *nadû*. The phrase *kussâm nadû* is well attested (cf. CAD K *kussû* mng. 2b–1′; *nadû* mng. 2–1′), but the syllabic value *dí* is not found otherwise in this text or in other peripheral dialects.

12′. The first verb has been variously interpreted:

9′. [He cast] it down; in the highest part of its wall he made a breach(?); he smote all of his wine-intoxicated men.

10′. [Sar]gon placed his throne before the gate. Sargon opens his mouth,

11′. [sp]eaking to his warriors, he declares, "Come on! Nur-Daggal, favorite of Enlil,

12′. "[Let him s]tir himself! Let him humble himself! Let me behold (it)!"

13′. [He was crowned] with a tiara of gemstones on his head, a footstool of lapis lazuli at his foot. Together with 55 deputies,

14′. [the *sukkallu*] sat before him, who just like him, is seated on a golden throne(s) (but) the king is seated like a god.

15′. [W]ho is exalted like the king? They made Nur-Daggal sit before Sargon. Sargon opens his mouth,

---

a. Rainey understands the verb as coming from *dâku* (*EA*, Glossary, p. 61) and translates 'let him smite it'.

b. Dhorme (p. 29) reads [*li-it*]*-tak-ki-šu* and translates 'Que Nour-Dagan, le favori du dieu Enlil, approche' and takes it from *nagāšu*, though *nagāšu* means 'to leave, go away', rather than 'to approach' (Did he mean *akāšu*?).

c. Meriggi (*Gedenkschrift W. Brandenstein* [Innsbruck, 1968] 262) tries to make the word not a verb but a noun, to be the object of *kanāšu*, which is usually *kišādu*. Meriggi wants to read another word for neck here: *tikku*.

d. Another possibility is to derive this verb from *dekû* 'to make rise' (D). For a similar usage of *dekû* with *kanāšu*, cf. *ultu kussī šarrūtīšu idkūniššumma uterrūniššu šaniāna ušaknišūš ana šēpēja* 'they (the gods) made him (the king of Elam) rise again from his throne; they made him bend down before my feet a second time' (Streck Asb. 44 v 33–46 v 35).

13′. Note the forms *rēšīššu* and *šupālāššu*, which are from **rēšēn* + *šu* and *šuplān* + *šu*. As has been pointed out by von Soden (*ZA* 41 [1933] 111 n. 2), the appearance of the pronominal suffix directly on the *-ān* morpheme is impossible in Old Babylonian. On the other hand, it could be another case of erratic doubling.

For the term *rābiṣu*, see the Hittite version, as well as the explanation of the term as 'bailiff' in the third-millennium texts by T. Jacobsen, *AfO* 26 (1978–79) 13 n. 50. Note that Sargon emphasized the size of his retinue in his royal inscriptions.

15′. The syntactical structure of the nominal interrogative sentence, *mannu kīma šarri il-lu-ú*, has bothered recent scholars, who have treated *il-lu-ú* as an adjective: 'Who is like the exalted king?' (Rainey, p. 11); 'Wer ist wie der

16′. [*e*]-*ip-pu-ša i-qáb-bi a-na* [1]*Nu-ur-dag-gal am*-⟨*ma-ta iz-za-kàr*⟩ *al-kà* [1]*Nu-ur-dag-gal mi-gi*$_5$-*ir* [d]*En-líl ki-ma táq-bi*

17′. [*a*]-*dì-ni* LUGAL.GI-*en la-a il-la-kà-an-na-ši li-ik-la-aš-šu*! *ki-ib-ru mi-lu-ú* ḪUR.SAG *ga-ap-šu*

18′. *li-pu-šu a-pu qí-il-ta li-ša-pí-šu ḫu-bu-tá qal*$_4$-*la* ⟨*ki-i*(?)⟩ *ki-*#*iṣ-ṣa-ri* ⟨*i-ta-wu-lu-ú*(?)⟩ [1]*Nu-ur-dag-gal* KA×U-*šu ep-pu-ša*

19′. [*i*]-⌜*qáb*⌝-*bi a-na* LUGAL.GI-*en mi-in-dì be-lí ú-ša*-⌜*du*⌝-*ka ú-še-bi-ru-ni-ik-ku* ERÍN.MEŠ DINGIR-*ka*

20′. [[d]*Za-ba*$_4$-*b*]*a*$_4$ ⟨*a*⟩-*li-li e-bi-ra* ÍD *a-i-ú* KUR!(wr. #QA) KUR.KUR.MEŠ URU.*Ak-kà-dá i-ša-an-na-an*

---

erhabene König?' (Franke, p. 189). The earlier commentators agree on a verbal interpretation: "Qui est élevé comme le roi?" (Dhorme, 30); "Wer is wie der König erhaben?" (Weidner, 69); "Who is exalted like the king?" (Albright, 10).

Although it is not grammatically impossible, the object of the preposition *kīma* is not found modified by an adjective in nominal interrogative sentences, most modifiers being pronouns and proper names. If *illû* (< *elium*) is an adjective, with initial intervocalic doubling, then it should modify *šarri* and be in the genitive, which it is not. The syntactic structure of a nominal interrogative sentence is: *mannu* + {pronoun}{noun}{*ša* clause}, e.g.:

1. *mannu šû* 'Who is this?' Lambert-Millard, *Atra-ḫasīs*, 84 II vii 45;
2. *amūt mannu šarru manni la šarru* 'omen portending anarchy (lit. omen who [is] king, who [is] not king?)' TCL 6 1 rev. 23 (SB ext.); for earlier examples of this phrase both in Sumerian and Akkadian, see Jacobsen, *Sumerian King List*, 52 and 112 vii 1;
3. *mannum ša kīma jāti irammuka* 'who loves you as I do?' PBS 7 9:3 (OB let.).

If *illû* is a verbal predicate of the subordinate clause in the subjunctive, the morphological form is correct and the syntactic structure is that of (3). Absent from the structure and essential to its proper understanding is the *ša*, the "determinative-relative" pronoun. The scribe has either been careless in omitting the *ša* or has confused the nominal interrogative sentence with verbal interrogative sentences, in which a *kīma* prepositional phrase can occur. In such verbal interrogative sentences, a *kīma* prepositional phrase can precede or follow the *mannu*, e.g.:

1. PN *kīma kāti mannum īdešu* 'Who knows PN like you?' (OECT 3 61:34–35);
2. *mannum kīma kunūti ra-ab* 'Who is as great(?) as you?' (VAS 16 88:19–20).

15′. Note the form *ultēšebū*, in which the phonological development *št* > *lt* has taken place. In Egyptian Akkadian, this development has not yet occurred.

16′. [s]peaking to Nur-Daggal, ⟨he declares⟩: "Come on! Nur-Daggal, favorite of Enlil, how could you say,

17′. '[Up] to now Sargon has not come to us. May the bank, the flood (or: high ground) prevent him! May the Mighty Mountain!

18′. 'May the reed thickets constitute forests against him, may it cause a copse to appear against him, and. . . . , as knots!'" Nur-Daggal opens his mouth,

19′. [he spe]aks to Sargon, "Who can tell who have revealed (the way to) you, O my lord, (or) have caused the troops to be conveyed for you—It is your god,

20′. Zababa, the hero of the trans-Euphrates region! What country among countries can compare with Akkade?

16′. As noted by Güterbock (*ZA* 42, 90 n. 1), the *-am-* after Nur-Daggal is the only remnant of the whole phrase introducing direct speech and is completely missing in line 19, as follows:

rev. 10′–11′PNKA×U-*šu eppuša* [*iq*]*abbi ana qarrādīšu ammata izzakar*
15′–16′ PN KA×U-*šu eppuša iqabbi ana Nur-Daggal am*⟨ ⟩
18′–19′ PN KA×U-*šu eppuša* [*i*]*qabbi ana Sargon*⟨ ⟩

17′–18′. See comments to lines 4′–5′.

19′–20′. These lines are full of uncertain words, uncertain verse division, and confusion between object and subject. The various suggestions are:

a. 'Wohlan, O Herr, ich werde Dich . . . es werden Dich hinüberbringen die Soldaten Deines Gottes. . . . überschreiten den Fluss' (Weidner, 69).
b. "However, my lord, can they have informed thee! The soldiers of thy god have brought thee. . . . I have crossed the river" (Albright, 11).
c. 'Vraiment je te proclaime mon maître. Les soldats de ton dieu t'ont fait passer . . . au delà du fleuve' (Dhorme, 30).
d. 'Your gods (emending DINGIR to DINGIR.MEŠ) brought your troops over here for you' (Güterbock, *JCS* 18, 5 n. 62).
e. 'Perhaps my lord has informed you (or) the hosts of your god have delivered (the message) to you! . . . to cross the river' (Rainey, 10).

Using these possibilities, I would select the most probable elements to give a sentence composed of the following three words: (1) *minde*, an adverbial expressing potentialis, so we must reject Dhorme's 'vraiment'; (2) *bēlī* 'my lord', a vocative in accordance with Weidner, and Albright; (3) *ušādûka* from *šūdû* 'to inform', third-person plural impersonal (see Albright).

20′. The space at the beginning of the line seems sufficient to restore [^{d}*Za-ba*$_4$-*b*]*a*$_4$ but leaves *li-li* dangling, which Aage Westenholz suggests is probably *ālilu* 'the warrior'. Note that *mātu* is construed as masculine in Boghazköy Akkadian (see Durham §49a, pp. 480–81).

21′. [*a-i-ú*] LUGAL *ú-ša-an-na-an kà-ša* ge_5*-ru-kà ú-ul i-ba-aš-ši na-ki-ir-šu-nu* KASKAL-*ru*

22′. [*i-š*]*a-tu* UDUN *qa-mu lìb-bi na-ki-ru-ka up-tal-*⟨*la*⟩*-ḫu-ma uš-ḫa-ra-ra-ma te-er-šu-nu-ti*

23′. [x x (x)] A.ŠÀ A.GÀR *baṭ-lu ša ri-ṣú-ú* UGU-*šu*

24′. [*im-ma-ti?*] ⌜*a*⌝*-na aš-ri-šu* ⟨*ú-ul*⟩ *ni-is-sà-ḫur in-ni-ib-ša li-iš-ši* GIŠ.ḪAŠḪUR GIŠ.PÈŠ GIŠ.ŠENNUR GIŠ.GEŠTIN

25′. [. . .] GIŠ.LAM.GAL GIŠ.ZÉ-ER-DU *ul-pa-nu im-ma-ti i-na aš-ri-šu ú-ul ni-is-sà-ḫur*

26′. [. . . *l*]*i-iš-ši lu pu-zu-uḫ* URU.KI *lu ut-ra-a ṭa-a-bi i-na a-la-ak*

21′. The signs at the end of the line are KASKAL-*ru*. Former treatments have been:

a. Reading according to signs *kas-ru* (cf. Borger, *Assyrisch-babylonische Zeichenliste*, for possible readings), Weidner (p. 69): "Ihre Feindschaft ist gehemmet," similarly CAD s.v. *kesēru*, Dhorme (p. 30): "Leur hostilité est endiguée."
b. Reading *gaš*($_x$)*-ru* (a reading not given by Borger): "their mighty opponent" Albright (p. 11), Rainey (p. 10), Franke (p. 190).

A third possibility is to read the signs as *girru* but to understand this not as *gerru/girru* A 'road, campaign', but as the homophonous *girru* B 'fire'. Note the wordplay between *gērû* and *girru*.

22′. The signs at the beginning of the line have been read:

a. A form of the possessive pronoun [*a*]*t-tu-*ᵓ without suffixes is completely unique; there seems to be no reference to this form in the grammars (GAG §44f) or the dictionaries. On the basis of the Aššur version, which reads *atta qamû l*[*ibbī*] (line 9), we might suppose that the scribe presumed that *attu* was the predicate nominative form of *atta*. Cf. Dhorme 'C'est toi' (p. 30); Albright, 'art thou' (p. 11); and Rainey, 'art thou' (p. 11). Note that Weidner assumes it to be another form of the nominative personal pronoun *at-ta* 'Du' (p. 69).
b. [*at-t*]*a tu-uq*!*-qa-mu* 'du verbrennst' (Güterbock, 90 n. 3; Franke, 190).

However, the sign form is neither ᵓ nor *uq*; it seems to be closer to UDUN, the pottery or brick kiln. Thus, we might restore [*i-š*]*a-tu* at the beginning of the line.

23′. The reading *baṭ-lu* was suggested by Walter Sommerfeld.

24′. The preposition at the beginning of the line has been restored to ⌜*i*⌝*-na* in AHw 1005b, on the basis of line 25′. However, the top of the vertical *a* is clear in

21′. "[What] king can compare with you? Your adversary does not exist. Their enemy is the blaze,

22′. "the (baking hot) kiln fire which burns hearts. Your opponents are afraid and I am dumbfounded. Send them back—

23′. "[the work on] the field(s) and the pastures is disrupted—those who could help with it."

24′. "[Never] to his place we will turn, even if it (the land) bears (all) its (kinds of) fruit, the apple, the fig, the medlar, the vine,

25′. "[. . .] pistachio, the olive, the bittersweet fruit/barley. Never shall we tarry in its place

26′. "even if [its fruit] it bears. Let the city be reviled. Let it be superfluous. What is good about coming (all)

---

the photograph. The remainder of the first clause is restored according to line 25′. The verb is in the present, with doubling of the first intervocalic consonant.

In the second clause, the identity of the nominal phrase and the verbal phrase is unclear. If the nominal phrase is *li-iš-ši* (cf. Güterbock, 90 n. 4, where he relates it to the word *līšu* 'Teig'), then the verbal phrase is the verb *innepša*. If the verbal phrase is *li-iš-ši*, it could come from *našû*. Dhorme (p. 30), Albright (p. 11), Rainey (p. 11), and Franke (pp. 191, 198) understood the passage in this way. However, then the nominal phrase must be *in-ni-ib-ša*, which is to be understood as a noun *inbu* + possessive pronoun *ša* with doubling of the first intervocalic radical.

25′. At the end of the list of fruits appears the word *ul-pa-nu*, which might be an unknown Assyrian variant of *alappānu*, *lappānu* 'bittersweet taste of fruit', 'barley yielding bittersweet beer'.

26′. For the meaning of the verb *b/puzzuḫu*, see Landsberger (references sub "Benno Landsberger's Lexicographical Contributions," compiled by D. A. Foxvog and A. Draffkorn Kilmer, *JCS* 27 [1975] 16), 'to insult, revile, defame, to treat not in accordance with station'. This meaning was accepted for our passage by von Soden (AHw 145b s.v. *buzzuʾu*), 'der Teig sei missachtet', and accepted in the above translation (also Güterbock, 90: 'aber dieses Essen soll verflucht sein'). Rainey (p. 86) takes this word as coming from the verb *pašāḫu* (also Weidner, 74, Z. 26; Dhorme, 30), while the CAD takes it from *bazāʾu* D 'to press (a person) for payment'. Franke takes it from *pasāḫu* D 'vertreiben' (p. 198).

The second verb *lu*(-)*ut-ra-a* has been interpreted as *tarû* 'to bring' (see Albright, 11 n. 43; Dhorme, 30; Rainey, 11). Unfortunately, *tarû* does not mean 'to bring'. Thus, we are left with the same three meanings as given above in the comment to line 7. However, another possibility is a predicate adjective *atru*/*utru* in the accusative pausal form. If a verbal adjective, the final *-a* should be

27′. [*u-ur-ḫí ù*] *a-ša-bi mi-nu* LUGAL.GI-*en ir*-TE-*e* URU *un-na-mi-šu* MU.3.KAM

28′. [ITI.5.KAM *i*]*t-ta-šab*

29′. [?] DUB.1.KAM *ša* LUGAL *tam-ḫa-ri qa-ti*

---

feminine plural. Further, this sentence is parallel with the preceding and should have negative connotations.

The next sentence seems to be a rhetorical question beginning with the adjective *ṭābi* and ending with the interrogative *mīnu*, 'good . . . is what', i.e., 'what is good', with the infinitival phrase as the third portion of the sentence.

27′. Although the majority of scholars take the verb *ir-te-e* from the verb *radû*/*redû* (Dhorme, 30 n. 11; Albright, 11, 'marched'; Rainey, *EA*, Glossary, p. 76, 'to lead, to accompany'; von Soden AHw 966a *redû* G 13, 'begleiten, leiten'; Franke, 191 'einhergezogen?'), it seems best to follow Güterbock's suggestion and derive it from the verb *reʾû* 'als Hirte regierte' (p. 90). As stated above, this text employs the perfect tense in narrative contexts. Thus, *reʾû* perfect fits

27′. [the way] and just staying here?" Sargon has ruled; (when) he gave orders to depart from the city, (at that time) it had been three years

28′. [and five months] he had sat (on the throne)/stayed.

29′. Tablet I of "King of Battle"—complete.

---

excellently, since as has been variously stated, this sentence has parallels in the chronicles and the omens.

Despite Güterbock's suggested reading *u namîšu* (p. 90 n. 6) and Dhorme's emendation *e-nu-mi-šu* (p. 31 n. 1), the verb *namāšu* D makes excellent sense in this passage (note Rainey's translation, p. 10), and the doubling of the first radical of the verb has been commented on above. The only problem, then, would be the apparent subjunctive *-u* on the verb without the necessary subjunction.

28′. This line is restored according to the Hittite parallel KBo 22 6 iv 9 (see Güterbock, *MDOG* 101, 21). The Hittite text seems to be describing the length of Sargon's stay, while the chronicles and omen texts mention the year of his reign.

9C
Amarna Fragment

Introduction

The attribution of this fragment to the "Sargon Saga" is uncertain because of its fragmentary nature. It does seem that the city of Akkade is mentioned. It was excavated by the Egyptian Exploration Society during their campaign in

---

Transcription

Obverse

(two-column tablet, uninscribed except for a few scattered traces)

Reverse

(break)
(blank)

---

1. [. . . UR]U(?).*Ak-kà-dì a-na* [. . .]
2. [. . .] URU *tar-ṣú-ú* [. . . .]
3. (traces of erased(?) signs)
4. (trace of one or two erased(?) signs)

(space)
(one broken sign in midfield)
(break)

1933–34,[32] Apparently this fragment was part of a group of texts and exercises belonging to an Egyptian school for cuneiform studies.

Manuscript

Akhetaten (Tell el-Amarna)

EA 375 = C. H. Gordon, *Orientalia* n.s. 16 (1947) 13–14 (transliteration), 20–21 (copy) = A. Rainey, *EA* (AOAT 8) 47–49 (transliteration).

[32] See J. D. S. Pendlebury, "Excavations at Tell el-Amarna," *JEA* 20 (1934) 137–38.

Translation

Obverse

(blank)

Reverse

(break)
(blank)

---

1. [. . .] the city of Akkade to [. . .]
2. [. . .] city period [. . .]

(illegible)
(break)

9D
Aššur Fragment

Introduction

This fragment contains the story segment of the confrontation between Sargon and Nur-Dagan, in which the latter makes his declaration of obeisance. In general, see Weidner.[33] According to Schroeder's copy, the upper edge of the tablet is preserved, and there seem to be only a few signs missing on the left edge of the tablet, according to the parallel text, **9B** rev. 17′–22′. The other side of the flake is destroyed. The fragment was found during the excavations in the

[33] Weidner, BoSt 6 (1922) 75ff.

Transcription

1. [*li-ik*]-*la-šú* [ ]
2. [. . . *t*]*e-pi-is-s*[*ú*]
3. [ˡZALA]G-ᵈ*Da-gan pa-a-šú* [*i-pu-uš*]
4. [*izzakara*(?)] *a-na* LUGAL.GI.N[A]
5. [. . . ?] *a-i-tu ma-a-*[*tu*]
6. [. . . ?] *a-a-ú* MAN *kiš-šá-*⸢*a*⸣*-t*[*e*]
7. [g]*i-ru-ka ul ib-ba-áš-ši* [ ]
8. [. . . ?]⸢x⸣ *at-ta qa-mu l*[*i-ib-bi*]
9. [?] ᵈUTU *šá* ˡZALAG-ᵈ*Da-gan*[ ]
10. [LUGAL].GI.NA *pa-a-šú i-pu-uš*[ ]

(break)

city of Aššur by the Deutsche Orient-Gesellschaft. Its exact provenance is not known.

Since there are no Middle Assyrian sign forms,[34] the text must be dated to the Neo-Assyrian period. This manuscript closely resembles the Amarna recension. The comparison of **9D** with **9B** is as follows:

9D	**9B**
1–4	17b′–19a′
5–8	20b′–22a′
9–10	—

Manuscript

Aššur

VAT 10290 = KAV 138 = Weidner, BoSt 6 (1922) 75 (see photograph, p. 388).

[34] Cf. Weidner *AfO* 16, 201.

Translation

1. "May the [bank, the inundation] hold him back
2. " . . . him. . . . "
3. Nur-Dagan opened his mouth to speak
4. [saying] to Sargon,
5. "[. . .] What land [can compare with Akkade]?
6. "[. . .] What king of the totality [. . .]?
7. "Your enemy does not exist . . .
8. ". . you are the consumer of the heart(?) . . . "
9. The sun(?) of Nur-Dagan . . .
10. Sargon opened his mouth to speak . . .

(break)

9E
Nineveh Recension

Introduction

In this recension, the fragmentary discourse comprises narrative elements that have been seen in previous texts. The existents are basically the same. The characters are Sargon, the merchants, and the goddess Ištar. Divine approval for the enterprise is apparently actively sought in this text. The setting seems to be the palace, as in **9B**, but may move to include the temple. The events concerning the merchants probably reflect the previous stories. However, there is one additional action on the part of Sargon. He seems to have gone to the temple to communicate with Ištar. This communication may have taken the form of a dream as in text **4**.[35]

The story segments are as follows:

a. a fragmentary account of the merchants' tale (line 2′);
b. a disturbed reaction on the part of Sargon (lines 3′–4′);

[35] Cf. J. S. Cooper, "Sargon and Joseph: Dreams Come True," *Biblical and Related Studies Presented to Samuel Iwry* (ed. A. Kort and S. Morschauser; Winona Lake, Ind., 1985) 33–39.

Transcription

(break)

1′. (traces)

2′. [. . .] ⌜x⌝-*ka liš-šá-a bi-lat-su šum-ma ul* x [. . .]

3′. [. . .] *a-mat* DUMU.MEŠ DAM.GÀR *ina še-me-šu im-ra-aṣ lì*[*b-ba-šú* . . .]

4′. [. . . ˡLUGAL.G]I.NA *a-mat* DUMU.MEŠ DAM.GÀR *ina še-me-šu im-ra-aṣ* [*lìb-ba-šú* . . .]

5′. [. . .] GIŠ.TUKUL.MEŠ URUDU.*qul-mi-i ši* x [. . .]

6′. [. . . *ana*] É.DINGIR *ina pu-ri-di-šú il-lik i-ru-*[*ub* . . .]

Philological and Textual Notes

6′. The phrase *ina purīdīšu* 'on his own feet' emphasizes the rapidity of Sargon's progress.

c. a fragmentary reference to weapons, maces, and copper battleaxes (line 5′);
d. Sargon proceeds to inquire the will of Ištar, Queen of the Eulmaš (lines 6′–9′);
e. Ištar's fragmentary response, in which there is a reference to Sargon's dominion over the four quarters of the earth (lines 10′–13′).

General Observations

This story is written on a blackened flake; it is impossible to decide the type or length of the tablet from which it comes.

Poetics

As in text **7**, this text preserves a poetic structure involving couplets with particularizing verses (e.g., 3//4, 8//9).

Manuscript

Nineveh

K. 13228 = W. G. Lambert, "A New Fragment of the King of Battle," *AfO* 20 (1963) 161–62.

Translation

2′. ". . . should your [. . .] bear his taxes, if not . . ."

3′. . . . when he heard the word of the merchants, his heart was grieved . . .

4′. . . . when Sargon heard the words of the merchants, his heart was grieved . . .

5′. . . . maces, copper battleaxes . . .

6′. . . . to the temple, he strode quickly (lit. on his own feet), he entered the [sanctuary(?) . . .]

7′. [. . . *ana* ^{d}]*Iš-tar šar-rat É-ul-maš* [*iqrub* . . .]
8′. [. . .] x ^{d}*Iš-tar šá* x [. . .]
9′. [. . ^{d}*Iš-tar šar*]-*rat É-ul-maš šá* x [. . .]
10′. [. . . *i-qa*]*b-bi-i*(?) *a*-[*na* . . .]
11′. [. . . *ki*]*b-rat er-bet*-[*ti* . . .]
12′. [. . .] x-*a-tum* x [. . .]
13′. [. . .] x *nu šá* x [. . .]
14′. (trace)
(break)

7′. . . . to Ištar, Queen of the Eulmaš, [he approached . . .]
8′. ". . . Ištar who. . . .
9′. . . . Ištar, Queen of the Eulmaš, who . . . "
10′. . . . she speaks to [Sargon(?) . . .]
11′. "[. . . ruler of the f]our quarters . . .
12′. . . . the words . . .
13′. . . .

Chapter 5

The Sargon Letters

The following two texts purport to be copies of letters sent by Sargon to various unknown persons whose names are only extant in the Ur letter. In both letters, the initial communication precedes a list of persons of certain status, rank, profession, or occupation. This unique juxtaposition of the introductory communication followed by a list of persons needs explanation. It has been stated in reference to the Ur letter that "the occupations listed in this text are in the accusative, and thus form part of the letter."[1] On the other hand, the Nippur letter is said to be a type II/2 Proto-Lu source (MSL 12 27), which normally contains a short extract of a different lexical series or a literary composition on the obverse and the Lu extract on the reverse. From this account, it would seem that a combination such as appears in the Nippur letter is accidental rather than deliberate. However, since the Nippur letter containing the canonical list can be compared to the Ur letter containing the noncanonical list, the working hypothesis is that precession of the fictional letter is deliberate and intentional.

If the opening formula of the Sargon letters was deliberate, it may have served as a mnemonic device for learning that was employed in the edubba. These letters were written in the centers of Sumerian learning and were perhaps a calque on the literary letters of the Sumerian kings contained in the Royal Correspondence. It may also be a remnant of traditional schoolboys' pastimes. Such a formula could have been just the opening of a game of memory in which the students took turns adding the titles haphazardly or according to some system, alphabetic or thematic. Such a game of memory is known to me from one of the childhood games of my children in Denmark that begins, "I went to tea with the Emperor of China and there I met. . . ." As it progresses

[1] C. Wilcke *apud* Steinkeller, ZA 72 (1982) 253 n. 58; see further C. Wilcke, "Zum Geschichtsbewußtsein im Alten Mesopotamien," *Archäologie und Geschichtsbewußtsein* (Kolloquien zur Allgemeinen und Vergleichenden Archäologie 3; ed. H. Müller-Karpe; Munich, 1982) 51 n. 67.

each child adds a name, and the whole list of names must be correctly repeated in order to succeed in the game. The key words of the Akkadian game of memory are presumably: (to . . . thus says your lord Sargon. . .) *unnedukkī ina amārīkunu* 'when you see my letter. . . .' The characteristic syntactical phrase *unnedukkī ina amārīkunu* is peculiar to the southern tradition of Old Babylonian letter-writing. Likewise, the lexeme *unnedukku*, a Sumerian loanword in Akkadian, is present only in letters from Southern Babylonia.[2] This dates and locates this Sargon game in early southern Old Babylonia.

For this fictive letter type, compare the celebrated "Letter of Gilgameš," treated by Gurney and by Kraus. Note also a possible Old Akkadian example treated by Foster.[3] A further example is the "Weidner Chronicle," which was composed in the form of a literary letter supposedly written by a king of Isin, possibly Damiq-ilišu (1816–1794) to a king of Babylon (or Larsa).[4] The outward form of the letter in this composition is advice given by the writer to the addressee as to how to keep Babylon under his control; he does so by recounting a spurious history of the rise and fall of past kings.

The last example of this genre is the letter of Samsu-iluna to his minister concerning the erection of a monumental inscription (*narû*). The letter contains a tirade against the priesthood of all the Babylonian cult-centers, who are accused of profanity and sacrilege.[5]

[2] See Lieberman, *Loanwords*, #537.

[3] Gurney, *AnSt* 7 (1957) 127ff.; Kraus, *AnSt* 30 (1980) 109ff.; Foster, *AnSt* 32 (1982) 43–44.

[4] F. N. H. Al-Rawi, "Tablets from the Sippar Library, I: The "Weidner Chronicle"— A Supposititious Royal Letter concerning a Vision," *Iraq* 52 (1990) 1–13.

[5] F. N. H. Al-Rawi and A. R. George, "Tablets from the Sippar Library, III: Two Royal Counterfeits," *Iraq* 56 (1994) 135–39.

10
Nippur Letter

Introduction

On the obverse of the tablet from Nippur is preserved the beginning of the letter of Sargon to his subordinates. This traditional piece of Akkadian folklore is not a narrative, but it does contain certain story elements previously seen. The land of Akkade is referred to as the land that the goddess rules and Sargon governs. On this occasion, the goddess is referred to by her older epithet Annunītum.

The reverse contains Old Babylonian Proto-Lu, forerunner of the late canonical series LÚ = *ša* (lines 365–82, 392–405).[6] The analysis of these lines reveals that their content consists of terms for the stages of human development and for kinship groupings. The question remains whether it is accidental or intentional that this part of canonical Proto-Lu occurs here.

General Observations

The top edge and left side of the tablet are preserved. The tablet seems to have been sliced off deliberately on the right side to preserve the section with the letter. Note that it is impossible to judge the number of columns that are missing, since the two columns on the reverse equal the width of the single column on the obverse.

Circumstances of Discovery

According to the Catalogue of the Babylonian Section of the University Museum, nothing is known about the findspot of this tablet at Nippur.[7]

Orthography and Language

The letter has typical southern Old Babylonian orthographical and morphological forms and accords lexicographically with its provenance. Orthographically, it is classical Old Babylonian. There is one archaic element: the use of *ù*-, at the beginning of the verb in line 15′.

Manuscript

Nippur

CBS 15217 (see photographs, p. 388).

[6] See MSL 12 32, where this tablet is source D_3.

[7] See P. Gerardi, *A Bibliography of the Tablet Collections of the University Museum* (Occasional Publications of the Babylonian Fund 8; Philadelphia, 1984) 189.

Transcription

Obverse

Column i

1. [*ana* . . .] // [x x] ⸢x⸣ *ri-a-*⸢x-x⸣
2. [*qí*]-*bí-ma*
3. [*um-m*]*a Šar-ru-um-ki-in* //[*be-el-k*]*u-nu-ma*
4. [x x (x)] *iq-ta-bi*
5. [x x x x]-*la-ak* // [x x] *ḫa* [x] *am*
6. *un-ne-du-uk-ki*
7. *i-na a-ma-ri-ku-nu*
8. *i-na ma-tim*
9. *ša An*!-*nu*!-*ni-tum*
10. *i-bi-el-lu-ši-ma*
11. *Šar-ru-um-ki-in*
12. *ù-wa-e-ru-ši*
13. x [. . .]

(break)

Reverse

Column i′

1. [. . .]
2. x [. . .]
3. gina (TUR.[DIŠ?])

Philological and Textual Notes

Obverse

3. The second-person plural indicates that there was more than one addressee.

8–13. These subordinate clauses contain two verbs, one in the present aspect and one in the past. It apparently demonstrates a two-tiered political philosophy with a divine permanent and immanent dominion and human temporary and transitory rule. An alternative idea is that Sargon is quoting an enemy concerning land that he has lost.

9. Between the *ša* and *-ni-tum*, the misbegotten signs look like:  (coll. A. Westenholz).

Translation

Obverse

Column i

1. To PN and [. . .]
2. speak
3. thus says your lord Sargon,
4. "[. . . .] has spoken:
5. '. . . depart. . . .
6. my letter
7. when you read (it),
8. in the land

9–10. which Annunītum rules

11. and which Sargon
12. governed

(break)

Reverse

Column i′

1–2. (too fragmentary for translation)

3. newborn(?)

Reverse

i′ 1–6. For these age groups and their Akkadian equivalents, see C. Wilcke, "Familiengründung im alten Babylonien," *Geschlechtsreife und Legitimation zur Zeugung* (ed. E. W. Müller; Freiburg and Munich, 1986) 215–16.

ii′ 1–5. These definitions are speculative, based on the literal meanings of the words: edin 'steppe', $bara_3$ 'to spread out' (PSD s.v.), líl-lá 'phantom' (CAD *zaqīqu*). Note also that these lines of Proto-Lu are duplicated in 820ff.

4. bungu (UŠ.G[A])
5. ga-ti-b[a-kú-kú]
6. mur-r[a-ku_4-ku_4]
7. ḫenzer (IGI.[DIM?])
8. ḫenzer (IGI.⌜DIM⌝)
9. níta
10. munus
11. árad
12. géme
13. gú-bí-dub-ba
14. gú-bí-⌜gul-gul⌝
15. gal_4-la
16. gal_4-la
17. síg-gal_4-la
(break)

Column ii′
1. (er.?)
2. [EDIN].BÀRA
3. [EDIN].LÍL.LÁ
4. [SAG].ḪAR
5. [ama-érin]-na
6. [im]-ri-a
7. [zag]-bar
8. [íld]u
9. [um]-ma
10. [um]-ma
11. [um-m]a-gal
12. [ab]-ba
13. [ab]-ba
14. [ab-ba]-uru
(break)

---

ii′ 4. For this designation, see the discussion of text **19**, line 7.

ii′ 6–8. For these kinship terms, see Å. Sjöberg, "Zu einigen Verwandtschaftbezeichnungen im Sumerischen," *Studien Falkenstein*, 202.

4. infant
5. suckling child
6. toddler(?)
7. child in crawling stage(?)
8. child in crawling stage(?)
9. mature male
10. mature female
11. male servant
12. female servant
13. ....
14. ....
15. female sexual parts
16. female sexual parts
17. hair of the female sexual parts

(break)

Column ii′

1. (illegible)
2. nomads spread out over the steppe(?)
3. the steppe region haunted by phantoms
4. Chief of the Harians (?)
5. mother of the people
6. kinship group
7. kinship group
8. kinship group
9. old woman, dowager
10. female elder
11. venerable female elder
12. father, chief
13. father, male elder
14. city elder

(break)

---

ii′ 9–13. These lines are the only ones of this section to survive in the canonical Lu series; cf. Lu III iv 72ff. (MSL 12 127–28).

11
Ur Letter

Introduction

The contents of this letter can be analyzed as follows: the addressees (lines 1–8), Sargon's communication (lines 9–16), the list of professions, etc. (lines 18–187), and conclusion (lines 188–90 ??). The pivotal line, line 17, does not yield any clear sense. Likewise, due to their broken condition, it is impossible to decide whether lines 188–90 form a conclusion or are three more entries in the list. If they are three more entries, then the text may be unfinished.

The names of the addressees reflect Old Babylonian onomastic formations but Old Akkadian gods and places. In particular, the first name Ìl-a-ba$_4$-AN.DÙL-šu is similar to the énsi of Aššur in the list of énsis in UET 8 14 v′ 4′, Ìl-a-ba$_4$-AN.DÙL.

In his communication Sargon proclaims that he has received divine approval for a campaign against Purušḫanda. After this declaration appears the phrase *unnedukkī ina amārīkunu* (discussed above, p. 142).

The list of 185(?) entries may be roughly subdivided into the following apparent groupings: (a) priests (lines 18–21); (b) royal court attendants (lines 22–31); (c) professions that are part of the ancient courier service: messengers, emissaries, and dispatch riders (lines 32–36); (d) lion hunter and elephant warden (lines 37–38); (e) public officials in charge of various levels of city and state administration (lines 39–52); (f) male and female members of the aristocracy and royal family (lines 53–58); (g) keepers of the royal herds on land, at sea, and in the air (lines 59–70); (h) people in charge of various religious offerings (lines 71–73); (i) craftsmen of various sorts, including artisans and builders, as well as the professions of doctor, barber, and gardener (lines 74–91); (j) persons involved with the river trade (lines 92–95); (k) processors of various raw materials (lines 96–100[?]), which curiously enough are not listed here; (l) two entertainers (lines 101–2); (m) persons in charge of the encampment on the road (lines 103–7); (n) persons in charge of food preparation (lines 107–15[?]); (o) officials: the secretary, clerk, steward, and commissar (lines 116–19); (p) two types of guards, the forest rangers and the household guard (lines 120–21); (q) personnel who work on ships and canals, with certain exceptions (lines 122–34); (r) a long list of performers (lines 135–66); (s) people who have some connection with animals (lines 168–75); (t) palace officials, diviners, and prophets (lines 176–81); (u) the butcher (line 182); (v) the people of the merchant (line 183); and (w) more singers (lines 185–87). There does not appear to be a governing organizing principle to the entries. Thus, the ordering may be accidental and not significant. The reason for much of the uncertainty is that many of the entries are rare or completely unknown.

General Observations

This is one of the few complete tablets, with four columns on the obverse and five columns on the reverse. The writing on the tablet fills the four columns on the obverse but only the top third of the first column on the reverse, leaving four and two-thirds columns empty. This is another indication that the tablet might have been unfinished.

Circumstances of Discovery

This text was found in controlled excavations at Ur; unfortunately the field number was lost, so it is not possible to reconstruct its findspot.

Orthography and Language

The mixture of Sumerian logograms and Akkadian words does not lead to easy comprehension. It is interesting to note that this text is exemplary in its use of LÚ = *ša*, and one wonders if it could be an exercise in using such forms in a composition, some in Sumerian and some in Akkadian. Many of the terms are obscure, hapaxes that never entered the lexical tradition and professions known only from the archaic lists of names and professions.

On the whole, the sign forms are hastily executed and poorly composed. Note the shapes of the signs *tim* in line 14 and ḪÚL in line 102. The A sign is written occasionally with two and not three wedges (lines 12, 13, but not lines 11, 16) and the NU sign with one horizontal alone (lines 10, 85, but not line 6). The BAR sign is written with the vertical running through the horizontal, as in later periods (see line 96).

As expected, the text is written in the southern orthography with the differentiation of the labials BI:PI and the renderings of the affricated */ts/ by ZA ZI *ZU in syllabic-initial position and *AZ *IZ UZ in syllabic-final position. There seems to be one exception in line 145, *ma-ás-su-*⸢x⸣, which cannot be an example of a sibilant plus suffix. Strange plene writings occur, such as *-ku-nu-u* (line 16) for the possessive pronoun.

The syntax of the letter as a whole is unclear. The Sumerian logograms are ostensibly singular but the Akkadian nouns show either genitival constructions in the absolute (lines 26–27, 33, 38, 111) or plural oblique (lines 40ff., 98, 119, 146, 150[?], 151, 170, 175[?], 181–82). There are cases of nominative where an oblique case is expected (lines 49, 145[?]). The correct case may be rendered in lines 96 and 129. An accusative suffix may be found in line 166.

In general, see C. Wilcke, "Geschichtsbewußtsein" (above, p. 141 n. 1).

Manuscript

Ur

IM 85544 = UET 7 73 (collated by C. Wilcke, March 1983).

Transcription

Column i

1. *[a-n]a Ìl-a-ba*$_4$-AN.DÙL-*šu*
2. ^{1}*E-tel*-KA-^{d}*Za-ba*$_4$-*ba*$_4$
3. ^{1}*Ma-[nu]-um-ma-ḫi*$^{?}$-*ir*$^{?}$-*šu-nu*
4. ^{1}*Nu-úr-Šuruppak*^{ki}
5. ^{1}*Ga-še-ir*-^{d}*Ul-maš*
6. ^{1}MES.SAG-*id-nu-um*
7. ^{1}MAR.TU
8. *ù* ^{1}[A(?)]-*ḫu-nim*
9. *qí-[bí]-ma*
10. *um-ma Šar-ru-ki-*⸢*in*⸣ *be-el-ku-nu-ma*
11. *a-*⟨*nu*⟩*-[u]m-ma* ^{d}*Šamaš qú-ra-dam*
12. *Ìl-a-*⸢*ba*$_4$⸣ ^{d}*Za-ba*$_4$-*ba*$_4$ U.⸢DAR⸣ *An-*⟨*nu-ni*⟩*-tum*
13. *a-na Pu-ru-uš-ḫa-an-da*
14. ⸢*ṣa*⸣*-ba-tim a-na-am ap-la-a-ma*
15. *un-ne-du-uk-ki*
16. *i-na a-ma-ri-ku-nu-ú*
17. DINGIR.X NIN.DINGIR(-)ŠU IŠIB SANGA

Philological and Textual Notes

1–8. For Old Babylonian onomastic formations, see H. Ranke, *Early Babylonian Personal Names from the Published Tablets of the So-Called Hammurabi Dynasty (B.C. 2000)* (Babylonian Expedition of the University of Pennsylvania, Series D, vol. 3; Philadelphia, 1905).

2. Wilcke ("Geschichtsbewußtsein," 51 n. 67) suggests an alternative reading: ^{1}*Ma-a[n-n]u-um-ba-lum-*⟨*ì*⟩*-lí-šu-nu.*

6. Wilcke ("Geschichtsbewußtsein," 51 n. 67 and Nachtrag) suggests an alternative reading: DUB.SAG ⟨*Di-*⟩ *id-nu-um*, for 'chief, sheikh' of the Didnu-nomads, though the nominative on the gentilic is difficult.

10. This line is read according to the collations of Wilcke ("Geschichtsbewußtsein," 51 n. 67 and Nachtrag). Further support for this reading can be found in **10**:3: [*be-el-k*]*u-nu-ma.*

11–12. This list of five gods should be compared to those in the "Naram-Sin" texts. Six are typical of the OB texts: *Ištar, Ilaba, Šullat u Ḫaniš Šamaš u Ūmumšû* (**16B**:21–22); *Ištar Ilaba Šullat u Ḫaniš Šamaš u Ūmšum* (**19**:1–2). Seven are typical of the SB tradition: *Ištar Ilaba Zababa Annunītum Šullat Ḫaniš Šamaš qurādu* (**22**:12–13 et passim). Our five are identical to five of the

Translation

Column i

1. To Ilaba-andullašu (or: ṣulūlašu)
2. Etel-pī-Zababa
3. Mannum-māḫiršunu
4. Nūr-Šuruppak
5. Gašer-Ulmaš
6. Messag-idnum
7. Amurrû
8. and Aḫuni(m)
9. thus speaks
10. Sargon, your lord:
11. "Now, O Šamaš, the hero,
12. "Ilaba, Zababa, Ištar, Annunītum
13. "to Purušḫanda
14. "in order to capture, give a positive response and
15. "when my letter
16. "you see,
17. "the nin-dingir priestess of god X, the purification priest, the chief administrator (of the temple)

---

last list, although they appear in a different order. Wilcke ("Geschichtsbewußtsein," 51 n. 67) corrects the last divine name into ^{d}LUGAL! = Ḫaniš. Nevertheless, the sign does not look like LUGAL (cf. line 23 et passim), and Ḫaniš almost never occurs alone. Hirsch (*AfO* 25 [1974–77] 192) reads '^{d}Uttu («zadim»)', but the name of this goddess is usually written with the combination TAG.TÚG, while $uttu_4$ = zadim, which does resemble our sign (cf. line 81). Since the petition is directed towards the gods, they are the subject of the plural imperative *aplā*. The accusative form *qurādam* is incorrect.

14. Wilcke ("Geschichtsbewußtsein," 51 n. 67) reads *a-na-am ap-la-a-ku(/ma)* 'Nunmehr habe ich dem . . . zugesagt', or 'Gebt nun . . . die Zusage für die Eroberung von B'. There is at least one other example of *annu* written *a-na-am* (CT 33 21:16 in Old Babylonian). Normally the positive answer is given by a god, usually through extispicy, to the human query, which makes *aplāku* suspect. We are then left with the imperative, as Wilcke points out.

17. On the pivotal nature of this line, see Wilcke, "Geschichtsbewußtsein," 51 n. 67. The reading of this line is not clear. In his collations (Nachtrag), Wilcke suggests reading a list of cultic functionaries in this line: EN(!) LAGAR(!)

18. ⌈GUDU$_4$⌉.GUDU$_4$.ZU+AB
19. LÚ.MAḪ
20. ÈŠ.A.AB.DU$_7$
21. NAM.LAGAR
22. LÚ.EGIR
23. ⌈*ša a-na*⌉ ŠU! LUGAL
24. A
25. *ú-ka-al-lu-ú*
26. *na-aš šu-ši-ip-pi-im*
27. *na-aš za-ap-pi-im*
28. *ša* AN.DÙL
29. *na-aš* GU.ZA
30. *ša* GIŠ.PISAN.ŠID
31. *ša ma-an-za-az-tim*
32. RA.GABA
33. *ma-ar ši-ip-ri-im*
34. *ša* INIM.MA.BI
35. *ša* BAN

NIN.DINGIR(-)*šu* IŠIB SANGA, or the first two signs as ^{d}X, to whom the possessive suffix (-)*šu* would refer.

18–21. If this section of four priests is compared to the section of four priests of Enlil's temple Ekur, en, lagar, nu-èš, gudu$_4$ (Proto-Lú 205–8, MSL 12 40), we see that our text begins with *gudapsû* and ends with NAM.LAGAR. In between are the LÚ.MAḪ (*lumaḫḫu*) and AB.A.AB.DU$_7$ (*ababdû*). Both are known from the Old Babylonian period, and both words are obviously Sumerian loanwords. The former is an archaic title of a consecrated priest chosen by liver omen (cf. MSL 12 40:219), while the latter is an administrative temple official (cf. MSL 12 36:82). For a recent discussion of the position and function of the *ababdû*, see D. Charpin, *Le Clergé d'Ur au siècle d'Hammurabi* (Paris, 1986) 214ff. For the correct reading èš-a-ab-du 'he walks into the sanctuary', see P. Steinkeller, *Sale Documents*, 81 n. 238.

22–31. These seem to be royal court attendants; see Wilcke, "Geschichtsbewußtsein," 51 n. 67.

22. LÚ.EGIR.MEŠ explained as supplemental troops of the army occur in the headings of many lists from Mari (cf. ARMT 23 369ff.).

23–25. This reading follows the suggestion of Wilcke in "Geschichtsbewußtsein," 51 n. 67, where he emends the text to read *ša ana* ŠU! LUGAL A *ú-ka-al-lu-ú* 'den, der Wasser für die Hände des Königs bereithält'.

18. "a *gudapsû*-priest,
19. "a *lumaḫḫu*-priest,
20. "an *ababdû*-administrative temple official,
21. "a *lagāru*-priestess,
22. "a retainer,
23. "who for the king's hand(??)
24. "water(?)
25. "he presents,
26. "scarf-bearer,
27. "brush-bearer,
28. "holder of the parasol,
29. "chair-bearer,
30. "comptroller(???)
31. "holder of a service obligation,
32. "mounted envoy,
33. "messenger,
34. "holder of the word/witness(?),
35. "bowman,

26–27. For *nāš za-ap-pi-im*, there are two possible interpretations: *zappu* 'comb, brush' (AHw 1511a, where our reference is cited); and *sappu* B 'a lance', which could be compared to the lexical GÍR.LÁ (MSL 12 36:99). Cf. Wilcke, "Geschichtsbewußtsein," 51 n. 67: *na-aš šu-ši-ip-pi-im, na-aš za-ap-pi-im* 'den (Lenden?)tuchträger, den Kammträger'.

28–29. The only example known from lexical texts is *nāš kussêm* = GU.ZA.LÁ (MSL 12 33:17).

30. The reading and meaning of the signs is not known. Perhaps this office is similar to NB *ša ina muḫḫi quppi* 'official in charge of the cash box'.

31. The term *ša manzaztim* seems to denote men under service obligations to the crown.

32–36. These professions are part of the ancient courier service: messengers, emissaries, and dispatch riders. Horse riders are not an anachronism, since excavations in the Keban reservoir area and at Demircihöyük in western Anatolia suggest that the first domestic horses entered Anatolia towards the end of the fourth millennium B.C.E.

34. The profession *ša* INIM.MA.BI does not seem to fit the context if it is the equivalent of LÚ.INIM.MA.BI, from Sumerian lú-inim-ma /lú-inim-ak/ 'man of transaction/legal case', the standard term for 'witness' (cf. Steinkeller, *Sale Documents*, 105ff.).

35. For [lú.ban] = *ša qaštim*, cf. MSL 12 171:453.

36. *ra-ki-ib*! ANŠE.KUR
37. ŠU.PEŠ UR.MAḪ
38. *ma-ṣa-ar pi-ri-im*
39. SUKKAL
40. *ma-li*$^{!?}$*-ki*
41. ⌈LÚ⌉ *mi-ki*
42. MÍ *mi-ki*

(space at end of column).

Column ii

43. *da-*⌈*a*⌉*-a-ni*
44. AB.BA [URU].KI$^{!}$
45. LÚ.SAG$^{!}$.BA
46. LÚ.GI$_6$.[D]U.DU
47. UGULA DAG.GI$_4$.A
48. *ša* A.LÁ
49. *šu-ut* GI.PISAN *nu-us-ḫu*
50. UGULA GAR
51. *ša* É.PAP
52. KIŠIB.DU$_8$
53. MÍ.AN.DÙL
54. IDIM
55. MÍ.IDIM
56. DUMU.LUGAL
57. DUMU.MÍ.LUGAL
58. ÉNSI
59. SIPA
60. ŠÀ.DARA$_3^{!}$(wr. MAŠ+SUMAŠ)

---

36. For the writing ANŠE.KUR without .RA, cf. UET 7 76 rev. 8 (Proto-Diri).

37–38. The lion-hunter and the elephant warden might afford some kind of protection to the royal figure on the march. For the latter term, see most recently Steinkeller, *ZA* 72 (1982) 253 n. 58.

39–52. Public officials in charge of various levels of city and state administration: beginning with the top level, the *sukkallu*, the vizier, and the *mālikī*, the counselors in charge of directing the political affairs of the whole country; and then descending to the city level, the *dajjānī*, judges, and the AB.BA.URU, city elder, who have under them the LÚ.SAG.BA, the man who administers the oath (SAG.BA = *māmītu*), LÚ.GI$_6$.DU.DU, the night watchman (= *hāʾiṭu* MSL 12 116:11), the UGULA.DAG.GI$_4$.A, the head of the city quarter (MSL 12 39:167), *ša* A.LÁ, the

36. "horseman,
37. "lion-hunter,
38. "elephant warden,
39. "vizier,
40. "counselors,
41. ". . . . ,
42. ". . . . ,

Column ii
43. "judges,
44. "city elder,
45. "oath administrator,
46. "night watchman,
47. "magistrate of city quarter,
48. "steward of the water clock,
49. "overseers of the *nusḫu*-containers,
50. ". . . overseer,
51. "superintendent of allotments (?)
52. "superintendent of opening seals,
53. "a (sequestered?) woman of high rank,
54. "nobleman,
55. "noblewoman,
56. "prince,
57. "princess,
58. "governor,
59. "shepherd,
60. "gamekeeper(?)

---

man responsible for the water clock (= *ša maltaktim* MSL 12 163:171), the *šūt* GI.PISAN *nusḫu*, those responsible for the warehouses, the *ša* É.PAP, the man responsible for some municipal building(?), and finally the KIŠIB.DU$_8$, the person responsible for opening sealed objects. The É.PAP may be related to the É×PAP found once in an Adab text and frequently in Eblaite administrative texts; see most recently M. Baldacci, "É×PAP and the Eblaite Administrative Terminology," *WO* 22 (1991) 10–20.

53. For SAL.an.dùl = *sekretu*, cf. MSL 12 124:12′.

54–55. Another possible equivalency is lú.idim = *saklu* 'simpleton' MSL 12 143 v 51, but such a person does not fit the context.

61. SIPA.ÙZ
62. SIPA.ŠÁḪ[!]
63. *ša* $BURU_5$
64. MUŠEN.DÙ
65. ŠU.PEŠ
66. ŠU.PEŠ.⟨ḪÁD⟩.DA
67. LÚ.A.AB.BA
68. LÚ.KAR
69. *ša* A.KU_5.DA
70. *ša* KU_6.UR
71. *ša* GI.NA
72. *na-aš* SÁ.DUG_4
73. *šu-ut* GA
74. SIMUG
75. TIBIRA
76. BUR.GUL
77. KÙ.DIM
78. AŠGAB
79. $BAḪAR_x$
80. NAGAR
81. ZADIM

---

66. For šu-ḫa-hád-da = *šuḫaddāku* 'inland fisherman' (AHw 1260b), cf. *bāʾir* UD.DA 'inland fisherman' (CAD B 32a). A. Salonen (on basis of Landsberger) translates 'fisherman who dries fish (for future use)' from hád 'to dry' (*Fischerei*, 46ff.).

67. For LÚ.A.AB.BA = *bāʾir tâmti* 'sea fisherman', cf. CAD B 32b; A. Salonen, *Fischerei*, 43ff.

68. The logogram LÚ.KAR covers certain diverse meanings, see OB Proto-Lu (MSL 12 59:725–31), where the following glosses are found: *lasāmum*, *eṭērum*, *nērubum*, *šībum*, *abum*, *ekēmum*, *karûm*. Furthermore, there are many Ebla references, in particular the treaty B13a (TM 75 G2420, Sollberger, *SEb* 3 [1980] 142, where he translates 'harbor master, fugitive'). For a review of all the evidence, cf. H. Waetzoldt, " 'Diplomaten', Boten, Kaufleute und verwandtes in Ebla," *Il Bilinguismo a Ebla* (ed. L. Cagni; Naples, 1984) 416–19, where he concludes that the term refers to 'Handelszentrum-Kaufleute'.

69. Literally, 'the one of cutoff waters'; cf. lú.GIŠ.ku_5-da (MLS 12 49:458), lú.é-ku_5-da = *ša bīti parsi* (MSL 12 166:265); probably to be related to a-ku_5

61. "goatherd,
62. "swineherd,
63. "birdkeeper,
64. "fowler,
65. "fisherman,
66. "inland fisherman,
67. "sea fisherman,
68. "harbor master/local tradesman,
69. "regulator of the sluice channel,
70. "functionary in charge of the otter(??),
71. "supervisor of the *ginû*-offerings,
72. "bearer of the *sattukku*-offerings,
73. "those of milk (offerings?),
74. "blacksmith,
75. "metalworker,
76. "stonecutter,
77. "silversmith,
78. "leatherworker,
79. "potter,
80. "carpenter,
81. "jeweler,

'sluice channel' found in gag-a-ku_5, lú-gag-a-ku_5 'the one who opens the sluice channel' PSD A/1 98.

70. KU_6.UR could be the name of a fish, although none such is listed in A. Salonen's *Fischerei*. The translation is based on the lexeme ur.a = *kalab mê* 'otter', cf. CAD s.v.

71–73. The people in charge of various religious offerings. The supervisor of the *ginā*ᵓ*u* offerings is a post that becomes important in the Middle Assyrian period; cf. his official archive in Aššur, O. Pedersen, *Middle Assyrian Libraries and Archives* (Uppsala, 1985) Part I, 43–53. For the lú.sá-dug_4 = *ša santukki* 'person in charge of regular offerings' (MSL 12 139:364, 170:416), who occurs in all periods, see the references in the dictionaries. The *šūt* GA is a hapax.

74–91. These lines consist of commonplace craftsmen of various sorts, including artisans and builders, as well as the professions of doctor, barber, and gardener.

79. This sign is not a variant of EDIN, U+EDIN, or BAR+EDIN but similar enough to warrant the suggestion of $BAḪAR_x$.

82. AD.KID
83. A.ZU
84. ŠU.I
85. NU[!].KIRI$_6$
86. LÚ.TÚG.DU$_8$.A
87. *šu-ut* GADA

Column iii

88. LÚ.TÚG
89. LÚ.KÉŠ.TÚG.RA
90. ŠITIM
91. LÚ.Ì.RÁ.RÁ
92. GA.RAŠ
93. *šu-ut* NÍG.KUD
94. A.GIGRÍ (GIR$_5$.GIR$_5$)
95. LÚ.MÁ[!].GÍD.DA
96. *ša* NI-*bar-bar-ra-ki*
97. LÚ.SUR.RA
98. LÚ *ṣa-ri-pi*
99. GA.RI.RI
100. LÚ.GUG È
101. *šu-ut* ŠU.KAL(= LIRUM).DÙ

---

92. For GA.RAŠ = *kaʾeššu* 'trader', cf. MSL 12 137:267ff.

93. For *šūt* NÍG.KUD, cf. lú.níg-ku$_5$-da = *mākisu* 'customs official' (MSL 12 137:271, 186:45).

94. For A.GIGRÍ, see a.GIR$_5$.GIR$_5$-re 'canal worker, dike worker', PSD A/1 90.

95. For lú.má-gíd-da = *ša makitti* 'boatman', cf. MSL 12 167:300.

96. This line is unintelligible. The reading of NI is unknown. The signs bar-bar are really written maš-maš, but with the Auslaut -ra, we must assume that they are to be so read. For bar-bar A, the PSD gives as meanings: (1) shuttle of a loom (giš.bar-bar) and (2) projectile of a weapon (gi.bar-bar).

97. There is apparently no explicit product listed as object for the processor. Note that *ṣāḫitu* 'preparer of sesame oil' is usually written (LÚ).Ì.SUR.(RA), and 'the beer presser' is usually written lú.kaš.sur (MSL 12 132:108).

98. For a description of the work of the *ṣāripu* in the leather industry, see M. Stol, "Leder(industrie)," *RlA* 6 (1983) 532.

82. "reedworker,
83. "doctor,
84. "barber,
85. "gardener,
86. "felter,
87. "linen/flaxworkers,

Column iii

88. "fuller,
89. "supervisor of wrapping/binding of beaten/lined textiles,
90. "builder,
91. "oil presser,
92. "traveling trader,
93. "customs official,
94. "canal worker,
95. "boatman,
96. " . . . .,
97. "manager of the (oil?) press,
98. "dyers,
99. " . . . .,
100. "disburser of monthly *guqqû*-offerings(?),
101. "strongmen(?),

---

99. The essential question is whether this word is to be read in Sumerian or Akkadian. If Sumerian, the root would be ri-ri 'to gather', and it would be related to other professions such as lag-ri-ri (MSL 12 140:379) and da-ba-ri-ri (MSL 12 58:700) or 'the action of the hoe' (Civil, *Kramer AV*, 94). If Akkadian, the root can be *garāru* A, *garāru* B, *qarāru*, and the result as CAD Q has it sub *qāriru* would be 'a profession or status'.

100. There is no evidence of this profession in the lexical texts and the monthly *guqqû* offerings are only attested in first-millennium texts. On the other hand, the well-attested *kukku* cakes are written with GÚG.

101. The signs are ŠU.KAL.DÙ, but the combination does not yield any sense, and note the term LÚ.LIRUM, line 140. In the Lu lists, there are also two entries, lú.lirum and lú.ŠU.KAL (MSL 12 167:320, 321, 193 C3 4–5, 208:223, 224), consistently translated *ša abārim*, *muštapṣu* but both rendered in the CAD as 'wrestler'. Probably both were body contact sports, such as boxing and wrestling today.

102. ḪÚL
103. KAR.DAB
104. LÚ.KAS$_4$.E
105. LÚ.EDIN.NA
106. *šu-ut* APIN
107. *ša* UNU(?) PÚ
108. KAŠ.⸢X⸣
109. LÚ.GIPAR$_x$(GÁ×ERIM).RA
110. MUḪALDIM
111. *e-pi-iš du-um-qí*
112. *ša si-bi-im-*⸢*di*⸣(?)
113. *ad-mi-*[x]
114. KA×UD.KA×UD.[X]
115. Á.[x]
116. GÁ.DUB.BA
117. ŠÀ.TAM
118. AGRIG
119. *ma-an-di-di*
120. EN.NU.UN TIR
121. EN.NU.UN É
122. MÁ.LAḪ$_4$
123. MÁ.LAḪ$_4$
124. MÁ.G[AL!].GAL
125. MÁ.GAL.GAL
126. *e-di-ki*

---

102. For ḪÚL as a profession, see the various copies of the "Names and Professions List": for Abū Ṣalābīkh, see R. Biggs, OIP 99, 67, line 189: LAK 183; and for Ebla, see A. Archi, *SEb* 4 (1981) 186, line 200: LAK 183. For a comparison of these copies, see Archi, *RA* 78 (1984) 171–74.

103. Although *kartappu* is usually written logographically as kir$_4$(KA)-dab, I assume that we have here a pseudo-logographic spelling. Note that kir$_4$(KA)-dab also precedes lú.kas$_4$-e in MSL 12 103:242–43, 139:344–45.

105. This is just a guess in context. Other possibilities include: *ālik ṣēri* 'a type of soldier', *ša ṣēri* 'country dweller' (CAD s.v.).

112–15. Unclear. For Á in the Lu lists, see MSL 12 110:211ff.

116. For *šandabakkum* at Ur, see D. Charpin, *Le clergé d'Ur au siècle d'Hammurabi*, 241, 272ff.

102. "entertainer,
103. "horse groom,
104. "express messenger / military scout,
105. "desert police,
106. "plowmen,
107. ". . . .,
108. "(Someone involved in beer production?),
109. "man of the *gipāru*,
110. "cook,
111. "confectioner,
112. ". . . .,
113. ". . . .,
114. ". . . .,
115. ". . . .,
116. "secretary,
117. "clerk,
118. "steward,
119. "commissar official supervising delivery or distribution of staples,
120. "forest ranger,
121. "household guard,
122. "boatwright,
123. "boatwright,
124. "sea-going ship(per),
125. "sea-going ship(per),
126. "basket menders,

---

119. The *mādidu* official supervising the delivery or distribution of staples is not attested hitherto before the MB period.

120–21. Two types of guards, the forest rangers and the household guard. For EN.NU.UN TIR = *maṣṣar qišti/qišāti*, cf. references collected in the CAD s.v. *maṣṣaru* mng. 1b)-3′; and for EN.NU.UN É = *maṣṣar bīti*, cf. MSL 12 37:129, 116:22, 207:162.

124–25. Wilcke had assumed that lines 124–25 refer to ships and not to persons but corrected this in an addition to the footnote referring to the profession in the Old Sumerian period (Wilcke, "Geschichtsbewußtsein," 51 n. 67).

126. For *ēdiku*, see CAD s.v. *ēdiḫu*.

127. LÚ.A.IGI.DU_8
128. KUN.GÁL
129. *ša zi-di*
130. *ša* ADDIR (A.PA.PAD.BI.IZ)
131. *ša* UR.GI_7

Column iv

132. *ša* GA(wr. BI)-AN-⌈DÚR⌉(?)
133. *šu-ut a-ma-*[*tim*?]
134. ŠITIM.G[AL(?)]
135. LUL.[x (x)]
136. *ḫ*[*u*]*-ub-*⌈*bi*⌉
137. NAR *a-ú*
138. LÚ.AN.TI.BAL
139. LÚ.A.TAR.LÁ.LÁ
140. LÚ.LIRUM
141. LÚ.ŠU.TAG

---

127. For LÚ.A.IGI.DU_8 = *sēkiru*, cf. MSL 12 163:170.

128. Note the unusual spelling KUN.GÁL for *gugallu*, usually written GÚ.GAL or KÙ.GÁL. Since KUN is the weir of the canal, it is probably the original form of the word.

129. The only known word that fits is one of the fixed pair *ṣiddu u birtu*.

130. ADDIR is written A.PA.PAD.BI.IZ rather than the normal A.PA.BI.IZ.PAD.DIR.

131. For *ša* UR.GI_7 = *ša kalbē*, cf. CAD K 73a.

132. For ga-an-dúr = *aššābu*, cf. CAD s.v. For the frozen Sumerian verbal forms used as active participles in designating a status, cf. Civil, "Išme-Dagan and Enlil's Chariot," *JAOS* 88 (1968) 10, note on gáb-íl.

135. For LUL.[X], caretaker of x-animal, cf. P. Steinkeller, "The Sumerian Verb lug_x (LUL)," *Studi Epigrafici e Linguistici* 1 (1984) 5–17.

136. For *ḫuppû* 'gymnast', see MSL 12 54:583, 136:233, 165:254. The first reference is to the Old Babylonian Proto-Lu section of entertainers, musicians, and music, in which ḫúb-bé precedes a-ù-a, possibly our entry, line 137. In the second reference, Lu IV, it appears in a section between instrumentalists and singers and dancers and precedes our entry line 138. See further, CAD and AHw s.v. *ḫuppû*, and note to AbB 9 193:14 for other references. Note that the labial is clearly /b/ in this entry.

137. In the same Lu IV section appears a-u_5, which could be related to NAR *a-ú* rather than 'ferryman' (MSL 12 136:230), but there also appears *addir*

127. "canal worker,
128. "canal inspector,
129. "the official responsible for the foreigners, riffraff(?),
130. "ferryman,
131. "keeper of hunting dogs,

Column iv

132. "tenant, resident(?),
133. "those of rafts(?),
134. "builder,
135. "keeper of [x-animal],
136. "acrobats,
137. "singer of woe,
138. "sign bearer,
139. "jester,
140. "wrestler,
141. "musician,

(MSL 12 136:231; cf. line 130 above). Both are seemingly out of place in this section. However, the determinative NAR might weigh in the balance. Moreover, in Proto-Lu of this section, a-ù-a occurs between ḫúb-bé and [è]š-ta-lá (MSL 12 54:584). Note that addir is also the name of an octave (cf. Kilmer, "A Music Tablet from Sippar(?)," *Iraq* 46 [1984] 79). The signs nar a ú might also be read KA_5. On the other hand, nar a-ù-a occurs in other texts from Ur (cf. YOS 5 163:21; see D. Charpin, *Le clergé d'Ur au siécle d'Hammurabi*, 250 and n. 3).

138. Although the LÚ.AN.TI.BAL is equated in the lexical lists with the *assinnu*, the transvestite functionary in the Inanna cult (MSL 12 134:190), it is also equated in the same Lu IV section with the *ša ṣaddi* 'a sign bearer(?)' (MSL 12 136:234).

139. For the equation LÚ.A.TAR.LÁ.LÁ = *epēšu ša namûti* 'to make jests', cf. MSL 16 108 Nabnitu VII (E) 129. Furthermore, for a discussion of LÚ.A.TAR.LÁ.LÁ = *šutēṣû*, see Sjöberg, "Beiträge zum sumerischen Wörterbuch," *Or* 39 (1970) 78–79, and see further PSD A/1 190–91.

140. For lú.lirum, cf. note to line 101.

141. The lexeme šu-tag has a large semantic range dependent on the direct object of its activity. In the realm of music, it connotes 'to play an instrument', see Sjöberg, "Beiträge zum sumerischen Wörterbuch," *Studies Landsberger*, 64 n. 2.

142. LÚ.KA[!].TAR
143. LÚ.GÉŠPU (ŠU.ḪAL.ḪAL)
144. *aš-ta-la*(coll.)
145. *ma-ás-su-ḫu*(?)
146. *an-za-li-li*
147. *ša* GI.GÍD
148. LÚ.PA.PA
149. LÚ.DAM.DAM.DI
150. *li-la-i*(coll.)
151. *ḫa-bi-bi*
152. LÚ.GI.DI.DA.A
153. LÚ.I.LU
154. LÚ.[BALA]G.DI
155. LÚ.[x].BA
156. [x R]A.RA
157. [X X] IB [X]
158. LÚ.[X].ḪU.LA.A[T](?)
159. LÚ.GIŠ.U+[x]

---

142. For lú.ka-tar-ri-a = *ša dalālim* 'the one of praise', *nutturum* (mng. unknown), cf. MSL 12 160:77–78. Furthermore, see the discussion by Sjöberg, "Der Vater und sein missratener Sohn," *JCS* 25 (1973) 128 n. to line 117; Römer, "Einige Beobachtungen zur Göttin Nini(n)sina," *Lišan Mitḫurti* (AOAT 1; Kevelaer, 1969) 299 n. to line 112.

143. For lú.géšpu = *ša umāši* 'wrestler, acrobat', see MSL 12 109:192, 167:319; géšpu = *emūqu, umāšu* 'strength, acrobatics', see MSL 12 110:218. For the association of the acrobat/wrestler in the games/sports of the Ištar cult and other references, see Kilmer, "An Oration on Babylon," *AoF* 18 (1991) 19. For another but less likely possibility, read here LÚ.ŠU.ḪAL.ḪAL 'drummer on the *ḫalḫallatu*-drum'.

144. The singer *eštalû* is found in the same Lu IV section written èš-ta-lú = MIN-*ú* (MSL 12 136:243, as well as MSL 12 54:585–86, 124:21, 103:224; and cf. references collected in Kilmer, "A Music Tablet from Sippar(?)," *Iraq* 46 [1984] 75 n. 6).

146. For *anzalīlu*, see CAD s.v. *anzanīnu*. Possibly a transvestite entertainer in the Ištar cult; see Kilmer, "Oration on Babylon," 17–18.

147. For *ša* GI.GÍD = lú.gi-gíd = *ša enbūbim*, cf. MSL 12 165:243, 208: 244. Note the confusion in the lexical texts between this entry and entry line 152.

148. As has been proven (Sweet, *AfO* 18, 360) LÚ.PA.PA = *ša haṭṭātim* 'military officer, captain'. However, such a meaning does not fit in this context. More-

142. "praise poet(?),
143. "acrobat/wrestler,
144. "singer(?),
145. "experts(?),
146. "performers,
147. "*embūbu*-flutist,
148. "musician on the clackers, a percussion instrument,
149. "noisemaker(?),
150. ". . . .,
151. "*ḫābibu*-flutists,
152. "*malīlu*-flutist,
153. "singer of laments,
154. "professional mourner,
155. ". . . .,
156. ". . . .,
157. ". . . .,
158. ". . . .,
159. ". . . .,

---

over, sìg(PA) = *maḫāṣu* and one of the specialized meanings of *maḫāṣu* (CAD sub mng. 3b) is 'to play a musical instrument'. Perhaps this functionary beats out the rhythm with a stick like a conductor so that the musicians and singers keep in time together. Perhaps he plays the instrument giš.PA or giš.PA.PA = *ṣinnatu* 'clackers' (cf. MSL 6 125, Hh 7B 114–15; MSL 16 253, Nabnitu 32 iii 15–16).

149. This entry might be related to the phrase dum-dam-za 'to make noise, rejoice' (cf. Civil, "Notes on Sumerian Lexicography, I," *JCS* 20 [1966] 119ff.).

151. For the *ḫābibu*-flute, see CAD and AHw s.v.

152. For lú.gi-di-da = *ša malīlim*, cf. MSL 12 165:242; = *ša inbūbi*, cf. MSL 12 208:243.

153. For lú.i-lu = *ša nubê* 'singer of laments', cf. MSL 12 208:249.

154. For lú.balag-di = *ṣāriḫum*, *munabbû* 'singer of laments', cf. MSL 12 134:175, 165:252–53, 208:251, and references cited in PSD B 79–80.

155–58. Too damaged for treatment. A possible restoration of line 155 is LÚ.[GUB].BA = *maḫḫû* 'ecstatic' (cf. MSL 12 102:213), preceded by i-lu-a-li (132:117) = *muḫḫû* (cf. MSL 12 158:23, 177:26–27, 207:147–48).

159. The single *Winkelhaken* could fit any of the percussion instruments, the *lilissu*, *manzû*, and *uppu* drums, but rarely do they have a determinative of wood, whereas all the string instruments usually have the giš determinative. The most probable would be giš.mi-rí-tum, but the space is not sufficient. Other possibilities include GIŠ.MI or GIŠ.NÁ, the umbrella or the bed.

160. LÚ.RAB.U+NÍNDA×RAT.ZU/K[A(?)]

161. *mu-ša-ar*$^{!}$*-di ša* TIR.AN.NA

162. *mu-uš-me-li-il ku-lí-lí* (coll.)

163. Ì.DU$_8$

164. KISAL.LUḪ

165. LÚ.ḪI.LI$^{!}$ [x] ab si

166. *mu-bi*(?)-[x]-*lam*

167. *ḫa*-[x]-*li*(?)

168. LÚ.SÌG

169. LÚ.GIŠ.BAN.SÌG

170. *za-ḫi-di*

171. LÚ.⌜ŠE⌝

172. LÚ.TAG

173. *šu-ut* ⌜DAG.[x].KISIM$_5$⌝

174. zu ma ma ⌜x⌝ [(x)]

175. *mu-šar*$^{!}$*-bi-di*

Column v

176. LÚ.É$^{!}$.GAL-*lim*

177. *šu-ut* NIN ⌜x⌝

178. LÚ.GIŠ.KAK

179. LÚ.MÁŠ.ŠU.GÍD.GÍD

180. LÚ.ENSI(EN.ME.LI)

181. *ka-zi-i*

182. *ṭa-bi-ḫi*

---

160. Possibly alam-zu = *aluzinnu*??

161. This phrase is unknown. For another unknown *mušāridu*, see Veenhof, *Old Assyrian Trade*, 318 n. 439. However, it is more likely that *mušardi* is an Š participle of *redû*. For TIR.AN.NA = *manzât* 'rainbow', cf. CAD and AHw s.v.

162. The hapax *mušmellilu* is seemingly a ŠD participle form of *mēlulu* verb 'to play', from which the nominal forms *mēlulû* 'player, actor', *mummillu* 'dancer, player, actor' are constructed.

163. For ì-du$_8$ = *atû*, cf. CAD s.v.

164. For kisal-luḫ = *kisalluḫḫu*, cf. CAD s.v.

169. This word is understood as a synonym of lú.(giš).ban-tag-ga = *māḫiṣu*; cf. CAD s.v.

160. “. . . .,

161. “followers of the rainbow(??),

162. “dancer (adorned) with wreaths(?),

163. “doorkeeper,

164. “court sweeper,

165. “the man filled with charm(??),

166. “. . . .,

167. “. . . .,

168. “hunter/scout,

169. “bow-armed hunter,

170. “stalking hunters,

171. “animal fattener,

172. “. . . .,

173. “. . . .,

174. “. . . .,

175. “. . . .,

Column v

176. “the man of the palace(!)

177. “those of the queen(?) . . . ,

178. “claviger,

179. “diviner,

180. “dream interpreter,

181. “grooms,

182. “butchers,

---

171. For LÚ.^{niga}ŠE = *marû*, cf. MSL 12 122:37.

175. There is a homophonous lexeme, *mušarbidu* ‘a soft leather hide’, that might be related to this entry. Furthermore, it is interesting to speculate on the possibility of a variant rendering of MU.DA.SÁ written MU.DA!.BI SÁ = *mudasû* ‘list (of names)’; cf. CAD s.v.

178. LÚ.GIŠ.KAK does not seem to belong among the diviners and prophets. In this title *sikkatu* should probably be related to the Old Assyrian word for military expedition or army.

181. The word written *ka-zi-i* is most probably a byform of *kizû* ‘groom’.

182. The butcher seems to come as an afterthought, since he could have been placed in some of the earlier groupings.

183. *ṣa-bi* DAM.GÀR

184. ⸢X⸣

185. NAR

186. NAR.GAL

187. NAR.GAL.2

188. *na-z*[*a*/*ḫa*-x x] PAP

189. *ṣa*-[*bi*(?) x]-*lim*

190. *a-na* ⸢*a*⸣? ⸢*bala*/*am*⸣? SIG_4?-*tim*

---

183. Classes of merchants have been listed above, but this item could possibly include all the tradesmen and their dependents ('the people of the merchant'), though this idea seems out of place on this list, or more probably the 'army of the merchant', native people hired to protect them in foreign parts.

183. "army/people of the merchant,
184. " . . . ,
185. "singer,
186. "chief singer,
187. "assistant chief singer,
188. " . . .
189. "people of the . . . / seize!
190. "to the . . . of the brickwork."

---

189. A possible reading might be *ṣa-[bi a-]lim* 'the people of the city'. Wilcke (personal communication) suggests reading: *ṣa-[ab-ta-n]im*!? 'seize', which would be the expected verb at the end of the letter.

190. Wilcke (personal communication) suggests reading: *a-na ḫa-al-qu-tim* 'as missing (persons)'.

Part B

Naram-Sin

Chapter 6

Naram-Sin and the Lord of Apišal

12
"Naram-Sin and the Lord of Apišal"

Introduction

This narrative composition has been considered the "Naram-Sin Epic."[1] The central event is a conflict between Naram-Sin and an unnamed ruler of the city of Apišal. This conflict is known from the omen tradition and the chronicles. The historicity of the event has been disputed by many scholars.[2] Nonetheless, a royal inscription was published by B. Foster (*ARRIM* 9 [1990] 25–44), in which Naram-Sin describes his defeat of a coalition army of Sumerian cities and Amorites that assembled in the vicinity of Mount Bašar (modern Jebel Bišri, mountain of the land of the Amorites) to do battle with the Akkadian king. The head of the coalition, King Lugal-AB, hailed from a city the reading of whose name is uncertain; it appears in the text as RÉC 349 (= AB×U/ŚUŚ).KI. Foster suggests that this writing might represent the city of Apišal but identifies it with the Sumerian city of the same name in southern Mesopotamia (ibid., 35–36). Newest collations of the text have shown that this king and country are Lugal-gírid of Uruk; see the forthcoming article by Walter Sommerfeld ("Narām-Sîn, die 'Große Revolte' und MAR.TU^{ki}") in the Oelsner Festschrift.

Although the fragmentary nature of this composition precludes definitive statements about its narrative structure, the story elements are clear. The actions involve a military expedition to the city-state of Apišal. The violent character of Naram-Sin attracts notice: *išāt libbi muti napiḫtum* 'the burning fire

[1] Hecker, *Epik*, 37.

[2] See the discussion by J.-J. Glassner, "Narām-Sîn poliorcète: Les Avatars d'une sentence divinatoire," *RA* 77 (1983) 3–10.

within the hero' v 11; *šarram ezzam* 'the furious king' vi 7. In this text he is presented as a terrifying conqueror endowed with an awesome aura, whose essence is epitomized by the word *lion*. Examples from the text are: *kīma nēšimmi nāḫirim tabašši* 'You are as a raging lion' (v 2); and *bēlī attāma lū labbu* 'My lord, verily you are a lion' (v 18). He is ably seconded by his *sukkallu* 'vizier'. On the divine level, he is fulsomely praised as being escorted by divine attendants: Ilaba, Zababa, Annunītu, and Ši-labba (ii 4′ff.), as well as Irnina (v 4), whom we met in text **7**. In this divine assembly, Naram-Sin appears as *il mātim* 'god of the land' (ii 3′). The god Enlil appears, if not as his antagonist, at least as a wily deceiver (v 10, 16; vi 5).

The setting is not described. Despite the well-known small Sumerian town of Apišal situated to the east or southeast of Umma,[3] it is most probable that the Apišal of this siege refers to another Apišal near Alalakh.[4] As Glassner points out, Riš-Adad is known as king of Apišal in the literary tradition but as king of Armanum (= Aleppo?; cf. RGTC 1 18) in the historical tradition. The literary evidence to which he refers is the mention of Apišal in the list of the coalition of the foreign kings who rebelled against Naram-Sin in the Great Revolt (**16B**:31: Riš-Adad *šar* Apišal between the king of Nawar and the king of Mari). Further, the Apišal of this composition might have some vague connection with the nomadic chieftain Apiašal, seventeenth king of Assyria according to the Assyrian King List, as well as with the enigmatic state of A.BAR.SÌLA.KI with which the state of Ebla contracted a treaty.

The narrative contains the following story segments. The first section is reminiscent of the Sargon tale, *šar tamḫāri* "King of Battle" (text **9**), in which the king desires to undertake a military campaign but his soldiers are reluctant. The next extant section gives a description of Naram-Sin, apparently proceeding with the campaign, surrounded by a divine guard. The reverse concerns an exchange of messages between Naram-Sin and the lord of Apišal, who is not designated by name in this text. In col. v there is a poetic speech by a messenger of the lord of Apišal. The message apparently enrages Enlil, while it appeases Naram-Sin, who then consults with his vizier. At the instigation of Enlil, the vizier proceeds to persuade Naram-Sin to wage battle against his enemies. After a break, the text continues. Enlil is in conference with the lord of Apišal, who does not know how to respond to Naram-Sin's daily challenge. He pleads with Enlil to help him, and Enlil's response is, "You will rule Apišal." This answer is clearly ambiguous, since it might apply either to Naram-Sin or to the lord of Apišal. This negative image of Enlil is also found in the Sargon tale "King of Battle." The narrative probably continued on several tablets, of which this tablet was the first.

The discourse mode is one of dialogue, between the messenger and the king, and between the god and the king. The transitions, which are minimal, are

[3] Cf. Steinkeller, *ZA* 72 (1982) 242–43 n. 18; see also Foster, *ARRIM* 9 (1990) 40–43.

[4] Cf. Glassner, *RA* 77, 10. The Alalakh reference is 409:45 (OB), listing expenses in connection with the marriage of a prince of Alalakh and the daughter of the Lord LÚ URU.*A-pí-šal*.KI.

given by an omnipresent covert narrator. The literary text reflects topoi of Naram-Sin's royal inscription (mentioned above). This inscription begins with the sending of messages to the lords of the Upper Lands and the rulers of Subartu. Their actions are also circumscribed by the statement that they feared Enlil (Ilaba according to collations by W. Sommerfeld).

The use of dialogue and the characterization of the protagonists in this text reflect a closer relationship to the Sargon texts than to the other Naram-Sin texts. Another significant point is the presence of the gods in the background moving the players. In particular, as noted, it is Enlil who wants war and not peace between the antagonists.

General Observations

The tablet was originally part of the collection of Lord Amherst of Hackney at Didlington Hall, Norfolk, when Pinches made his original copy. After Pinches's death, the copy was given to the editor of *Archiv für Orientforschung*, and the text was sold. Güterbock published the copy immediately, but the original text against which it could be checked was not located. Recently the text reappeared as Lot #81, Sotheby's Auction House, on July 17, 1985, when it was purchased by the British Museum and handed over to their conservation department.

This text is written on a three-column tablet, of which the bottom seven/eight lines are extant on the obverse and the top twenty/twenty-one lines are preserved on the reverse. It seems to be the product of a scholarly hand rather than a school exercise. However, it is replete with scribal errors both of addition and subtraction. Note the addition of syllables (-⟨⟨*bi*⟩⟩- i 6′; -⟨⟨*ta*⟩⟩- ii 5′) and the omission of syllables (-⟨*ra*⟩- v 17; -⟨*li*⟩- vi 6), which may account for the absence of mimation on a few words. The lack of manuscript reliability coupled with the employment of rare words and abstruse epithets (see below) make it difficult to conjecture the meaning of broken and unclear readings.

Orthography and Language

The paleography of this text shows early noncursive Old Babylonian sign forms. Its linguistic features identify the composition as originating in the south of Mesopotamia. As for the graphemes used to render the syllables, the BI:PI (*bi-ir-bi-ru-ka*, v 1; *li-pi-ti-a-nim*, i 3′) contrast expresses in writing the voiced/voiceless distinction in the labials, which is characteristic of the southern tradition of orthography. Also significant are the rendering of the emphatic dental /ṭu/ by the DU sign (*ṭù-da-at*, i 3′) and the emphatic velar /qi/ by GI (*qì-bi-tum*, v 9). In marking the affricated */ts/, this text follows the method encountered in the "Code of Hammurapi" and letters of Šamši-Adad I and his son.[5] Initially and medially, where geminated, the set ZA, ZI, *ZU is employed (*lu-us-sà-qá-ar*, v 7; *ku-us-sí-i-im*, vi 11); medially, whenever single, the set *SA, SI, *SU is

[5] See Goetze, *RA* 52 (1958) 144, 146.

employed (*i-si-ru*, ii 1′). In the instances where the */ts/ is geminate, the syllable ending with the */ts/ is rendered by *AZ, IZ, UZ (*ku-us-sí-i-im*, vi 11). The plene writings reflect the system discussed in general by J. Aro[6] and in particular in reference to the hymn to Bēlet-ilī, discussed by C. Wilcke.[7] However, these writings probably have nothing to do with the orthographic tradition but are dictated by prosody (see below). The morphology is consistent with an early Old Babylonian date for the text. The vowels *u* and *i* are not contracted (see further below).

Poetics

This composition and the next are representative of the highly evolved Old Babylonian "hymno-epic" poetic idiom. This style is characterized by its

[6] J. Aro, *StOr* 19/11, 13.
[7] C. Wilcke, *ZA* 67, 154–55.

Transcription

Obverse

Column i

(break)

1′. [x] *aš ka*(?) *ak ta am ša a-ta-a-ú ba-na-ta*

2′. *at-lu-uk* x(er.?) *ma-a-ta-am na-ki-ir-ta-am // ù za-ir-ta-am*

3′. *a-ta-al-ka-am-ma li-pe-ti-a-nim // ṭù-da-at ša-du-ú-i ta-ab-ra-at // e*!*-ni*

Philological and Textual Notes

Obverse

i 1′. The verb at the end of the line seems to be a second-person masculine stative, but it cannot come from *banû*, since the expected form would be *baniāta*. Another possibility would be to emend the text by adding the mimation -⟨*am*⟩ to create a noun in the accusative.

i 2′. The first word in the line should be a verb. It was originally read by Güterbock as *šu-lu-uk-ni*, from the verb *šūluku*, governing a double accusative, the pronominal object *-ni* 'us' and *mātam* 'land'. In form it is an infinitive; the imperative would be *šūlik*. If one could assume a scribal error and take the verb as an imperative, there would be two possible interpretations of the line: 'Lead

archaisms, convoluted syntax, rare words, and abstruse epithets. Examples are: (a) archaisms, the use of the preposition *išti* instead of *itti* (ii 3′, v 4), the use of nunation (ii 5′), the lack of contraction of *u* and *i*; (b) free syntax, subject-verb-prepositional phrase (ii 3′), prepositional phrase-verb-subject (next line, ii 4′), subject-prepositional phrase-verb (v 4); (c) rare words, *uzibu* (i 6′), *šalbubum* (v 10); (d) abstruse epithets, *pālil urḫim . . . eddam qarnīn* (ii 4′–5′). Other hymno-epic traits found in this text include the shortened assimilated form of the prepositions *ina* and *ana* to *i*(*n*)- and *a*(*n*)-, and the use of the terminative-locative suffixes. Further, this text is unique in its apparent reflection of prosodic features, with its lengthened short vowels, additional syllables, and elided syllables (for instance, *kilal kilalal . . . qarnam qarnaʾam*, obv. ii 6′–7′).

Manuscript

Unknown Provenance

BM 139965 = Güterbock, *AfO* 13 (1939–40) 46–49 (see photographs, p. 389).

Translation

Obverse

Column i

(break)

1′. "[. . .] . . . , of which I speak . . .

2′. "When the departure for the strange and hostile country

3′. "I have launched, let the paths through the mountains be opened for me, the . . . s of springs."

---

us through the hostile land' or 'Make the hostile land serve us'. However, it is likewise conceivable that the first sign is not *šu* but *la* or *at*. The last possibility results in an infinitive Gt of *alāku* in status constructus, which should be the object of the verb *attalkamma* in line 3′, but the following nouns are in the accusative rather than the genitive case.

i 3′. For *ṭù-da-at*, see *ṭūdu* 'Weg, Pfad' (AHw 1393b). Von Soden interprets the last two words as follows: (1) *ta-ab-ra-at*, plural of *tabrītu* (AHw 1299b) '(staunendes) Anschauen', with cross-reference to *tašīltu*; (2) under *tašīltu* (= GIRI$_x$.ZAL) (AHw 1338a), he makes a cross-reference to *tabrītu* B2, our reference, and one must assume he reads KA.NI as GIRI$_x$.ZAL. There are obstacles to both readings: (a) the plural of *tabrītu* should be *tabriātum*, since there is no vowel contraction

4′. [*i nu-ka-a*]*l-li-im-ka a-la-ak ša-aš-mi-i* // *a-ka-al pi-i-tim*

5′. [. . .]-*ni ša-ta-a-i*(er.?) *me-e na-da-tim*

6′. [. . .]-*ib* A-*kà-dé*.KI *ú-zi-*⟨⟨*bi*⟩⟩-*i-bu*

Column ii

(break)

1′. *i-si-ru* [. . .] // *er-ṣe-tum ša* x [. . .]

2′. *Na-ra-am*-^{d}EN.ZU *ur-ḫ̯a-šu i-la-ak-ma*

3′. *il ma-tim i-la-ku iš-ti-šu*

---

in this text, and (b) the reading GIRI$_x$.ZAL would be the only logogram to be used in this text. The word *ta-ab-ra-at* probably should be understood as a malformed substantive plural feminine in apposition to *ṭūdāt*. According to the photograph, the sign before the *ni* seems to be *un*. If we read it as a logogram KALAM-*ni* or UN-*ni* 'our land' or 'our people', it would fit the context admirably, but again it would be the only logogram to be used in this text. A slight emendation would produce *e*!-*ni* 'spring'. Cf. the description of opening springs in mountains in the inscription of Ilu-šumma (Grayson, RIMA 1, 17, A.0.32.2:30–48).

The identity of the subject is not clear. Glassner suggests (*Akkadica* 40 [1984] 28) it is the gods who open the roads for the army. However, the verb *li-pe-ti-a-nim* is feminine plural. If we do not analyze the verb as D (as von Soden does, AHw 860b) but as N, then the subject of the sentence is the roads, which makes excellent sense.

i 4′. The noun *pi-i-tim* may derive from *pemtu*/*pentu* 'charcoal', which occurs in the form *pettu* and *peʾettu* in Middle and Neo-Assyrian. It also means 'firestone, stone for making fire' (cf. Hallo, *JAOS* 103 [1983] 179). The phrase refers to the consuming of bread baked directly on coals, since no oven exists in an army camp. Similar sentiments are expressed by the Sibitti when they urge Erra to battle: "([Why] are you lingering at home like a weak child? Like those who do not stride into the battlefield, shall we have to eat women's bread?. . .) *akal āli lullû ul ubbala kamān tumri šikar našpi duššupi ul ubbalu mê nādi* city-bread, though plentiful, is not comparable to loaves (baked) in embers. Sweet *našpu*-beer is not comparable to water from the water-skin" (I 57–58).

i 6′. The verb at the end of the line is perplexing. It could be a Dt form of a verb with the root *s*/*ṣ*/*z-b-b* referring to the city of Akkade in the subjunctive. No apparent verb suggests itself: *ṣabābu* D 'to keep something aloft on wings' (CAD Ṣ, AHw Ṣ) or **zabābu* D 'to be in a frenzy, to act crazily' (CAD Z) are the only apparent verbs with this root. If we emend the signs to read *ú-zi-*⟨⟨*bi*⟩⟩-*i-bu*, grammatically the only possible solution to such a form would be a preterite plural of the verb *waṣābu* 'to add, enlarge'. On the other hand, another possibility is to view this word as a noun. Two rare nouns come into consideration: *uzību* 'abandoned, orphaned child' (AHw 1447b) and *uzubbû*/*uzibbû* (AHw 1448) 'divorce settlement, parting gift'.

4′. "[Let us sh]ow you the manner of battle, the bread (baked) on coals,
5′. "[. . .] the drinking of water from waterskins."
6′. "[the . . .] of Akkade," they added.

Column ii

(break)

1′. They will surround [. . .] (and) the land of [. . .].
2′. Naram-Sin proceeds on his way.
3′. The God-of-the-Land—they go with him.

---

ii 1′. Cf. *amūt Šarrukīn ša ummānšu rādu īsirūma* 'the omen of Sargon, whose troops a rainstorm immobilized (lit. hemmed in)' (CT 20 2 rev. 9–10 and dupls., ibid. 3a:1–2, 8 80-7-19,157 rev. 6). In our text, the troops are probably hemming someone else in, i.e., laying siege.

ii 3′. The expression *il mātim* is relatively rare, being found only on three other occasions in the singular:

(1) The gate of the temple of Aššur, which was part of the stepgate (*muš-lālu*) and the place of judgment, is called *bāb nīš il māti* 'the gate of the oath of the God of the Land'. The referent is obviously Aššur (Adad-nirari I, Grayson, RIMA 1, 140, A.0.76.7:36 = AOB I 68:36 = Grayson, ARI I, 63 §409];

(2) In a variant to a *tākultu* text, a similar expression occurs: ᵈ*Ni-iš*.DINGIR.MEŠ.KUR with variant [ᵈ*Ni*]-*iš*.DINGIR.KUR, referring perhaps to the deified gatepost mentioned in (1) (B. Menzel, *Assyrische Tempel* II, T 138, no. 61 i 27, and var. no. 62:1′; see note to text on T 145 to line I 27);

(3) In a poem to Šušinak found in an Elamite grave of Old Babylonian date, he is described as *tabkat puluḫtakama ì-lí ma-ta-ti* 'your awesomeness is poured out, O God of the Lands' (Scheil, *RA* 13, 172, no. 5:4 = Dossin, MDP 18, 255:4 = Ebeling TuL 21 iv 4).

For an example of the plural, cf. *ilī mātim ištarāt mātim* 'the gods of the land, the goddesses of the land' (*ZA* 43, 306:5: "Prayer to the Gods of the Night"). In the singular, however, it seems from the few examples above that it refers to the chief god of the local pantheon. *Il-mātim* may appear as a divine name in the Early Dynastic god-lists. The writings AN-*ma-tum* 'god, the land' (Deimel, SF 1 viii 1, Fara; see M. Krebernik, *ZA* 76 [1986] 166) and *ìl-má-ti* 'god of the land' (OIP 99 82 rev. i′ 2, Abū-Ṣalābīkh; see P. Mander, *Il Pantheon di Abū-Ṣalābīkh* [Naples, 1986] 29, no. 297) could be so interpreted, but it seems more likely (in view of the nominative on the former example) that they should be interpreted as ᵈ*Mātum* 'Death'. In our text, it is possible that the phrase *il mātim* refers to the king Naram-Sin. This would also remove the difficulty of the singular subject and the apparently plural verb. The subject of the sentence is the troops, as in line 1, who accompany the god of the land, Naram-Sin. For Naram-Sin as *il Akkade*, see Seux, *Epithètes*, 107–8; and for Šar-kali-šarri as *il māti* X.KI, see ibid., 109. Note that the equivalent and more common Sumerian

4′. *im-ma-aḫ-ra I-la-ba pa-li-il ur-ḫi-i-im*
5′. *i-wa-ar-ka Za-ba-ba e-da-⟨⟨ta⟩⟩-am qá-ar-ni-in*
6′. *šu-ri-in An-nu-ni-ti ù Ši-la-ba ki-la-al // ki-la-la-al* x (er.?)
7′. *i-mi-ta-am ù šu-we-la-a-am qá-ar-na-am // qá-ar-na-a-am*

Column iii

(break)

1′. x[. . .]
2′. *ra-am* [. . .]
3′. *id* x [. . .]
4′. *šu ḫi me* [. . .]
5′. *mu-ki-i*[*l* . . .]
6′. *ut-ta ši/ru/ar/ḫi* [. . .]
7′. *na-ar* [. . .]
8′. *ḫu* [. . .]

Reverse

Column iv

1. *šar-ra-*[*am* . . .]
2. *mi-na-am t*[*a-* . . .]
3. *Na-ra-am-*^{d}[EN.ZU . . .]
4. *mi-na-am* [. . .]
5. *šar-ra-am* [. . .]
6. *ri-i-du*(?)-[*um* . . .]
7. *e-is* [. . .]
8. *ma-an-*[. . .] // [. . .]
9. *i-ni* [. . .] // [. . .]

---

title dingir-kalam-ma is used both of kings and gods (see Seux *Epithètes*, 389; Å. Sjöberg, ZA 63 [1974] 16, note to line 26′; and *Orientalia Suecana* 23/24 [1974–75] 177, note to line 10).

ii 4′. It is now clear from the photograph that the second word is to be read *i-la-ba*, and from the parallel line, it could be expected that this word contains the name of the god followed by a two-word epithet. Although the patron deities of the king are written with logograms in col. v 6, ^{d}INANNA *ù Ìl-a-ba*$_4$, it is still possible that the writing *I-la-ba* refers to the same god as *Ìl-a-ba*$_4$.

For the epithet *pālil urḫim*, see the note by Güterbock (*AfO* 13, 48). For a discussion of *Pālil* and *palālu*, see E. A. Speiser, "Palil and Congeners: A Sampling of Apotropaic Symbols," *Studies Landsberger*, 389–93. Note the gloss *ālik*

4′. To the fore, Ilaba, the pathfinder,
5′. to the rear, Zababa, the sharp-horned,
6′. the emblems of Annunītum and Ši-labba, two by two,
7′. right and left, horn by horn.

Column iii
(too fragmentary for translation)

Reverse

Column iv
1. The king [. . .]
2. What are you [. . .]?
3. Naram-S[in . . .]
4. What are [you . . .]?
5. The king [. . .]

(the remaining lines are too fragmentary for translation)

---

maḫri for *pālilu*. The reference is to a divine bodyguard who protects Naram-Sin while he is on the road.

ii 5′. The word *e-da-ta-am* is emended according to the suggestion of von Soden (*JNES* 19, 164), who understands *e-da-ta-am* as a scribal error and reads *eddam qarnīn* 'mit spitzen Hornen'. Cf. in broken context in reference to the chariot of Marduk, *e-di-id qar-*[*ni*] 'with sharp horns' (Lambert, *Symbolae Böhl*, 279:8).

ii 6′. For the goddess Annunītum, see the survey by K. B. Godecken, "Bemerkungen zur Göttin Annunītum," *UF* 5 (1973) 141–62; and for the goddess Ši-labba(t), see Deimel, *Pantheon*, 258:3206. Although Pinches copied *ki ki la al*, the photograph has only *ki la al*.

10. *mi* [. . .]
11. *uš*-[. . .]
12. *ur*-[. . .]
13. *ri*-[. . .]
(break)

Column v

1. *bi-ir-bi-ru-ka gi-ri ri-gi-im-ka ad-du-um*
2. *ki-ma ni-e-ši-im-mi na-ḫi-ri-im ta-ba-aš-ši*
3. *ba-aš-mu-um-mi pi-i-ka* ᵈIM.DUGUD *ṣú-up-ra-ka*
4. *Ir-ni-na iš-ti-ka i-la-ak*
5. *la-a ti-i-šu ša-ni-ni ša ki-ka ma-an-nu-um*
6. *nu-uḫ-ma* ᵈINANNA *ù Ìl-a-ba$_4$ li-ra-ma-ka*
7. *e-et-qá-ni-i-ma lu-us-sà-qá-ar ni-iš-ka // lu-ut-ma*
8. *a-di ma-ri ši-ip-ri-⟨im⟩ ú-ša-an-nu-ú sé-eq-ra-⟨am⟩*
9. *ú-ta-ki-iš-ma a-di-ši-za-az qì-bi-tum // ib-ta-a*

10. *iq ta az da* ᵈ*En-líl ša-al-bu-bu-ú-um // i-nu-uḫ ša-ar-ru-ú-um*

Reverse

v 1. These similes appear in other literary texts. The fire image usually refers to the mouth: cf. ka-zu giš-bar-re-ḫuš-a (CBS 4503+:21′; Sjöberg, *Ex Orbe Religionum: Studia Geo Widengren* (Leiden, 1972) 61 [prayer for Hammurapi]; *pīšu* ᵈBIL.GI-*ma* (Gilg. Y v 17 [speaking of Huwawa]). On the other hand, the roar is commonly compared with the god of the thunderstorm: šeg$_x$-gi$_4$-a-ni ᵈiškur-gin$_x$ In-nin-šà-gur$_4$-ra, line 52 (Sjöberg, *ZA* 65, 182); za-pa-ág-zu ᵈiškur (CBS 4503+:20′; Sjöberg, *Studia Geo Widengren*, 61 [prayer for Hammurapi]). For a similar spelling of (Ḫ)addum, cf. "The Epic of Zimri-Lim," 141: *illak ad-du-um ina šumēlīšu* 'Addum goes on his (Zimri-Lim's) left' (D. Charpin, *MARI* 5 [1987] 661).

v 2. For the phrase *nēšu nāʾiru* as a formulaic epithet, see Hecker, *Epik*, 164.

v 3. These similes paint a terrifying picture: the venom-laden mouth with protruding tongue of the viper and talons of the monstrous, lion-headed eagle. For the identification of the *bašmu*-snake as the venomous horned viper, see F. A. M. Wiggermann, *Mesopotamian Protective Spirits: The Ritual Texts* (Groningen, 1992) discussion, pp. 166ff. and illustration, p. 186, fig. 2; and J. Black and A. Green, *Gods, Demons and Symbols of Ancient Mesopotamia* (London, 1992) 168. For the latest discussion of Anzû the lion-headed eagle, see Wiggermann, *Mesopotamian Protective Spirits*, discussion, pp. 159ff. and illustration, p. 187, fig. 11; and Black and Green, *Gods, Demons and Symbols*, 107–8.

Column v

1. "Your radiance is fire, your voice is the thunderstorm.
2. "You are as a raging lion.
3. "Your mouth is a venomous viper, your nails are (those of) the Anzû.
4. "Irnina walks beside you.
5. "You have no equal. Who is like you?
6. "Be calm! Let Ištar and Ilaba love you!
7. "Spare me and I will take an oath and swear (allegiance) to you."
8. When the messenger had delivered (his) speech,
9. He removed (himself). Meanwhile he is standing(?), the utterance overcame (him).
10. Enlil, the raging one, had . . . (or: the raging one had . . . ed Enlil). The king was appeased.

---

v 5. For the phrase *lā tīšu šānini* as a 'Versanfangsformel', see Hecker, *Epik*, 171.

v 7. This line is elliptical in that the verbs *lussaqar* and *lutma* seem to refer to the same object, *nīška*. The idea seems clear enough: the messenger of Apišal is asking Naram-Sin to spare him and his country, Apišal, during the military campaign and promising in return a loyalty oath.

v 9. The verb *uttakkišma* has been taken by the dictionaries as a Dt form of *akāšu* 'to drive out of the way, to displace', but *nakāšu* 'to set aside, set on fire' is also plausible.

The subordinating conjunction *adi* should govern a verb in the subjunctive, as in the preceding line, which *ši-za-az* is not. The form of the verb is not clear. A possible interpretation of the phrase is that it contains a sandhi writing of *adišu* (adverbial) + *izzaz* = *a-di-ši-za-az* 'while he is standing'. The third-person referent may be Enlil, who appears in the next line. On the other hand the referent may be the word *qibītum*.

The last verb is also problematic: a tentative suggestion is to take the verb as *bâʾu* 'to walk along, to meet, to sweep over destructively', but whether to understand the form as G perfect or Gt present is not clear.

v 10. The first four signs are quite clear. Therefore, the reading *iq-bi*!-*šum*!-*ma*! 'he said to him' (von Soden, AHw 453) must be rejected on the grounds that it makes no sense in the context, since there is no speech by Enlil in the following lines and the verb should convey the contrast between raging

11. *i-ša-at li-ib-bi mu-ti na-pi-iḫ-tum* // *ib-li*
12. *Na-ra-am-*^{d}EN.ZU *pa-a-šu i-pu-ša-am-ma*
13. *is-sà-qá-ra-am-ma šu-uk-ka-li-iš-šu*
14. *a-te-re-et A-pi-ša-li-im te-eš-me-e*
15. *mi-im-ma iš-pu-ra-am i-in-ka ma-aḫ-ra-a*
16. *i-na a-wa-at* ^{d}*En-líl-li ma-ma-li-iš* // *i-pa-al-šu*
17. *is-sà-aq-qá-ar a-na Na-⟨ra⟩-am-*^{d}EN.ZU *e-*[*te*]//*-li-*[*im*]
18. *bé-li at-ta-a-ma lu-ú la-bu na-ki-r*[*u-ka*] // *šu-nu lu-ú ši-li-bu-ma a i-ra-*[(x)]

19. [x] *ra aḫ ad*(?) *ri-ig-mi-i-ka li-ru-bu* // *a-na ḫu-ur-ri-šu*!-[*nu*]
20. [. . .] *i ni i ni ki a* [. . .]
21. [. . .] ⌜x x x x⌝ [. . .]

(break)

Column vi

1. [. . . *aš-šum du-ul-lu*]*-uḫ te-⟨er⟩-ti-im*
2. [. . .]*ig*(?)*-ta-ra-ni-iš-šu*
3. [. . . *it*]*-ta-qì te-e-ir-ta-am* [// . . .]*mu-ši-šu ù ši-ri-i-šu*

4. [. . .] *ú-ma-ka-al ši-ip-ru-um*
5. [. . .] *i-ṭe*$_4$*-eḫ-ḫi* ^{d}*En-lil a-na A-pi-ša-⟨li⟩-im* // *ip-tu*
6. [*i*]*š-*[*t*]*a-ap-ra-ak-ku Na-ra-am-*^{d}EN.ZU // *ši-ip-ra-am*
7. *mi-na-am ta-pa-al šar-ra-am iz-za-am*

Enlil and pacified Naram-Sin. No obvious verb suggests itself. Although the form of the adjective *šalbubu* occurs only in a lexical text and in our text, the form of the adjective *šalbābu* occurs as an epithet of Marduk, Nabû, Nergal, and Erra. This is the only occurrence of the adjective as an epithet of Enlil. On the other hand, it may not be an epithet of Enlil; the raging one could be Naram-Sin, and the object could be Enlil. The syntax of lines 8–10 could be: *adi*-subordinating clause, main clause with verb in a *-t-* form (*uttakkišma*), *adi*-clause, main clause with two verbs in a *-t-* form (*ibtâ, iktasda*). Line 10 would then be transitional to line 11 with two preterite verbs (*inūḫ, ibli*). The verbs in the *-t-* form would be perfect aspect, describing Naram-Sin's feelings before the speech of the Apišalian messenger, and the verbs in the preterite would be narrative past tense, describing Naram-Sin's feelings after the speech of the messenger.

v 13. For the form *šukkalliššu*, the terminative adverbial *-iš* plus pronominal suffix, see B. Groneberg, "Terminativ- und Lokativadverbialis in alt-

11. The burning fire within the warrior was extinguished.
12. Naram-Sin opened his mouth,
13. and speaks to his vizier:
14. "You have heard the message of the Apišalian.
15. "Has anything he delivered found favor in your eyes?"
16. He answers him fully upon the command of Enlil.
17. He speaks to Naram-Sin, the young nob[le]:
18. "My lord, verily you are a lion. Your enemies—they are foxes, may they not [. . .]!
19. "At the ⌜. . .⌝ of your roar—may they slink into [their] hollows!"
20. . . .

(break)

Column vi

1. [. . .] because of the ambiguity of the omen.
2. [. . .] they (pl. fem. / dual) . . . for him.
3. [to/before Enlil he offered] sacrifices, the omen // [(he sought)] night and day (lit. his nights and his mornings).
4. A message [(arrives)] every day.
5. [. . .] Enlil approaches the Apišalian, they met(?).
6. "Naram-Sin has sent you a message.
7. "What answer will you give the furious king?"

---

babylonischen literarischen Texten," *AfO* 26 (1978–79) 15–29; our example is listed on p. 25, sub B I (d) 4. The *sukkallu* appears also in the texts concerning Sargon, discussing military tactics and desire for combat: **6**:33, **9B** obv. 13.

v 14. The form *a-te-re-et* contains the shortened form of the preposition *ana* + *têrtu* in status constructus.

v 18. In this line, there may be a reference to the "Fable of the Fox." In that tale, one of the fox's antagonists is the lion. The position of the lion in that fable is obscure, but it seems that he has both might and right on his side and that he is the instrument of divine punishment (Lambert, BWL, 188). Note also that the fox is known in the fable and outside it as the proverbial trickster.

vi 1–3. In these lines, the lord of Apišal seeks oracular guidance from Enlil in the extispicy performed after the royal sacrifice. Note that in this text the word *têrtu* means both 'message' (cf. col. v 14) and 'oracular message'. In addition, the word *šiprum* is used to denote 'message' (lines 4 and 6).

vi 6. The phrase *šipram šapāru* is unique to this text.

8. *at-ta-a-ma lu-ú i-li a-pa-al-šu*
9. *id-na-am-ma pi-i-ka lu-uš-ta-na-an* // *it-ti-i-šu*
10. *at-ta-di-ik-kum te-bi-e-il* // A-*pi-ša-al*.KI
11. [x x x (x)]-*ma i-na ku-us-sí-i-im* // [. . . *ta*/*š*]*a-ri-i-iš ma-a-ta-am*
12. [. . .] *i-na la-a ṭù*(?)-*bi at-ḫu*
13. [. . . *Na*]-*ra-am*-^{d}EN.ZU [// . . .] *az*/*uq*/*gìr ba-a-am*
14. [. . .] x *ma-ḫa-ar-šu*
15. [. . . *i-na ku*-]*us-sí-im* [// . . .] *bi*
16. [. . .] x
17. [. . .]
18. [. . .]-ta

(break)

---

vi 9. Note that the author seems to vacillate between the poetic *išti* and the more ordinary form of the preposition *itti*: *alāku išti* (ii 3′–4′) and *šitannunu itti* (vi 10).

8. "You are my god, answer him!
9. "Give me your answer and I shall struggle with him."
10. "I have given to you (so that) you will rule Apišal,
11. "[You will sit] on the throne and [make] the land rejoice.
12. "[. . .] without good relations, equals."
13. [. . .] Naram-Sin [. . .].
14. [He repeats the answer(?)] before him.
15. ["You will rule Apišal and sit] on the throne."

(remainder too fragmentary for translation)

---

vi 11. Although the sense of the line is clear, the verbs are not. The verbs that usually appear with the phrase *ina kussêm* are either *ašābu* or *elû*, neither of which fits the traces. Likewise, the only verb that could possibly appear with *mātam* as the object is *riāšu*. Cf. *murīš Barsipa* 'He who makes Borsippa rejoice' (said of Hammurapi) (CH iii 11–12). The grammatical form is not obvious.

Chapter 7

Erra and Naram-Sin

13
"Erra and Naram-Sin"

Introduction

Notwithstanding the lacunae, the narrative of this tale can be defined and detailed. Erra, the god, and Naram-Sin, the king, join forces to fight unnamed enemies backed by Enlil. This event is linked to the erection of a temple to Erra and his consort Laz. The tale, whose historical kernel is unknown, is both mythic and heroic.[1] In this composition, the actions are graphically portrayed, and one feels the fury of the attack. It is a tale of action rather than of happenings.

In the list of characters, there are Sin (written ^{d}EN.ZU), whose part is not obvious; Erra (written syllabically, *Er-ra*, with no divine determinative), who wants to battle Enlil; Laz (written syllabically with and without a divine determinative, $^{(d)}$*La-az*), his queen, who determines the fates; battle-thirsty Annunītum/Ištar (the epithet, syllabically written *An-nu-ni-tum*, alternates with the logogram ^{d}INANNA), the grantor of *irnittu* 'victory'; and one human being, Naram-Sin, whose aid Erra enlists in his battle. This text abounds in the use of epithets: Erra is *ilum* Erra 'Erra-the-god', or *qurādum* Erra 'Erra-the-hero'; Naram-Sin is *šarrum* 'the king'. Erra needs Naram-Sin because, apparently, Ištar will only join forces with him if Naram-Sin participates. Again, we see Enlil as the antagonist, the enemy.

[1] Although a proposal has been made to link the action of this text with a year-date of Naram-Sin of Ešnunna describing the erection of *mušḫuššu*-monsters on a gate (B. Foster, *Finkelstein Mem. Vol.*, 79 n. 11; D. R. Frayne, *JAOS* 102 [1982] 511–13; D. Charpin, *MARI* 3 [1984] 66 n. 65), the arguments seem baseless beside the known relationship between Naram-Sin of Akkade, Erra/Nergal, and Kutha (cf. W. G. Lambert, *JAOS* 106 [1986] 793–95); Frayne changed his opinion: *BiOr* 48 (1991) 380 n. 5.

The setting is the Meslam, the temple of Erra, and its *gigunnû* 'the high temple on the ziggurat', probably in the city of Kutha. More information is not offered in the text. The close connection between this temple, the city of Kutha, and Naram-Sin is also found in text **22**.

The narrative is almost complete; only a few lines of the introduction and the conclusion are missing. This unusual composition deals with Naram-Sin's acquisition of weapons in return for a promise to build a temple for Erra and Laz, according to the advice and inspiration of Ištar. Thereafter, the two warriors, Erra and Naram-Sin, set out for battle. After the successful conclusion of the military campaign, the king builds the temple. The text ends with a blessing on Naram-Sin the wise, who takes pleasure in justice.

The story segments are as follows:

a. Narrative introduction of characters Erra, Sin, King Naram-Sin, and Annunītum (lines 1–6);
b. Speech of Ištar to Naram-Sin promising victory in battle and bestowing weapons to insure it (lines 7–15);
c. Narrative transition describing Naram-Sin's receipt of the weapons (lines 16–17);
d. Speech of Erra to Naram-Sin asking for his aid in battle against Enlil (lines 19–23);
e. Speech of Naram-Sin offering to join Erra in battle, to build a temple for him and Laz, and to bring Ištar with him to battle (lines 24–32);
f. Description of battle (lines 33–45);
g. Description of the building of the temple by the king (lines 46–58);
h. Scene in which Laz asks her consort Erra to bless Naram-Sin (lines 59–68).

The discourse mode varies between narrative description and dialog.

General Observations

This composition is found on an almost complete, single-column tablet. The left side of the tablet presently bears some red stains.

Orthography and Language

This text's linguistic features identify it as probably coming from the south of Mesopotamia. In orthography, the opposition of voiced/voiceless labials is maintained on the whole (see BI:PI, *lu-ša-pi-iš* . . . *lu-ša-al-bi-iš*, lines 28–29; as well as BA:PA, *ba-bi-im*, line 48 and *pa-ra-ak*, line 27), but there is an occurrence of BA for /pa/ in line 49 (*sí*-BA-*ra*). Note that in the Larsa region, PI and BA do occasionally render normal /pa/.[2] The emphatic dental /ṭ/ is represented by the DI sign in lines 50–51 but is represented by the TU sign in line 51. A

[2] See the review of Walters, *Water for Larsa*, by M. Stol in *BiOr* 28 (1971) 366.

similar dichotomy is seen in the inscriptions of the kings of Malgium.[3] As in the text of "Naram-Sin and the Lord of Apišal," the syllable with emphatic velar /qa/ is represented by GA (*qá-ab-lu-um*, line 44), while /qu/ is represented by KU (*qú-ra-du-um*, line 36). The syllable /qi/ is represented by both GI (*i-qì-ir-bi-šu*, line 27) and KI (*lu-ša-aš-qí*, line 25). In marking the affricated */ts/, this text follows the previous text: initially and medially where geminated, the set ZA ZI ZU is employed (*sí-pá-ra*, line 49); and medially, whenever single, the set *SA SI SU is found (*i-si-ir*, line 45; *ra-ak-su*, line 47). The semivowel /j/ is represented by the sequence A-A (*a-a*, line 14), a southern characteristic according to Goetze. Certain exceptional orthographic writings are limited to particular lexemes: *gigunnû* in which *k* replaces g (*ki-ku-un-nu*), *šarru* with CVC ŠAR, *Mišlam-mum* with CVC LAM, and *An-nu-ni-tum* with CVC TUM. No logograms are used in writing this text.

Phonologically, there are a few archaisms. The vowels *u+i* are not contracted, and there are verbal forms in which the vowel has not undergone phonetic change: *iqrab* (line 46) and *tašab* (line 27). On the other hand, there is a unique case of a nasal assimilating to an adjacent labial: *mb* → *bb* (line 38).

The morphology is indicative of an early Old Babylonian date for the text, and mimation is used consistently. Also preserved in this text are the dual form of the noun (line 49), the nominative case ending in the construct (line 66), and third-person feminine forms (precative lines 30–31, finite lines 60–61). Moreover, there is a shortened form of the Gtn present (line 36), which is probably a poetic form due to metric considerations, since it is found in other pieces of Old Babylonian poetry and later. It is interesting to note the frequent use of various adverbial formations.

The lexicon contains the preposition *išti*, found commonly in early Old Babylonian poetry.[4]

Poetics

The highly evolved Old Babylonian hymno-epic poetic style is revealed in this composition. The obvious poetic forms found in this text are: the shortened suffixed pronouns, shortened forms of prepositions, the use of the terminative adverbial, as well as inverted word order. Besides this influence of cadence, there is prominent play on sounds. A striking example of assonance can be found in lines 47ff., in which *u* in the first line is followed by *i* in the second and *a* in the third. Likewise, a clear instance of alliteration with *l*, *š*, and *k* is found in lines 28–29.

The poetic structure is achieved by repetitions of identical words and phrases as well as whole lines, to create ring constructions. The text is divided by rulings into sections. The deciding factor seems to be an indication of direct

[3] See Kutscher-Wilcke, "Eine Ziegel-Inschrift des Königs Takil-ilišśu von Malgium," ZA 68 (1978) 105.

[4] See von Soden, ZA 41 (1933) 138–39.

speech as far as the obverse is concerned, but the rulings on the reverse seem to be narrative transitions, perhaps indicating changes of scene. These rulings do not indicate stanzas as such, since they divide sections of variable length.

Manuscripts

The tablet was acquired by the trustees of the British Museum in 1928. It is said to bear a remarkable affinity to the Morgan tablet with the Old Babylo-

---

Transcription

Obverse

1. [x] ⸢x⸣ [. . .]
2. ^{d}EN.ZU *ur*-[. . .]
3. *ki-ku-un-na i*-⸢x⸣-[. . .]
4. *Er-ra wa-ši-i*[*b*! *bi-it Mi-iš-lam-mi-im*]
5. *iš-ši-iq qá-qá-ra-am a-di* 10+[. . .]
6. *e-mu-uq šar-ri-im* ⸢^{d}⸣EN.ZU *ú*-[x x (x)]
7. *An-nu-ni-tum is-sà-q*[*á-ar*] ⸢*a*⸣-*na Na-ra-a*[*m*-^{d}EN.ZU]
8. *ši-ta-ra-a*[*t*? x (x) *sí*]-*iq-ri*-[*ša*]

---

9. *la ta-ap-pa-la*-[*as-sà-aḫ*] ⸢*x*⸣ *ma-ḫa-a*[*r-šu*(?)]
10. *ši-ti mi-im-ma* [*ša aš-ku*]-*nu-ku-um mi-it-ḫa*-[*aṣ*]
11. *ip-pa-ti-a-ma b*[*a*? x x x]-*ú šu-ṣi-a-ku*-[*um*]
12. *ka-ki ir-ni-ti-i*[*m* x x (x)] ⸢*x x*⸣ *li-im-ḫu-ra ṣi-im-di-i*[*š* (x)]

Philological and Textual Notes

Obverse

8. The word *ši-ta-ra-x* is possibly used as an epithet of Annunītum. Note the word *šitʾāru* 'iridescent (of eyes)' (AHw 1251), used in the description of Ištar in the Old Babylonian Hymn, *RA* 22 (1925) 172:12. Thus, I would restore *ši-ta-ra-a*[*t*].

10. The verb at the beginning of the line may come from *šeʾû* Gtn, although the expected form would be *ši-te-i*.

11. The meaning of the line could be that a siege will be lifted and Naram-Sin will be able to leave the city to fight. The subject of the verb *petû* (N

nian recension of the legend of "Etana" (Kinnier Wilson, *Etana*, 28). In general, see the edition of the text by W. G. Lambert, "Studies in Nergal," *BiOr* 30 (1973) 357–63. In the following, only notes and comments are added.

Unknown Provenance

BM 120003 (1928-7-6,3) = W. G. Lambert, "Studies in Nergal" (see photographs, pp. 390–91).

Translation

Obverse

1. [. . .]
2. Sin [. . .]
3. The *gigunnû* [. . .]
4. Erra, who dwel[ls in the Meslam],
5. kissed the ground x+10 times(?) [. . .].
6. Sin [increased?] the strength of the king.
7. Annunītum spoke to Naram-Sin,
8. the Iridescent-[of-Eyes expressed] her utterance.

---

9. "Do not prostrate (yourself) before him (? the enemy?)!
10. "Seek what[ever I s]et before you and fight!
11. "[(The gates)] will be opened [. . .]. Despatch (the troops) for yourself!
12. "The weapons of victory, let [(your hands)] receive. . . ."

---

stem) is lost in the break, but it must end with the *-ú*. The reading *ú-šu-ṣi* suggested by Lambert seems unlikely, since such a form is only attested in Old Akkadian, the Old Babylonian form being *ú-še-ṣi* (cf. text **20** iii 2). The verb therefore must be an imperative in parallelism with *mitḫaṣ* in the line before, and note that both appear together in line 15. In the context, the verb *šūṣû* means 'to send forth the army' (cf. *ajû zikri tāḫāzašu ušēṣika* 'what man has sent a battle array against you', En. el. II 110).

12. The subject of the dual verb should be a part of the body that occurs in a pair. Note that the parallel line (line 16) on the receipt of the weapons reads *Naram-Sin . . . imḫur kakki ina* ⟨*qā*⟩*tīšu*. Unfortunately, the traces do not

13. ^{d}INANNA *te-l[i$^{!}$-tum iq-bi a-n]a šar-ri-im ir-ni-ti-i-ša*
14. *a-a tu-um-mi-[id (tubqāti) ḫ]a$^{?}$-ṣí-in-ni ka-ak-ki*
15. *šu-im-ma a-na* [. . .] x *da?-la-at bi-it Er-ra ra-bi-ṣi-ka* // [(???)] *šu-ṣi-a-ku-um mi-it-ḫa-aṣ*
16. *Na-ra-[am-*^{d}EN.ZU (. . .) *im-ḫ]u-ur ka-ak-ki i-na* ⟨*qá*⟩*-ti-šu*
17. *da-m[i na-ki-ri-ja* x-*l]u-ú še-li li-iš-ti*
18. *mi*-x [x x x] ⌜x⌝ *ša-a-ti*
19. *Er-r[a pa-šu i-pu-ša-a]m-ma a-na N*⌜*a-ra-am-*^{d}EN⌝.ZU *šar-ra-šu is-sà-qá-ar*

---

20. *iš-t[a-tu qá-ab-la-am* ^{d}]*En-líl na-ak-[ri-iš] ù ra-i-ša-ku*
21. *ra-b[i-ṣa-ak na-a]b-la-ak [i-ša]-ta-ak*
22. *mi-ša/qá*[(?) . . . *n*]*i* [x x (x)]-*ti*
23. *qá-ab-l[a-am* x x] *wa-ar-ri/ḫ[u-um* x]-*ta-i*
24. *šar-ru-u[m iq-ta-]bi ru-a q[ú-ra-da-a]m Er-ra*
25. *qá-ab-l[a-am* x x]-*wa-ar wa-ri ka-ka-*⟨*am*⟩ *lu-ša-aš-qí*

---

26. *lu-pu-uš-ku-*⌜*um*⌝ *b[i-t]a-am ša ta-ši-la-tu li-ib-bi*

---

fit a reading of *qá-ta-ka*. The traces seem to fit [^{d}E]N.ZU, but a weapon of Sin does not fit the context. The meaning of the last word is not certain, and thus the postposition *-iš* could be understood as a terminative adverbial or a comparative adverbial (as in line 42).

13. The last word, *ir-ni-ti-i-ša*, is to be understood as an adverbial formed with either *-išam* or *-iš*; see W. R. Mayer, "Zum Terminativ-Adverbialis im Akkadischen," *Or* 64 (1995) 184, although the lack of mimation would make the second alternative preferable (cf. line 32).

15. The word *šu*ʾʾ*imma* is taken as a D imperative of *šummu* 'to conceive, reflect, ponder' (AHw 1274a), rather than of *šūdû* 'to inform', as in Lambert and Mayer (*Or* 63 [1994] 120). For the gods as *rābiṣu* of kings, cf. "Hymn to Hammurapi" (CT 21 40 i B 22): Šamaš and Adad are *rābiṣūka* 'your guardians'; Samsu-iluna (C 75): Enlil instructed us (Zababa and Ištar) to be *rābiṣūtika* 'your guardians'.

18. This line is paralleled by line 22, but unfortunately both are so broken that they cannot be restored.

19. Note that although the word *šarrašu* is in the accusative, it is in apposition to a proper noun in the genitive.

20. The first verb could also be from *šatû*, as in line 17. The verb *râšu* in the D-stem is used of 'crushing enemies' in Old Akkadian royal inscriptions (cf. *aK* 256:51, "Narāmsîn C 5") as well as Old Babylonian poetical texts (cf. VAS 10

13. Skillful(?) Ištar [(spoke to)] the king about her desire for victory.
14. "You may not [(leave in the corner)] my axe or my mace!
15. "Consider and to . . . doors(?) of the temple of Erra your protector // [?] send out for yourself and fight!"
16. Naram-Sin [?] received the weapons in his hands.
17. "Let the [. . .], my sharp one, drink the blood of [my enemies]!
18. "[. . .] him/that."
19. Erra o[pened his mouth] and spoke to Naram-Sin, his king,

---

20. "Enlil has wo[ven battle like an e]nemy but I am a destroyer.
21. "I am a crouching one, I am a [fla]me, I am [fi]re.
22. ".[. . .].
23. "Batt[le, . . .] . . . of [. . .]."
24. The king spoke, "Friend, Hero Erra,
25. "batt[le,] . . . the weapon(?) let me raise up!"

---

26. "Let me build you a t[em]ple in which joy (is found)!

213:12, "Hymn to a Goddess"). Cf. *ana ra-si napišti* (text **17** ii 32 and note to line). It is listed in AHw Ntrg. 1585b, *râs/šu*. Note that the verb appears in first-person stative, so Erra is referring to himself in these words.

23, 25. These two parallel lines are difficult to restore. A tentative suggestion for [x]-*wa-ar* is [*ka*]-*wa-ar* from *kamāru* B 'defeat, annihilation'.

24. In our text Erra is referred to as the *rūʾu* of Naram-Sin (here and in line 34), and in an Old Akkadian votive text Naram-Sin is referred to as the *rūʾu* of the deity NIN-KIŠ-UNU (MDP 6 pl. I 2:7). The latter deity has been tentatively identified as Erra (see P. Steinkeller, "The Name of Nergal," ZA 77 [1987] 164 n. 18a). For a king as a friend (ku-li) of a god, see C. Wilcke's discussion of the word ku-li (ZA 59 [1969] 70–71, sub 6.2.3ff.). Cf. the east wind as the ku-li of Naram-Sin: tu_{15}-sa_{12}-ti-um im-ḫé-gál-la ku-li-^{d}Na-ra-am-^{d}Suʾen 'the east wind, the wind of abundance, is the friend of the divine Naram-Sin' (E. I. Gordon, *JAOS* 77 [1977] 71 Proverb Coll. 4 no. 9:3; and see Wilcke, ZA 59 74 sub 6.3).

The epithet *qurādum* is apparently in the wrong case, accusative for nominative.

25. The sign sequence PI-*ri-ka-ka* does not make much sense. Lambert did not attempt to understand it, and von Soden left it as "unkl." (AHw Ntrg. 1593). It is possible to see in this lemma the word *pirikkum* 'Löwensymbol', as a martial banner that Naram-Sin raised in battle. For the lion staff as the symbol of Nergal, see *RlA* 6 488 s.v. Göttersymbole. Another possibility, if one emends the

27. *ta-ša-ab i-qì-ir-bi-šu ri-mi pa-ra-ak šar-ru-ti-im*
28. *lu-ša-ri-ik e-li-ik lu-ša-ar-pi-iš*
29. *ki-ku-un-na-a-ak lu-ša-al-bi-iš wa-ar-qá-am*
30. *i tu-šu-li-il šar-ra-šu i ta-ḫi-iš*
31. *i tu-ši-im La-az i-na mu-ut-ti-ka*
32. *ta-am-ḫa-ri-ša e-re-di-ši* dINANNA
33. *i-lu-um Er-ra ù* (er.) *Na-ra-am-*dEN.ZU
34. *pu-úḫ-ri-iš il-li-ku ru-šu ù šu*
35. *ta-at-ta-ak-pi-iš ma-ta-am qá-ba-al-šu*
36. *it-na-al-la-ak iš-ta-šu qú-ra-du-um Er-ra*

Reverse

37. *wi-ru-um ša-ka-al-mu-šu a-aš-šu-um e-zu-*x [...]

---

38. *ki-ma ib-ba-ri-im i-*[...]
39. *a-li na-ki-ri ti-bu-uš* x [...]
40. *uz-zi na-ki-ri i-lu-u*[*m Er-ra* ...]
41. *i-ša-ka-an šu-um šar-ri-im mu-*[...]
42. *il-li-li-iš la ta ar ni ni-ši* (-)[...]
43. *e-li-tu-um ù ša-ap-li-tu-um* [...]

---

44. *qá-ab-lu-um Er-ra za-*[*i-ri-šu*(?) ...]

---

text and assumes that there has been a dittography of the *-ka-*, is to read *wa-ri-ka* 'of your leadership' from the verb *wâru* + suffix *ka*. Moreover, it may be related to the *wa-ru-um* in line 37. Furthermore, *ka-ka* could be read *kakkam* if the mimation is emended in. For the writing with single consonant, cf. line 12.

27. For the contraction *i-qè-er-bi-šu*, see B. Groneberg, *AfO* 26 22.

28. The word *e-li-ik* is understood by von Soden (AHw Ntrg 1553) as coming from *elû* I 'das Obere', so perhaps it refers to the ceiling.

30. On the grammar of the third-person feminine precative, see Lambert-Millard, *Atra-ḫasīs*, I 295ff. In his analysis of tablet I of Atra-ḫasīs (ZA 68 [1978] 82), von Soden discusses our reference. However, he corrects his understanding of the root of *i taḫḫiš* in ZA 71 (1981) 172 n. 11, where he analyzes it as coming from the verb *naḫāšu*.

34. For the coordinated subject found frequently in Old Babylonian poetry, cf. d*Ištar u šū puḫur urdūnim* 'Ištar and he went down together' (CT 15

27. "Reside within it, sit on the royal dais!
28. "Let me spread [the roof] long and wide over you!
29. "Let me clothe your *gigunnû* with green!
30. "Let her acclaim its king!, let her prosper!
31. "Let Laz determine (the fates) before you!
32. "I will escort Ištar to her battle."
33. The god Erra and Naram-Sin
34. went together, his companion and he.
35. His battle overwhelmed(?) the land.
36. The Hero Erra went with him.

Reverse

37. The mighty one, the terror(?), the overwhelming(?), the furious(?) .. [. . .]

---

38. like a mist, he [. . .].
39. His attack (on) the cities of the enemies [. . .].
40. The hostile fury, the god Erra [subdued(?)] . . .
41. Establishing the name of the king who [. . .].
42. Like Enlil. . . .
43. The highlands and the lowlands [. . .].

---

44. In the battle Erra [(slew his enemies)].

---

2 viii 4; see Römer *WO* 4 [1967] 13, "Hymn to Bēlet-ilī"); *imtallikū šī u ḫamuš* 'they consulted, she and her husband' (*RA* 22 [1925] 173:36, "Hymn to Ištar"); [*att*]*a u šī mitlikā ina puḫri* 'you and she, confer in the assembly' (Lambert-Millard, *Atra-ḫasīs*, III vi 44).

35. In AHw Ntrg. 1571, von Soden reads the beginning of the line as *ta-la*!-*ta-ak* and takes it from the verb *latāku* 'to test, try out, check', which is grammatically correct but does not add much sense to the line, as Lambert points out (*JSS* 27 [1982] 285), for then the element PI-*iš* would stand alone. However, von Soden (AHw Ntrg 1583) has the lemma *p/wišmatum*.

36. For the form *itnallak*, see Lambert's note to this line. For the preposition *išta*-, see AHw 1564b.

37. Cf. Lambert's note and add von Soden (AHw Ntrg 1495) *werrum* V 'starker?'

45. *šar-ru-um i-si-ir ta-ḫa-zi ir-bi* [. . .]
46. *šar-ru-um iq-ra-ab e pi* ⸢x⸣ *bi tu* x x [. . .]
47. *ra-ak-su ṭú-ur-ru-šu tu-uk-ku-šu tu-*x[. . . *-a*]*m*
48. *i-na ši-ga-ri-im mu-ri-bi-im ba-bi-im ka-*[*wi-i*]*m*
49. *ša-ak-na ba-aš-ma-an sí-pá-ra re-ti-ta-an da-al-ta-an*
50. *ù šu-um Er-ra* ⟨⟨*Na-ra-am-*^{d}EN.ZU⟩⟩ [*e*]*l-šu-nu ša-ṭi-ir ta-ḫa-zu-um*
51. *ša-ki-in šu-um ša*[*r-ri-im el-šu-*]*nu ša-ṭi-ir ṭú-ub-bu-um*
52. *eṭ-lu-ut Er-r*[*a a*?-*li*?-*ku*?-*ut*?] *im-ni-šu*
53. *ma-al lu ḫu/ri*[. . .] *ni-lu*
54. *ip-ḫu-ur ki* x [. . .] x-*ti ma-da*
55. *bi-tu-um pi ta* [. . .] *ši-ma ad-da-ar pa-la-i nu-úḫ-ši*
56. *ki-iṣ-ṣú-šu* x [. . .]⸢x⸣-*ku-šu*
57. *el-lu mu-šu* x [. . .]-*šu-šu*
58. *i-ri-ib qì-ir-b*[*i-šu* . . .]*ar/ri ka la aq ru ša-ar-ri*
59. ^{d}*La-az šar-ra-t*[*u-um pa-r*]*a-ka-am ma-li-a-at*
60. *tu-uš-ša-am-ma* ^{d}[*Er-ra*(?)] *tu-ḫi-a-al*
61. *im-mu-ut-ti na-ra-mi-iš ta-ka-ra-ab šar-ra*
62. *tu-ku-ul-ti A-ni-im na-ra-mu Du-ra-an-ki*
63. *šar-ru Mi-iš-lam-mi-im a-ša-re-du I-*gi_4-g[i_4]
64. *Er-ra na-ra-mu Du-ra-an-ki šar-ru Mi-iš-lam-mi a-ša-re-du* [*I-*gi_4-gi_4]
65. *i-di-in a-na šar-ri-im ka-ak-ka-am da-an-na-am ši-bi-ir-*[*ra-am*(?)]
66. *er-ši-im ḫa-di mi-ša-ri-im ba-nu bi-ti-*[*ka*]
67. *a-na Na-ra-am-*^{d}EN.ZU *ši-bi-ir-r*[*a*]-[*a*]*m*? [*i-din*(?)]

---

47. For the idiom *ṭurram rakāsu*, see AHw 1397a.

48f. For the *bašmu*-snake, see notes to text **12** v 3.

49. In this line the only use of the sign BA occurs to express the value /pa/. It is found in a Kulturwort *siparru* 'bronze', which is written ZABAR(UD.KA.BAR) in Sumerian. This word is not written out syllabically in any Old Akkadian text (MAD III s.v.), so it is unknown what the traditional spelling was; the last sign of the logogram is said to be a phonetic indicator. For a syllabic writing in Old Babylonian, see *Idiglat ina kutlāti sí-pa-ri isker ina kutlāti sí-pa-ar-ri šigarī wērîm Idiglat isker* 'the Tigris with bronze fences she dammed up, with bronze fences and bolts of copper she dammed up the Tigris', CT 15 2 viii 8–9 ("Hymn to Bēlet-ilī for Hammurapi"). According to the references collected in the dictionaries, it is usually written with the PA or PAR signs, so the writing of the word with BA is unusual. Note that it appears in the stative, referring to the bronze doors and not the bolt.

45. The king held back the battles, presents [(he accepted)].
46. The king drew near, . . . [. . .].
47. Tied were its fastenings, its warning signals [(extinguished)].
48. On the bolt, the entrance of the outer gate,
49. were placed two vipers; bronze were the fixed double doors.
50. and the name of Erra ⟨⟨and of Naram-Sin⟩⟩ was inscribed on them: "Battle."
51. Affixed was the name of the king, inscribed on them: "Prosperity."
52. The men of Erra who went (?) at his right side,
53. as many as. . . .
54. He gathered. . . . , ... were many.
55. The temple. . . . her and for an eternal reign of abundance.
56. Its chapel. . . .
57. Pure were its rites. . . .
58. The presents in its midst [(he offered)] . . . the . . . of kings.
59. Queen Laz filled the dais.
60. Reclined, making Erra(?) writhe.
61. In the presence of her beloved, she invokes blessings upon the king.
62. "Anu's help, beloved of Duranki,
63. "monarch of Meslam, foremost of the Igigi,
64. "Erra, beloved of Duranki, monarch of Meslam, foremost of the Igigi,
65. "give the king the mighty weapon, the scimitar!
66. "The wise one, who takes pleasure in justice, who built (your) temple,
67. "to Naram-Sin, [give] the scimitar!

---

55. In place of Lambert's *ši-ma-at da-ar*, B. Groneberg (*AfO* 26 22) reads *ad-da-ar* for *ana dar.*

56. The word *kiṣṣu* must be the word for chapel; cf. *ušalpit ki-iṣ-ṣa-am*, VAS 1 32:22 ("Ipiq-Ištar of Malgium") rather than *kisû* 'supporting wall'; cf. *ki-sa-a-am rabiam . . .* [*i*]*šdāšu kīnā* [*a*]*lwīšuma*, ZA 68 [1978] 127:14–18 ["Takil-ilišśu of Malgium"]).

59ff. Closely resembling Old Babylonian royal hymns addressed to various deities, this composition concludes with a blessing for the king. The convention in the hymns to female deities is for the female deity to be addressed and for her in turn to beseech her spouse for blessings on the king.

60. On the broken writing of *tu*-ḪI-*a-al*, see B. Groneberg, "Zu den 'Gebrochenen Schreibungen,'" *JCS* 32 (1980) 158 and 163.

65, 67. The word *šibirru* is restored in these two lines on the basis of both phonology and semantics. According to the orthographic system outlined above,

68. *er-ši-im ḫa-di mi-ša-ri-*[*im ba-nu bi-ti-ka*]
69. *mu-um-ma iš-tu sí-ip-p*[*i* . . .]
70. *i-ša-am-ma na-ra-am a-na* [. . .]
71. *ik-la-am* x x x [. . .]
72. x [. . .]

---

the sign BI should represent /bi/ rather than /pi/. Semantically, investing Naram-Sin with the weapon of kingship, the *šibirru*, makes good sense. For *šibirru* as a weapon of kingship, cf. Etana OB Tablet I I/A 10 and SB Tablet I I/A 8. Note the following references: (1) *enūma Aššur bēlī ana palāḫīšu kīniš utannīma ana šūšur ṣalmāt qaqqadi ḫaṭṭa kakka u šibirra iddina agâ kīna ša bēlūti išruka* 'when Aššur, my lord, faithfully chose me for his worshiper, gave me the scepter, the mace, and the scimitar to (rule) properly the black-headed people, and granted me the true crown of lordship' (Grayson RIMA 1 183:22–26 A.0.77.1 [Shalm. I]); (2) *ina mēzez šibirrīka tušeškin ana* IM.4 *gimir tubqāte* 'with the fury of your scimitar you subjugated the entire inhabited earth in all four directions' (Tn.-Epic "ii" 9); (3) (Aššur, father of the gods, regarded me with favor and. . .) *šibirru lā pādû ana šumqut zāʾiri ušaṭmeh rittūʾa* 'an unsparing scimitar for the overthrow of my enemies he put into my hand' (OIP 2 85:5 [Senn.]).

68. "The wise one, who takes pleasure in justi[ce, who built (your) temple]."
69. The beam from the doorframe . . .
70. he raised and a stela at [that place he wrote].
71. He finished . . .
72. . . . .

---

69. The rare lexeme *mummu* B is a wooden object described by the CAD as 'a curved stick or beam'. From the present context and that of the literary composition, the Old Babylonian "Man and His God," where it occurs in relation to a gate (*patijetma abul šulmim u balāṭim mu-um-ma qerbuš erub ṣi lū šalmāt* 'For you the gate of prosperity and life is open, the pivot beam (is) in it; go in and out of it and prosper' [W. G. Lambert, *Studies Reiner*, 192, lines 66–67 and note to lines on p. 201]), it can be inferred that the beam in question is the pivot beam of the door. Another interpretation of this lemma is offered by B. Groneberg in a comment on Lambert's essay in her review of *Studies Reiner* (*JAOS* 112 [1992] 125); she relates it to *mummu* A 'craftsman'.

70. The verb at the beginning of this line is difficult. Since there is no vowel assimilation in this text, the verb *našû* is impossible. Phonologically, the only verb that fits is *šâmu* 'to buy'.

Chapter 8

Elegy on the Death of Naram-Sin

14
"Elegy on the Death of Naram-Sin"

Introduction

This unique composition is inscribed on a prism. The story of the great deeds of Naram-Sin is cast in the form of a panegyric or praise poem, perhaps a calque on the royal hymns addressed to the king. Note, however, that the king is not deified in this poem. Rather, he is depicted as the sun of his people, a most appropriate metaphor for a text from Larsa, whose tutelary god was Šamaš, the sun-god. The greatest king during the period of the Old Babylonian Larsa Kingdom, Rim-Sin, was also addressed as the sun of his people.[1] As in the story of the sun-god's visiting the netherworld at night, Naram-Sin appears to descend to the realm of the dead and to enjoy a night of sleep while the bolt and door of the netherworld are locked (col. iv). The netherworld is depicted as a place where the darkness cannot be illuminated (col. v 3), thus incorporating the theme of light versus darkness. The great unknown goddess in this composition is probably to be identified as Ereškigal, goddess of the underworld (col. i 16′).

This composition is unique and fragmentary, but the existing content suggests that there was little narrative. The discourse is a monologue, partly in third and partly in second person.

The contents of the prism's seven columns can be schematized as follows:

a. Column i 1′–9′: Praise hymn to Naram-Sin in third person, spoken by a goddess(?);
b. Column i 10′–11′: Narrative description of the approach of Naram-Sin to the great goddess, Ereškigal;
c. Column i 12′–14′: Direct speech toward a specific man;
d. Column i 15′–16′: Narrative transition;

[1] Cf. YOS 11 24 i 17–18, and see further references to other kings as suns of their people in AHw 1159 s.v. *šamšu* sub 5.

e. Column ii: Monologue partly directed outward toward an audience, concerning Naram-Sin and his offspring, in third person; partly undirected rhetorical questions; perhaps blessings on a son born to Naram-Sin and presented to the gods or blessings on the son's ascension to the throne after the death of Naram-Sin;
f. Column iii: Monologue addressed to a female (wife or goddess?), comparing Naram-Sin to Šamaš;
g. Column iv 1′–9′: Addresses directed to the audience in common first person and to Naram-Sin in second-person singular, depicting his lying-in-state;
h. Column iv 10′–18′: Address in second-person plural to Naram-Sin or to the audience extolling Naram-Sin;
i. Column v: Monologue describing mourning ceremonies with rhetorical questions on the inevitability of death;
j. Column vi: Monologue directed to Naram-Sin, relating to the moon and unnamed females;
k. Column vii: Address directed to a male; mention of Ištar-kakkabi, the Venus star; and command to end battle, to extinguish the flames of warfare, perhaps a cry for pacifism. This column may be reminiscent of the conclusion of "Naram-Sin and the Enemy Hordes" (text **22**) in its concepts but cannot be compared as far as vocabulary is concerned. On the other hand, it is similar in vocabulary to col. iv of the statue of Hammurapi, which contains a bilingual hymn in his praise (LIH 60 = CT 21 42). There the image of Hammurapi as the one who makes an end to war is coupled with his destruction of all enemies, thus ushering in an era of peace; see also *nakrī eliš u šapliš assuḫ qablātum ubelli šīr mātim uṭīb* 'I eradicated the enemies everywhere (lit. above and below), I extinguished battle, I healed the flesh of the land' (CH xlvii 30–34).

Binary oppositions between light and darkness are embedded in the deep structure.

Circumstances of Discovery

This text was found during 1974 in the sixth campaign of the Délégation Archéologique Française en Irak at Larsa. I would like to express my thanks to Daniel Arnaud for permission to publish the prism. It was found in situ on the floor of room 3 of the Ebabbar Temple of Šamaš.[2] Like the Mari tablet of the "Great Revolt" (text **16A**), it was discovered together with administrative texts, in this case concerning the Ebabbar and other temples connected to it, from the period of Rim-Sin to the eleventh year of Samsuiluna. It was accompanied by

[2] For the archaeology of room 3, see Calvet et al., *Syria* 53 (1976) 18; and for the catalogue of the cuneiform tablets and inscribed objects, see D. Arnaud, "Larsa: Catalogue des textes et des objets inscrits trouvés au cours de la sixième campagne," *Syria* 53 (1976) 77; idem, "French Archaeological Mission in Iraq: A Catalogue of the Cuneiform Tablets and Inscribed Objects Found during the 6th Season in Tell Senkeren/Larsa," *Sumer* 34 (1978) 175.

another Old Babylonian literary text. Arnaud suggests that the tablets had been abandoned in antiquity and the various archives were stored in the room sometime after the eleventh year of Samsuiluna, perhaps put there by builders from the time of Burnaburiaš during the cleaning and rebuilding of the Ebabbar. There are other literary texts that are said to have come from Larsa, such as "Gilgameš" P and/or Y, incantations, and the "Hymn of Sin and Išum."[3]

General Observations

One of the most interesting aspects of this text is the shape of the clay object on which it was inscribed. Prisms with Sumerian literary texts and reference works are known from the third millennium through the second millennium, and examples with Assyrian building inscriptions are known from the second millennium through the first millennium,[4] but prisms with Akkadian literary texts are almost unknown. It is interesting to note that another example of an Akkadian literary text written on a prism is the Boghazköy version of "Naram-Sin and the Enemy Hordes" (text **21A**).

The prism is four-sided, and there are two columns per side. Of the eight possible columns, seven are filled and one is left blank, thus clearly indicating the beginning and end of the composition. The reading of this text is dependent on the field photographs and copies made by Daniel Arnaud. After excavation, the prism was housed in the Iraq Museum, where it could not be located for collation. Consequently, the new copy and the transliteration must be considered tentative.

Orthography and Language

Its linguistic features identify this text as probably coming from the south of Mesopotamia, which is consistent with its being found in Larsa. In orthography, the opposition of voiced/voiceless in the labials is maintained on the whole (BI:PI, [*iḫ-bi-it* in iii 5, *pi-ti-a-at* in v 4]; as well as BA:PA). The emphatic dental /ṭ/ is represented by the DA *DI *DU signs (*ṭa-bu-um* iv 20). As in text **12**, the syllables with emphatic velars, /qa/ and /qi/, are represented by GA (*qá-be-šu*, i 11) and GI (*qè-re-eb*, v 12), but also by KI (*qí-bi-tu*, i 14); /qu/ may be rendered by KU (example in vi 10′ is uncertain) or by GU (example in v 11 is also uncertain). In marking the affricated */ts/, the set *ZA ZI *ZU is employed. The syllable ending with */ts/ is represented by *AZ IZ and *UZ. The plene writings are characteristic of the southern Old Babylonian texts: they are used to indicate phonologically long vowels (including vocalic endings before *-ma* and suffix) in penultimate and antepenultimate open syllables. An early or archaizing feature of the writing system is the appearance of uncontracted vowels. On the other hand, various groups of CVC signs are used: TUM, TIM, ŠUM, ŠAR, DAN, and QUM (*tu-qum-ta-am*, vii 9).

[3] For these texts, see respectively: Hecker, *Epik*, 27; van Dijk, *Or* 41 (1972) 348 and VAS 17 8; CT 15 5–6 and Römer, *JAOS* 86 (1966) 141.

[4] See R. S. Ellis, *Foundation Deposits in Ancient Mesopotamia* (New Haven, 1968) 108–14.

Morphology of the nominal declensions is consistent, and mimation is used systematically in the text. In verbal morphology, the *t*-prefix appears for the third-person feminine singular, reproducing the same system as in text **13**.

Poetics

Poetic diction is evidenced in this text by its shortened suffixed pronouns, shortened forms of the prepositions, the use of the terminative adverbial, as well as by inverted syntax. For example, a peculiarity of this text is the writing of *ki* with a short *i*, which is also found in other pieces of Old Babylonian poetry: *ki* ᵈ*Šamaš*, VAS 10 215:24; *ki nannarim*, ibid. 52 (OB, "Hymn to Nanaya

---

Transcription

Side a

Column i

(break)

1. [. . .] *tim* [x] *i* [. . .]
2. [. . .] ⸢x⸣ *ša-am-šum*
3. [. . .]⸢x⸣ *in ni ši-ga-um*
4. [. . .] *al*? *ra* [*n*]*a ni-bi-ú-um*
5. [(. . .)] ⸢x⸣ *ki-ib-ra*?*-tum*
6. [. . .] x *li ša-am-ša-a*[*m*] *lu-wa-ir* [//(?)] *ki*! *ma-i*
7. [*du-ul-lu*]*-ḫu di-ma-tim na*!?*-ra-tum ḫa-ab-ba*
8. [*Na-ra-am*]-ᵈEN.ZU *im-ma-ki-a-ma*
9. [. . .]*-ab-bu-di-iš ša-ni bi-il-ka* [//(?)] *ša-a-ru-ma*
10. [(?)] *ra*?*-bi-it ru*?*-ḫi*?*-šu*
11. [x x]*-ši-i ta-i-ša ki la qá-be-šu*

Philological and Textual Notes

i 2. There are various possible readings for the signs *ša-am-šum*, *ša-ga-šum*, *ša-bi-šum*. In view of the poor condition of the tablet and the broken context, it is not possible to choose between them. The sun, *šamšum*, appears as god and as cosmic body in this text; as the former it is written ᵈUTU, and as the latter syllabically. Moreover, it seems that the sun as a cosmic body is construed as feminine with respect to gender agreement (see iv 18–19). For a discussion of the writings of *šamšum* in OB "Gilgameš," see Jacobsen, "*Inūma ilu awīlum*" (*Finkelstein Mem. Vol.*, 114). Another possibility is to read *ša-ga-šum* and to

for Samsuiluna"); *ki ūmi*, CT 15 4 ii 10 (OB, "Hymn to Adad"); *ki ūmi*, Genouillac Kich B 472 ii 4′, 6′ (love poem).

The poetic structure is built of repetitive verses: ABAC. Such a quatrain forms one strophe, and it is followed in one instance by a tercet DED, forming the second strophe. These two strophes form a stanza in col. ii. In other columns, there may be repetition of lines and verses, even where the above-mentioned poetic structure does not appear.

Manuscript

Larsa

L 74.225 (see photographs and copy, pp. 392–99).

Translation

Side a

Column i

(break)

1. [. . .] . . . [. . .]
2. [. . .] x the sun
3. [. . .] x the raging one
4. [. . .] . . . the brilliant one
5. [(?)] the quarters
6. [. . .] the sun, let me command(?) [(?)] like water
7. [disturb]ed by tears. The rivers(?) murmured.
8. [Naram]-Sin is lacking and
9. [. . .]. . . . he is changed, your (masc. sg.) lord is wind (i.e., nothing).
10. [(?)] The great female one of his magic spell (?!)
11. [. . .] she is(?). Toward her, not according to his behest

---

compare this phrase with *š[a]-gi-is la gammal ūbil[ka]* 'The merciless Destroyer has brought you' (W. G. Lambert, "A New Babylonian Descent to the Netherworld," *Studies Moran*, 291, line 6).

i 9. The reading of *bi-il* from *bēlu* is forced upon the reader because of the orthographic distinctions of this text. For a similar writing, see **7** iv 4′.

i 11. Cf. *atkašī ta-i-iš-ša* 'move off toward her' (VAS 10 214 vi 35, OB "Hymn to Agušaya"). For the prepositional expression *daʾiš*, see M. Krebernik, ZA 81 (1991) 137.

12. [*ša*(?)] *wi-ri-im ša-ap-tu-uk*!
13. [*pi-ti*] *ša-ap-ta-ak ki-la ta-ka-al-šu*
14. [... -*r*]*a-am i-ši-ru qí-bi-*⟨*a-*⟩*tu*
15. [//(?)] *me-a-am* x-[x-(x)]-*aš*
16. [...] . *uš* gi_4 ^{d}*Er*[*eš-ki-gal*] [...]

(break)

Column ii

(break)

1. *al ki/di* ⌜x⌝ [...]
2. *wi-il-di-iš ku-ub-*[*bi-it a-na*] // *šu-mi-šu ra-*[*bi-im*(?)]
3. *a-na Na-ra-am-*^{d}EN.ZU *lu-ub-*[...]
4. *wi-il-di-iš ku-ub-*[*bi-it a-na*] // *šu-mi-šu ra*[*-bi-im*(?)]
5. *pa*(!)-*ši-šu ka-la* [...]
6. *il-li-im šar i-*[*na šar-ri* ...] // *mi-iš-š*[*um* ...]
7. *Na-ra-am-*^{d}EN.ZU *da-*[*an-nu-um* ...]
8. *il-li-im šar i-*[*na šar-ri* ...] // *mi-iš-*[*šum* ...]
9. *mi-iš-šum la iš-*[...]
10. *i-lu šu-ut ut* x [...] // *ma-ḫa-ar-šu-nu* [...]
11. *mi-iš-šum la ú-*[...]
12. u_4*-mi-iš ka* x [...]

(break)

Side b

Column iii

(break)

1. [...] *iš ša am* ⌜*a-na*-x⌝
2. [...] *ki na*(sign: PI)-*pi-iš-tim*
3. [*ina pu-úḫ-r*]*i ka-la i-li-ma*

---

ii 2. Cf. CAD *ildu*, AHw *wildu* 1496. Also, in description of foreign land, *ul mātum ša Amurrîm ... me-ri-sú*! *rapaštam wi-il-di-ša li-*[*x-x*]*-ma* (text **7** ii 13′).

ii 5. For *pašīšu* as a royal epithet, see Seux, *Epithètes*, 222.

ii 6ff. For a similar repetition of rhetorical questions, see the bilingual "Hymn to Hammurapi," CT 21 40 iB, which has as a refrain: *atta mannam tuqâ* 'whom are you waiting for?' Cf. also *miššu danānu qarrādūtīka* 'what has become of your great valor?' (addressing Enkidu), Gilg. Y iv 145.

ii 6. The genitive of the form *illim* is inexplicable, unless one assumes a shortened form of the preposition *ina* in which the *-n-* has assimilated to the *-l-*

12. "[of ?] the mighty ones are your lips.
13. "[Open] your lips! Hold back (masc. sg.) his trusting!"
14. .... the divine pronouncements have come straight down
15. .... he has heard (?) ....
16. [...].... Er[eškigal] ....

(break)

Column ii

(break)

1. ....
2. Pay honor to his offspring for the sake of his great name!
3. To Naram-Sin pray!...
4. Pay honor to his offspring for the sake of his [great] name!
5. The anointed one of all the....
6. Among a thousand, the king among kings.... why....
7. Naram-Sin, the mi[ghty ....]
8. Among a thousand, the king among kings.... why....
9. Why did he not....
10. The gods who.... before them....
11. Why did he not....
12. Like a storm....

(break)

Side b

Column iii

(break)

1. [...]....
2. [...] like life.
3. [In the assembly of] all the gods

---

of *līm*(*u*).

iii 2. For *ki* written with a short *i*, see above. The scribe must have made a mistake and written the sign PI twice, because there is no such word as *pi-pi-iš-tu*. Therefore, I emend the text to read *na*!*-pi-iš-tim*. Note *kīma na-ap-ša-ti-ku-un* in iv 27.

iii 3. The broken sign at the beginning of the line does not resemble TU, as in line 6, but is most probably to be read RI, and therefore I propose to restore [*ina pu-úḫ-r*]*i*.

4. [. . .] *e-lu-uk-ki*
5. [. . . *ma-a*]*n-nu-um iḫ-bi-it*
6. [. . .]*-tu ka-la i-li-ma*
7. [. . .] ⸢x⸣ *e-lu-uk-ki*
8. [. . *ma-an*]*-nu-um iḫ-bi-it*
9. [. . .] *tu-ka-al-li-mi-ma*
10. [. . .] *ta*??*-ra-a-mi-i-šu*
11. [. . .]*-iš la i-wi*
12. [. . .]*-an-šum ša-ma-i-ša-am*
13. [. . .]*-am-ma ki* ᵈUTU
14. [. . .] *la ša a i-ni-iš-šu*
15. [. . .] *ša-di e-re-ni-im*
16. [. . .] x *li-ṣí*
17. [. . .]*-ma ir-šu-ú-uš*
18. [. . .]*-a-an ši*? *bi mu* x?
19. [. . .] x *sa šu*
20. [. . .] *el-ki*
21. [. . .] *di i-li*
22. [. . .] *aš-šu*

---

iii 4. Note the use of the locative adverbial. Cf. [*uḫ*]*tannamu elušša* [x]*-nabu* 'blooming about her are . . .', VAS 10 215:5 (OB "Hymn to Nanaya for Samsuiluna").

iii 5. The verb is *ḫabātu* C (CAD Ḫ 11b) = *ḫapātu* (AHw 321b) 'to prevail, to triumph'; see discussion by F. R. Kraus, *RA* 69 (1975) 33. The labial is most probably voiced, as known writings are with -BI- or at syllable-end -VB, where one cannot differentiate between voiced/voiceless consonants in Akkadian.

iii 6. One could possibly restore at the beginning of the line [*labbat*]*u* or [*rabīt*]*u* or [*têlīt*]*u*.

iii 11. Cf. *awīliš īwe* 'he became a man', Gilg. P iii 25; [*iqbi ša irrar*]*u iwwi ṭiddiš* 'If he speaks, the one he curses shall turn to clay', OB "Epic of Anzu" 22; see M. Vogelzang, *Bin šar dadmē* (Groningen, 1988) 96.

iii 12. Perhaps the last word, *ša-ma-i-ša-am*, could be *šamû* 'heavens' with a terminative adverbial ending *-išam*, meaning 'toward heaven'. Cf. *īteli š*[*a-me*]*-e-ša* '(Anu) had gone up to heaven', Lambert-Millard, *Atra-ḫasīs*, 42 I 13; *īlû ša-me-e-ša* '(after Anu) had gone up to heaven', ibid., 17. The first could be a temporal adverbial.

iii 13. The beginning of this line must contain a verbal phrase. For a comparison with Šamaš in OB poetry, cf. *abrātišin palsāšim* (sic) *ki* ᵈ*Šamaš nišū*

4. [. . .] more than you.
5. [. . .] who has triumphed?
6. [The great one/lioness(?)] of all the gods
7. [. . .] more than you
8. [. . .] who has triumphed?
9. [. . .] you revealed.
10. [. . .] you loved him.
11. [Into . . .] he did not change.
12. . . . . for him, to the heavens
13. [He ascended(?)] and like Šamaš
14. [. . .] . . . in his eyes.
15. [. .] the mountains of cedar.
16. [. . .] let him go out.
17. . . . they desired him.
18. [. . .]. . . .
19. [. . .]. . . .
20. [. . .] upon you.
21. [. . .] of the gods.
22. [. . .]. . . . to him.

---

nūriški '(O Lady of all habitations) their peoples look on you(!) as on Šamaš, (thus, look) the people towards your light' (VAS 10 215:24; see von Soden, *ZA* 44 [1938] 32; and B. Groneberg, *WO* 12 [1981] 180, note to S. 44 Z. 3–5 [OB "Hymn to Nanaya for Samsuiluna"]); *šulmam u balāṭam ša kīma* ^{d}*Sin u* ^{d}*Šamaš darium ana qīštim liqīšūšum* 'may they give him as a gift health and life, which are eternal like the moon and the sun' (Samsuiluna C 148–52; and see in general Seux, *Epithètes*, 284 n. 115).

iii 15. The cedar is the tree most closely connected with Šamaš; cf. ^{d}Utu kur-šim-giš-erin-na-ta è-a-ni 'when Utu comes forth from the mountain perfumed by cedars' (CT 36 34 3 and 5); and epithets of Utu, giš-erin a-nag 'drinking water of cedar' (R. Kutscher, "Utu Prepares for Judgement," *Kramer AV* 307:10). The mountain of sunrise is referred to as the 'cedar mountain' (see W. Heimpel, "The Sun at Night and the Doors of Heaven," *JCS* 38 [1986] 144).

iii 17. The pronominal subject is either third-person plural or third-person singular subjunctive: 'they desired him' or 'whom she/he desired'. Of gods making requests of humans, cf. *ina šurrî Ea Damkina ana wardū⟨ti⟩šunu iršūninni* 'from the very first Ea and Damkina desired me for their service' (VAS 1 32 ii 8–9, "Ipiq-Ištar of Malgium").

23. [. . . *i*]*š-ku-nu*
24. [. . .]*tu-qá-i-šu*
25. [. . .] *ka-la-a-ma*
26. [. . . *ru-a*]*-mi*? *a-wi-li-im*
27. [. . .] *ri*

(break)

Column iv

(break)

1. [x x] *ma nu* [. . .]
2. *ḫu-um-ma-a-*[*ta* . . .] // *li-*⌈x⌉-[. . .]
3. *ba-al-lu-ki* [. . .]
4. *iš-ka-al-l*[*i-iš* . . .] // *i ni-*[*li-ik ga-ab-ba-ni*?]
5. *Na-ra-am-*^{d}EN.[ZU . . .]
6. *iš-ka-al-*⌈*li-iš i ni*⌉-[*li-ik*] // *ga-ab-*[*ba-ni*?]
7. *šar-ri ṣí-iḫ-tu-uk tu-ul-*[x x]
8. *ir-šu-tim bi-ni i-qá-ru li-ib-bi*
9. *Na-ra-am-*^{d}EN.ZU *ṣí-iḫ-tu-uk* // *li-it/da-tum*
10. *nu-ur-bi ša-am-mi di-ša-tim* // *te-it-te-i*
11. *ša a ta pu ur ru-ḫu-ú la-lu-ku-un*
12. *e-ru-ú ut-lu-ku-un ša-nu-ḫi-iš* // *ta-at-ti-la*

---

iv 3. For the perfume of this tree used to freshen beds, cf. *ša kanakāti munī ba-lu-ku-ú* 'my bed of incense is *ballukku*-perfumed' (Genouillac Kich B 472 i 8′).

iv 4. The *ešgallu* is a Sumerian loanword found in first-millennium Akkadian texts, meaning: (1) great temple, from its Sumerian etymology 'the great sanctuary/temple', (2) a name of the netherworld. In Sumerian texts, the èš 'sanctuary' is used in connection with most of the holy places of Sumer, while èš-gal is a much rarer lexeme. For instance, the Ebabbar itself is called an èš; cf. èš-é-babbar-ra (UET 6 90 rev. 15, "Hymn to Rim-Sin of Larsa"). As a proper noun, the reading of ÈŠ-gal as iri_{12}-gal for the temple of Inanna in Uruk has been suggested (cf. Å. Sjöberg, *Temple Hymns*, 90). It also occurs as a common noun: Sin-iddinam of Larsa builds for Nanna/Sin of Ur a ganunmaḫ referred to as an èš-gal-maḫ (see I. Kärki, *Die sumerischen und akkadischen Königsinschriften der altbabylonischen Zeit* [Helsinki, 1980] 58 Sid 2:14).

iv 7. For the reading *zi-iḫ-tu*, there are only two possible meanings: *siḫtu* 'invalid tablet' and *ṣīḫtu* 'delight, laughter'. For laughter as characteristic of love-making, cf. [*eli*] *ṣīḫātim u ruʾāmi tuštazna*[*n*] 'you are endowed with laughter and love-making' (VAS 10 215:7; see von Soden, ZA 44 [1938] 32; and B. Grone-

23. [. . .] they established.
24. [. . .] you waited for him.
25. [. . .] all(?).
26. [. . .] love of man.
27. [. . .]. . . .

(break)

Column iv

(break)

1. . . . .
2. You gave confidence. . . .
3. The incense. . . . .
4. To the temple, let us go, all of us!
5. Naram-Sin [and. . . .]
6. To the temple, let us go, all of us!
7. O king, your delight [. . . s you]
8. Create wise ones/wisdom, they summon my heart,
9. O Naram-Sin, your delight is offspring(?)
10. (With) the succulent portion of the abundant grass you are bedecked.
11. . . . . . Magic are your (pl.) charms.
12. Naked are your (pl.) loins, exhausted you slept.

---

berg, *WO* 12 [1981] note to S. 43 Z. 3 and 4, "Hymn to Nanaya"). Note that the city of Larsa is connected in the literary tradition with the theme of love: *ūm x ina Larsam ṣīḫātu izīqā* 'When (I was) in the city of Larsa, dalliance came wafting through the air' (KAR 158 vii 37, catalogue of cultic and secular love songs) and cf. the following incipit of another love song, *rīšī* ^{d}*Nanaja ina kirî Ebabbar ša tu-rammī* 'Rejoice O Nanaya in the garden of the Ebabbar which you love' (ibid., 38).

iv 8. Cf. the Old Babylonian euphemism for dying: *ištu* PN *ilūšu iqterû* 'after his gods have summoned PN'.

iv 10. Cf. *ina nurub šammē iraʾīši* 'he (Sin) pastured her (the cow) among the luscious grasses' (W. G. Lambert, *Studies Landsberger*, 286:23; see Römer, *Or* 54 [1984] 262:A16); the eagle *nurub šīri ište[neʾi]* 'sought the juicy part of the meat' (Kinnier-Wilson, *The Legend of Etana*, 56 MA I/B 20). For the term 'abundant grass', cf. also *arqū dešūtu* (VAB 4 160 A vii 11 [Nbk.]), as well as *dīšu*, meaning 'spring grass'. The verb could be from *têʾu* 'to be covered, bedecked', second-person perfect? N-stem?

iv 12. Cf. *ina utlīja nišī māt Šumerim u Akkadim ukīl* 'in my lap I hold the people of the land of Sumer and Akkad' (CH xlvii 49–52). The verb is *i/utulu* to sleep.

13. *e li be li ik nu ša-am-ša-ku-un* // *na-wi-ir-tum*
14. *ṭa-bu-um ṣí-il-la-ku-un* // *e-ri-im-ku-um ki-nu-um*
15. *ṣí-*⸢*ru*⸣*-um du-ur-ku-un* // *šu ta-ka-la-tim*
16. *Na-ra-am-*^{d}EN.ZU *ka-ap-pa-ku-un* // *ša-gi-ku-un*
17. *wa-ak-lum ki-ṣí-ir-ku-un*
18. *ul/uk!?-ku-mu ki-ma na-ap-ša-ti-ku-un*
19. [*d*]*an-nu-um sí-ik-ku-ru-um? da-*[*al-tu-um?*] // x [. . .]

(break)

Side c

Column v

(break)

1. (traces)
2. [. . .] *a ši-ma-tim-ma*
3. [*eklet*] *la na-wa-ri-im-ma ḫi-i-im* ⸢x⸣
4. [x (x) x] *an-nu-um pi-ti-a-at a-bu-ul-la-šu* // *e-re-bi-iš*
5. [x (x) x] *sé-ek-re-et-ma* // [(x) *m*]*u-ṣe-a-am la ti-šu*
6. [. . .] x *ma-a ḫi-ra-tum*
7. [*a*]*n* [. . .] *im-mu-ti-ši-in* // *ù ma-ri-ši-in*

---

iv 13. Whether *nawirtum* is a predicate adjective or a part of the nominal phrase, it is clear that it is in the feminine gender, and it describes the sun *šamšum.* A common epithet of Šamaš is *namrum* 'brilliant'. The referent behind the term *šamšu* 'sun' could be the god Šamaš, the king, or even a goddess. For the sun as an epithet of kings, see Seux, *Epithètes*, 283ff. For a goddess called the sun, cf. the "Hymn to Nanaya": *iltam šamaš nišīša* 'goddess, the sun of her people' (VAS 10 215:1).

iv 14. Cf. *ṣillam šuku*[*n elīja*] 'bestow (O Šamaš, your) protection on me' (Gilg. Y 220); *ṣillī ṭābum ana ālīja tariṣ* 'my (Hammurapi's) comforting protection is cast over my city' (CH xlvii 46–48). The second hemistich is more difficult, although it appears to be parallel to the first hemistich. The first word could be a noun *erimu* from the verb *arāmu* 'to cover' plus the second-person plural possessive suffix *-kun*, which the scribe has incorrectly written as the second-person singular dative suffix *-kum*, or it could be a verbal form from *arāmu* with the second-person singular dative. The change from plural to singular in one hemistich is peculiar.

iv 15. Cf. *dūr makî šarru* 'the king is the (protecting) wall of the weak' (ABL 1250 rev. 15 [NA]).

iv 16. The line may hold an allusion to the description of the netherworld, *labšūma kīma iṣṣūrī ṣubāt kappi* 'where they (the dead) are clad like birds in

13. Above, let.... your (pl.) shining sun.
14. Good is your (pl.) shade, your(!) cover is reliable.
15. August is your (pl.) (protecting) wall, it is of trustworthiness.
16. Naram-Sin, your (pl.) arms (are?) in your (pl.) shrine(?).
17. Faithful is your (pl.) army.
18. Taken away by force/wreathed in mist as your (pl.) lives.
19. Strong is the bolt, the door is....

(break)

Side c

Column v

(break)

2. [She who allots the?] fates—
3. [Darkness] which cannot be illuminated and brightened,
4. (imposed is) the punishment, opened is its gate for entering.
5. [...] is closed [...] It has no exit.
6. [...] .. Wives.
7. [...] from their husbands and their sons.

---

garments of wings', Gilg. VII iv 38; also CT 15 45:10 ("Descent of Ištar"); STT 28 iii 4 ("Nergal and Ereškigal").

iv 19. On the basis of the word-pair *sikkūrum* : *daltum* 'bolt' : 'door', we have restored *daltum* at the end of the line. Perhaps there is a reference here to Šamaš, who opens up the bolts of the doors of heaven.

v 2. For the decreeing of fates by the gods in royal inscriptions, cf. *RA* 61 41:27–30 (Samsuiluna B); *RA* 63 33:19 (Samsuiluna C).

v 3. In order to make sense out of this line, the last word has been emended to read *ḫilîm* from *ḫelû* 'to brighten'. Another possibility is *ḫi-i-im-ṭi-im* 'heat', but the nomens regens would then not be *ekletu*. For the restoration [*eklet*] *lā nawārim*, cf. *eklet lā nawārim... ana šīmtim lišīmšum* '(may the gods) determine for him a never-ending darkness as his fate' (CH xlix 68–72).

v 4. The word *erebiš* could be: the infinitive *erēbu* 'to enter', the noun *erebu* 'sunset' or the 'west', the noun *erbu/erebu* 'locust', or *erēb/pu* 'to become dark, dusky' with the addition of the terminative adverbial postposition *-iš*.

v 5. Etymologically, the correct form of the lexeme for 'exit' should be *mūṣāʾum*. However, there do occur rare examples in Old Babylonian of a byform *mūṣium*; cf. *mu-ṣe-e-am*, CT 47 6:2.

8. *ša-aṭ an-nu-um mu*-x-x-*ra-tum*
9. *ša-am-nam ù* ⸢x x x x x⸣ // *la ra*?-*ab-ba*!-*ni-im*
10. *ṣú-ur-ru ù na-ag-la-bu ku-ri-nu-ši-in*
11. *i-gu-ši-in di-ma-a-tum* // *ša-ma-an-ši-in ep-ru-um*
12. *iš-ta-ap-pu ki li-i-im* // *qè-re-eb* ⸢*um*⸣-*mi-ka*
13. *šar-ru-um iš-si/e* x x *ni-iš-šu* // *da tu ud ni mi*?? *ja*??
14. *i-ni-im-ma-am-ma-a-an la i-mu-ut-tu e-nu*
15. *i-ni-im-ma-am-ma-an la i-mu-ut-tu a-ši-ú*
16. *i-ni-im-ma-am-ma-an la i-mu-tu-ni-im*
17. *ma-al-ku na-i-lu-ut ú-zi-x-ru*
18. [x]-*ši-da/it-tum wa-ši-bu-ut wa*-x-[. . .]
19. [. . .] *i na ab ru* [. . .]

(break)

Column vi

(break)

1. *be-lí* [. . .] // *k*[*a* . . .]
2. *na-wi-ru-u*[*m* . . .]
3. *wa-ar-ḫu-um* x(*dam*?)-[. . .] // *ik li šum mi ik* [. . .]
4. *Na-ra-am*-^{d}EN.ZU *im*?? *ra*? x [. . .]
5. *wa-ar-ḫu-um tu-um*-[. . .] // *ik li* [*šum mi ik* . . .]
6. *mi is*?/*šu*?/*ki i*? *ḫu-uz*? *i* ⸢x⸣ [. . .] // x x *a-na ši-na-ši*-[*im* . . .]
7. *ga-ni-nu-um wa* ⸢*ar*? x x⸣ [. . .]
8. *Na-ra-am*-^{d}EN.ZU *ba-al-ṭam* [. . .] // *ši-na* [x (x)] *mu* [. . .]
9. *ga-ni-nu-um* x [x] *i ma*(?) [. . .]
10. *qú-ra-du*!-*um*? [x (x)] *ša ra/at*? [. . .]

---

v 9. This line may express the custom of not anointing oneself during the mourning period.

v 10. The flint knives and razor blades were used for slashing oneself in mourning ceremonies. The predicate noun could be *šurinnu* 'symbol', *šūrīnu* 'eyebrows', or *kurinnu* 'necklace, neckguard'.

v 11. According to a suggestion by W. G. Lambert, the first word is taken as a nominal formation from the verb *eqû* 'to daub (eyes) with medicine or cosmetics', referring to eye make-up, such as mascara. Other possibilities include: (a) *igu*, a Sumerian loanword from igi 'eye', (b) *igû* B 'prince', (c) *ikku* 'temper' with -g- for /kk/, (d) *egû* 'antimony paste'. The second word can either be from *dimātu* 'tears' or *dimmatu* 'moaning lamentation' (cf. Lambert-Millard, *Atra-ḫasīs*, 94 III iii 47). Of the various possible combinations, eye and eye make-up

8. Borne is the guilt, the . . . -females
9. with oil and . . . they are not softened(?).
10. Flint knives and razor blades will be their necklaces.
11. Their eye make-up will be tears. Their oil will be dust.
12. The bowels of your (masc. sg.) mother cry out like a bull.
13. The king cried out in his misery from suffering(??).
14. Alas, will they not die, the *ēnu*-priests?
15. Alas, will they not die, the nobles?
16. Alas, will they not die?
17. The rulers who sleep. . . .
18. . . those who dwell in [. . .].
19. [. . .] . . . . [. . .]

(break)

Column vi

(break)

1. My lord. . . .
2. Shining one. . . .
3. The moon. . . .
4. Naram-Sin . . .
5. The moon. . . .
6. . . . . to them (fem.) . . . .
7. The store house / (burial) chamber. . . .
8. The living Naram-Sin. . . . they (fem.). . . .
9. The store house / (burial) chamber. . . .
10. The Hero(?). . . .

---

including antimony paste goes with *dimātu* 'tears', while 'temper' goes together with lamentations. All these solutions have obvious problems.

v 12. Cf. *mātum kīma liʾi išappu* 'the land is bellowing like a bull' (Lambert-Millard, *Atra-ḫasīs*, 66 I 354; 72 II i 3; 94 III iii 15); (the sufferer brays like the weaned foal of a donkey) *iš-⌜ta⌝-pu maḫar ili*[*m*] 'he has got loud in the god's presence' (Lambert, "The Babylonian 'Man and his God,'" *Studies Reiner*, 190:7). The image of the mother weeping over a slain king is found in Sumerian (e.g., "Death of Ur-Nammu," lines 15–16) and in Akkadian (UET 395 rev. 12). For bovine noises (and *šapû*) as figures of human grief, see also the image of Ninsiskurra bellowing like a cow (Lambert, "A New Babylonian Descent to the Netherworld," *Studies Moran*, 292–93 rev. 12, 21).

v 14ff. The first word is *inimma*, the interjection 'alas', plus *man*, the particle denoting irrealis.

11. *id* ⌜x-x-x⌝ *ru* [. . .]
12. *a i ki*? ⌜x (x)⌝ *šum* [. . .]
13. *ik* x *la ka* x[. . .]
14. *la-ab-šu* ⌜x x⌝ [. . .]
15. *be-lí iš*? *si*? ⌜x⌝ [. . .]
16. ⌜x⌝ [. . .]
(break)

Side d

Column vii
(break)
1. [. . .] *it/da*
2. [. . .] *da* ⌜x⌝ *am*
3. [. . .]-*am ki-ib-ri-ka*
4. [. . . *it-*]*ta-am-ḫa-ar-šum*
5. [*a-gu-*]*úḫ*? *šu-mi-li-ša ki qá-ad-mi-im*
6. *im*?-*nu*?-*um* U.DAR *ka-ak*?-*ka*?-*bi* // *šu-ku-un* ⌜*šu*⌝-*ṣí-šum*
7. *na-pi-iḫ-ta-am di-*[*i*]*t-pa-ar* // *tu-qum-ta-am*
8. *bu-ul-li a-na-na-tim šu-up-pi* // *ri-ig-ma-*[*tim*]
9. (er.?) *i-ša-ar-šum i-ni-a* [*irtam* . .]
10. *ur*!?-*ḫi-iš la ka* x x [. . .]
(traces of 3? more lines)

---

vii 5. The *aguḫḫu* is a piece of apparel worn by the gods, especially Ištar.

vii 7. This verb is a G stem related to the D stems of the verbs *dubburu*, *duppuru*, *ṭuppuru* (see Moran, *JCS* 33 [1981] 44–47). On p. 44 n. 3, Moran disposes of the few examples of the G stem of the verb *dapāru* (CAD D, 'to become sated') and defines the verb 'to become strong, aggressive'. The latter meaning does not fit the present context, where it is with *bullû*, *šuppû*. Thus one must postulate that there exists a G stem of the verb *dubburu* 'to drive away, go away' with similar meaning.

11. ....
12. ....
13. ....
14. They are dressed....
15. My lord....
16. ....

(break)

Side d

Column vii

(break)

1. ....
2. ....
3. .... the ... of your banks
4. .... has been received for him
5. The sash of her left like a god.
6. Place on the right Ištar of the star, go out for him!
7. Drive away conflagration, warfare!
8. Extinguish battles, silence battle-cries!
9. It is right/appropriate for him, let us turn the chest/withdraw(??)
10. Quickly....

(break)

---

vii 8. These two lines are very similar to lines found in the bilingual "Hymn to Hammurapi," as well as in the Code. Cf. giš-giš-lá te-en-te-en sùḫ-saḫ$_4$ si-si-a : *mubelli tuqmātim mušeppi saḫmašātim* '(Hammurapi) who makes an end to wars, he who silences turmoil' (CT 21 42 iv 10–11 [= LIH 60]) and *qablātim ubelli* 'I put an end to wars' (CH xlvii 32); *tēšî lā šuppîm* 'disorder that cannot be suppressed' (a curse of Enlil; CH xlix 59).

Fragments

A

(remains of traces of one sign per line and possibly the lower edge of the prism at the bottom of the fragment)

B

1. [x (x)] *za*? *am* [. . .]
2. [x (x)] *lu ut* x [. . .]
3. [x (x)] *ki* ? *ib*/*is*? *ku*/*ma* [. . .]

(lower edge of prism)

C

Column i′

1. [. . .] *i da*? x x *gi* ?
2. [. . .] *e-wi-ma*
3. [. . .] x *ù* ^{d}*En-líl*
4. [. . .] *an*
5. [. . .] x -*ja*

Column ii′

1. *šar-ri*? *ša*? *ma*? [. . .]
2. *mi-iš-ša-am* x [. . .] // *ša te ru z*[*i* . . .]
3. ? *Na-ra-am*-^{d}EN.ZU(??) x [. . .]
4. *mi-iš*-[. . .]

D

1. x *za ak*/*ḫar ši šu*
2. x *ga ba mi im*
3. [. . .] *li-bi-iš*

Chapter 9

The Great Revolt against Naram-Sin

This tale comes down to us in both historical and literary texts. The historical evidence is found in Old Babylonian copies of the inscriptions on the royal monuments set up by Naram-Sin in the Ekur at Nippur. There are two duplicate but fragmentary manuscripts: (a) N 3539 + PBS 5 37 (+) PBS 5 36[1] and (b) BT 1.[2] Further allusions to the revolt are scattered in various other royal inscriptions.

The literary legend is extant in four different versions: (1) an Old Akkadian exercise tablet (text **15**), (2) two Old Babylonian excerpt tablets containing a version based closely on the historical descriptions (texts **16A**, **16B**), (3) one incomplete Old Babylonian recension (text **17**), and (4) an Old Babylonian excerpt tablet (text **19**), which has points in common with both texts **16** and **18** but which concludes with a curse formula of the type found in votive inscriptions.

This is the first long list of characters in this corpus, with no unnamed opponents; if anything, there is a plethora of characters. Naram-Sin stands alone against his opponents. It is true that he has an army but there is no aide-de-camp. Unlike Sargon, he does not ask the advice and assistance of his subordinates before he hazards them and himself in battle. He is placed above them, and in text **19** he is put on the level of the divine, which reminds us of his title *il mātim* 'god of the land' in text **12**. His army is numbered in the tens and hundreds of thousands in text **17**. The opponents are many but deserve the retribution that Naram-Sin is dispensing. They are not only disloyal but they have broken their oath; they have returned evil for good. In one text, **17**, for the first time an enemy appears who is not flesh and blood—the inhuman adversary.

[1] Published by P. Michalowski, "New Sources Concerning the Reign of Naram-Sin," *JCS* 32 (1980) 234ff.

[2] Published by R. Kutscher, *The Brockmon Tablets at the University of Haifa: Royal Inscriptions* (Haifa, 1989) 13–48. In the following, my transliteration of the text BT 1 is based on the copy and transliteration made by Aage Westenholz and thus will not agree in every detail with that given by R. Kutscher. Further, both manuscripts have been republished in *aK* 226–43, "Narāmsîn C 1."

Further, Naram-Sin's piety toward his divine allies is portrayed. Texts **16B** and **19** both contain an invocation of the gods: Ištar, Ilaba, Šullat and Ḫaniš, Šamaš and Ūmšum, while text **22** ("Naram-Sin and the Enemy Hordes") contains an invocation of the gods Ištar, Ilaba, Zababa, Annunītum, Šullat, Ḫaniš, and Šamaš. However, at no point in the narrative does any of these gods take any action. The invocation by Naram-Sin reflects the religious piety of the hero.

The action of the narratives concerns the rebellion against Naram-Sin, possibly at the time of his coming to power or more probably in the wake of his undertaking the rebuilding of the Ekur, the action that Sumerian tradition holds responsible for his downfall. This tale recounts the gathering of the city-states of the northern heartland of the land of Akkade: Kiš(i), Kutha, Tiwa, Wurumu, Kazallu, Giritab, Apiak, Ibrat, Dilbat, and Sippar and the crowning of Ipḫur-Kiši of Kiš(i) to be king over them. A separate rebellion begins under Lugal-Anne of Ur according to **15** and of Uruk according to **16**, who joins in the coalition under Ipḫur-Kiši and brings along with him the states of the Sumerian south. The excerpt texts **15** and **16** end at this intriguing point.

The setting of the assembly and the coronation of Ipḫur-Kiši of Kiš(i) is described in texts **16A** and **16B** in accordance with the geographical setting of the battle in the royal inscriptions of Naram-Sin. At the conclusion of **16B**, there is a list of kings of outlying provinces of the Akkadian empire. In **17** is the tale of the uprising of these kings under Gula-AN, king of Gutium. Under Gula-AN are seventeen kings, whose territories extend from Kaniš in the northwest to Elam in the southeast. There are incomplete descriptions of battles, after which Naram-Sin magnanimously gives back to Gula-AN his freedom, which he misuses. A vivid description of a bloody battle between the two adversaries is given, in which Gula-AN seems to be the victor. The text ends with a final battle at the walls of Akkade, at which point the text breaks off. This text has four points in common with the texts of chapter 10, "Naram-Sin and the Enemy Hordes": (a) a description of an enemy who is not flesh and blood, (b) the Amanus and the Silver Mountains as the location from which the enemy arises in final battle, (c) the number of allied kings, seventeen, who join the enemy hordes on their devastating march, and (d) the numbering of the army forces. Text **18** contains a Hittite version that also offers a list of seventeen rebellious kings. Both lists of kings seem to go back to the same oral tradition.[3]

In text **19** we have an excerpt concerning the nine battles, after each of which Naram-Sin shows his magnanimity by giving his enemies their freedom, and then the text breaks off as Naram-Sin prepares to wage his tenth battle. These nine battles are historically documented in original Old Akkadian inscriptions contemporary with the events and are there related to the crushing of the revolt: (a) five door sockets dedicated to Naram-Sin,[4] (b) an inscription on

[3] See my forthcoming article, "Relations between Mesopotamia and Anatolia in the Age of the Sargonic Kings," *XXXIV Uluslararsi Assiriyuloji Kongresi* (Istanbul, 1987), in press.

[4] See YOS 1 10 = *aK* 102–3, "Narāmsîn A 1."

the base of a copper statue from Bāseṭkī,[5] and (c) an inscription on the base of a diorite statue from Susa.[6] Further evidence is found in Old Babylonian copies of an inscription on a royal monument set up by Naram-Sin in the Ekur at Nippur.[7]

These compositions have not only the outward form of a royal inscription but also the diction found in them. There is use of certain formulas known from the royal inscriptions. Reflecting the narrative style of the period, the third-millennium text is written in the third person, while second-millennium and later texts are characterized by first-person narration. In these texts, the overt narrator Naram-Sin relates his exploits for the edification of his implied audience, his people and/or future rulers. In first-person narration, the protagonist as narrator presents us with a record of the speech of a single character, Naram-Sin. This discourse mode of first-person narration offers a one-sided view of the events from the speaker's perspective. There is no dialogue as in the previous texts. Poetic diction is evident in only one of these texts, text **17**.

In all these texts, there are the underlying themes of loyalty and honor. The enemies have acted ignobly: they have returned evil for good. Although Sargon freed the Kišites from the yoke of Uruk, they turned traitor to his descendant. Amnesty was given to the Gutian king in text **17**, and nine times Naram-Sin freed the rebels after they revolted in text **19**, yet they dealt falsely with him.

15
The Old Akkadian Exercise

Introduction

This fragment of a student's poor exercise is the only extant proof that literary works were composed on the theme of contemporary historical events.[8] The triumph of Naram-Sin over the rebellious city-states was probably celebrated with pomp and circumstance. News of the parading of the three rebel kings in fetters through the streets of Nippur accompanied by a royal proclamation may have reached the ends of the far-flung provinces. In the city of Ešnunna, situated in the Diyala Valley, which was an essential part of the Akkadian heartland, a teacher made this subject the topic of an assignment of a written composition for a student.

[5] *Sumer* 32 (1976) 63–75 = *aK* 81–83, "Narāmsîn 1."

[6] Sb 52; MDP 6 pl. 1 no. 1 = *aK* 89–90, "Narāmsîn 3."

[7] N 202+ ii, *JCS* 32 (1980) 244; and BT 1 rev. v′ = *aK* 226–43, "Narāmsîn C 1."

[8] In the view of B. Foster, this text is a Sargonic student's copy of a genuine inscription (*ARRIM* 8 [1990] 44 n. 14). His proposal has been followed by B. Kienast in his publication, *aK* 272–73, "Narāmsîn C 15," and by Frayne (*JAOS* 112 [1992] 631).

In this composition, the events covered are the coronation of Ipḫur-Kiši by the people of Kiš(i) (lines 1–4) and the arrival of his ally Lugal-Anne of Ur (lines 5–7) with his confederate, the unnamed king of Uruk (lines 8–12).

As stated above, the discourse mode of this third-millennium composition is that of third-person narration. For similar surface structure in both contemporary royal inscriptions and later literary works, see philological notes to lines 1–4.

General Observations

The text is recorded on the obverse of a single-column Old Akkadian tablet. It is subdivided into sections with rulings, and the whole composition has been crossed out. On the reverse and the edges of the tablet are stray wedges and a few signs (see copy, p. 401).[9]

Circumstances of Discovery

The archaeological context within which this text was found is well known; it was found outside a private house in Ešnunna, evidently thrown out as refuse in the area between houses XXX and XXXI (H 18:14, level IVb).[10]

[9] A. Westenholz, *AfO* 25 (1974–77) 96.
[10] Ibid.; OIP 88, pl. 27.

Transcription

1. [*in* KIŠ.KI(?)]
2. [ÙKU *gul-la*(?)-]*zi-in*

Philological and Textual Notes

1–4. In this section, it seems best to see some description of the raising of Ipḫur-Kiši as rebel king of Kiš(i) in accord with the Old Babylonian texts **16A**:13–16 and **16B**:24–28:

16A:13–15 *birīt* GN_1 *u* GN_2 *ina* GN_3 *birīt* GN_4 *Kiši ipḫurma* ⟨*Ipḫur*⟩-*Kiši* . . .
16B:14–27 *birīt* GN_1 GN_2 *ina* GN_3 *birīt* GN_4 *Kiši ipḫurma Ipḫur-Kiši* . . .

16A:16 *ana* ⟨NAM⟩.LUGAL *iš-šu-ni-*[*i*]*š-šu*
16B:28 *ana ša*[*r*]*-ru-tim iš-šu-ma*

So also begins the copy of the royal inscription, BT 1 (= *aK* 226–27, "Narāmsîn C 1") obverse col. i:

[*in* KIŠ.KI]
⸢*Ip-ḫur*⸣-KIŠ
sar-ru$_x$(URU×A)-*zum*
i-se$_{11}$-*ù*

Orthography and Language

This school text was produced as an exercise by a very poor student. One should bear in mind that this is a discarded, crossed-out student exercise that must have contained some errors. One possible error is the writing of the third-feminine plural suffix as *-zi-in* in place of the correct *-si-in*, in line 2. Another seems to be the repetition in lines 10–11 of one phrase twice in the attempt to write it correctly.

In general, see the discussion of the text by Thorkild Jacobsen, "Ipḫur-Kīshi and His Times," *AfO* 26 (1978–79) 1-3.

Notes on the Transliteration System

The following transliteration system uses the more common values for the cuneiform signs rather than the innovations created to fit Old Akkadian, thus preferring *se*$_{11}$ rather than *śé* (Borger, *Zeichenliste*, no. 592).

Manuscripts

Ešnunna

TA 1931-729 = Gelb, MAD 1 172 (transliteration) = A. Westenholz, *AfO* 25 (1974–77) 97 (copy) (see new copy and photographs, pp. 400–401).

Translation

1. [In the city of Kiš(i)(?),]
2. [all of] its [people(?)]

ù
in UNUG.KI
Amar-gírid(KIŠ×GÁNA *tenû*)
sar-ru$_x$(URU×A)*-zum-ma*
i-se$_{11}$*-ù*

Presumably, the text should be translated something like this: '[When the four corners of the world all rebelled against him, in Kiš(i)] they raised Ipḫur-Kiši to kingship and in Uruk, they raised Amar-girida likewise to kingship'.

1. In accordance with the Old Akkadian and Old Babylonian versions, this line should contain the location of the event or possibly the subject of the verb.

2. On the basis of *ana šarrūtim* in the Old Babylonian versions, we would like to restore a similar phrase in this line (but note the Old Akkadian idiom in line 10, *śarrūssum*). A restoration such as [*ana sar-ri*]*-zi-in* for 'their king' is impossible, since the third-person feminine plural suffix is written *-si-in* (cf.

3. ⌜*Ip-ḫur*⌝-KIŠ.KI
4. [*a*]-*pu-na na-se*$_{11}$-*nim*

---

5. [*I*]*p-ḫur*-KIŠ.KI
6. [*u*]-*sá-lí-ma Lugal-An-né*
7. *ig-ru-sa-am* LUGAL // (er.) ŠEŠ.AB.KI

---

8. ⌜*ù*⌝ *la ma-al-ku*[*m*]

MAD 2^2 130 nn. 20 and 21). The ZI sign may represent the assimilation of the dental and the sibilant of the suffix. Thus, if we assume that line 1 contains the subject of the sentence, possibly the citizens of Kiš(i), then perhaps a word such as *kullassin* 'all of them', in apposition to the subject, is a likely restoration.

4. The verb *našû* is found in this section in the Old Babylonian texts. Likewise, it is found in the original royal inscription from Bāseṭkī i 16–19 (*Sumer* 32 [1976] 63–75 = *aK* 81–83, "Narāmsîn 1"): *ù* LUGAL-*rí šu-ut i-se*$_{11}$-*nim i-ik-mi* 'and took captive the kings which they had raised'. For this interpretation, see W. Farber, *Or* N.S. 52 (1983) 68–69 and note to lines 17–18; note that H. Hirsch prefers to see in *i-se*$_{11}$-*nim* a genitive substantive (*AfO* 29 [1983–84) 59–60 and n. 1). On the basis of these parallels, despite the lack of the plural morpheme ⟨*ū*⟩, *na-se*$_{11}$-*nim* is translated 'they raised'. A similar form of the verb is found in the Naram-Sin royal inscription (UET 1 275 ii 23 = *aK* 256:52–55, "Narāmsîn C 5"): GIŠ.ÍL *Ìl-a-ba*$_4$ *ì-lí-su na-se*$_{11}$-*nim* 'they (the people whom Dagan gave into the hands of Naram-Sin) bear the corvée-basket of Ilaba, his god'; note that CAD G *gamāru* renders this line in quite a different manner: GIŠ.ÍL *Ìl-a-ba*$_4$ *ì-lí-su Na-ab*(sic)-NUM *ù A-ma-nam sa-tu* GIŠ.ERIN *i-ig-mu-ur* 'the . . . -weapon of DN, his personal god, annihilated the cedar mountains, Lebanon and Amanus'. The second sign of *na-ab-nim* is copied as ÁB and Sollberger's collations agree with that reading (UET 8 32). In both cases it has been said that the verb shows the assimilation or dropping of the verbal plural morpheme -*ū*-/-*ā*-. There are Old Akkadian examples of *našû* in which the plural morpheme is written; cf. *li-se*$_{11}$-*ù-ni-kum-ma* (*JRAS* 1932 296:19). Most scholars insert the missing vowel into the text; cf. Farber, *Or* N.S. 52, 68, *i-se*$_{11}$-⟨*ù*⟩-*nim*. Since this form of the verb is found in at least two texts in a context suggesting plural forms, we have to accept the form as it stands.

5–7. After Ipḫur-Kiši's successful insurrection, Lugal-Anne joined the rebellion. In our text, he is called king of Ur. The tradition that he is king of Uruk is dependent on the Old Babylonian text **16B**:36, an obviously unreliable tradition, since the other two kings listed in lines 36–38 are unknown. As to the supposed reference to Lugal-Anne by Enḫeduanna in her song "The Exaltation of Inanna," there are three possible interpretations of lines 74–77: (1) Hallo and van Dijk's rendition (*The Exaltation of Inanna* [New Haven, 1968] 25) has Enḫeduanna refer to the person Lugal-Anne in lines 74 and 77; (2) Jacobsen's rendition (*AfO* 26 11 and n. 40) has Enḫeduanna refer to the person Lugal-Anne in

3. Ipḫur-Kiši
4. [in]deed, they raised.

---

5. Ipḫur-Kiši
6. [made] an alliance and Lugal-Anne
7. came, the king of Ur.

---

8. And that non-(entity of a) king,

---

line 74 and to the kingship of heaven in line 77; while (3) Kramer's translation (ANET^3 581) renders the words lugal an-ne in both lines as a common noun 'king of heaven / kingship of heaven'. Since Naram-Sin in BT 1 mentions another candidate, Amar-girida, for the throne of Uruk (see above), we should believe the testimony of this Old Akkadian text over the Old Babylonian text and accept that Lugal-Anne was king of Ur. Thus we have three kings: Ipḫur-Kiši of Kiš(i), Lugal-Anne of Ur, and Amar-girida of Uruk, who joined together in rebellion against Naram-Sin. According to the door sockets of Naram-Sin that refer to his victory, there is mention of his capture of three kings: *iśtum taʾhāzī śunūti yišʾaru u śarrīśunu 3 yikmīma maḫriś Enlil yuśaʾrib* 'after he was victorious in these battles, then he took captive their three kings and brought them before Enlil' (YOS 1 10:9–18 = *aK* 102:9–18 "Narāmsîn A 1").

6. Suggestions for the verb in this line are: (1) [*i*]-*se*$_{11}$-*ì* 'he sought', from the verb *šeʾû*, as Jacobsen has understood it; (2) [*na*]-*se*$_{11}$-*ni-ma* 'he was raised', subjunctive of the verb *našû*, as in line 4, or less probable, 'they raised', with the elision of the vowel; (3) [*u*]-*se*$_{11}$-*lí-ma* 'he brought up', from the verb *elû*; (4) [*i*]-*se*$_{11}$-*ni-ma* 'of . . . ', a noun in the genitive, as in the Hirsch interpretation of the Bāseṭkī inscription above (note to line 4); (5) according to the new copy (see p. 401), the space for the broken sign at the beginning of the line is very limited: there is hardly room for *i-* or *na-*, only for *u-*. Furthermore, the first visible sign can be either DI or SIG. Thus a new possibility would be to read [*u*]-*sá-lí-ma* = *yuśallim-ma* 'he made an alliance' (suggestion of A. Westenholz).

7. For the verb *garāšu* 'to come', cf. Jacobsen, 3 and compare, in a different context:

> (Naram-Sin, the great, heard this and)
> *iš-t*[*um*] KIŠ.KI *da-i*[*s-su*] *ig-r*[*u-us*]-*m*[*a*]
> he hurried from Kiš(i) to him (and)
> (the two joined battle and fought each other) BT 1 v 32′–35′

Note the attempt to delimit the meaning of this verb to 'sexuellen Umgang haben' by B. Groneberg (*UF* 6 [1974] 66 n. 4), quoting our example.

8–11. I find it difficult to accept Prof. Jacobsen's interpretation of this text as a royal hymn; its proof lies in this quatrain. I would prefer to see these lines as describing the battle or preparations for it.

9. [*u*]*r-ki-um i-dì-iš-s*[*u*]
10. [*s*]*ar-ru*$_x$(URU×A)-*uz-zum ù s*[*u-x*]
11. (er.)-*un* (space) *su*-[x]
12. *iš-ku*-(er.)-*un*

---

13. *du*-[. . .]
14. *u-rí*-[*id* . . .]
15. BALA *a* [. . .] // [. . .]

---

9. The form *urkīum* 'later' (so Jacobsen) is not good Old Akkadian. It is attested in Ur III and in Assyrian dialects, beginning with Old Assyrian. The form *warkīum* is the expected Old Akkadian form; see MAD 3 64 sub $^{ʾ}{}_6$RK, and AHw 1470. Instead, we could take *urkīum* as 'the Urukian', the unnamed leader of Uruk, whom we know from BT 1 as Amar-girida. In that text, mention is made several times of 'the Kišite', written KIS.KI-*ši-um*. Likewise, in the Old Babylonian text, Ipḫur-Kiši is referred to as 'the Kišite', *Ki-iš*-[*šu*]-*ú-u*[*m*.K]I **16A**:15; LÚ.KIŠ.KI **16B**:27. Of course, it is not certain that the first sign in line 9 is really UR. It could be MA, or possibly NE, GIŠ, or several other signs.

The word *i-ti-iš-su* could be either a noun in terminative locative or a verb. If it is a verb, *i-dì-iš-su* might be understood as *idīš* + *śu* 'he trampled (*diāšu*) him'.

10. The form *sar-ru*$_x$-*uz-zum* is composed of *śarrūt* + *śum*, in which -*śum* is a poorly understood morpheme (see GAG §67g). It has been transcribed as if the -*zum* was a simple mistake for the possessive suffix -*śu* with the reading -*śu*$_{14}$ (BT 1 i 2′, 7′; *aK* 226:14, 19, "Narāmsîn C 1"; *aK* 272:11, "Narāmsîn C 15"). The various interpretations of this morpheme are: (1) combination of deictic element /š/ and the locative adverbial suffix -*um* forming adverbials of time and space (B. Groneberg, *AfO* 26 [1978–79] 17); (2) an allomorph of the morpheme -*išam* (D. Frayne, *BiOr* 48 [1991] 385); (3) a combination of the terminative and locative adverbial postpositions -*iš* and -*um* (D. Frayne, *JAOS* 112 [1992] 630). There seems to be a consensus on the understanding of the phrase as 'to kingship' (A. Westenholz *apud* Frayne, *BiOr* 48 [1991] 385). The same form occurs

9. the Urukian, at his side(?)
10. for kingship and . . .

11–12. He established.

---

13. .[. . .]
14. he descen[ded (??) . . .]
15. reign [. . .].

---

in BT 1 i, quoted above. There are two other attestations of this composite morpheme in Old Akkadian: *e-tá-ra-ab sa-tu-šum* 'he entered into the mountain' (BT 3 i 12′; cf. the idiom *šadâšu emēdu*) and *ūmśum* (see discussion sub **16B**:21–22). After the conjunction *ù*, there is probably one object beginning with *su-* at the end of this line, and it would be appropriate if it could be a substantive referring to battle.

11–12. In these two lines, it is probable that the student tried twice to write *su-*[. . . .] *iš-ku-un*, each time with mistakes.

13–15. These lines are extremely fragmentary and no connected sense can be made of them.

14. The first sign on the line is U; the horizontal before it in the copy is one of the stray wedges on the edge. It is this stray horizontal wedge that led Gelb to read BE (MAD 1 92)

15. The word BALA occurs only in PN's in Old Akkadian texts, according to MAD 3^2 213–14. For this word, it is perhaps best to look at its myriad meanings in Sumerian (see PSD B 67ff.). When the word means 'reign', it can refer to the reign of a person or of a city. Among its rarer meanings, bala-2-šè 'for the second . . . ' could also fit the context of this line. Cf. (Naram-Sin pursued Ipḫur-Kiši to Kiš(i)) *u al lēti Kiši bābi Ninkar taʾḫāzam yišniāma yiśkunāma* [*yitt*]*aḫzāma* 'and near (lit. on the cheek of) Kiš(i), at the gate of Ninkar, the two of them set down to battle a second time, and they fought one another' (BT 1 iii 18′–23′).

16
The Old Babylonian Excerpt Versions

The following two texts, despite their near identity in subject matter, differ in narrative content and in the surface structure of their discourses. As far as content is concerned, text **16A** treats only the revolt of the northern cities from the so-called Akkadian area. There is no apparent mention of the foreign provinces. Both refer to the past history of the conflict during the times of Sargon and mention his demonstration of mercy to the people of Kiš(i) by giving them "freedom," shaving off their slavemarks, and breaking their shackles. In his inscriptions Sargon states: sar-um-GI lugal kalam-ma-ke$_4$ Kiši^{ki} ki-bi bí-gi$_4$ uru-bi ki-gub e-na-ba // *sar-ru-*GI LUGAL KALAM.MA.KI KIŠ.KI *a-ša-rí-su i-ni* URU.KI-*lam u-sá-ḫi-su-ni* 'He restored(!?) Kiš(i) to its place and caused those two(?) to hold the city (or: let them settle the city?)' (PBS 5 34 + PBS 15 41 iii 27–34 // iv 28–35; *aK* 159:95–102, "Sargon C 1"). Note that the motif of shaving the heads occurs in text BT 1 at the beginning of col. ii 'the man of Kiš(i) gouged out their eyes and shaved their heads'. Both texts include the catalogue of cities and text **16B** also has a catalogue of kings. It is possible that the latter is added to draw a picture of kings coming from far and wide to witness the coronation of the king of Kiš(i).

The story segments are:

a. the dedication to Enlil and Ilaba (**16B**:1);
b. the introduction of Naram-Sin with his various epithets (**16B**:2–9);
c. the introduction of the rebellion, including the list of the cities of the northern coalition (**16A**:1–4, **16B**:10–15);
d. a description of the state of affairs during the reign of Sargon (**16A**:5–11, **16B**:16–20);
e. the coronation of Ipḫur-Kiši of Kiš(i) (**16A**:12–16, **16B**:21–28);
f. the catalogue of the kings of the foreign provinces and of the southern coalition (**16B**:29–38);
g. description of nine battles(?) (**16A** rev.).

The surface structure of the discourses takes the form of a royal inscription of the Old Akkadian kings. In its introduction, text **16B** reproduces the formula found in one Old Akkadian royal inscription, namely that of N 3539 + PBS 5 37 (+) PBS 5 36 (*aK* 226–43 "Narāmsîn C 1"). In particular, these texts have the form of a dedicatory inscription.[11] Note van Driel's analysis of the Old Akkadian royal inscriptions as dedicatory inscriptions.[12] However, the form posed difficulties where an account of the past was forced into it. The composer of text

[11] Cf. discussion by A. Poebel, "The 'Schachtelsatz' Construction of the Narām-Sîn Text *RA* XVI 157f.," *Miscellaneous Studies* (AS 14; Chicago, 1947) 23–42.

[12] G. van Driel, "On 'Standard' and 'Triumphal' Inscriptions," *Symbolae Böhl*, 99–106.

16A was most successful in his use of the adverbial *inūmīšūma* but the writer of text **16B** did not manage as well in his attempt to employ the parallel *inūma . . . inūmīšūma*. In place of referring to action simultaneous or subsequent to the first clause, the *inūmīšūma* clause should have referred to action prior to the first clause. Further, these texts are written in the first person, addressing their audience directly. As stated above, the royal inscriptions of the third millennium were couched in the third person, while the royal inscriptions of the second millennium were written in the first person. Moreover, these texts lack the poetic diction exhibited in many other texts in this corpus and perhaps should be considered more as prose sagas than as poetic tales. Note that in text **16A** there is written enjambement in that the clauses run over the ends of the lines of texts and also end in the middle of lines.

The similarity and occasional identity of the extant portions of texts **16A** and **16B** have been demonstrated by Grayson and Sollberger; in this edition, the texts are presented separately in order to display their divergences. The same oral traditions are reflected in these two texts, but their written forms clearly demonstrate the lack of any written contact.

16A
Mari Version

Introduction

Circumstances of Discovery

The archaeological context of the finding of this tablet is not as clear as one could wish. It was discovered during the fifth campaign at Mari in 1937.[13] Apparently it was lying in room 108 on the west side of court 106 of the palace among a miscellaneous assortment of texts: incantations, texts in Hurrian, liver models, a fragmentary royal inscription, and administrative texts. Although there were several rebuildings of the room, the levels to which the various texts belong are unknown. Thus we are left with a mixed archive without clear archaeological strata to which to assign the different texts, unless the collection consisted of a group of tablets thrown hastily into storage.

General Observations

The composition is a one-column text whose upper half is preserved, with seventeen lines extant on the obverse and five lines extant on the reverse. There

[13] A. Parrot, "Les Fouilles de Mari: Cinquième campagne (automne 1937)," *Syria* 20 (1939) 20; G. Dossin, "Les Archives economiques du palais de Mari," *Syria* 20 (1939) 99; Parrot, *MAM II: Le Palais architecture* (Paris, 1958) 102.

are probably about thirty lines missing. The copy is obviously unfinished; not only does it stop in the middle of a line, but also no line division follows the final line. Note the layout of the signs along the crack in the center of the tablet in the new photograph made by the Mari mission, which does not correlate with the published copy by Grayson and Sollberger.

Orthography and Language

The orthographic system of this text is in accordance with what is known from the Mari dialect area: SA for /ša/ in *mu*-SA-*li-il-šu-nu* in line 8;[14] the ḪA sign represents /ʾa/.[15] Furthermore, all words are written syllabically, including toponyms, with the exception of a few logograms: A.ŠÀ, A.GÀR, É, LUGAL. The clumsiness shown in the one attempt to write a logogram for the name of Lugalzagesi demonstrates the inability of the scribe to handle such writings. The sign BI is employed to render the syllable /pi/ and the sign PI the syllables wa/wi/wu/. The characteristic Mari phonological form of the first-person accusative suffix -*ne* is also found in this text.[16]

[14] See GAG §30e, as well as Finet, *L'accadien des lettres de Mari*, 18, §11b.
[15] Finet, *L'accadien des lettres de Mari*, 17 §10a; Grayson-Sollberger, *RA* 70 123–24, note to line M 11.
[16] See Finet, *L'accadien des lettres de Mari*, 31–32, §17a.

Transcription

Obverse

1. [*Ki-ši*.KI *Ku-tu-*]*ú*.KI *Ti-wa*.KI *Wu-ru-mu*.[KI]
2. [*Ka-zal-lu*.KI *Gi-r*]*i-it-ta-ab*.KI *A-pí-wa*(a over er. KI?)-*a*[*k*.KI]
3. [. . .] ⌜x x⌝ [*Ib-ra-at*.KI *Di*]-*il-ba-at*.KI
4. [. .-*b*]*i*.KI *Ú-ru-uk*.KI *ù Sí-ip-pí-ir*.KI

Philological and Textual Notes

Obverse

1. For *ti*-WA, one might compare the suburb of Kiš(i) with the name *Ti-me* (MAD 5 67 ii 4). It is written A.ḪA in BT 1 i 15′, 25′; see the discussion of Kutscher, *Brockmon Tablets*, 39–40, and D. Frayne, *BiOr* 48 (1991) 386–87, who identifies it with Sippar-Amnānum. For the city and province of Urum, see P. Steinkeller, *JCS* 32 (1980) 23–33; G. McEwan, *JCS* 33 (1981) 56; M. W. Green, *Acta Sumerologica* 8 (1986) 77–83; and Kutscher, *Brockmon Tablets*, 40–42, and D. Frayne, *BiOr* 48 (1991) 387–88.

In morphology, syntax, and lexicon, text **16A** differs from **16B** in the following ways: (1) it employs the ventive *-ūnim*, while **16B** uses the nonventive *-ū*; (2) it clearly coordinates the sentences following the *inūmīšūma* in lines 6–10: *inêrma* . . . [*ù*] . . . *ù* . . . *ù* . . . *ù*; (3) it uses the Š-stem of the verb *galābu*, while **16B** employs the D-stem of the verb. Note that BT 1 ii 5′ employs the D-stem. Plene writings are limited to occurrences of the city of Kiš(i) and one plural noun *kurṣū* (line 7). In the lexicon this text contributes a few new words (see comments to lines 8, 9, and rev. 4–5).

In general, see the discussion of A. K. Grayson and E. Sollberger, "L'Insurrection générale contre Narām-Suen," *RA* 70 (1976) 103–28; as well as that of T. Jacobsen, "Ipḫur-Kīshi and His Times," *AfO* 26 (1978–79) 3–14.

Manuscript

Mari

A 1252 = Grayson and Sollberger, *RA* 70 (1976) 113–14 (see new photograph, p. 402).

Translation

Obverse

1. [Kiš(i), Kuth]a, Tiwa, Wurumu,
2. [Kazallu, Gir]itab, Apiak,
3. [. . .], Ibrat, Dilbat,
4. [. . .]bi, Uruk and Sippar

---

2. For references to Giritab in OAkk, see RGTC 1 59 and to Api(w)ak, see RGTC 1 16.

3. Ibrat is not found in OAkk sources but in the form Iabrad, it is found in Ur III sources (see RGTC 2 82). The writing Ibrat occurs in Isin-Larsa sources (see RGTC 3 104; and for the most recent discussion of its location in relation to Malgium, see M. Sigrist, "Mu Malgium Basig," *RA* 79 [1985] 168). Dilbat, written *Dal-ba-at*.KI, occurs in BT 1 iv 15′ and in an economic text (see RGTC 1 156 sub Talbat).

5. [*i-nu-m*]*i-šu-ma* LUGAL-*ki-in a-bi a-lam Ú-ru-uk*.KI *i-ne-er-ma*
6. [*an-du-r*]*a-ar ki-iš-ši-i-im*.KI *iš-ku-un*
7. [*ù*(?) *ap-pa-ti-š*]*u-nu ú-ša-ag-li-ib ù* [*k*]*ur-ṣe-e-šu-nu*
8. [*ú-ḫa-aṣ*]*-ṣí-ib ù Lugal*-LUGAL.ZA.GÌN.GI.NA *mu-sa-li-il-šu-nu*
9. [*a-na A-kà*]*-dè*.KI *ú-ru ù i-ia-ti in-ši-iš lam-ni-iš*
10. [*i-ta-a*]*k-ru-ni-ne i-na di-*[*i*]*n* U.DAR *ù An-nu-ni-ti*[*m*]

11. [*i-na ta*]*-ḫa-zi-im iš*-ḪA-*ar-šu-nu-t*[*i*] *ú*-[Ḫ]A-*ab-bi-ta*$^{?}$*-am-*[*ma*]
12. [x x (x) *K*]*i-iš-šu-ú-um*.KI *la na-ka-ar a-ḫu-ti-i*[*-im* x (x)?]
13. [*bi-ri-i-i*]*t Ti-wa*.KI *ù Wu-ru-mu*.KI *i-na* A.ŠÀ A.GÀ[R-^{d}EN.ZU]

14. [*bi-ri-i-i*]*t* É-*sa-ba-ad* É ^{d}*Nin-kar-ra-a*[*k*]
15. [*Ki-š*]*i*.KI *ip-ḫu-ur-*⟨*ma Ip-ḫu-ur*⟩*-Ki-ši*.KI *Ki-iš-*[*š*]*u-ú-u*[*m*.K]I
16. [DUMU *Ṣú-mi*]*-ra-at*-U.DAR [*m*]*u-ṣa-ri-iḫ-tim a-na* ⟨NAM⟩.LUGAL *iš-šu-ni-*[*i*]*š-šu*

---

5. The adverb *inūmīšūma* appears here in the rare independent usage found also in the Lipit-ili doorsocket, a building inscription, introducing the construction of the temple of Lugal-Marada (YOS 1 10 ii 1), written *in u-mi-su* (cf. van Driel, *Symbolae Böhl*, who refers to Kupper, *Oriens Antiquus* 10, 98), as well as Samsuiluna C 129 and Šamši-Adad I (Grayson RIMA 1 50:73, A.0.39.1). Normally the adverb *inūmīšūma* heads a clause that follows a subordinate clause headed by the conjunction *īnu* or *inūma*. The second clause that is headed by *inūmīšūma* is usually pluperfect to the action of the main clause. However, at Mari and in southern Babylonia, the subjunction *inūma*/*inūmi* serves as a preposition in the sense of 'at that time' (see von Soden GAG §115s and Finet, 112, §46d). Consequently, *inūmīšūma* could be understood as *inūmi* + *šu* + *ma* as 'in his time'.

6. Grayson and Sollberger (*RA* 70, 123) list the equations between the syllabic writings of the gentilics of our text and the logographic writings of **16B**. Cf. the mixed writings: KIŠ.KI-*ši-um*, KIŠ.KI-*ši-am* in the Old Akkadian royal inscriptions: PBS 5 36 ii' 9′ and BT 1 ii 21′ and iii 34′. On the phonetic realization of the city as Kīši, see Jacobsen, *AfO* 26, 1 n. 3. The gemination of the consonant rather than the vowel is characteristic of the Mari dialect; see Finet, 12, §8e. Note that the gentilic is construed as a singular in form, but the pronominal reference is in the third-person plural rather than singular.

8. As suggested by Grayson and Sollberger, a verb such as *ḫasāpu* A or *ḫaṣābu* A would fit the context as well as *kasāpu*, which is not yet found in the D-stem. For the participle, the use of the sign SA to represent /ša/ is an Old Akkadian as well as a Mari value, and there does not seem to be any reason to establish a lexical item *sullulu* v. 'to despoil(?)' on the basis of this one reference (the other two are already questioned by the CAD S sub *sullulu*).

5. [In his] days, my (fore)father Sargon conquered the city of Uruk and
6. established [fre]edom for the Kišite (people),
7. [and] had their [slavemarks] shaved off and their shackles
8. [smas]hed(?) and escorted their despoiler Lugalzagesi
9. [to Akka]de, and (yet) me, in a . . . and evil manner
10. [they reb]elled against me. (When) according to the verdict of Ištar and Annunītum,
11. he defeated them [in ba]ttle and destroyed
12. [. . .] the Kišite was not an enemy. Of brotherhood [. .].
13. [(Nevertheless) on the common bounda]ry of Tiwa and Wurumu in the field, Ugar-Sin
14. [on the common bounda]ry to Esabad, the temple of Ninkarak
15. did [(the people of) Kiš]i assemble and they raised Ipḫur-Kiši, the Kišite
16. [son of Ṣummi]rat-Ištar, the lamentation priestess, to kingship.

---

9. As Grayson and Sollberger state, the word *inšiš* is a hapax. It might be possible to connect it with the verb *enēšu* 'to be weak'. As an adverb it should modify the verb, but it makes no logical sense describing an act of rebellion ('they rebelled weakly'). W. Mayer suggests (*Or* 64 [1995] 183 n. 40) seeing here a case of nasalization: *in-ši-iš* for *eššiš* 'anew'.

10–11. One sentence ends with the verb *ittakrūninne* and another begins with *ina dīn*. . . . The first sentence (lines 5–10) describes Sargon's relationship to the people of Kiš(i) in contrast to the present relationship between the people of Kiš(i) and Naram-Sin. The second sentence (lines 10–11) describes Sargon's victory and the past reaction of the people of Kiš(i). This sentence is similar to the one describing the victory of Naram-Sin over the Kišites: *in dīni* ᵈINANNA-*annunītim Narām-Sîn dannum in taʾḫāzim in Tiwa Kišiam yišʾar* 'by the verdict of ˁAštar-annunītum, Naram-Sin, the Great, defeated the Kišite in battle at Tiwa' (BT 1 ii 14′–22′ = *aK* 228:82–89, "Narāmsîn C 1"; cf. also iii 26′–35′ et passim). The last verb in the line is understood as coming from *abātu* A 'to destroy', the object of the action being lost in the break at the beginning of the next line.

13–14. These toponyms Ugar-Sin and KÁ-ᵈNinkar both occur in BT 1 as battlegrounds of the conflict between Naram-Sin and Ipḫur-Kiši. Esabad appears only in this text; see discussion by Kutscher, *Brockmon Tablets*, 42, and Frayne, *BiOr* 48 (1991) 388.

15. As pointed out by Grayson and Sollberger, there is a haplography in this line, made by the inexperienced scribe.

16. As Grayson and Sollberger state (p. 124), the form *muṣarriḫtum* is a participle from the same root as the noun *ṣarriḫtu*. While the CAD M/2 241 accepts this interpretation, von Soden prefers to read a proper noun here: Ṣarriḫum

17. [. . . *Ku-t*]*u-ú*.KI
(break)

Reverse

(break)
1′. [. . .] *ab/ad* [. . .]
2′. [*aṭ*(?)]-*ru-ud du*-[*un*? . . .]
3′. [. . .]-*a*$^{?}$-*ab*$^{?}$ x-*šu-nu* [x x *b*]*u-ut*$^{?}$ [x x (x)] *man*$^{?}$ *ra ka u*[*t* x x]
4′. [x]-*bu-ut* [. . . .] A-*kà-dè*.KI-*ma* 9 *ṣú-ub-bi*-[x x (x) *i*]*m*
5′. [*ú-ša*]-*at-bi-šu-nu-ši-im*
(unfinished)

'lies PNF!' (AHw Ntrg. 1588). But such an interpretation is impossible; the name of the mother is already given, and we have the evidence of the parallel version **16B**. Collation does not confirm the suggestion of Jacobsen (*AfO* 26, 6 n. 29) to read MUNUS rather than *mu*-. The position of his mother is given here to indicate Ipḫur-Kiši's pedigree. For royal princesses as BALAG.DI = *ṣarriḫtum*, note Lipuš-iāum, the balag-di of Sin, daughter of Nabi-Ulmaš, ensi of Tutu, son of Naram-Sin. For the meaning of the term, see PSD B 79 balag-di B 'lyre player, lamentation singer, mourner'.

Reverse

2′. Cf. **17** ii 38: [. . .]*a šuāti lu aṭruda*[*ššunūti*?].

4′–5′. The number nine in this line must refer to the nine battles in which Naram-Sin was victorious in one year: *šāʾir* 9 *taʾhāzī in* 1 *šattim* (Susa, Sb 52, MDP 6 pl. 1, no. 1:6–8; Bāseṭkī, *Sumer* 32 70:13–15; *JCS* 32, 239 II N

17. [Kiši, ... Kut]ha(?)
(break)

Reverse

(break)
1′. [. . .] . . . [. . .].
2′. [I se]nt forth the str[ong . . .]
3′. . . . .
4′. [I dest]royed(?) [. . .] Akkade and nine military expeditions [. . .]
5′. [I ra]ised against them
(text unfinished)

202+ ii 1; YOS 1 10 5–7). Jacobsen's interpretation of Grayson and Sollberger's reading of these lines is: [*i-na ti*]*-bu-ut* [*um-ma-an*] *A-kà-dè*.KI*-ma* 9 *ṣú-ub-bi-*[*i*]*m* [*ú-ša*]*-at-bi-šu-nu-ši-im* 'in calling up solely the forces of Akkade, nine military expeditions I raised against them' (*AfO* 26, 11 and n. 44). However, for the paradigmatic usage of the number 9 as meaning last and final, see Klengel, *MIO* 11 (1965) 352–53, referring to Šulgi's year-date 44: "the year he smote Simurrum and Lullubum for the 9th time (a.rá.9.kam)." Compare, referring to Sargon's battles: *ana tišīšu awīlam alpam būlam u immeram ikmi* 'for the ninth time, he took captive men, oxen, cattle, and sheep and goats' (**7** iii 14′–15′). Note that the conquests in the speech in text **6** are also nine in number. On the verb *ṣabāʾum* 'zum Felde ziehen', see AHw 1071, and cf. *īnu šašniš iṣab-baʾūma* 'when they go to battle' (CT 15 4 ii 17; see Römer, *Studien Falkenstein*, 187 [*kummu*-Hymn to Adad]). For the D-stem, see BT 1: *Ipḫur-Kiši . . . u-ṣa-bi-àm-ma* (i 9′–12′).

16B
Geneva Version

Introduction

This version of the story of the "Great Revolt against Naram-Sin" is the closest to the description given in the royal inscriptions. Because the first three lines are almost identical to the royal inscription, this version, unlike all other literary texts of the Sargonic cycle, begins with an invocation of Enlil, the capricious leader of the Sumerian pantheon,[17] and of Ilaba, the stalwart head of the Old Akkadian royal pantheon.

Furthermore, the king is presented as the rightful king by the grace of the gods, against whom any transgression is not just perversity but willful disobedience. This attitude is reflected in the exaltation of Naram-Sin through the employment of all possible epithets: "the great king, the king of Akkade, king of the four quarters of the world, who proclaims Ištar and Annunītum, anointed priest of Anum, the military commander of Enlil, regent of Ilaba, guardian of the sources of the Irnina, the Tigris and the Euphrates, who dispatches the strength of the . . . against all the kings."

Circumstances of Discovery

The origins of this tablet are unknown. It was collected by Swiss Assyriologist Alfred Boissier, who in turn sold it to the Musée d'art et d'histoire de Genève in 1938.[18]

[17] For the relationship between the Sargonic kings and Enlil, see Glassner, *La chute d'Akkadé*, 18.

[18] See E. Sollberger, "The Cuneiform Collection in Geneva," *JCS* 5 (1951) 20, §6.4.

Transcription

Obverse

1. [^{d}*E*]*n-líl id-zu Ìl-a-ba*$_4$ *e-ṭel* D[INGIR.MEŠ *il-la-at-su*(?)]

Philological and Textual Notes

1–3. For the parallel lines in the OAkk royal inscription, see P. Michalowski, *JCS* 32 (1980) 234–35, and *aK* 226ff., "Narāmsîn C 1." Ilaba also appears with the identical epithets in the inscription of Erridu-Pizir (BT 2 i 9–11 = *aK* 303:9–11, "Gutium C 1"). As can be clearly seen in the published photograph,

General Observations

This composition is complete; it is missing only a few signs. It is preserved on a one-column tablet tightly covered with writing on both sides and edges. The script is that of a clear concise hand of an Old Babylonian scholar.

Orthography and Language

The labials are distinguishable by voicing, a "southern" trait, and the sign ZÉ renders /ṣi/, but there is no other evidence for the writing of the emphatic stops and the sibilants. The semivowel /y/ is apparently written A-IA, a "northern" dialectical trait. The plene writings are limited to the long vowel in closed syllable, but this is not consistently carried out (line 3, *ki-ib-ra-a-at* vs. line 10, *ki-ib-ra-at*). The morphology is classical Old Babylonian. The syntax shows the *inūma*-subordinate clause followed by the *inūmīšūma*-clause but, as stated above, the *inūmīšūma*-clause refers to action prior to the first clause rather than simultaneous or subsequent action. Lexically, there are no hapaxes, rare, or unusual words. Moreover, there is clear substitution of lexical items: for example, *nabalkutu* replaces *nakāru* in the meaning 'to rebel'. To sum up, its few diagnostic linguistic features are not sufficient to identify the source of this text.

This text reproduces the formula found in one Old Akkadian royal inscription, namely that of N 3539 + PBS 5 37 (+) PBS 5 36 (*aK* 226–43, "Narāmsîn C 1").

In general, see A. Boissier, "Inscription de Narâm-Sin," *RA* 16 (1919) 157–64; A. Poebel, "The 'Schachtelsatz' Construction of the Narâm-Sîn Text *RA* XVI 157f.," *Miscellaneous Studies* (AS 14) 23–42; A. K. Grayson and E. Sollberger, "L'Insurrection générale contre Narām-Suen," *RA* 70 (1976) 103–28; and T. Jacobsen, "Ipḫur-Kīshi and His Times," *AfO* 26 (1978–79) 3–14.

Manuscript

Unknown Provenance

MAH 10829 = Dossin *RA* 16 (1919) 157–64 = Grayson and Sollberger, *RA* 70 (1976) 109–10.

Translation

Obverse

1. (For) Enlil—his strength, Ilaba—the young man of the gods—his clan god,

---

there is no room for both the DINGIR-sign and the NA in the break. Therefore, there is no reason to expect that Naram-Sin was deified in this text.

1. The second word, written ID/Á-ZU, might derive from *idu* A mng. 7 'strength' + *šu* third-person possessive suffix. Enlil appears with such an epithet

2. [*N*]*a-ra-am*-^{d}EN.ZU LUGAL *da-an-nu-um* // LUGAL *A-kà-dè*.KI
3. LUGAL *ki-ib-ra-a-at ar-ba-i*
4. *mu-ša-pi* U.DAR *ù An-nu-ni-tim*
5. *pa-ši-iš A-nim* GÌR.NITÁ ^{d}*En-líl*
6. PA.TE.SI *Ìl-a-ba*$_4$
7. *ra-bi-iṣ bu-ra-a-at* ÍD.*Ir-ni-na* // ÍD.IDIGNA *ù* ÍD.UD.KIB.NUN.NA
8. *mu-še-ṣi du-*[*un-ni*] ⌜GIŠ.ZU⌝
9. *a-na ka-la šar-ri*
10. *i-nu-ma ki-ib-ra-at ar-ba-i*
11. *iš-ti-ni-iš ib-ba-al-ki-tu-ni-in-ni*
12. KIŠ.KI GÚ.DU$_8$.A.KI *Ti-wa*.KI *Ú-ru-mu*.KI
13. *Ka-zal-lu*.KI *Gíri-tab*.KI *A-pi-a-ak*.KI
14. *Ib-ra-at*.KI *Dil-bat*.KI UNU.KI *ù* UD.KIB.NUN.KI
15. *iš-ti-ni-iš ib-ba-al-ki-tu-ni-in-ni*
16. *i-nu-mi-šu-ma* LUGAL-*ki-in a-bi*
17. UNU.KI *i-ni-ir-ma*

---

in personal names, e.g., ^{d}*En-líl-is-sú* 'Enlil is his strength' (see CAD I sub *idu* for references). The word *idu* is a substitute for Old Akkadian *ilu*. The end of the line has been restored according to the Old Akkadian royal inscription. For the interpretation of *illatu* as 'clan god, family god' in this context, see *aK* 239, ad line 5).

4. For this unusual title, cf. *mut* ^{d}*Ištar-annunītim*, Seux, *Epithètes*, 173.

5–6. For *pašīš Anim* of the Old Akkadian kings, see Seux, *Epithètes*, 222. On the other hand, *šakkanak Enlil* is in place of the usual *iššiak Enlil*; see Seux, *Epithètes*, 116. The title *šakkanak* DN does occur; note the clay nail containing a building inscription of Ur-gigira, son of the king Ur-nigina of Uruk who has the title GÌR.NITÁ Dumuzi (UET 8 15 i 2–3). In the cruciform monument of Maništušu, a pious forgery, the king is titled *šakkanak Ilaba* and *iššiak Enlil*, as well as in the newly-published text of Naram-Sin (B. Foster, "Naram-Sin in Martu and Magan," *ARRIM* 8 [1990] 30 viii 29–32), which is precisely the reverse of the epithets in this literary text. For other references to GÌR.NITÁ DN, cf. UET 8 3, as well as Seux, *Epithètes*, 279–80.

7. For *rābiṣu* as an epithet of the king, see Seux, *Epithètes*, 233–34. It is the equivalent of the logogram MAŠKIM.GI$_4$ used in the royal inscriptions. For the Irnina canal, see RGTC 2, 269–70, and the review by H. Waetzoldt, ZA 65 (1976) 278. For the significance of the title, see Jacobsen, *AfO* 26, 13 n. 50. Naram-Sin also emphasized his reaching the sources of the Tigris and the Euphrates in his year-date: *in* 1 MU ^{d}Naram-^{d}EN.ZU *nagab* IDIGNA.ÍD *ù* UD.KIB.NUN.ÍD *yikśudu* (MAD 1 231 iv 1–5; 236:8–12; 4N-T48 = *aK* 52 D-14, "Narāmsîn 7") and in his royal inscriptions (see *aK* 84 and Neumann, *JCS* 42 [1990] 205, lines 3′–7′).

2. (I,) Naram-Sin, the great king, the king of Akkade,
3. the king of the four quarters of the world,
4. who proclaims Ištar and Annunītum,
5. the anointed priest of Anum, the military commander of Enlil,
6. the regent of Ilaba,
7. guardian of the sources of the Irnina, the Tigris, and the Euphrates,
8. who dispatches the strength of the . . .
9. against all the kings—
10. When the whole world
11. broke out in united rebellion against me,
12. (also) Kiš(i), Kutha, Tiwa, Urumu
13 Kazallu, Giritab, Apiak,
14. Ibrat, Dilbat, Uruk, and Sippar
15. together rebelled against me,
16. at that time my fore(father) Sargon
17. after he had conquered Uruk,

---

8. The text is read in accordance with the published collations of Grayson and Sollberger. I have not seen the original tablet. The meaning of this phrase is unclear. In general, the word *mušēṣû* can mean 'he who brings forth, evicts, dispatches, removes, drives away, releases', etc. In particular in the OB period, it refers to a person in charge of safe passage through a hostile area (see R. Frankena, *Kommentar zu den altbabylonischen Briefen aus Lagaba* [SLB 4; Leiden, 1978] 200). It depends on the meaning of the object, which is uncertain. If GIŠ.ZU is the correct reading, are we dealing with *lēʾu* 'wooden writing board'? One could adduce the reference from "Curse of Agade," line 20: Mar-ḫa-ši.KI li-um-ma gur-ru-dè 'to put the (people of) Marḫaši back on the tablets' (Jacobsen), 'that (even) Marḫaši would be reentered on the (tribute) rolls' (Cooper). Then one could render the phrase 'he who removes the severity of the (tribute) rolls for all kings', which does not seem to be an epithet to be applied to Naram-Sin. One would prefer a reading GIŠ.KU (i.e., GIŠ.TUKUL = *kakku*), which would give us a meaning such as 'he who brings forth the mighty weapon against all the kings'. Foster not only suggests (*ARRIM* 8 [1990] 38, note to lines ix 4ff.) that the signs may be for DINGIR-*su*, but also brings the parallel from his text, which he reads *muttarri dunnim ana kali in bīt Enlil* 'commander of the stronghold for all in the house of Enlil'. Cf. also *muttarri* ÉRIN-*rí Ilaba* 'commander of the troops of Ilaba' (*aK* 251:10–12, "Narāmsîn C 4"). It does seem that the present text is garbled and that *du*-[x-x]-*iz-zu* 'his . . . ' is the most probable object.

10–11. This subordinate phrase appears for the first time in the royal inscriptions of Naram-Sin and is repeated in later Akkadian royal inscriptions, e.g., Ašduni-erim (CT 36 i 6ff. = *RA* 8 65 i 4ff.).

Edge

18. *an-du-ra-ar* ERÍN KIŠ.KI // *iš-ku-un*

Reverse

19. *ap-pa-ti-šu-nu ú-ga-*⌈*al-li*⌉*-i*[*b*]
20. *ku-ur-ṣe-šu-nu ú-ḫe-ep-pi*
21. U.DAR *Ìl-a-ba*$_4$ $^{d.šu}$PA *ù* ^{d}LUGAL
22. ^{d}UTU *ù U*$_4$*-mu-um-šu-ú*
23. KIŠ.KI *la na-ka-ar a-ḫu-tum a-ia-*[*ši*]
24. *bi-ri-i-it Ti-wa*.KI *Ú-ru-mu-um*.KI
25. *i-na* A.GÀR.^{d}EN.ZU *bi-ri-i-it* // *É-sa-bad*.KI É.^{d}*Gu-la*
26. KIŠ.KI *ip-ḫu-ur-ma*
27. ^{1}*Ip-ḫu-ur*.KIŠ.KI LÚ KIŠ.KI // DUMU *Ṣú-m*[*i-r*]*a-a-at*-U.DAR *ṣa-ar-ri-iḫ-tim*

28. *a-na ša*[*r*]*-ru-tim iš-šu-ma*
29. ^{1}*Pu-ut-ti-ma-da-al* // LUGAL *Ši-mu-ur-ri-im*

---

19. Cf. BT 1 ii 1′–5′: [*e-ni-su*]*-nu u-na-zí-*⟨*iḫ*⟩ *ù bí-bí-in-na-at-zu-nu u-gal-li-ib* 'he gouged out their [eyes] and shaved their heads' (subject uncertain).

21–22. This list of gods is duplicated in **19**:1–2. The last divine element there is written ^{d}U$_4$*-um-šu*(*-um* erased, collated). There does not seem to be any reason to emend text **19** according to text **16B** to read ^{d}U$_4$-⟨*mu*⟩*-um-šu-*[*ú*]. The word when not deified has been understood as: 'that day' (Poebel, AS 14 24); 'heutzutage' (F. R. Kraus, AbB 1 68:15, 17); 'täglich' (von Soden GAG §67g, *BiOr* 23 54 ad AbB 1 68:15, 17 assuming it as a variant of *ūmišam*); 'an seinem (für die Opfer reservierten ?) Tage' (W. H. P. Römer, "Studien zu den altbabylonischen Hymnische-Epischen Texten," *Studien Falkenstein*, 198); 'bis heute' (F. R. Kraus, "*ūmšum* und Verwandtes," *RA* 62 [1968] 77–79), which meaning was accepted by von Soden in AHw 1418, *ūm-šu*(*m*) (from *ūmu* + *šum*) 'bis zu diesem Tag'. A deified day ^{d}Ūm or Ūmum exists; in the former form, it appears among the gods in the curse formula of the OAkk royal inscriptions (see Roberts, *Earliest Semitic Pantheon*, 150:8) while in the latter shape it occurs in a personal name (ibid., 55:74). The deified Ūmšum only appears in the two literary texts in our corpus. Therefore, Grayson and Sollberger translate "Ūmum lui-même(?)." On the basis of context, Jacobsen suggested that 'that day' is the personification of the day of the assembly of Kiš(i) and that the day is called upon as witness to what took place on it (*AfO* 26, 6 n. 30). This explanation cannot be used of the text in **19**. Therefore, it must refer to 'this day' of the oath of the king. Note, in

Edge

18. had established the freedom of the population of Kiš(i),

Reverse

19. had shaved off their slavemarks,
20. (and) had broken their shackles.
21. By Ištar, Ilaba, Šullat, and Ḫanish
22. Šamaš and Ūmšum,
23. Kiš(i) was not an enemy—(was in) brotherhood with me.
24. (Nevertheless) on the border between Tiwa and Urumu,
25. on Ugar-Sin in the region between the Esabad and Gula temples,
26. did (the citizens of) Kiš(i) assemble
27. (and) Ipḫur-Kiši, the man of Kiš(i), son of Ṣummirat-Ištar, the lamentation-priestess,
28. they elected to kingship.
29. Puttimadal king of Simurrum

---

this regard, that the idea that each day had a distinct personality was formulated by Jacobsen in a lecture given to the Biblical Society of the Hebrew University of Jerusalem. The gods are called upon to observe the fact that Kiš(i) was breaking their oath of allegiance in hope that they might rain down upon Kiš(i) the curses entailed in the breaking of oaths.

25. For the site of Egula, see RGTC 2 44.

29–35. The Coalition of the Seven Kings of the outlying provinces of the Akkadian Empire: There does not seem to be any geographical order to the listing of these provinces. These lands surrounding the heartland of Mesopotamia are known to have been subjugated by the Old Akkadian kings. The personal names and the toponyms have been reviewed by Grayson and Sollberger. Additional references will be given in the following notes.

29. For Simurrum, the gateway to the Hurrian territory, whose exact location is unknown, see RGTC 1 143–44 and Hallo, "Simurrum and the Hurrian Frontier," *RHA* 36 (1978) 71–83. On the basis of the Old Babylonian royal inscriptions from Simurrum, (see A.-H. Al-Fouadi, "Inscriptions and Reliefs from Bitwata," *Sumer* 34 [1978] 122–29), its location must be placed east of the Tigris between the Lower Zab and the Diyala. Naram-Sin commemorated his conquest of Simurrum in his year-dates (*aK* 51 D-11, D-12, "Narāmsîn 5a," "Narāmsîn 5b"). Note the references to Sargon's conquest of Simurrum in his year-date and literary texts nos. **6–7** (see discussion at **6**:68–70).

30. [1]*In-gi* LUGAL *ma-at Na-ma-ar*.KI
31. [1]*Ri-iš*-[d]ISKUR LUGAL *A-pí-šal*.KI
32. [1]*Mi-gir*-[d]*Da-gan* LUGAL *Má-rí*.KI
33. [1]*Ḫu-up-šum-ki-pí* LUGAL *Mar-ḫa-ši*.KI
34. [1]*Du-uḫ-su-su* LUGAL *Mar-da-ma-an*.KI
35. [1]*Ma-nu-um* LUGAL MÁ.GAN.NA.KI

Edge

36. [1]*Lugal-An-na* LUGAL UNU.[KI]
37. [1]*Ìr*-[d]*En-líl-lá* LUGAL GIŠ.ÙḪ.[KI]
38. [1]*Amar*-[d]*En-líl-lá* LUGAL EN.LÍ[L.KI]

---

30. Opinions vary whether the toponym Namar/Nawar is to be equated with Nagar (probably to be identified with Tell Brak) or whether there are two different sites in the Khabur region with phonetically similar names; see D. Matthews and J. Eidem, "Tell Brak and Nagar," *Iraq* 55 (1993) 203–7. However, the expression *māt Namar*^{ki} 'the land of Namar' in our text is very similar to the *māt Nagar*^{ki} 'the land of Nagar' in the late Old Akkadian seal published by Matthews and Eidem (ibid., 201–3).

31. For Apišal, see discussion in the introduction to text **12**, where it is maintained that it is located in the vicinity of Aleppo.

32. For Mari, a known Old Akkadian province already conquered by Sargon, see RGTC 1 117–18. The dynastic list of Mari reaches back to the Old Akkadian period, where the founder is named Ididiš, but there is no mention of any Migir-Dagan; see J.-M. Durand, "La situation historique des Šakkanakku," *MARI* 4 (1985) 152–59.

33. For Marḫaši under the Old Akkadian kings, see P. Steinkeller, "The Question of Marḫaši," *ZA* 72 (1982) 237–65. He identifies it as the region of Kerman in Iran.

34. For Mardaman, known in a Naram-Sin year-date, see RGTC 1 118 sub Maridaban. On the location of Mardaman, which most commentators place somewhere in the Upper Tigris region of northern Mesopotamia, see most recently D. O. Edzard, "Mardaman," *RlA* 7 (1989) 357–58; and K. Kessler, *Untersuchungen zur historischen Topographie Nordmesopotamiens* (TAVO Beiheft Reihe B 26; Wiesbaden, 1980) 64 and notes.

35. The location and Mesopotamian connections of the land of Makkan have excited much interest in recent years; see W. Heimpel, "A First Step in the Diorite Question," *RA* 76 (1982) 65–67; W. Eilers, "Das Volk der Maka vor und nach den Achameniden," *Archäologische Mitteilungen aus Iran*, Ergänzungsband 10 (1983) 101–19 (discussing both cuneiform and classical sources); D. Potts, "The Booty of Magan," *Oriens Antiquus* 25 (1986) 271–85; W. Heimpel, "Das Untere Meer," *ZA* 77 (1987) 22–91 (who gives a most thorough review of

30. Ingi king of the land of Namar
31. Riš-Adad king of Apišal
32. Migir-Dagan king of Mari
33. Ḫupšumkipi king of Marḫaši
34. Duḫsusu king of Mardaman
35. Manum king of Makkan

Edge

36. Lugal-Anne king of Uruk
37. Ir-Enlila king of Umma
38. Amar-Enlila king of Nippur

---

all known evidence); E. Braun-Holzinger, "Nochmals zu Naramsins 'Beute von Magan,'" *OA* 26 (1987) 285–90; P. Michalowski, "Magan and Meluḫḫa Once Again," *JCS* 40 (1988) 156–64; and W. Heimpel, "Magan," *RlA* 7 (1989) 195–99. It is to be located in the Oman Peninsula and perhaps also in the Iranian coast opposite it.

The original form of the name of the king of Makkan has been a subject of controversy. For a summary of the various suggestions, see D. Potts, "The Booty of Magan," *OA* 25 (1986) 276–77; these mainly alternate between Manium, based on our text, and Manitan, based on the "Chronicle of Early Kings." R. Zadok (*The Elamite Onomasticon* [Supplemento no. 40 agli Annali di Istituti Universitario Orientale di Napoli; Naples, 1984] 55) analyzes the latter form, spelled *Man-nu-da-an-nu* ("Chronicle of Early Kings" = Grayson, *Chronicles*, no. 20:27) = *Ma-ni-t[an]* ("Naram-Sin Statue A," MDP 6, pl. 1), as an Akkadianized Elamite name composed of two elements: *man* (p. 27:137), of unknown meaning, and *dan*, an Akkadian loanword 'strong' (p. 43:241). On the other hand, Grayson (*Chronicles*, 224, 291) suggests that it is a garbled version of a foreign name that Babylonian scribes have given a form meaningful in Akkadian: 'Who is strong?' Notwithstanding, our text has *Ma-nu-um*, which Grayson and Sollberger suggest emending to *Ma-nu-⟨da-an-nu⟩-um*. Glassner has two conjectural readings for the original name: *Ma-ni-*URUDU = *Ma-ni-ṭāb* or *Ma-ni-*KUM = *Ma-lí-kum* (*La Chute d'Akkadé*, 15 n. 65).

36–38. These three cities appear in the list of seven rebel cities of the Southern Coalition under the leadership of Amar-girida of Uruk (*aK* 232–33, 240–55, "Narāmsîn C 1"): Ur, Lagaš, Umma, Adab, Šuruppak, Isin, and Nippur. Their captured rulers are mostly in the broken sections; cf. the ensi of Nippur, ibid., 234:315, which has been restored as Luga[l-nì-zu] by Frayne, *JAOS* 112 (1992) 630. As mentioned above, line 36 contains the famous incorrect reference to Lugal-Anne of Uruk, in company with the unknown Ir-Enlila of Umma and the equally unknown Amar-Enlila of Nippur.

17
"Gula-AN and the Seventeen Kings against Naram-Sin"

Introduction

As stated in the introduction to this chapter, text **17** has many similarities to "Naram-Sin and the Enemy Hordes," in the characters, setting, poetic discourse, and close relationship to the Hittite text **18**.

This composition can be divided into the following story segments:

a. a break of unknown dimensions;
b. a catalogue of kings of various countries and peoples who rose in rebellion against Naram-Sin (col. i′);
c. a break of sixty to seventy lines;
d. the first confrontation between Naram-Sin and his two enemies, Mengi of Nagu and Gula-AN of Gutium. The former was taken to Akkade by Naram-Sin, and the latter was released on his own recognizance (col. ii′ 1′–13′);
e. the return of Gula-AN in a victorious assault on the forces of Naram-Sin (col. ii′ 14′–29′);
f. a prayer of Naram-Sin beseeching the gods for help (col. ii′ 30′–34′);
g. events in Akkade concerning two Akkadians by the names of Puzur-Ulmaš and Riš-Zababa (col. ii′ 35′–44′);
h. a break of unknown dimensions.

This text and text **23**, "The Curse of Agade," are the only two literary texts that claim Gutium as the aggressor.[19] The negative assessment of these mountaineers should be balanced by the peaceful economic relations exhibited in administrative archives,[20] as well as by the fact that there existed three statues of a Gutian king in Nippur in the Old Babylonian period and that a scribe took the trouble to copy down their inscriptions.[21] It should be noted that Gutium falls to the invading hordes in "Naram-Sin and the Enemy Hordes." On the other hand, the name *Gu-la-an* is similar to the sound and shape of *Gú-tar-lá*, the Gutian, who ravished southern Mesopotamia at the beginning of the Ur III dynasty and whose name was synonymous with 'hostility' and 'enemy'.[22]

The discourse features are similar but not identical to those of previous texts. The text is written in the first-person narrative mode but not obviously in the form of a royal inscription.

[19] Even for this text this claim could be questioned on the basis of the writing [*G*]*u-tu-um*. Note that Gutium functions as the instrument of Enlil's wrath in Sumerian city laments: cf. "Uruk Lament" 4.11, 20 (M. W. Green, *JAOS* 104 [1984] 272) and "Lamentation over Sumer and Ur," line 75 (P. Michalowski, *The Lamentation over the Destruction of Sumer and Ur* [MC 1; Winona Lake, Ind., 1989]).

[20] J. J. Glassner, *La Chute d'Akkadé*, 46–47.

[21] Kutscher, *The Brockmon Tablets*, 67.

[22] M. Civil, "On Some Texts Mentioning Ur-Nammu," *Or* 54 (1985) 27–32.

General Observations

Only the bottom half of two columns is preserved of the original three-or-more-column tablet. There are two unusual features of these two preserved columns: they wrap themselves around the edge, continuing on the reverse as if each were an individual single-column tablet; and their widths are unequal, the first appearing to have been much wider than the second column.

Orthography and Language

The linguistic features of this text provide the following picture. Orthographically, the labials are rendered according to the northern pattern. The sign BI renders both /bi/ and /pi/, BA renders /ba/ and PA renders /pa/. The sibilants exhibit initial SI- and final -ÁŠ to render the affricated */ts/ and the sign ZÉ to render /ṣi/; these are also all "northern" dialectical traits. On the other hand, the emphatic stop plus the vowel *i*, /ṭi/, is written with the DI sign, a "southern" trait but one also found in another Sippar text (cf. Lambert-Millard, *Atra-ḫasīs*, 29). A more puzzling "southern" trait is the apparent writing *e-pi*-IS-SU rather than -IZ-ZU (see Goetze, *RA* 52, 141); however, -SU is half broken on the edge of the tablet and might be read -ZU. This text distinguishes carefully between the vowels /e/ and /i/ and employs the whole range of e+C and C+e signs. Vowels are written plene in initial and final position to represent morphologically short or long vowels; examples are: *i-ir-du-ud*, *ú-ub-la*, *-ni-i*. There are a few CVC signs, as in the word *dan-nim*. There are no distinguishing morphological, syntactical, or lexical features in this text.

Poetics

Of all the literary texts with the theme of the rebellion against Naram-Sin, this composition is the only tale cast in poetic form. A poetic syntactical structure exists: inverted word order within clauses and repetition of refrains, words, phrases, and clauses. Nevertheless, there are no "hymno-epic" traits to be found.

The refrains divide the poem into stanzas: (1) *ina taḫāzīja dannim adūk* appears in lines ii′ 8′, 12′ and, as a transitional repetition, in 15′; (2) *lū idūk lū igmur u lū udaʾʾiš* in lines ii′ 22′, 29′.

There seems to be a case of enjambement in lines 32′ff., where a new sentence begins midline.

In general, see A. K. Grayson and E. Sollberger, "L'Insurrection générale contre Narām-Suen," *RA* 70 (1976) 103–28. On the basis of the British Museum inventory number 89-10-4, 537, a Sippar number, it is very probable that this text originated in that area.

Manuscript

Sippar(?)

BM 79987 (89–10–14, 537) = Grayson and Sollberger, *RA* 70 (1976) 116–19.

Transcription

Column i′

(break)

Obverse

1′. [. . . *e-ni*]*-ir*
2′. [^{1d}*Gu-la*-AN LUGAL *G*]*u-tu-um*.⌈KI⌉
3′. [. . .]*-el* LUGAL *Ka-ak-mi-im*.KI

Philological and Textual Notes

Column i′

This list of personal names and topographical names has been compared with the list of seventeen kings in the Hittite composition, text **18**, by Grayson and Sollberger (*RA* 70, 126–27) and also by the author ("Relations between Mesopotamia and Anatolia in the Age of the Sargonic Kings," *XXXIV Uluslararasi Assiriyoloji Kongresi* [Istanbul, 1987], in press). Note the preponderance of names ending with AN or *-el*. It has been said that "Gutian" personal names end in *-an* or *-ka-an* (Hallo, *RlA* 5 sub Gutium). The titles vary among "king" (lines 2′–6′, 14′), "man" (lines 7′–13′), and "king of the land of" (lines 15′–21′). This division must reflect some political hierarchy.

Eleven out of the eighteen countries, states, or peoples listed in this composition are known already from OAkk. documents; see Gutium (RGTC 1 65–66), Lullubum (RGTC 1 111), Ḫabḫum (RGTC 1 68), Amurru (RGTC 1 14; also Mardu, 115–16), Dēr (RGTC 1 22), Meluḫḫa (RGTC 1 121), Aratta (RGTC 1 17), Marḫaši (RGTC 1 116–17), Elam (RGTC 1 42ff.), Gišgi (a place with the same name in the heartland is RGTC 1 59), and Armanum (RGTC 1 18). However, one of the above eleven, Gišgi, is more probably to be equated with the Old Babylonian toponym Apum. The toponym Kakmium appears at Ebla, e.g.: TM.75.G.2420:340 ("the treaty"); TM.75.G.1570 ii 1; cf. A. Archi, "Notes on Eblaite Geography, II," *SEb* 4 (1981) 11; and the summary chart in A. Archi, *ARET* 1 224–25. However, it may not be identical to Old Babylonian Kakmum since its geographical situation differs. The city of Kaniš did exist in the Old Akkadian period according to archaeological evidence (see T. Özgüç, "New Observations on the Relationship of Kültepe with Southeast Asia and North Syria during the Third Millennium B.C.," *Ancient Anatolia: Aspects of Change and Cultural Development: Essays in Honor of Machteld J. Mellink* [Madison, Wis., 1986] 31–47). Of the remaining five, some toponyms reflect the period of its written redaction during the Old Babylonian period: the inclusion of both Kakmum and Turukkû reflects the conquests of Hammurapi in his year 37. In his "40th" yeardate the toponym Arallum, which may be the Ararrû of our text, occurs. The Kas-

Translation

Column i′

(break)

Obverse

1′. [. . .] he conquered.
2′. Gula-AN, king of Gut(i)um,
3′. [. . .]-el, king of Kakmum,

---

sites and the Land of Ḫana only appear in late Old Babylonian times. The last toponym, the Land of Fifty, is unknown.

These lands do not seem in be in any exact geographical order but seem to be systematized according to certain geographical areas: (a) the northern area: the piedmont uplands, spanning the Hurrian territories surrounding the Mesopotamian heartland (lines 2′–11′); (b) the eastern area: the mountains, Iranian plateau, and the coastal plains (lines 12′–18′); and (c) the western area (lines 19′–21′).

i′ 1′. The first sentence does not end in KI, the geographical determinative. The restoration is conjectural, based on text **6**, in which Sargon lists his conquests: GN *enīrma* . . . GN_2 *enīrma.*

i′ 2′. The problem of the location of Gutium has been succinctly stated by R. Henrickson:

> Although Gutium in the Akkadian period is often located in (central) western Iran (e.g. Edzard, Farber and Sollberger, 1977, 65–66 and map [RGTC 1]; Gadd, 1971b, 454–61 [CAH 1/2]), there is no archaeological evidence from Mesopotamia, such as Godin III: 5-4 pottery, to suggest any connection with central western Iran at this time. 'Gutian' material culture remains to be identified. Contemporary sources indicate that Gutium in the Akkadian period is to be located on the mid-Euphrates; the trans-Tigridian Gutium begins with Old Babylonian traditions (Hallo, 1971, 719 [RlA sub Gutium]). Thus, the waves of Gutian barbarians descending from the Zagros lack historical or archaeological confirmation" ("A Regional Perspective on Godin III Cultural Development in Central Western Iran," *Iran* 24 [1986] 23).

Cf. also Henrickson, "Šimaški and Central Western Iran," *ZA* 74 (1984) 98–122. Despite this opinion, the campaigns of Erridu-pizir, the Gutian king, did take him to the lands east of the Tigris (cf. Kutscher, *The Brockmon Tablets*, BT 2+3 and discussion, pp. 68ff.).

i′ 3′. The Old Babylonian toponym Kakmum is identified with the area south of Lake Urmia (see RGTC 3 129–30) or the northwest Zagros mountain

4′. [. . .]-*a-el* LUGAL *Lu-ul-lu-im*.KI
5′. [. . . -*a*]*n-da* LUGAL *Ḫa-aḫ-ḫi-i*.KI
6′. [. . . *l*]*i-i*-AN LUGAL *Tu-ru-uk-ku-um*.KI
7′. [. . .]-*ḫa*-AN LÚ *Ka-ni-šum*.KI
8′. [. . .]-*du*-AN LÚ MAR.TU.KI
9′. [. . .]-*me-e*-AN LÚ BÀD.AN.KI
10′. [. . .]-*bu-na*-AN LÚ A-*ra-ar-ru-ú*.KI
11′. [. . . -*i*]*t-lu-uḫ* LÚ *Ka-aš-šu-ú*.KI
12′. [. . .]-*ib-ra* LÚ *Me-luḫ-ḫa*.KI
13′. [. . . -*d*]*u-na* LÚ SU.KUR.RU.KI
14′. [. . .]-*en* LUGAL *Mar-ḫa-ši*
Edge
15′. [. . . -*k*]*i*/[*t*]*u* LUGAL *ki-iš-ša-at* NIM.MA.KI
16′. [. . . -]**bur*-AN LUGAL KUR GIŠ.GI.KI

---

area (see *RlA* 5 289 s.v.), while the earlier Kakmium is perhaps to be located in the Khabur region or even further to the west (see references above).

i′ 4′. The omission of the syllable ⟨*bi*⟩ in Lullubum may not be accidental; note the Hurrian rendering *Lu-ul-lu-*(*e-ne-we*) (KUB 27 38 iv 14, containing Old Hurrian King List[?]) and Hittite rendering **Lu-ul-li-u-i* (KBo 3 13:10′; see the *Chicago Hittite Dictionary* sub Lullu), as well as the Old Babylonian rendering Lullû (RGTC 3 154). The mountains of the Lullubians are pictured in the victory stela of Naram-Sin (Stele B set up in Sippar) and are located in the area of modern Suleimaniya; see further H. Klengel, "Lullubum: Ein Beitrag zur Geschichte der altvorderasiatischen Gebirgsvölker," *MIO* 11 (1965) 349–71; and "Lullu(bum)," *RlA* 7 (1989) 164–68. For Anubanini, king of Lullubu, in later Naram-Sin traditions, see **22**:39.

i′ 5′. Ḫaḫḫum has been located in the upper Euphrates area at various sites: Elaziğ, Malatya, Elbistan, and Gaziantepe. Gudea's mountain of Ḫaḫḫum is usually placed in the Elbistan Plain or in the Malatya region. It has now been identified by Liverani (*OA* 27 [1988] 165–72) with the newly excavated tell of Lidar Höyük on the Euphrates in the district of Samsat. It may possibly lie nearer to Elaziğ and the tributaries of the Murad Su, where alluvial gold was worked until recently (cf. K. R. Maxwell-Hyslop, "Sources of Sumerian Gold," *Iraq* 39 [1977] 84–85). Sargon is said to have crossed the Euphrates and defeated the troops of Ḫaḫḫum but not to have destroyed the city, according to the bilingual annals of Hattušili I (cf. Güterbock, "Sargon of Akkad Mentioned by Hattušili I of Hatti," *JCS* 18 [1964] 1–6). Thus, Güterbock locates Ḫaḫḫum on the western side of the Euphrates. Note that the Hittite writings reflect nunation as does the Sargonic inscription ii′ 4, *Ḫa-ḫu-un*.KI (P. Michalowski, "The Earliest Hurrian Toponymy: A New Sargonic Inscription," ZA 76 [1986] 4–11).

4′. [...]-a-el, king of Lullu(b)um,
5′. [... -a]n-da, king of Ḫaḫḫum,
6′. [... l]i-i-AN, king of Turukkum,
7′. [...]-ḫa-AN, man of Kaniš,
8′. [...]-du-AN, man of Amurru,
9′. [...]-me-e-AN, man of Dēr,
10′. [...]-bu-na-AN, man of the Ararrites,
11′. [... -i]t-lu-uḫ, man of the Kassites,
12′. [...]-ib-ra, man of Meluḫḫa,
13′. [... -d]u-na, man of Aratta,
14′. [...]-en, king of Marḫaši,

Edge

15′. [...], king of the Confederacy of Elam,
16′. [...]-bur-AN, king of the Land of Apum/the Canebrake,

---

i′ 6′. With Turukkû, an Old Babylonian toponym, compare Tukru of the "Sargon Geography," line 38: the land of Amurrû from Lebanon to Tukru. This toponym has also been compared with Tukriš; see A. Kammenhuber (*Or* 45 [1976] 141 n. 28), who identifies it with the area north of Kermanshah on the eastern border of the Hurrians (idem, *Acta Antiqua* 26 [1978] 213). For a survey of the location of Tukriš and its gold-bearing mountain Ḫarali, see G. Komoróczy, "Das mythische Goldland Ḫarali im alten Vorderasien," *Acta Or* 26 (1972) 113–23; and most recently P. Michalowski, "Magan and Meluḫḫa Once Again," *JCS* 40 (1988) 162–63. Thus, the substitution of an original Tukriš with a later Turukkû is a possible hypothesis.

i′ 12′. Although Makkan and Meluḫḫa form a pair, note that text **16B** lists only Makkan, and text **17** lists only Meluḫḫa. On the location of Meluḫḫa, see D. Potts, "The Road to Meluḫḫa," *JNES* 41 (1982) 279–88; W. Heimpel, "Das Untere Meer," *ZA* 77 (1987) 22–91, and W. Heimpel, "Meluḫḫa," *RlA* 8 (1993) 53–55.

i′ 13′. Grayson and Sollberger's proposal to consider the writing SU.KUR.RU.KI (= Šuruppak) as LAM.KUR.RU.KI (= Aratta) is accepted here on the basis of its position in the list between Meluḫḫa and Marḫaši. This country, the memory of whose location was lost in hoary antiquity, appears mostly in Sumerian literary texts. Hansman identified the city of Aratta with Shahr-i Sokhta in the Iranian Sistan (cf. J. Hansman, "Elamites, Achaemenians, and Anshan," *Iran* 10 [1972] 118 n. 97), while in his thorough review of the subject, Majidzadeh identified it with the Kerman region ("The Land of Aratta," *JNES* 35 [1976] 105–13). Note that the Kerman region has also been equated with Marḫaši by Steinkeller (*ZA* 72 [1982] 255).

i′ 15′–16′. As pointed out by Grayson and Sollberger, these lines are inadvertently repeated at the beginning of the reverse of the tablet. They could be

Reverse

17′. [. . .] LUGAL *ki-iš-ša-at* NIM.MA.KI

18′. [. . . *-bu*]*r*-AN LUGAL KUR GIŠ.GI.KI

19′. [. . . -g]*e-e* LUGAL KUR 50.KI

20′. [ᴵ*Ma-d*]*a-gi-na* LUGAL KUR.*Ar-ma-nim*.KI

21′. [. . .] LUGAL KUR.*Ḫa-na*.KI

22′. [. . .]*-am-ma*

23′. [. . .] ⌈*iš*⌉*-mi-i*

24′. [. . . *i-i*]*k-mi*

(break)

Column ii′

(break)

Obverse

1′. [. . .]

2′. [. . .]-x-*ú ù* x [. . .]

3′. [. . . KASK]AL.GÍD UŠ *ur-tám-*[*mi-ku da-ma*(?)]

4′. *u*[*m-m*]*a-ni-i* PÚ.ME.EŠ *ú-ḫe-ru-*[*ú* . . .]

5′. *e-pí-ri lu iš-pu-uk-ma iṣ-*[. . .]

6′. *eš-me-ma an-ni-a-am e-pí-is-su* [. . .]

7′. *ḫa-am-ṭi-iš eš-te-i-šu a-na-k*[*u* . . .]

8′. *i-na ta-ḫa-zi-ja dan-nim* [*a-du-uk-šu* . . .]

9′. *a-šar* BÁRA *ì-lí-ja* ᵈ·ˢᵘPA *ù* [ᵈLUGAL . . .]

10′. *ás-ku-ru te-li-tam* U.DAR *u*[*m-mi* . . .]

---

related if one read *qí-iš-ša-at* as a form of *qištu* 'forests' with doubling of the *š* in the feminine plural. These two lines would then refer to the forested highlands of Iran and the lower marshlands on the coast. The linkage of GIŠ.TIR/*qištu* and GIŠ.GI/*apu* is very common in Akkadian literature. Nevertheless, it is more likely that the word is *kiššatu* 'totality', referring to the confederate character of the Elamite state (on which see F. Vallat, *Suse et l'Elam* [Éditions recherche sur les civilisations, Mémoire 1]; Paris, 1980]). Consequently, we must look further afield for the location of KUR.GIŠ.GI. It has recently been proposed to connect it with the land of Apum in the Upper Khabur basin, on the Old Assyrian route to Cappadocia (D. Charpin, "Šubat-Enlil et le pays d'Apum," *MARI* 5 [1987] 138 n. 45), which would place this toponym with section (c), the western group.

i′ 19′. The unknown Land of Fifty may be related to the GN Ḫamšā (ARM 1 4:20; see RGTC 3 88) or to the more famous Ḫaššum (see RGTC 3 94). A Hit-

Reverse

17′. [. . .], king of the Confederacy of Elam,
18′. [. . . -bur]-AN, king of the Land of Apum/the Canebrake,
19′. [. . .]-ge-e, king of the Land of Fifty,
20′. Madagina, king of the Land of Armanum,
21′. [. . .], king of the land of Ḫana,
22′. [. . .] and
23′. he heard [. . .].
24′. He captured [. . .].
(break)

Column ii′

(break)

Obverse

1′. [. . .].
2′. [. . .].
3′. [x] double miles / double hours they were was[hed in blood].
4′. My men dug pits [. . .].
5′. But he (the enemy) did heap up earth (on them) [. . .].
6′. I heard what he had done [. . .].
7′. Quickly, I sought him out, I [. . .].
8′. With my strong battle [I defeated him . . .].
9′. At the place of the sanctuary of my gods, Šullat and [Ḫaniš . . .],
10′. where I had invoked skillful Ištar, my mother, [. . .],

---

tite fragment KBo 8 63 names an Atra-ḫasīs son of Ḫamšā (Lambert-Millard, *Atra-ḫasīs*, 21 n. 1).

Column ii′

ii′ 3′. The restoration *ur-tám-*[*mi-ku da-ma*(?)] is uncertain; cf. a metaphor in describing battle, *urtammakā dāma ālettān* (**6**:21). Another possibility is to take the verb from *ramû*: *ur-tám-*[*mu-ú* . . .] 'they were let loose', but it is not clear how this would fit the context.

ii′ 9′–11′. These lines describe the place of the battlefield. Note that Naram-Sin met the forces of Ipḫur-Kiši at Esabad, the temple of Ninkarak, also called the temple of Gula.

ii′ 10′. Cf. **7** i 14, 15: *têlišam iskur* 'he (Sargon) spoke distinctly'. For *telîtu* as an epithet of Ištar, see AHw 1345a; W. G. Lambert, *Kraus AV*, 213–14; A. R. George, *Babylonian Topographical Texts* (Louvain, 1992) 44 Tintir II 6.

11′. *ú-de-eš-šu-ú si-ra-aš ú-g*[*a-* . . .]
12′. ^{I}*Me-en-gi* LUGAL *Na-gu i-na t*[*a*]*-ḫa-*[*zi-ja dan-nim a-du-uk-ma*]
13′. *a+na kar A-kà-dè*.KI *ú-ub-la-aš-*[*šu* . . .]
14′. ^{Id}*Gu-la-*AN LUGAL *Gu-tu-um*.KI [. . .]
15′. *ša i-na ta-ḫa-zi-ja dan-nim a-*[*du-ku* . . .]
16′. *a-na* KUR-*ti-šu ú-wa-aš-še-ru-šu a-na* ^{Id}[. . .]
17′. *la ši-ru-um la da-mu-um šu-ú lu* x [. . .]
18′. *i-na Ḫa-wa-an-nim* KUR GIŠ.ERIN *bi-ri-š*[*u* . . .]
19′. *a-na pa-ni pí-ir-ṣi ra-bi-i ša ša-di* [KÙ.BABBAR(?)]
20′. KÁ.GAL-*ša iṣ-ba-ta-am-ma ḫal-la-al-l*[*a-ni-iš*]
21′. *i-na mu-ši-im it-bi-a-am-ma u*[*m-ma-na-ti-ja*]

Edge

22′. *lu i-du-uk lu ig-mu-ur ù l*[*u ú-da-i-iš*]
23′. *te-še-e gu-ru-un ša-al-ma-ti-ši-n*[*a iš-ku-un*]
24′. *da-mi-ši-na šu-pa-lu ù na-ḫal-l*[*u um-tal-lu-ú*]

Reverse

25′. *a-di na-pa-aḫ* ^{d}UTU-*ši* 6 KASKAL.GÍD *i*[*t* . . .]
26′. *la ú-ša-ap-še-ḫu*[. . .]
27′. *wa-ar-ki-ja i-ir-du-ud a-na pa-ni-ja a*[*-gi-iš it-bi-a-am*]
28′. 90 *li-mi um-ma-na-ti-ja ša i-na qá-a*[*t* . . .]
29′. *lu i-du-uk lu ig-mu-ur ù lu ú-d*[*a-i-iš*]
30′. *i-na* 6 *šu-ši li-mi um-ma-na-ti-ja a-na-ku* [. . .]
31′. DUMU *ma-am-ma-na ni ri ḫa* [. . .]
32′. *is-ḫu-ra-am-ma a-na ra-si na-pí-iš-ti* LUGAL.GI.NA [*a-bi-ja*]

---

ii′ 11′. Cf. **21A** b:22–23: *aja īṣen* [*nip*]*iš širaš mê lištima* 'may he not smell the fragrance of beer, may he drink (only) water'.

ii′ 12′. Mengi of Nagû is not mentioned in the catalogue in col. i′. Nagû is unknown as a specific geographical term, only as a general term for district, see W. Horowitz, "The Babylonian Map of the World," *Iraq* 50 (1988) 156–58, and note that there is no geographical determinative KI on *Na-gu*. On the other hand, there may be an aural mistake here, and Mengi of Nagû may be identical with Ingi of the Land of Namar in **16B**:30; cf. already Grayson and Sollberger, *RA* 70 127.

ii′ 18′. For the Amanus as the cedar forest mountain in royal inscriptions of Naram-Sin, cf. *Amanam śadu* GIŠ.ERIN (UET 1 275 ii 25–27 = *aK* 256:57–59, "Narāmsîn C 5"); for its appearance in legends of Sargon, cf. *uštētiq ummānšu Ḫamanam qišat erīnim ikšud qāssu*, **7** i 11′–12′.

11′. where I had provided beer abundantly, I [. . .],
12′. Mengi, king of the Far Territory(?), by my [strong b]attle [I defeated him and]
13′. brought him back to the harbor of Akkade [. . .].
14′. Gula-AN, king of Gut(i)um, [. . .],
15′. whom I [defeated] in my strong battle [. . .],
16′. and whom I had released to return to his land (but) PN [he joined],
17′. he who is not flesh nor blood, verily he is [. . .].
18′. In the Amanus the cedar mountain his oracles [he consulted].
19′. Before the great divides of the [silver(?)] mountains,
20′. its gate he captured and stealthily
21′. in the night he attacked and my a[rmed forces]

Edge

22′. he did kill, he did decimate and he did [trample down].
23′. [He made] a confusing mass of their corpses.
24′. The depressions and the wadis were [filled] with their blood.

Reverse

25′. Until the sunrise, for six double hours he [made a forced march].
26′. They did not let (me?) rest [. . .].
27′. He pursued me, he [attacked] me frontally fu[riously].
28′. 90,000 of my troops, who were under the command of [PN],
29′. he did kill, he did decimate and he did tra[mple down].
30′. In my 360,000 troops I [had confidence].
31′. Son of a nobody [. . .],
32′. He encircled me. For the sake(?) of life of Sargon [my fore(father)]

---

ii′ 20′. For *ḫallall*[*āniš*], see discussion by W. R. Mayer, *Or* 64 (1995) 174–76, who also evaluates von Soden's suggestion (ZA 67 [1977] 235–36) *ḫal-la-al-l*[*a-at-tam*/*ta*].

ii′ 22′. For *gamāru*, cf. *i-ig-mu-ur* (UET 1 275 ii 28 = *aK* 256:60 "Narām-sîn C 5").

ii′ 23′. Von Soden (ZA 67 [1977] 236) suggests that *te-še-e* is a writing of the numeral 90 in which *tešê* < *ti*/*ešiā* exhibits the *e* < *ia* contraction known at Mari and Ešnunna. However, I have shown that the origin of this tablet is probably Sippar, so there should not be any examples of such contractions on this tablet.

ii′ 27′. For *radādu*, cf. **16A**:rev. 2 and **22**:121.

ii′ 32′. The subject of the verb *isḫuramma* is not obvious. The word *ra-si* has been connected with the verb *râs*/*šu* by von Soden (AHw Ntrg. 1585b) 'er-, zerschlagen'; cf. *raʾišāku* in text **13**:20.

33′. [*ù*(?) *e*]*p-še-tim ù ma-ar-ṣa-tim ša i-te-ep-pu-š*[*u* . . .]

34′. [. . . A]-*kà-dè*.KI *la e-ru-bu-ma* [. . .]

35′. [. . .]-*la a-na kar* A-*kà-dè*.KI [. . .]

36′. [. . . ^{1}P]Ù.ŠA-*ul-maš ù Ri-iš-*^{d}*Za-ba*$_4$-*ba*$_4$ [. . .]

37′. [. . .]-*li* A-*kà-dè*.KI *ki* x[. . .]

38′. [. . .]-*a šu-a-ti lu aṭ-ru-da-*[*aš-šu-nu-ti*?]

39′. [. . . *ù*] *Ri-iš-*^{d}*Za-ba*$_4$-*ba*$_4$ ALA[M . . .]

40′. [. . . A-]*kà-dè*.KI *ki* x[. . .]

41′. [. . .]-x-*ne*.ME.EŠ *lu ip-q*[*i-id*]

42′. [. . . *š*]*u-ši li-mi um-m*[*a-na-ti-ja* . . .]

43′. [. . .]x *ni in* x[. . .]

44′. [. . .]-x-*ḫu*-[. . .]

(break)

33′. [and] the acts and tribulations that he continually suffered [. . .],
34′. [. . .] Akkade, they should not gain entrance [. . .].
35′. [. . .] to the harbor of Akkade may they [. . .].
36′. [. . .] Puzur-Ulmaš and Riš-Zababa [. . .].
37′. [. . .] in the midst of Akkade [. . .].
38′. [. . .] I did send them to [. . .] that [. . .].
39′. [. . .] Puzur-Ulmaš and Riš-Zababa the statue of [. . .].
40′. [. . .] to Akkade [. . .].
41′. [. . .] he appointed(?) them as commanders(?) [. . .].
42′. [. . .] my 360,000 troops [. . .].
43′. [. . .] strengthen [. . .].
44′. [. . .].
(break)

19
"The Tenth Battle"

Introduction

For the historical background of this text, see the discussion in the introduction to this chapter.

The story segments in this short exercise are:

a. an invocation of the gods (lines 1–2);
b. historical background concerning the nine previous battles (lines 3–6);
c. the tenth battle (lines 7–12);
d. a gap of unknown length;
e. a curse formula (rev. 5–10).

As noted above in the introduction to this section, Naram-Sin is deified in this text. He is portrayed as a forgiving and merciful sovereign who shows his magnanimity by giving his enemies their freedom after each of the first nine battles.

The enemy of Naram-Sin is named: $^{1(aš)}$*Ba-na-na* SAG *ḫa-ri-a-am* 'Banana the Harian chief' (line 7). The name has a similar sound to that of Anu-banini, the leader of the enemy forces in "Naram-Sin and the Enemy Hordes" (see next chapter). The term SAG.ḪAR is found in OB Proto-Lu,[23] of which an excerpt, including this term, is found in text **10** ii′ 4 of our corpus. It occurs among terms for peoples of the steppe and kinship groups.

[23] MSL 12 47:394a.

Transcription

Obverse

1. ^{d}INANNA *Ìl-a-ba*$_4$ ^{d}PA *ù* ^{d}LUGAL
2. ^{d}UTU *ù* ^{d}*U*$_4$*-um-šu-*(er.)
3. 9-*šu ik-ki-ru-ni-in-ni-ma*
4. 9-*šu lu ak-mi-šu-nu-ti*

Philological and Textual Notes

Obverse

1–2. For the discussion of the gods mentioned here, see above comments to **16B**:21–22.

This composition is formulated as a royal inscription, in the first person, as is typical of the Old Babylonian period. In general the text resembles a royal inscription, since it concludes with a curse formula. In particular it reflects the Naram-Sin text.[24]

General Observations

Only a few remarks can be offered on this short text. First, it is an incomplete, one-column tablet, of which the lower two-fifths are extant, containing twelve lines of text on the obverse and ten lines of text on the reverse. The text seems to end abruptly in the middle of a sentence, suggesting that this, too, is an excerpt text like **16A** and **16B**. A continuation something like "not judge his case" is expected. However, according to the collations of Aage Westenholz, there is nothing written either on the end or the edge of the tablet.

The provenance of this text is unknown; it was apparently bought on the antiquities market.[25] It seems to have the early ductus resembling the texts from the southern area around Larsa. However, the sample is too small to analyze the orthographic system.

Manuscript

Unknown Provenance

VAT 7832a = van Dijk, VAS 17, no. 42 (see photographs, p. 403).

[24] UET 1 276 col. ii (*aK* 259–60).
[25] See van Dijk, VAS 17, 7.

Translation

Obverse

1. (By) Ištar, Ilaba, Šullat and Ḫaniš,
2. Šamaš and Ūmšu(m),
3. Nine times they rebelled against me.
4. Nine times I captured them.

3–6. Cf. *inūmi kibrātum erbeʾim ikkirāninnīma samāni šanātim taḫāzam ēpušma ina samuntim šattim* 'when the four quarters rebelled against me and I fought battles for eight years and in the eighth year . . . ' (CT 36 i 6–15 = *RA* 8 65 i 4–13, "Ašduni-erim").

5. 9-*šu lu ú-wa-ši-ir-šu-nu-ti*
6. *i-na eš-ri-im a-na ta-ḫa-zi-im it-bu-nim-ma*
7. $^{1(aš)}$*Ba-na-na* SAG *ḫa-ri-a-am*
8. [x+1] *šu-ši li-mi ù* 5 *li-mi*
9. [*i-n*]*a wa-ṣí-im-ma lu am-ḫa-aṣ*
10. [x-x]-*um* ^{d}*Na-ra-am-*^{d}EN.ZU
11. [*i-na*] GIŠ.TUKUL *Ìl-a-*ba_4
12. [*i-na*] GIŠ.PA ^{d}*En-líl*

(break)

Reverse

(break)

3′. $^{d?}$[x] x *wa-ar* [. . .] x-*ki-im*
4′. ^{f}*aš+ni* (break) *a-am* ^{f}*ú/el*? x *šu*(?) [x x] *ri*
5′. ^{d}*É-a na-ar-šu da-me-e-am*
6′. [. . .] *li-im-tu-ud*
7′. *i-na še-ir-ḫi-šu* ^{d}NIDABA *a ḫa-ni-ib*
8′. ^{d}*Nergal be-el* GIŠ.TUKUL
9′. GIŠ.TUKUL-*šu li-iš-bi-ir*
10′. ^{d}UTU *be-el di-nim* (written over erasures)

(edge of tablet)

---

7. The horizontal wedge is possibly a *Personenkeil*, the personal name being *Ba-na-na*, a real "banana name." Another possibility is that the name begins *Aš-*.

10. The broken word at the beginning of the line may be an adverb.

11. Cf. *in* ŠÍTA (KAK+GIŠ) *Ìl-a-*ba_4 (PBS 5 34 + PBS 15 41 vii 60–61 = *aK* 171:17–18, "Sargon C 4"; and also Foster, *ARRIM* 8 [1990] 30 viii 10–11, OB copy of a "Naram-Sin royal inscription").

12. Cf. ^{d}En-líl giš-tukul in-na-sum (Ni 3200 viii 6–8 = *aK* 169 Beischrift (a) V08 4–6, "Sargon C 3"), as well as the curse formula: PA *ana Enlil* 'the scepter for Enlil (he shall not wield)' (UET 1 276 ii 9–10, OB copy of a "Naram-Sin Royal Inscription" = *aK* 259:161–62, "Narāmsîn C 5").

Reverse

5′–6′. This curse is similar to but different from the puzzling versions found in the royal inscriptions: (1) ⌜^{d}EN.KI⌝ ÍD-*zu* A *li-im-tu-ud* 'may Enki measure out (scantily) the water in his canal' (UET 1 276 ii 29, OB copy of "Naram-Sin royal inscription"); see 'Enki möge sogar(?) (im(?)) Flusse . . . "darmessen"' (Hirsch, *AfO* 20, 78 and note on p. 82); 'Enki soll seinem Kanal nicht "voll machen" (reading a {*li*} *im-dú-ud*)' (*aK* 260:180–82, "Narāmsîn C 5"); (2) ^{d}EN.KI ÍD-

5. Nine times I let them go free.
6. In the tenth time they arose in battle against me and
7. Banana, the Harian chief,
8. [with 3]60,000 and 5000 (of my troops),
9. [whe]n he went out to battle, I did fight.
10. [At that time(?)], (I,) the divine Naram-Sin,
11. [with] the mace of Ilaba,
12. [with] the scepter of Enlil,

(break)

Reverse

(break)

3′. ....
4′. ....
5′. May Ea, his canal ....
6′. measure out!
7′. In his furrow may grain not grow abundantly!
8′. May Nergal, lord of the mace,
9′. break his mace!
10′. May Šamaš, the lord of justice

(end of text?)

---

su$_4$ *sà-ki-kà-am li-im-dú-ud* 'may Enki measure out (only) mud for his water-courses' (Foster, *ARRIM* 8 [1990] 32 xiii 6–9); (3) ^{d}EN.KI ÍD-*s*[*u a*]*na sakīkim limtud* 'may Enki block up (?) his canal with silt' (CT 32 4 xii 24; see Sollberger, *JEOL* 20 62:370, NB Cruc. Mon. Maništušu). All commentators treat the verb as being derived from the verbal root *madādu* (cf. CAD M/1 *madādu* A mng. 2 [uncert. mng]). Therefore, assuming the subject is the god of the waters, Enki/Ea, the aim of his curse would be to let little of the precious water reach the accursed. The means of doing this would be to block up the canals with silt or reduce the amount of water measured out, as in times of drought. The proper formulation of this curse seems to have been confused in the above versions. In the present composition the object that is measured out is a hapax and the reading of the first sign is not certain.

7′. Cf. (may Adad and Nisaba) *si-rí-iḫ-su a ù-si-si-ra* 'not prosper his furrow' (UET 1 276 ii 25–26; see UET 8 33 = *aK* 259:176–79, "Narāmsîn C 5"; see also *ARRIM* 8 [1990] 32 xiii 1–5).

8′–9′. For this expression, see von Weiher, *Nergal*, 29–30; and Charpin, "Inscriptions votives d'époque assyrienne," *MARI* 3 (1984) 62–63 no. 10, Malédictions: Fin de la dédicace d'une arme à Nergal; as well as Dossin, *Syria* 32 (1955) 17 v 20–21 ("Foundation Inscription of Yaḫdun-Lim").

Chapter 10

"Naram-Sin and the Enemy Hordes": The "Cuthean Legend" of Naram-Sin

The tale known as the "Cuthean Legend" was the most popular of all the legends, according to the available written evidence. To capture the essence of this legend in its title, I have suggested designating it "Naram-Sin and the Enemy Hordes."[1] The native title of this composition was stabilized in the written tradition as early as the Old Babylonian period, and is given in the colophon of Old Babylonian edition **20B** vi 3′: *ṭupšenna pitēma* 'Open the Tablet Box'.[2] It is presumably identical with the broken title *ṭup-šin-na pi-*[. . .] listed in a catalogue of the library of Aššurbanipal.[3] The incipit is fully preserved on K.1351, a document parodying this Naram-Sin composition to ridicule Bēl-ēṭir of Bīt-Ibâ: *ṭup-šin-na* BAD-*ma* NA_4.NA.RÚ.A *ši-t*[*as-si*].[4]

Although the title was fixed, the length and thus the text was not fixed. This composition is preserved in two Old Babylonian manuscripts (**20A**, **20B**); two(?) manuscripts in Akkadian from Boghazköy (**21A**); a late version in six copies from Nineveh, one from Sultantepe, and one from Kiš (**22**); in addition to four possible Hittite versions from Boghazköy (**21B**). The extant manuscripts indicate that the Old Babylonian edition was at least two tablets long, perhaps as many as 600 lines, whereas the first-millennium edition only consisted of approximately 180 lines. This difference is significant, despite the fact that the Old Babylonian line is shorter than the Standard Babylonian line.

1 *JAOS* 103 (1983) 330.

2 See the discussion by C. Walker, "The Second Tablet of *ṭupšenna pitema*: An Old Babylonian Naram-Sin Legend?" *JCS* 33 (1981) 193–94.

3 K.13684+:8; see W. G. Lambert, "A Late Assyrian Catalogue of Literary and Scholarly Texts," *Kramer Anniversary Volume* (AOAT 25; Neukirchen-Vluyn, 1976) 314; and the collation of S. Parpola, "Assyrian Library Records," *JNES* 42 (1983) 28.

4 Ibid.; and A. Livingstone, *Court Poetry and Literary Miscellanea* (SAA 3; Helsinki, 1989) 64.

The character of Naram-Sin is more fully fleshed out in this tale than in any other. In the other tales he is a man of action; in this tale he is a man of introspection as well. Initially he is depicted as a self-willed individual, putting himself above the gods. Since Naram-Sin defies the will of the gods, he must be punished. He must realize and acknowledge his tragic error before he can receive assistance from the gods. Whereas the focus of the texts in chapter 9 was the disloyalty of the adversary, the focus of these texts is the hubris of the hero. In these texts he has become the true hero, with the fatal flaw known from heroic epics of other nations.

In this composition the hero, Naram-Sin, has a foil against whom his deeds can be measured. As in all Mesopotamian royal inscriptions, the king must surpass the accomplishments of his royal predecessors. The royal predecessor and foil for Naram-Sin is Enmerkar,[5] whose tutelary gods are Inanna and Enki/Nudimmud—but not Enlil.[6] According to the Sumerian King List, the historical Enmerkar was the second king of the dynasty of Uruk and the founder of the dynastic city. He is one of the three kings of Uruk around whom a cycle of epics was composed: Enmerkar, Lugalbanda, and Gilgameš. Each of these heroes was treated differently. Enmerkar alone remained a mortal king, while the others were deified and worshiped as gods. Thus, of all the Sumerian and Akkadian epic heroes he alone had no cult. The reason may be that given by this composition, "Naram-Sin and the Enemy Hordes": he did not inscribe a *narû* for future generations to read. This omission is the focus of attention in the composition "Naram-Sin and the Enemy Hordes," but it is only a consequence of the ignoble fate decreed for Enmerkar by the gods. In the historiographic tradition, Enmerkar appears in the "Weidner Chronicle," where he and Naram-Sin stand accused of a grave sin, the despoiling or destruction of the inhabitants of Babylon ("Weidner Chronicle," lines 32 and 53–54 respectively). It has been suggested by Gurney[7] that line 32 should be read: *En-me-kiri šar Uruk nam-maš-*[*še-e*] *ú-šal-pit-m*[*a umm*]*an*(?)*-man-da*. The two parallel lines would then read:

> *Enmekar šar Uruk nam-maš-*[*še-e*] *ú-šal-pit-m*[*a* ER]ÍN*-man-da šá a* [. . .]
> 'Enmerkar, king of Uruk, destroyed the settlements and the Ummān-manda who. . . .'
>
> *Narām-Sîn nam-maš-še-e Bābilī ú-šal-pit-ma adi šinīšu ummān Qutî idkâššumma*
> 'Naram-Sin destroyed the settlements of Babylon, and twice he (Marduk) brought up against him (Naram-Sin) the army of the Gutians'.[8]

Thus, the Ummān-Manda are involved in Enmerkar's misfortune, as well as Naram-Sin's.

[5] For Enmerkar, the meaning of his name and literature about him, see C. Wilcke, *Das Lugalbandaepos* (Wiesbaden, 1969) 41–48.

[6] Enlil is also the enemy of Enmerkar in "Enmerkar and Ensuḫkešdanna"; see Wilcke, *Das Lugalbandaepos*, 66–67.

[7] Gurney, *AnSt* 6, 163 and cited by Grayson, *Chronicles*, 285.

[8] This is a composite reading based on the new Sippar text; see F. N. H. Al-Rawi, *Iraq* 52 (1990) 6, line 20.

According to the literary tradition, the identification of Naram-Sin's adversary is uncertain, with a bewildering number of possibilities. Whether out of ignorance of the past or due to the unintelligibility of the documentary sources, the authors of the various versions agree neither on the characterization of the enemy hordes nor on their identity. In the first composition, text **20**, an unknown hapax appears in a broken and difficult context: the Harians. The Harians' first appearance was in text **19**:7: $^{1(aš)}$*Ba-na-na* SAG *ḫa-ri-a-am* 'Banana, the Harian chief . . . (I fought)', and their second appearance is in **20A** iii 17–19: [L]Ú.KÚR *danna idkiamma* [(*iš*)]-*ši-a-*⟨⟨*ga*⟩⟩*-am ḫa-ri-a-ti Mal-gi-a* [x x (x)] *gu uk ka ni a* 'He summoned against me a mighty foe and raised the Harians(?) (of) Malgium. . . .' Note the designation SAG.ḪAR among the terms for peoples of the steppe and kinship groups.[9]

In the Boghazköy Akkadian version, the enemy is described but not named. The oral tradition carried on the folk memory of the Harians, using a word that was understood as 'cavefolk'. The caves, *ḫurru*, entered the tradition: see **21A** b 5 [*a*]*wīlūtum īrub ana pānīšunu ana ḫurrī* 'before them mankind scurried into caves' and **22**:31 *ṣābu pagri iṣṣūr ḫurri amēlūta āribū pānūšun* 'warriors with bodies of cave birds, a race with ravens' faces'. The elements are parallel and are either identical or similar: *awīlūtum* // *amēlūta*, *īrub* // *āribū*, *ana pānīšunu* // *pānūšun*, *ana ḫurrī* // *iṣṣūr ḫurri*, but the difference in sense is profound.[10]

Modern scholars have expended much ink in writing about the Ummān (ERÍN.MEŠ)-Manda as the quintessential opponents of Naram-Sin. With them, the oral saga continues into the modern era despite the written sources,[11] which offer little support for the contention that they are savage fiends. Although they are mentioned in Middle Babylonian and later texts pertaining to Naram-Sin,[12] they appear neither in the description of the enemies nor in their raiding expeditions. The gentilic Ummān-Manda occurs in the speech of the gods to Naram-Sin urging him to desist in his intentions, as well as in a broken context in the Hittite version. In the Standard Babylonian recension, the Ummān-Manda are mentioned once in a difficult line (line 54), apparently in the list of victims.

The term Ummān-Manda may contain two elements that have a prehistory in historical and literary records. The word *ummānum* as a place-name is found in a Sargonic royal inscription, perhaps of Naram-Sin: (the one who broke the "weapons" of Subartu) *mukīn* SUḪUŠ.SUḪUŠ *Um-ma-nim*^{ki} 'The one

9 MLS 12 47, OB Proto-Lu 394a, and text **10** ii′ 4.

10 Another possibility is to take into consideration ḫur-ru-um-kur-ra-(k) 'the cave of the mountain', the place of refuge of Lugalbanda. For a discussion of the sense of this term, see Wilcke, *Das Lugalbandaepos*, 36–37; J. Klein, *JAOS* 91 (1971) 296–97 n. 7; Civil, *JNES* 31 (1972) 386; S. Cohen, *Enmerkar and the Lord of Aratta*, 52; Hallo, *JAOS* 103 (1983) 165.

11 Gurney, "It is a fact that in line 54 the invaders are described as *Ummanmanda*," *AnSt* 5 (1955) 97.

12 References all: KBo 3 16 rev. 16, see H. Güterbock, ZA 44 (1938) 56 and H. Hoffner, *JCS* 23 (1970) 18; Bo 1309 rev. 16, see H. Otten, ZA 63 (1974) 86; and text **22**:54. For a most thorough investigation of the term Ummān-Manda, see G. Komoróczy, *Acta Antiqua Academiae Hungaricae* 25 (1977) 43–67.

who strengthened the foundation(s) of *Ummānum*' (UM 29-16-103 i 10′–12′).[13] Michalowski interprets *ummānum* not as a specific toponym but rather as a general word for an army camp. He compares it to UGNIM.KI (RGTC 2 203). However, note ù-ma-núm ḫur-sag me-nu-a-ta 'from Umānum, the mountain of Menua' (Gudea Stat B vi 3). In the Enmerkar-Lugalbanda epic cycle the toponym ma(n)du(m)[14] occurs, for which Wilcke has suggested 'flatland',[15] but it may be a geographical entity that was located on the route from Aratta to Uruk.[16] Moreover, this toponym may be related to the class of soldiers found in Proto-Lu and OB Lu (CAD *mandu*, M/1 209b), which is also known in the west in Hittite laws, Hittite literature (see RGTC 6 259, Manda, considered there as a toponym in ÉRIN.MEŠ *ma-an-da*), Ugaritic records, and Mari texts. On the other hand, the Manda of *ummān* Manda may be related to the PN Manda, which appears as the name of an enemy leader in a letter from Ešnunna.[17] Furthermore, the Ummān-Manda are mentioned in the apodosis of Old Babylonian omina (see AHw 1413b for examples). Although his Indo-European etymology is suspect, Cornelius[18] understands the term to mean a type of steppe nomad whose culture is based on the horse and wagon, an appealing speculation.

The present story line concerns a devastating invasion of Babylonia by certain barbarian hordes, who are the creatures of the gods. Naram-Sin decides to attack them, but his forces are annihilated so that "not one comes back alive." Deeply depressed and seriously doubting whether he is at all fit to be king, Naram-Sin does not know in which direction to turn. The conclusion is only preserved in the late recension, which seems to indicate that Naram-Sin finally succeeds in battle. However, he is not allowed to pursue his victory and exterminate the enemy. The late version closes with an admonition to a future ruler: his moral message is one of pacifism.

In the deep structure of the narrative are embedded binary oppositions: warfare : peace; action : non-action; divine : human; human : animal. Confrontation and conflict of wills provide the action in the narrative. The motif of writing for the guidance of future generations in return for future blessings is emphasized.[19]

This narrative is encapsulated in a discourse framework: there are an introduction and conclusion that refer to the text as a stela, a *narû*, to be read aloud, and whose injunctions should be observed. Consequently this text has been labeled a piece of *narû*-literature and has not been included in discussions of literature in general or epics in particular.

13 P. Michalowski, "The Earliest Hurrian Toponomy: A New Sargonic Inscription," ZA 76 (1986) 5, republished in *aK* 286–91, "Fragment C 5."

14 "Lugalbanda and Enmerkar," line 342.

15 Wilcke, *Das Lugalbandaepos*, 213–14.

16 S. Cohen, *Enmerkar and the Lord of Aratta*, 53–54.

17 R. Whiting, *Tell Asmar*, 37–38, no. 2:1(?), 7.

18 Cornelius, *Iraq* 25 (1963) 167–70.

19 See my article, "Writing for Posterity: Naram-Sin and Enmerkar," *Kinattūtu ša dārâti: Raphael Kutscher Memorial Volume* (Tel Aviv, 1993) 205–18.

20
The Old Babylonian Edition

Introduction

The following two texts, **20A** and **20B**, contain parts of tablets I and II of the Old Babylonian edition of the tale of "Naram-Sin and the Enemy Hordes." Although there is positive evidence that **20B** and **22** are older and later recensions of the same composition with the same title, such evidence is lacking for **20A**. There is a remote possibility that **20A** represents a different composition.[20]

The depiction of Naram-Sin as hero is most developed in text **20**. The passage in I iii 8–13 shows a revelation of character, if we assume that the question "what has God brought upon my reign?" is answered by "what have I brought upon myself and the cycle of reigns?" "It is not in the stars but in ourselves that the tragic fault lies," is what Naram-Sin may be saying in this paragraph. Unfortunately, another interpretation of the second line is "what has my reign brought upon me?" which exhibits a very self-centered individual. This pivotal question of interpretation involves the next two lines (I iii 14–15), which may be interpreted either "how can I set about to put myself out (for my country)?" or "how can I manage to extricate myself (from the present situation in order to save myself)?"

The composition may be divided into the following story segments:

a. a break of unknown dimensions (tablet I i);
b. Naram-Sin takes counsel and acts (I ii);
c. the defeat of the forces of Naram-Sin three times in three years (I iii 1–7);
d. the depression of Naram-Sin (I iii 8 through the end);
e. the destruction of the land of Akkade (I iv);
f. a break of unknown dimensions (I v–vi);
g. a short description of battle and destruction, mostly broken (II).

The description of the destruction of the land of Akkade in section (e) has echoes in text **23**:147–50.

The discourse mode is that of first-person monologue. The overt narrator is Naram-Sin, who is heard revealing his innermost thoughts. This brings the immediacy of the narration closer to the audience. The discourse contains a surface structure similar to that of the later **22** in only one block. The parallel texts are: **20** I iii 1–15 and **22** 84–93.

[20] See discussion by J. J. Finkelstein, *JCS* 11 (1957) 87–88; H. Hoffner, *JCS* 23 (1970) 17 n. 8; and J. Cooper, "Symmetry and Repetition in Akkadian Narrative," *JAOS* 97 (1977) 510 n. 14.

General Observations

The manuscript of Tablet I is found on the upper right-hand corner of a three-column tablet with sections of cols. ii, iii, iv, and v preserved. The manuscript of Tablet II is found on the lower left-hand corner of a three-column tablet of which parts of cols. i and vi are extant.

Orthography and Language

The linguistic features of **20A** provide the following picture: In orthography, there is no evidence concerning the treatment of the labials, because the sequence /pi/ does not occur. The reflex of the affricated */ts/ is spelled with the SA SI SU set of sibilants, a "northern" characteristic (*sa-pa-nu* iii 20, iv 15′, *es-si-*[*ḫi*] iii 8, *is-su-ú* iv 4′). However, in syllable-final position there is an occurrence of -UZ for /us/ (*šu*-UZ-*ḫu-ra-at* iv 13′), a 'southern' trait, as well as -ÁS for /as/ (*ik-ta-ba*-ÁŠ iv 5′, 16′), a 'northern' feature. An apparent exception is found in *uz-za-aḫ-ḫi-ir* iv 12′, where the double -zz- renders -st- unless the root of this verb is *ṣḫr*, in which case this exception is not diagnostic. The same diversity is found among the renderings of the emphatic stop /ṭ/—the syllable /ṭe/ is represented by the TE sign, a 'northern' trait, while the syllable /ṭi/ is represented by the DI sign, a 'southern' feature. The latter feature is also found in the "Atra-ḫasīs" texts from Sippar; see Lambert-Millard, *Atra-ḫasīs*, 29. The sign ZÉ renders both /ṣi/ (*lu-še-ṣi* iii 15) and /ṣe/ (*ṣe-ri* iii 16). There are almost no plene writings to be seen; a few examples occur in word final position in final weak verbs and nouns as well as *ja-a-ši-*(*im*) ii 9, 11, iii 13. CVC signs of the type Cum/am/im occur in abundance but only in word-final position. There are also a few logographic writings. In the morphology, mimation throughout is optional. The lexicon has a couple of hapaxes.

Poetics

The morphology does not exhibit any poetic forms, i.e., there are no obvious hymno-epic traits in this text. On the other hand, the poet has taken poetic license with the syntax. He has not only inverted the order of the words but also used the inversions to make ring constructions (e.g., iv 3′–4′, 10′–11′).

The poetic structure is tight. It is built on the repetition of words, half lines, and full lines. This structure is particularly evident in I col iv. Note, also, the repetition of the half line *imtaḫaṣ dabdâ* I iii 1 // 3 // 7 in which the last line is incremental *imtaḫaṣ dabdâ rabia*. For full lines, compare I iii 2 // 4. Parallelism is common: *anāku šarrum lā mušallim mātīšu u rēʾûm lā mušallim nišīšu* (I iii 11–12).

Devices of sound patterning are also employed. Note the assonance *essi[ḫi] enniši* (I iii 8) and even rhyme in *ispuḫ* // *ispun* I iv 5′–6′ or simple repetition of *ušēṣiamma* I ii 2 // 4.

In general, see J. J. Finkelstein, *JCS* 11 (1957) 83–88 and C. Walker, *JCS* 33 (1981) 191–95.

Provenance

Text **20A** is one of the Morgan Library tablets housed in the Yale Babylonian Collection. On the basis of the history of the tablet and its connection with the Morgan Library tablet of Atra-ḫasīs, MLC 1889 (now in the Morgan Library in New York), Finkelstein assigned his text to late OB Sippar. It may be significant to note that this tablet, MLC 1364, has an old number M-128, according to the MLC catalogue in the Yale Babylonian Collection. As we can see from the piece of Tablet II that was published by Walker, this text was definitely copied in the scribal schools of Sippar. However, the two manuscripts differ in that **20A** has already undergone the sound shift of the semi-vowel /w/ to /m/ in intervocalic position (in iv 7, 10 but note *ú-wa-at-te-er* in iii 5). Note that during the reign of Ammi-ṣaduqa, there were three widely different recensions of Atra-ḫasīs compiled in the single town of Sippar.[21] Whether the same scribe, KÙ-Aya is responsible for both the MLC "Naram-Sin and the Enemy Hordes" and the MLC "Atra-ḫasīs" is questionable.[22] The KÙ-Aya tablets have a wedge for 'ten' put against each tenth line and the semi-vowel /w/ is preserved in MLC 1889 i 10 (Tablet II).

Manuscripts

Tablet I

Sippar

MLC 1364 = Scheil, *Recueil de Travaux* 20 (1898) 65–67 = Finkelstein, *JCS* 11 (1957) 83–88 (see photographs, p. 404)

Tablet II

Sippar

BM 17215 (92-7-9, 331) = Walker, *JCS* 33 (1981) 191–95

[21] Lambert-Millard, *Atra-hasīs*, 34.

[22] For this suggestion, see Finkelstein, *JCS* 11, 83.

Transcription

Tablet I: Text **20A**

Column i (destroyed)

Column ii

1. [. . . .] x *it-ti-šu*
2. [. . .] *-il-tam*
3. [. . .] x *be-el ma-tim*
4. [. . .]x *a-na-ku am-ta-al-li-ik*
5. [. .MU/UD.X+] 1.KAM *ša ap ra*
6. [. . .]*-ra ša šar-ru-tim*
7. [. . .] *aṣ-ba-at-ma*
8. [. . .] *ša an-ni-tam*
9. [. . .] *ra a-na ja-a-ši-im*
10. [. . .] ⌜x⌝*-du-ú a-na-ku*
11. [. . .] *ú*(?) *ra a-na ja-a-ši*
12. [. . . *a-n*]*a* ⌜*ru*⌝*-qú-tim*
13. [. . . *i*]*š-tu ul-la*
14. [. . . *il*]*-li-kam-ma*
15. [. . .] *ib-ri-ja*
16. [. . . *a*]*ṣ-ba-at*
17. [. . . *a*]*m*

(break)

Column iii

1. *im-ta-ḫa-aṣ da-ab-da-a ú-ul i-zi-i*[*b*]
2. *i+na ša*!(WR.TA)*-ni-i* 2 *š*[*u-š*]*i li-mi um-ma-na ú-še-ṣi-am-ma*
3. *im-ta-ḫa-aṣ da-a*[*b-d*]*a-a ú-ma-al-li ṣe-ra*
4. *i-na ša-al-ši* 1 *šu-ši li-mi um-ma-na ú-še-ṣi-am-ma*
5. *e-li* ⌜*ša pa-na*⌝ *ú-wa-at-te-er šu-a-ti*

Philological and Textual Notes

Tablet I: Text **20A**

iii 3. In this context, the word *ṣēru* refers to the hinterland, the fields surrounding the city. It is found as the place of battle (cf. CAD Ṣ 146b), and as a battlefield it is described as being full of corpses, etc.

Translation

Tablet I: Text ***20A***

Column ii
(too fragmentary for translation)

Column iii
1. He inflicted a defeat; none escaped alive.
2. The second (year) 120,000 troops I sent forth, but
3. he inflicted a defeat; he filled the battlefield (with corpses).
4. The third (year) 60,000 troops I sent forth, but
5. he expanded that (defeat) beyond the previous.

---

iii 5. The anaphoric pronoun *šuāti* probably refers to the noun *dabdû* found in lines 1 and 3. There is no need to emend *šuāti* to *šunūti* as does the CAD A/2 sub *atāru* D, p. 490a. The D-stem of the verb *wutturu* 'to augment in number or size' fits the context very well, although von Soden questions this

6. *iš-tu* 6 *šu-ši li-mi um-ma-ni i-ni-ru*
7. *im-ta-ḫa-aṣ da-ab-da-a ra-bi-a*
8. *a-na-ku es-si-[ḫi] en-ni-ši*
9. *a-ka-ad a-na-aḫ a-šu-uš am-ṭi-ma*
10. *um-ma a-na-ku-m[a]* DINGIR *a-na* BALA-*ja mi-nam ub-lam*
11. *a-na-ku šar-rum la mu-ša-lim ma-ti-šu*
12. *ù* SIPA *la mu-ša-lim ni-ši-šu*
13. *ja-a-ši* BALA-*e mi-nam ub-lam*

14. *ki-i lu-uš-ta-ak-kan-ma*
15. *pa-ag-ri ù ra-ma-ni lu-še-ṣi*

---

derivation (AHw 1490 "dazu?"). Cf. *el ša pana utter* '(I restored the *ḫiburnu*-vats and the pipes and) made them larger than before' (Grayson RIMA 1 192:37 A.O.77.4, Shalm. I); *sisê . . . eli ša pana uttirma elīšu aškun* 'I imposed the delivery of more horses upon him' (Lie Sar. 71).

iii 6. This subordinate clause sums up the amount of men slaughtered during the three years of defeat: [180,000] + 120,000 + 60,000 = 360,000 men killed. The relationship follows the sexigesimal system of 3–2–1. In text **22**, the numbers of the slaughtered are not ordered in any system, but they probably do not reflect a more reliable tradition.

iii 8. The verbal phrase *enniši* (N *ešû*) appears not only in the Standard Babylonian recension but also in the omen tradition: BALA LUGAL *A-kà-dè*[ki] *in-niššì* (C. Virolleaud, ACh, Sup. 2 no. 24:6 (EAE 20); see F. Rochberg-Halton, *Aspects of Babylonian Celestial Divination: The Lunar Eclipse Tablets of Enūma Anu Enlil* [AfO Beiheft 22; Horn, Austria, 1988] 179:7).

iii 9. For the hapax *a-ka-ad*, see the suggestion of emending it into the SB *a-ka-la* by Zimmern, ZA 12 (1898) 330. Likewise, it has been suggested to read the SB *a-ka-la* as *a-ka-ad*. To escape from this circle, I suggest reading *a-ka-ad* and taking *nakādu* 'to worry, fear' as the verb with improper vocalization *a* for *u*.

iii 10, 13. The contrast between *ana* BALA-*ja* 'upon my reign' and BALA-*e* 'the reign(s)' is clear. However, the grammatical form of the latter is not. It might be a singular genitive or plural oblique; in either case the preposition ⟨*ana*⟩ is needed to make the sentence understandable. The late conflated text (**22**:90) has *ana pa-li-e mīna ēzib*, for which Gurney suggests 'what have I left to the (*not* my) reign?' meaning 'for my successor' (*AnSt* 6, 164). Another possibility is that the grammatical form is nominative with first-person possessive suffix: *palāʾum* + *i* = *palê* according to the paradigm *qabāʾum* + *i* = *qabê*. This would result in a very self-centered exclamation: 'What has my reign brought upon me?'

6. After he had slain my 360,000 troops,
7. he inflicted a comprehensive slaughter.
8. I became confused, bewildered.
9. I was worried, depressed, sunk in gloom, reduced in spirit.
10. Thus I thought: "What has god brought upon my reign?
11. "I am a king who has not protected his land
12. "and a shepherd who has not safeguarded his people.
13. "What has my reign brought upon me? / What have I brought upon myself and the cycle of reigns?
14. "How shall I ever continue to act so that
15. "I can get myself out (of trouble)?" / "I can put myself out (in order to save the country)?"

---

iii 11–12. These lines seem to represent typical royal epithets of the Old Babylonian period: *rēʾûm mušallimum* of Ḫammurapi (CH xlvii 43). The parallel pair of *mātu//nišū* is common; cf. CAD M/1 418b.

iii 14–15. The idiom *pagra u pūta šūṣû* is peculiar to this legend. It occurs in OB as *pagrī u ramanī lušēṣi* and in SB as *pagrī u pūtī lušēṣi* (**22**:93). There is one other occurrence in the "Sin of Sargon" text (H. Tadmor, B. Landsberger, and S. Parpola, "The Sin of Sargon and Sennacherib's Last Will," *SAAB* 3 [1989] 10:12–13): [*pūtī*] *u pagrī itti ili lušēṣi*. The translations that have been given for the whole sentence, *kī luštakkanma pagrī u ramanī lušēṣi*, are:

Zimmern (*ZA* 12 [1898] 325 iii 2): 'Aber also will ich tun: In eigener Person will ich ausziehen!';

Jensen (KB 6/1 295 iii 2): 'Wie soll ich . . . und: meinen Leib und meinen . . . hinausziehn lassen?';

King (STC 149 iii 2): 'But (this thing) will I do. In mine own person will I go forth!';

Güterbock (*ZA* 42 [1934] 68): "In eigener Person auszuziehen';

Finkelstein (*JCS* 11 [1957] 86): 'How shall I proceed? Shall I go forth myself?';

Gurney (*AnSt* 5 [1955] 103): 'How am I to proceed and keep myself out of trouble?';

Tadmor (*Eretz Israel* 5 [1958] 155, translating the "Sin of Sargon" text): 'I shall go forth proudly with the help of my god';

CAD A/2 372b (1968, uncert. mng.): 'How should I proceed to act with the approval of the gods?';

Labat (*Les religions*, 312): 'Comment agirai-je pour m'en sortir moi-même';

AHw 1137b (1974): 'Wie soll ich (es) i.w. leisten (und mich retten)?';

Longman (*Autobiography* [1991] 230): 'Indeed let me set it down for all time and let me publish my "record"';

16. *a-na ḫu-ul-lu-uq ṣe-ri Ak-ka-di-i*
17. [L]Ú.KÚR *da-an-na id-ki-a-am-ma*
18. [(*iš*)]-*ši-a-**⟨⟨*ga*⟩⟩*-am ḫa-ri-a-ti Mal-gi-a*
19. [x x (x)] *gu uk ka ni a*
20. [. . *ṣ*]*e-*⌜*ri*⌝ *Ak-ka-di-i sa-pa-nu* ⌜x x⌝
21. [. . .] x x [. . .]

(break)

Column iv

(break)

1′. x x [. . .]
2′. *eš-re-ti* x x x x x[. .]
3′. *ma-t*[*um šu*]*-ul-pu-ta-at qab*?*-li-at*? x x x
4′. x x x *ša* ᵈ*Adad is-su-ú e-li ma-*[*tim*]
5′. *ḫu-bu-ur-ša ik-ta-ba-ás* $ṭe_4$*-em-ša is-pu-uḫ*

Glassner (*La Chute d'Akkadé*, 83): 'Que dois-je faire? Echapperai-je au péril?' (OB) and 'Comment agirai-je pour m'en sortir moi-même(SB)';

H. Tadmor, B. Landsberger, and S. Parpola (*SAAB* 3 [1989] 11): 'With the god's help let me save myself';

B. Landsberger (ibid., 43): 'How (can I rid my country of all these catastrophes and failures) and put myself out for my country efficiently?'

In the first clause *šakānu* occurs in a unique usage. As Landsberger summed up the situation clearly, "It is nothing but a guess if one translates 'how can I manage to' (phrase), thus considering the two sentences an hendiadys: *ša-kānu* as *objektlos* ('absolute usage') and as Gtn" (ibid., n. 25).

In the second clause the objects *pagru* and *ramanu* occur, as well as the verb *šūṣû*. A well-known expression from Old Babylonian texts onward, the body parts *pagru* and *pūtu*, as well as *ramanu*, are used to express 'self' and as such occur in other literary texts: e.g., (Enlil has had enough of bringing about an evil command) *ana ramanīja u pagrīja ina ṣērījama rigimšina ešme* 'as a result of my own choice, and to my hurt I have listened to their noise' (Lambert-Millard, *Atra-ḫasīs*, III iii 42–43).

The meaning of the phrase depends on the combination of 'myself' as object and the verb *šūṣû* 'to bring out, make leave, dispatch, send away, let go free, escape, etc.' The above translations have two basic thrusts: one interprets *šūṣû* as 'to take oneself out in order to save oneself' and the other 'to put oneself out in order to save the country'. Philologically, both interpretations are possible.

iii 17. Cf. "Weidner Chronicle," line 54: *ummān Qutî idkâššumma* 'He (Marduk) raised the army of the Guti against him (Naram-Sin)'.

16. To destroy the plain of Akkade
17. he (the god) has summoned a mighty foe against me and
18. [rai]sed the Harians(?) (of) Malgium,
19. [.]. . . .
20. [. .] the plain of Akkade, the flatlands . .[. .]
21. [. . .] . . [. . .]

(break)

Column iv

(break)

1′. . . [. . .]
2′. The sanctuaries . [. .]
3′. The land was defiled. . . .
4′. The . . . . of Adad roared over the land.
5′. Having trampled its activity, it confused its mind.

---

iii 18. For parallels to this difficult line, see the introduction to chapter 10. The reading of Finkelstein is unlikely because *a-dì* with TI rendering /di/ is impossible in this text. One interpretation compatible with this line is to take *ḫa-ri-a-ti* from *arītu*, plural *ariātu* 'shields', and another the unknown Harians. The feminine plural oblique adjectival form *ḫa-ri-a-ti* could refer to *nišū* (cf. iv 9′). For Malgium, a territorial state located east of the Tigris and south of Ešnunna during the Old Babylonian period, see R. Kutscher, "Malgium," *RlA* 7 (1988) 300–4.

iii 19. This word has been treated in the dictionaries as unknown (CAD G) and as the name of a place (AHw 296b). The difficulty with this lexeme is the incompatibility of g with *k* in the same root in Semitic languages.

iv 3′. The verb *šulputu* can mean 'to overthrow, defeat, destroy' cities, etc., as well as 'to desecrate, defile' sanctuaries, etc. Both meanings are possible here; cf. *ana ešrēti māt Akkadî qāssu iddûma ušalpitu māt Akkadî* 'he (the Elamite king) who had laid hands on the sanctuaries of Babylonia and defiled all of Babylonia' (Streck, Asb. 178:14).

iv 5′. This bicolon line seems to have two paired verbs and objects. The objects are *ḫubūru // ṭēmu*. The latter has been variously understood as 'sense, personality, understanding', while the former has been understood as 'noise, tumult'. The 'noise' of mankind is a major motif of the flood narratives and thus basic to the flood metaphor employed in this column. It has been reinterpreted by W. von Soden as 'lautes Tun, larmende Aktivität' (*Symbolae Böhl*, 353). See most recently P. Michalowski, 'noise as activity, creation, independence' (*Studies Moran*, 387ff.), as well as the analysis of W. Moran (*Studies Reiner*, 251ff. and n. 37). On the other hand, for *ḫubūru* in the sense of 'deliberation, consideration' in addition to 'movement', see Å. Sjöberg (ZA 54 [1961] 58–59 n. 15), who bases

6′. *a-la-ni ti-la-ni ù* BÁRA.MEŠ *is-pu-un*
7′. *mi-it-ḫa-ri-iš ka-li-iš uš-te-mi*
8′. *ki-ma a-bu-ub me-e ša ib-ba-šu-ú*
9′. *i+na ni-ši* [(x)] *ma-aḫ-ri-a-ti*
10′. *ma-at* A[*k-ka*]*-di-i uš-te-mi*
11′. *uḫ-ta-al-li-iq ma-tam*
12′. *ki-ma la na-ab-ši-i ka-la-ša us-sà-aḫ-ḫi-ir*

13′. *s*[*a*]*-ap-na-at ma-tum šu-us-ḫu-ra-at ka-lu-š*[*a*]
14′. ⌈*i-na*⌉ *e-ze-ez* DINGIR.MEŠ *ma ru uš ib* [. . .]
15′. *a-l*[*a-n*]*i ub-bu-tu ti-la-nu sa-ap-nu*
16′. *ḫu-bu-ur ma-t*[*im*] *ú*-x-*eq-qí-ma ik-ta-ba-ás*
17′. *ki-ma a-bu-ub pa-al-gi ma-tam uš-te-m*[*i*]
18′. x x x *uḫ*[*-ta-a*]*l-li-iq wa-ri*-x (??)

Column v

(break)

1′. [. . .] x x
2′. [. . .] *ar pa*(?) *kam*?
3′. [. . .] x x [. .]
4′. [. . .] ^{d}INANNA
5′. [. . .]-*šu*(?)*-nu Me-li-li*
6′. [. . .] *i-na an-na bal* [x]
7′. [. . .]-*il-šu-nu-ti-ma*

---

his reasoning on the paired Sumerian nouns and their Akkadian counterparts: dím-ma // umuš :: *ḫubūru* // *ṭēmu*. Note the synonymous parallelism contained in the following line: a-ga-dè^{ki} dím-ma-bi ba-ra-è . . . umuš a-ga-dè^{ki} ba-kúr 'so was the good sense of Agade removed, . . . and Agade's intelligence was displaced' ("Curse of Agade," text **23**:147–48). It is interesting that the etymological correspondence dím-ma = *ṭēmu* is not employed in the same order. The present line may describe the complete cessation of physical and mental activities in the wake of devastation. For a detailed description of the flood imagery in these lines, see my article, "Symbolic Language in Akkadian Narrative Poetry: The Metaphorical Relationship between Poetical Images and the Real World," *Mesopotamian Poetic Language: Sumerian and Akkadian* (Groningen, 1996) 195–200. Both the collective nation and the individual person can possess dím-ma // *ṭemu*; for the former as the political balance of power and stability, see the discussion by P. Michalowski, *JAOS* 103 (1983) 244, and for the latter, see *ittad-*

6′. It leveled cities, tells, and temples.
7′. It transformed everywhere equally.
8′. Like the deluge of water that had been unleashed
9′. among the first peoples,
10′. It transformed the land of Akkade.
11′. It destroyed the land.
12′. As if it had never existed, it turned back/reduced it all (to almost nothingness).
13′. Leveled was the land, turned around was all of it.
14′. By the fury of the gods, ...
15′. Cities were obliterated, the tells were leveled.
16′. The activity of the land was . . . and trampled
17′. Like the flood (overflowing the banks) of the canal, it transformed the land.
18′. . . . destroying the . . .

Column v

(too fragmentary for translation)

---

laḫ ṭēmī ittešī mil[*ik* . . . *ia*] 'My reason has been disturbed, the counsel [of my . . .] confused' (W. G. Lambert, *Studies Sjöberg*, 327:117).

iv 10′–12′. Note that these lines are formed with a series of verbs in the perfect tense.

iv 14′. Could *ma-ru-uš* be the single example of shortened pronouns in this text?

iv 15′. Note that *alāni* is in the oblique case, but it must be the subject of the verb *ubbutu*.

iv 17′. The flooding of defeated cities was part of their destruction, as noted in an inscription of Naram-Sin; cf. (He took prisoners whom he drowned in the Euphrates, smote the city of Kiš(i), razed its wall) *ù* ÍD [*in*] *qirbīšu ušūṣi* 'and he let out the water into the (city's) center' (and thus slaughtered many in the city) (PBS 5 36 "ii" 18–20; and BT 1 iv 36′–39′ = *aK* 231–32:201–20, "Narām-sîn C 1").

8′. [. . .] *nu-ḫa um-ma šu-ú*
9′. [. . .] x x *ar iš-mu-ú*
10′. [. . .] *ud wa-ar-ba-ti*
11′. [. . .] *ši-id an-ni*
12′. [. . .] x *i-ib-*ka-nim*
13′. [. . .]x *ù ki*(?)*-lam za an ga*
14′. [. . .] *ud/na*(?)*-mu ši-na-ti*
15′. [. . .] *pu-ti-šu*
16′. [. . .] *bi-lu*
17′. [. . .] *ur*

Tablet II: Text ***20B***

Column i
1. *qá-ab-lam iš-ta-tu i-na mu-uḫ-ḫi-*⌈*ša*⌉
2. *ki-ma kar-mi uš-te-wi*
3. ⌈*ba la/ab* NE *te*?⌉ *im du*
4. [. . .] x [. . .]

(break)

Column ii

(traces of one sign each in lines 2–3)

Column v

(traces of one sign each in four lines)

Column vi

1′. [. . .] x x [. . .]
2′. [x] x ÉRIN GIŠ? MI x [.] x [.]

---

1. DUB.2.KAM.MA *ṭup-še-na pí-te-e-ma*
2. ŠU *Id-da-tum* DUB.SAR.TUR
3. ITI.ŠE.GUR$_{10}$.KU$_5$ UD.26.KAM
4. mu *Am-mi-ṣa-du-qá* lugal-e
5. ⌈urudu-du$_8$⌉-maḫ ⌈gal⌉-gal-la

---

v 8′. In this line, one might restore a form of *nâḫu,* either imperative or preterite, on the basis of "Naram-Sin and the Lord of Apišal," **12** rev. ii 6, 10.

v 14′. The parallel line is found in **21A** b 12. The two read as follows:

OB	ù ki-lam za	an-ga
Bo	ù ki-lam ša an-níš	an-ga

*Tablet II: Text **20B***

Column i

1. He wove battle against it.
2. He turned (it) into a ruin.
3. ....
4. ....

(break)

Column ii

(traces of one sign each in lines 2–3)

Column v

(traces of one sign each in four lines)

Column vi

1′. ....

2′. ....

---

1. Second Tablet of (the series) "Open the Tablet-Box,"
2. written by Iddatum, the junior scribe.
3. Month Addar, 26th day,
4. Year when Ammiṣaduqa, the king,
5. (presented) a very large high copper platform.

Neither makes much sense, although KI.LAM could be read GANBA, which does not add much in the context. However, note that the phonetic reading of the logogram according to the Ras Shamra edition of Diri is: *ša-ka-an-ka* KI.LAM = *ma-ḫi-rum* (see CAD M/1 93a). Thus the question is whether or not the above lines are to be read as a logogram and a full phonetic complement. The equivalent of disaster (KI.LAM) in the SB version line 95 is *ibissû* 'financial losses'.

21
The Middle Babylonian Recension

Introduction

In this section two texts are treated, only one of which (KBo 19 98) is definitely an edition of "Naram-Sin and the Enemy Hordes." The extant parts of the second (KBo 19 99) are not sufficient for positive proof of its identity. Consequently, the general statements below derive from the first text.

There are additional story elements that comprise the narrative statement of this edition. In particular the active roles of the divine characters attract notice. Ea, the trickster god, the creator of good and evil beings, decides to create an army of savages. This act is nevertheless ambivalent, for he restricts their power to obliterate mankind. Šamaš is the god of justice; Naram-Sin directs his prayers to Šamaš, whose city is exempt from savage destruction. In the human realm, Naram-Sin the king faces the enemy assault. Another thread of the story concerns Enmerkar, who at some time prior to this story forgot to write his memoirs. In the subhuman realm are uncivilized barbarians who lack the amenities of the urban Mesopotamian—the walled cities, the bread of life, and the aroma of beer. They are characterized as nomads of the mountains, herdsmen who live on the periphery of the Mesopotamian plan, but they are presented as a ranked society led by chieftains, the six equal "kings."

In the setting there are vague references to: (1) the mountains where the barbarians grew to maturity, and (2) "the city of Šamaš," which is said to be exempt from plundering by savages. The setting sharpens its focus on the main gate of the capital city of Akkade, at which point there is a parley between the aggressor and Naram-Sin.

The events are difficult to construct from this fragmentary text. It begins by stating that Enmerkar(?) did not write a stela(?) so that Naram-Sin could be guided and could proffer prayers to Šamaš on Enmerkar's behalf. Then, for an unknown reason, Ea creates the barbarians and endows them with certain attributes, including all sorts of plagues and disasters. The savages attack the Akkadian Empire, reaching the gates of Akkade itself. There the king meets them, and the text breaks off.

The intelligible story segments are:

a. the lack occasioned by Enmerkar who did not leave written memoirs with the result that Naram-Sin cannot be guided and cannot pray for him (lines b 2′–4′);
b. the creation of the nomads and the bestowal of plagues and disasters by Ea (lines b 5′–14′);
c. the destiny of the nomads declared by the gods (lines b 15′–25′);
d. the savages and their upbringing (lines b 26′–break);

e. the arrival of the enemy at the gates of Akkade and the parley with Naram-Sin (side c).

The discourse contains a surface structure identical with or similar to that of text **22** in certain blocks. The parallel texts are:

21A b 2′–4′	parallels **22** 29–30
21A b 5′	parallels **22** 31
21A b 7′–8′	parallels **22** 37–38
21A b 10′–14′	parallels **22** 94–97, 99–100

Circumstances of Discovery

The prism KBo 19 98 was found in controlled excavations in 1967 by the Deutsche Orient-Gesellschaft in the Great Temple, Temple I, on the eastern street in front of storeroom 4 in the rubbish pit or drainage canal. It was announced upon discovery by H. Otten and published in 1970.[23] On the other hand, KBo 19 99 was found in 1931 on Büyükkale, in locus x/8 directly under the surface.

General Observations

This edition is exceptional in that it is written on a five-sided prism. Although it has entered the literature as a six-sided prism, the geometry of the four extant sides indicates that their extension could only form a pentagonal figure. In the center of the prism, there is a perforation along the long axis in order that the standing prism could be rotated. One column of text is found on each of the five sides of the prism. The sides are blackened from burning, either from the destruction of the storeroom or in the original baking.

As in other Akkadian texts from Boghazköy, the text is divided into paragraphs, and the line division does not correspond to the syntactical divisions. The fragmentary state of the text is unfortunate, and it can only be hoped that more of the story will be found.

Orthography and Language[24]

This prism is the earliest extant exemplar of the Sargonic traditions to be found at Boghazköy. The writing has been dated by Gary Beckman to the Hittite Middle Kingdom (ca. 1500–1380).[25] Further, he states that the language of

[23] H. Otten, "Neue Entdeckungen in Boğazköy," *AfO* 22 (1968–69) 112; idem, *Aus dem Bezirk des Grossen Tempels* (KBo 19; WVDOG 84; Berlin) no. 98 Bo 1202/z.

[24] References in the following section are to: F. Böhl, Die *Sprache der Amarnabriefe* (LSS 2; Leipzig, 1909); J. Durham, *Studies in Boğazköy Akkadian* (Ph.D. diss., Harvard University, 1976); J. Huehnergard, *The Akkadian of Ugarit* (HSS 34; Cambridge, Mass., 1989); and R. Labat, *L'Akkadien de Boghaz-köi* (Paris, 1932).

[25] G. Beckman, "Mesopotamians and Mesopotamian Learning at Ḫattuša," *JCS* 35 (1983) 101ff.

prisms KBo 19 98 and 99 is "not the 'barbarisches Schreiber-Akkadisch'" and notes that the father of the scribe of KBo 19 99, who bears the name Anu-šar-ilāni, must have been a genuine Mesopotamian, probably a Babylonian, who lived, had a son, and probably died at Ḫattuša.[26] There are none of the characteristics of the dialects of western peripheral Akkadian. For an example of western peripheral Akkadian written at Ḫattuša, see text **9B**.

In relation to the paleography, Beckman mentions in particular the cramped spacing and the "stepped" ID and DA signs.[27]

The orthography is closer to late Old Babylonian than to Middle Babylonian: (1) irregular appearance of mimation (*u_4-mi-im*, b 17′ vs. *qa-qa-ru*, b 6′); (2) noncontraction of *i* + *a*; (3) negative particle /aj/ written *a-ja*; (4) written *w* (neither dropping at beginning of words nor undergoing the intervocalic shift to *m*). The determinative KI after GN's as well as the writing URU.KI occur only in the oldest tablets from Ḫattuša (Durham §11b). CVC signs are limited: BAT, ḪAR, ḪUR, KÀR, ŠAL; and CVm signs, ŠUM, LUM, NAM, NIM, TUM, TAM, TIM.

With a few exceptions, the stops are rendered by contrasting syllabograms: *ba* :: *pa*, and so on, reflecting the Babylonian series of stops, which distinguish voicing.[28] This contrast is also found on Akkadian scholarly tablets found at Boghazköy written in an Assyro-Mitannian ductus.[29] The only exceptions to this practice occur among the labials: the sign BI is used to render /bi/ and /pi/, and the sign PI is used to render /wa, wi, wu/, a contrast that we have noted was typical of northern Old Babylonian. Despite the confusion in other texts (Böhl, p. 20; Labat, pp. 13–14; Huehnergard, p. 35; Durham §7b, §26a), our text seems to distinguish between /pa/ and /ba/. The dentals are rendered as would be expected according to the Babylonian syllabary, with the exception of /di/, which is rendered by the TI sign (side b 20′) (see Durham §21d). According to Durham's note, this rendering is confined to tablets from the reign of Šuppiluliuma I or earlier.[30] Among the velars, the exception is the use of the sign KI to render /gi/ (side b 24′),[31] and /ki/ and the expected KI as well as GI are used to render /qi/ (side b 11′).[32] The rendering of /qa/ by QA is the normative writing in BoAkk.[33] The spellings with sibilants are consistent with expected Babylonian forms, the exceptions being due to the phonological form of certain lexemes rather than phonology. One lexeme is *siraš*, which undergoes phono-

[26] Ibid., 104.

[27] Ibid., 102 n. 27.

[28] Note that this is not true of the other peripheral Akkadian text in this corpus, text **9B**: *šar tamḫāri*.

[29] G. Wilhelm, "Zur babylonisch-assyrischen Schultradition in Ḫattuša," *Uluslararası 1. Hititoloji Kongresi Bildirileri* (Çorum, 1990) 88.

[30] Durham, 288 n. 56.

[31] See occasional references in Durham §21g.

[32] See rare occurrences of the latter listed in Durham §21q, as well as in text **9B**.

[33] See Durham §21o and p. 307 n. 254.

logical development over time: the initial sibilant /s/ changes to /š/, and the final /š/ becomes /s/ by dissimilation. The writing *ši-i-ra-aš* occurs in this text. Should we render the first syllable si_{17}? Such a rendering is possible.[34] Another problem is the writing *še-bi-it* (side b 11′), which seems to be *šibṭu*. According to Durham (§24p) the value $ši_x$ for the sign ŠE does not occur in the Boghazköy Akkadian corpus. Consequently, one may conclude that our text does not distinguish between /še/ and /ši/ but uses both signs, ŠE and ŠI, arbitrarily. No syllabograms starting with S occur; /sa/ is rendered by ZA, /si/ is rendered by ZI, which is quite normal in Boghazköy Akkadian, in particular before the reign of Šuppiluliuma I.[35] There is no use of emphatic syllabograms, except in a broken context, side c 17.

The plene spellings of vowels are not only limited to the traditional *-i-a-am/at* and CV-V contracted vowels in word-final position, but also to use as phonetic indicators of the vowel quality i/e: *ri-e-it-ti* (side b 3′), *li-iš-ki-e-nu* (side b 19′), *gi-i-li-e* (side b 11′), and *ni-i-nu* (side c 11′). The tendency to double consonants in intervocalic position in the first syllable of the word has been noted in connection with text **9B**. In this composition it appears in *ḫu-ul-lu-uq-qí* (side b 16′) representing *ḫuluqqû*.

Throughout this composition, the standard syntactic order of subject-object-verb has undergone inversion in accordance with poetic license.

Poetics

Hymno-epic elements are found sporadically in this text. There is the terminative adverbial postposition *-iš* in *qa-ti-šu* for *qātiššu* (side b 9′).

Parallelism forms the poetic structure of the composition. In particular there are frequent parallel couplets; one example is *ālum ana panīšunu ul ālum qaqqaru ana panī*[*šunu*] *ul qaqqaru*, side b 5′–7′.

Both texts have been treated in T. Longman, *Fictional Akkadian Royal Autobiography: A Generic and Comparative Study* (Winona Lake, Ind., 1991). These texts were collated in 1972 by Bob Biggs, who kindly permitted me to use his results. I also collated them in 1987.

Manuscripts

Boghazköy

Bo 1202/z = KBo 19 98 (five-sided prism)
Bo 316/a = KBo 19 99 (four-sided prism)

[34] See Durham §25b.
[35] See Durham §21s and notes, §25b.

Transcription, Text **21A**: *KBo 19 98*

Side a

(break)

1′. [. . . . .]

2′. [. . . . .]-an-gub me-en

3′. [. . . .]-*ib ra-ak-*⌈*su*⌉

4′. [. . . í]b.ús

5′. [. . . *ša*]-*me-e lu-ú-*[(x)]

6′. [. .] AN

7′. [. . . í]b.ús

8′. [. . . *i-*]*na ša-me-e*

9′. [. .] AN

10′. [ ] ti-la

11′. [. . . . *ib-lu-*]*uṭ*

(break)

Side b

(break)

1′. [. . .] *i ki na*? [. . .]

2′. [*En*]-*me-kàr*! *ú-ul iš-ṭú-ra-am-ma na-*x[-x]

3′. [*šu-ú ú*]-*ul a-ḫi-ma ù ri-e-it-ti ú-ul*

Philological and Textual Notes, Text **21A**

b 2′. This line is read [. . .] NA.DU$_8$ *ul išṭuramma* NA.DU$_8$ by Longman, *Autobiography* [1983] 310. However, *narû* is never written with the logogram DU$_8$. With slight emendation of the first two signs, I read [*En*]-*me-kàr*. For the use of the *kàr* sign in this text, see line 14: *iz-za-kàr*. Unfortunately, although one wants to read *na-ra*/DÙ-[*am*/*šu*] at the end of the line, the second sign does not fit.

Translation, Text **21A**: *KBo 19 98*

Side a (bilingual)

(too little of the text is preserved on side a to warrant a translation, and this side bears no obvious relationship to the rest of the text)

Side b

1′. (unconnected signs)

2′. [En]merkar did not inscribe a stela(?) for me.
3′. [He] was not my brother and he did not guide me (lit. [take] my arm).

---

b 3′. The suggestion of reading *ṣabātu* in the break at the beginning of line 4′ is based on the common phrase *qātam ṣabātu*. Normally, however, the verb used with *rittu* is *tamāḫu*, and *kullu* is used of holding items in the hand, but neither seems to fit the present context.

4′. [*iṣ-bat-ma*] *ma-ḫar* ^{d}UTU *ú-ul ak-ru-ub-*⸢*šu-ma*⸣

5′. [*a*]*-wi-lu-tum i-ru-ub a-na pa-ni-šu-nu a-na ḫur-ri* URU.KI
6′. *a-na pa-ni-šu-nu ú-ul* URU.KI-**lum qa-qa-ru a-na pa-ni-*[*šu-nu*]
7′. *ú-ul qa-qa-ru* 6 LUGAL.MEŠ *šu-nu at-ḫu-ú šu-*[*pu-ú*]

8′. *ù* 6 ME *um-ma-an-šu-nu* ^{d}*É-a be-lum* [x] ⸢x⸣ [?]
9′. [*a-n*]*a zu-mi iš-pu-ur qa-ti-šu ib-ni-šu-nu-*[*ti*]
10′. x-x-*šu-nu-ti-ma ša-lu-um-ma-at* UR.MAḪ.[MEŠ]
11′. *mu-ú-tam nam-ta-ra gi-i-li-e še-bi-iṭ* [*ša-ri*]
12′. [*ni-ib-r*]*i-ta ḫu-ša-aḫ-ḫa ù* KI.LAM *ša an-níš* (wr. *QA) *an ga*
13′. [x x] *ra-bu-ú it-ti-šu-nu iṭ-ru-ud* ^{d}*É-a* [*be-lum*]
14′. [*pa-šu*] *i-pu-ša-am-ma iz-za-kàr a-na* DINGIR.MEŠ ŠEŠ.MEŠ-*šu*

15′. [ÉRI]N.MEŠ *an-ni-a-am a-na-ku ab-ni at-tu-nu ši-ma-ti-šu*
16′. *ši-i-ma aš-šum la ḫu-ul-lu-uq-qí a-wi-lu-tim šum-šu*

17′. *lu-ú zi-ki-ir a-na wa-ar-ki-a-at* u_4*-mi-im*
18′. *l*[*i*]*-ip-la-ḫu-ma* BÀD *ù* SIG$_4$ BÀD *lu-ú* DINGIR-*lum*
19′. *šu-nu li-iš-ki-e-nu*

20′. *a-ja iṣ-bat* URU.KI ^{d}UTU *qú-ra-a-dì a-ja iš-lu-ul*
21′. *šal-la-tam-ma li-ib-ba-šu a-ja ib-lu-uṭ*
22′. *a-ja i-ku-ul* NINDA *bu-lu-uṭ li-ib-bi a-ja i-ṣí-in*
23′. [*ni-p*]*í-iš* ⸢*ši*⸣*-i-ra-aš me-e li-iš-ti-i-ma*
24′. [*li*]*-it-ta-ag-gi*$_5$*-iš a-na ka-la* u_4*-mi i-na mu-*[*ši*]

---

b 9′. The word *zu-mi* is perhaps related to the word *zummu* 'beraubt sein, entbehren' (AHw).

b 10′. For the phrase *šalummat nēši* 'the radiance of the lion', cf. [*ki*] *nēši šalummat*[*am lūṭ*]*erka* 'I will take from you (your) radiance as (from) a lion' (Tell Asmar, 1930, 117:7–8; see Whiting, ZA 75 [1985] 180) and parallel [*ki-ma*] UR.MAḪ-*im š*[*a*]*-l*[*um-m*]*a-tum li-ik-l*[*a*?]*-ka* '(May your heart) deny you splendor like (that) of a lion' (Wilcke, ZA 75 [1985] 202). Further, Sargon's terrifying leonine radiance is termed *šalummatu* in **8** rev. 5′.

b 11′. Note the emendation of von Soden: *gi-iḫ!-le-e* (AHw 1556b), taking this word from *giḫlu*, "an expression or gesture of mourning." If so, one won-

4′. So before Šamaš I did not pray for him.

5′. Before them, mankind scurried into caves. A city
6′. before them was not a city. Land (plots) before them
7′. were not land (plots). Six kings were they, partners in brotherhood, resplendent,
8′. and six hundred were their troops. Ea, the lord, ...
9′. to be dispensed with, he sent. With his own hand, he created them
10′. . . . . them and the terror of lions,
11′. death, plague, fever(?), storms/disease,
12′. [fa]mine, want, and (losses on) the market, which. . . .
13′. . . . . increased, with them, he sent. Ea, the lord,
14′. opened his mouth and spoke to the gods, his brothers.

15′. "I have created this people. You, its destiny
16′. "determine on the condition that they are not to annihilate mankind." "Its name
17′. "shall be a password. To the end of days,
18′. "may they fear walls, so that the very bricks of the walls will be a god
19′. "which they will worship.

20′. "May it not attack the city of Šamaš, the hero! May it not take
21′. "any booty, and may its heart not enjoy life!
22′. "May it not eat the bread of life! May it not smell
23′. "the aroma of beer! May it drink (only) water and
24′. "Let it roam all (its) days! In the night

---

ders if *še-bi-it-tam* could be a mistake for *sipittu*. On the other hand, more in keeping with the context would be another physical infection or infirmity. Therefore, the two words were interpreted as *qīlû*, and an unattested noun formation from *qalû* 'to burn' and *šebiṭ* [*šāri*] from *šibṭu* (AHw 1228a).

b 12′. See notes to OB version col. v 14′. Further, a reading *an-níš* is possible in Ḫattuša; the syllabogram *níš* does appear there (see Durham §21n). The clause *ša . . . rabû* forms a relative clause that ends in a stative subjunctive.

b 22′–23′. Note the parallel: *šikaram šiti šīmti māti* 'drink beer, the custom of the land' (Gilg. P iii 14).

b 24′. I take the verb to be *itangušu* 'to wander around, to run about'.

25′. [*li*]-*it-ti-la-ma a-ja i-še-a-*[*šu šittum*]

26′. [6 LU]GAL.MEŠ *šu-nu at-ḫu-ú šu-pu-*[*ú ba-nu-tu*(?)]
27′. 6? ME *um-ma-an-šu-nu* ḪUR.SAG.MEŠ [. . .]
28′. [x].HI.A *ú-ra-ab-bu-ú-šu-nu-ti* [. . .]
29′. [. . .]-*ri ki-ib-ri *dan-na!-t*[*im* . . .]
30′. [. . .]-*me*(?)-*su*(?) [x]-*al-la-at* [. . .]
31′. [. . . *t*]*i i-mu-r*[*u* . . .]

Side c

(break)
2′. [. . .]-*ma a-na* [. .]
3′. [. . .] SAL.TUKU-**na* [. . .]
4′. [. . .] *e*? *iṣ-ṣa-lu ú-*[. . .]
5′. [. . . *ša-*]*a-ru ú-ul* [. . .]
6′. [*a-na a-*]*la-ki-im ša-a-ru* [. . .]
7′. [*a-bu*]-*bu te im tam* [. . .]

8′. [*a*]-*na* KU[R A]-*kà-dè*.KI *is-sà-an-qú-nim a-na* K[AR . . .]
9′. [*is*]-*sà-a*[*n-qú*]-*nim-ma a-na* KÁ.GAL A-*kà-dè*-K[I *a-na*]
10′. ^{I}*N*[*a-r*]*a-am-*^{d}EN.ZU LUGAL *ki-a-am i-ša-*[*ap-pa-ru*]
11′. [*um-ma š*]*u-nu-ma* 6 LUGAL.MEŠ *ni-i-nu at-ḫu-*[*ú šu-pu-ú*]
12′. [x] *ba-nu-tum ù* 6 ME *um-ma-an-ni ù it-*[*ti-ni* x x]
13′. [?] x SIPA x *ka-bar qí-in-na-*[*a-at*(?)]
14′. [*ti-a*]*m-tim is-sà-an-qú-ni-ik-ku zi-mi* [. . .]
15′. [*a*]-*na*(?) *ma-aḫ-ri-*[*ka*]

16′. [x] ^{I}*Na-ra-*[*a*]*m-*^{d}EN.ZU-*ma id-dì-ma-*[. . .]
17′. *pa-ni-ti* [. . .] *ù* [*er*?]-*ṣe-tim lu* [(*dariaku*) . .]
18′. *i-il-la-a*[*k/ku*. . . . . . .] *li-ik* [. . .]
19′. ^{I}*Na-ra-am-*^{d}[EN.ZU . . .]
20′. *um-ma šu-ma* [. . .]
21′. *i-il-la-*[*ku*. . . . . . .]
22′. *ú-lu ma-a* [. . .]
23′. [*a-n*]*a*(?) LÚ [. . .]
24′. (traces of two signs)

25′. "let it lie down, but may sleep not find it!"

26′. Six(?) kings were they, partners in brotherhood, resplendent [in beauty?].
27′. Six hundred troops were their troops, the mountains. . . .
28′. . . . . raised them. . . .
29′. . . . .
30′. . . . .
31′. . . . . which they saw. . . .

Side c

(break)
2′–7′. (too fragmentary to warrant translation)

8′. To the land of Akkade they approached. To the quay of [. . .]
9′. they approached and to the (very) gate of Akkade to
10′. Naram-Sin, the king, thus, they send (messages),
11′. saying, "Six kings are we, brothers, resplendent
12′. "in beauty, and six hundred are our troops and w[ith us(?) . . .]
13′. " . . . shepherd, . . . , cowboy, comrades/clansmen
14′. "[of the seal] and they have come to you in massed force[. . .]
15′. "to oppose you."

16′. [. . .] Naram-Sin became downcast(?) . . .
17′. of former/before . . . and . . .
18′. he will go
19′. Naram-Sin [opened his mouth, speaking to . . .]
20′. saying, " . . . .
21′. he will go
22′–26′. (too fragmentary for translation)

25′. *šu*-x [. . .]
26′. *ú-lu* [. . .]
27′. (traces of one sign)
(break)

Side d

(break)
1′. (traces of one or two signs)
2′. [*a-n*]*a* DAM [. . .]
3′. [*a-n*]*a mu*? *kur* [. . .]

4′. [x] x *na* [. . .]
5′. [*ḫu-l*]*u-uq*(?)[. . .]
6′. [x] x *ta* [. . .]
7′. [?] *ki-ib-*[*ra-tim* . . .]
8′. [x] x [. . .]

9′. [x] x [. . .]
(break)

Transcription, Text ***21B****: KBo 19 99*

Side a

(break)
1′. [. . .] *ad/la* [. . .]

2′. [. . .] *uš-te-e-ri-*[*ib*? . . .] GIŠ [. .]
3′. [. . .] *ḫur-ri šum-*[*ma* . . .]
4′. [. . . *l*]*a*? *uš-te-e-*[*ri-ib*? X].MEŠ LUGAL(?).[MEŠ]
5′. [. . .]*ú-še-ṣi* [x] *ma-a/dan-*⌜x⌝ [x (x)]

Text ***21B***

a 2′–5′. Perhaps this section could be interpreted as 'if the enemy has invaded, then scurry into caves; if the enemy has not invaded, bring out. . . . '

Side d

(too fragmentary to warrant translation)

*Translation, Text **21B**: KBo 19 99*

Side a

(too little of the text is preserved on side a to warrant a translation)

6′. [. . .]x-*li-li*
7′. [. . . LUG]AL *a-li-e-tim*
8′. [. . . *i*]-*ta-mu-ú*
9′. [. . .] x *i-na-na* [*iq*]-*tab-bi*
10′. [. . .] x *ú-šar-ki*-[*ib*]
11′. [. . .] ⌈x⌉ *a-ḫi is*-[x]
12′. [. . .] x *ri*(?) *bi tu nim*
13′. [. . .] *ja* [x]
14′. [. . .] *⌈*ja*⌉ [x]
(break)

Side b

(break)

---

1. ŠU [l]*Ḫa-ni-ku-i-li* DUB.SAR [(x)]
2. DUMU [d]*A-nu*-LUGAL.DINGIR.MEŠ [D]UB.SAR BAL.BI [(x)]
3. ÌR [d]EN-*bi-lu-lu* [d][x-x] [d]*Nin*.[*maḫ*?]
4. [d]*Nin-é-gal* [d]*A-nim* [d]IM [d][. . .]
5. *Ìl-a-ba*$_4$ [d]*Aš-šur* [d]*Ḫa*-[*ni-iš*?]
6. [d]x [x].GAL *ù* [d]*I-na-ar* x[. . .]
7. *na-ra-am* [d]*Ḫé*?-*bat*? [d][. . .]
8. [d]*Ni*[*saba*(?)]

(break)

Side b

2. For a discussion of the sign BAL in Hittite texts and its meaning in this text and others, see C. Rüster and E. Neu, *Hethitisches Zeichenlexikon* (Wiesbaden, 1989) p. 90 sub no. 4.

(too fragmentary for translation)

7′. [. . .] King(?) of the Upper Lands

8′. [. . .] they swore

9′. [. . .] now, he has repeatedly said

10′. [. . .] he caused to ride

(break)

Side b

(break)

---

1. (By) the hand of Ḫanikuili, the scribe,
2. the son of Anu-šar-ilāni, the scribe, its translator(?),
3. servant of Enbilulu, [. . .], Ninmaḫ(?),
4. Ninegal, Anu, Adad, [. . .],
5. Ilaba, Aššur, Ḫa[niš],
6. [. . .]. gal, and Inar, . . .
7. beloved of Ḫepat(?) . . .
8. . . . .

(break)

22
The Standard Babylonian Recension

Introduction

The short Standard Babylonian recension of the powerful legend of "Naram-Sin and the Enemy Hordes" contains a narrative in which the several characters are sketched in rapidly, and the setting is depicted with short impressionistic brushstrokes. It is a story of action seen in the shadow of the character Naram-Sin, who is the focus of the tale.

A variety of characters appear in this text. In the divine realm, the gods are divided into two groups: (1) those who create and guide the enemy hordes—Enlil, Tiāmat, Bēlet-ilī, and Ea; and (2) those who guide Naram-Sin and whose guidance he seeks—Ištar, Ilaba, Zababa, Annunītum, Šullat, Ḫaniš, and Šamaš. Ea is again a liminal figure who helps the great gods with their devastation and then turns on them after the deed. A truer friend of mankind is Šamaš, forefather of Enmerkar, who reigns over the earth but who passes a severe sentence on Enmerkar. In the human realm stands Naram-Sin, the central person of the narrative. For reasons not given in the text, he is compared with Enmerkar. In many ways the two are similar.[36]

The cause of Enmerkar's punishment is not obvious. Certainly, his crime was not that he did not write down the way in which he extricated himself from the teeth of disaster. This was just an unfortunate consequence of his punishment.[37] Perhaps the crime for which he and his entire kin had to pay so dearly was rather his disobedience to the omen he received, which may be described in lines 11–21 of "Naram-Sin and the Enemy Hordes." Disobedience to omens is the sordid transgression for which Naram-Sin is treated so harshly.

In the subhuman realm are the enemy hordes, a people with partridge bodies and raven faces but with human blood running in their veins. Their leaders are named: Anubanini, his wife, and his sons. His sons become the seven equal kings and thus are not "in brotherhood" but are really blood brothers.

The setting is described sketchily. The path of the rampage begins at Purušḫanda (cf. chapter 4) in Anatolia, sweeps across northern Mesopotamia, the shores of the Van and Urmia lakes, the mountains and plateaus of Iran, and completes the circle in the southern lands of Dilmun, Makkan, and Meluḫḫa. The sites of the battles with the troops of Naram-Sin are not given. What is specified is the setting for the placement of the *narû* and its tablet box: the cult room of Nergal, in the Emeslam in Kutha. The same connection between the god Nergal, his sanctuary, and Naram-Sin is made in text **13**.

The events may be outlined as follows: There is a devastating invasion of Babylonia by barbarian hordes, who are the creatures of Enlil, suckled by

[36] See discussion at the beginning of this chapter.

[37] See further my article, "Writing for Posterity," *Kinattūtu ša dārâti: Raphael Kutscher Memorial Volume* (Tel Aviv, 1993) 205–18.

Tiāmat, and raised by Bēlet-ilī. The hordes are described as being led by seven brothers, sons of Anubanini, charging down from the mountains of the northwest to annihilate the whole Near East. On their march of destruction, they are joined by seventeen more kings. Having ascertained that these hordes are composed of human beings of flesh and blood rather than demons and evil spirits, Naram-Sin decides to attack them and asks the gods for an omen. His pious solicitude to obtain a correct omen is shown in his inquiring of not one but seven gods. Unfortunately, the omen is negative, but Naram-Sin in his hubris decides to ignore the answer and proceeds with his attack. For three years Naram-Sin pursues the enemy, but his forces are annihilated so that "not one came back alive." Deeply depressed and seriously doubting whether he is at all fit to be king, Naram-Sin does not know where to turn. At Ea's suggestion, he offers the New Year's offerings on the fourth year and then seeks counsel of the gods through omens. Apparently the answer is now positive, since Naram-Sin succeeds in battle. However, he is not allowed to complete his victory and exterminate the enemy. Ištar informs Naram-Sin that Enlil will take care of his enemies. This version concludes with an admonition to a future ruler.

The story segments are:

a. Naram-Sin's introduction (lines 1–3);
b. history of Enmerkar (lines 4–30);
c. creation of the enemy hordes (lines 31–46);
d. eruption of the enemy hordes and subsequent devastation (lines 47–62);
e. despatch of scout (lines 63–71);
f. first consultation of omens (lines 72–78);[38]
g. first reaction of Naram-Sin and its aftermath (lines 79–87);
h. second reaction of Naram-Sin and the intervention of Ea (lines 88–98);
i. second consultation of omens (lines 108–19);
j. capture of enemy soldiers (lines 120–23);
k. third reaction of Naram-Sin and the intervention of Ištar (lines 124–48);
l. admonition to future ruler (lines 149–80).

The narration is shorter than the earlier written versions of the tale. This condensation has resulted in abrupt shifts, without the transitions essential for bonding the individual segments into a unified whole. The clumsiness of the conflated text is reflected in the inverse order of the logical sequence of events in lines 105–7 and 108–10.

In section (k) a unique unit, lines 131–46, seems to be embedded. This unit is conspicuous for its lack of relationship to the preceding and succeeding sections. It reflects themes from the "Curse of Agade" and the Old Babylonian "Sumerian City Laments." In its formulas it contains phrases and clauses found in the prophecies and the omen literature. Labat speculates that the scribe may

[38] There would not be any reason for Naram-Sin to inquire of the will of the gods before this point in the story, despite opinions to the contrary (cf. Parpola's views in H. Tadmor, B. Landsberger, and S. Parpola, "The Sin of Sargon and Sennacherib's Last Will," *SAAB* 3 [1989] 37–38).

have copied out certain omens from astrological literature concerning Venus.[39] The unit is composed of a series of couplets.

The content of the couplets is as follows:

131–32: the withdrawal of divine favor from the enemies in some future time;
133–34: the demolition of the city of the enemies and its dwelling places;
135–36: the defilement of the earth and the disruption of the natural agricultural cycle;
137–40: death and discord among people, disruption of family life;
141–42: inversion of ethical standards;
143–44: attack of a foreign army;
145–46: collapse of economic life and the imposition of a new ruler as a result of foreign conquest.

This narrative is encapsulated in a discourse framework: an introduction and a conclusion refer to the text as a royal stela, a *narû*, which is to be read aloud and its injunctions observed. The narrative mode that characterizes this text has been said to be "autobiography," first-person narration by an overt narrator, Naram-Sin, who relates his exploits for the edification of his implied audience, his people. Thus Naram-Sin is at the same time the protagonist and the narrator, whose perceptual and conceptual points of view alone are conveyed. The perceptual point of view is that of his older self, who has learned wisdom from his experiences. The discourse time is possibly the end of Naram-Sin's life, and the story time is previous to the discourse time, with a retrospective order of events. Certain blocks of the discourse contain a surface structure identical with or similar to the structure of texts **20** and **21**.

Circumstances of Discovery

The standard recension of "Naram-Sin and the Enemy Hordes" is found on tablets that are Neo-Assyrian and Neo-Babylonian in provenance and script.

Most of the Neo-Assyrian tablets (A–F) were probably gathered from the site of Nineveh during the nineteenth-century explorations.[40] Accessioned by the British Museum in 1881, tablet A bears the stamp of the palace of Aššurbanipal, giving clear evidence of its original findspot. The remaining manuscripts were accessioned under the siglum of the palace mound, known by the Turkish name, Kuyunjik, at Nineveh, which was ransacked by British Museum agents during three periods in the nineteenth century.[41] While Layard uncovered Sennacherib's palace and its library in the southern part of the mound in 1849–51, it was Rassam who discovered the northern palace of Aššurbanipal

[39] Labat, *Les Religions*, 313 n. 5.

[40] For bibliography, see Chapter 1: Introduction.

[41] All were cataloged by C. Bezold in his *Catalogue of the Cuneiform Tablets in the Kouyunjik Collection of the British Museum*. For A, see vol. 4.1773, B in 2.715–16, C in 2.734, D in 3.942, E in 1.388, and F in 3.1304.

and other libraries in 1852. Excited by the discoveries, George Smith came in 1873 and 1874 to search methodically through the spoils from these excavations. Nevertheless, all we know at present is that the library of Aššurbanipal at Nineveh contained at least one copy of "Naram-Sin and the Enemy Hordes."

Manuscript G comes from Sultantepe, on the plain of Harran, ten miles southeast of Urfa. Excavations at Sultantepe were conducted by the British Institute of Archaeology at Ankara and the Turkish Department of Antiquities in 1951–52.[42] On June 5, 1951, the excavators came upon a cache of 572 unbaked tablets in sounding F.[43] These tablets were lying against the outer wall of a house on the earth pavement of an open space. "Whether they had been deliberately stacked in this position or had been thrown out as refuse remained uncertain."[44] They seem to be the remains of a provincial library of a priest of Zababa by the name of Qurdi-Nergal and are now housed in the Archaeological Museum at Ankara.

The Neo-Babylonian tablet, manuscript H, is said to come "probably from Kish."[45] Although the tablet has a 1924 accession number, indicating that it came from the first two seasons of excavation at Kiš, the Ashmolean Museum gave it this number in 1949 when it was found among other tablets lying unnumbered in a drawer. In the drawer were tablets published by van der Meer with the 1924 date, other fragments that could be joined to tablets of the 1924 Kiš collection, and still others that matched the ones photographed during the 1923–24 season.[46] Apart from certain exceptions, the tablets accessioned in 1949 probably do stem from the excavations at the site conducted by the joint expedition of the Ashmolean Museum of Oxford University and the Field Museum of Natural History (Chicago) from 1923 to 1933. Neo-Babylonian remains were found in both the western and the eastern mounds. In the western district of the site, Nebuchadnezzar, the famous builder, restored the splendor of the ziggurat and its temenos at Uḥaimir, while new building was undertaken in areas even further west. In the eastern part of the site, major construction took place around Ingharra; ancient Ḫursagkalama, the main ritual center; mound W, the main residential area; and at some of the other smaller mounds.[47] All these areas were explored during the first two seasons, so while most of the late tablets come from mound W,[48] tablet H could just as well have come from any other mound.

[42] See "Summary of Archaeological Work in Turkey during 1951," *AnSt* 2 (1952) 15; S. Lloyd and N. Cökçe, "Sultantepe: Anglo-Turkish Joint Excavations, 1952," *AnSt* 3 (1953) 27–51.

[43] See the locus on the plan in *AnSt* 3, 30, fig. 2 and p. 35, fig. 4.

[44] O. R. Gurney, *The Sultantepe Tablets*, vol. 1 (Occasional Publications of the British Institute of Archaeology at Ankara 3; London, 1957) iv.

[45] O. R. Gurney, *Literary and Miscellaneous Texts in the Ashmolean Museum* (OECT 11; Oxford, 1989) 11.

[46] Ibid., 1.

[47] McG. Gibson, *The City and Area of Kish* (Coconut Grove, Fla., 1972) fig. 29b.

[48] Ibid., 76.

General Observations

All Neo-Assyrian manuscripts are ostensibly written on two-column tablets; this is certain for texts A, B, C, F, and G, while D is a flake and E a corner. The upper half of A is preserved, the lower half of B, a portion of the left half of C, a portion of the bottom left of F, and most of G. D is a fragment of the middle of the tablet. There is an apparent difference in length of the columns (see score). Whereas there seem to be 46 lines per column in A, B, C, and E, although C might possibly be shorter by a line or two (see beginning of col. iv in A iii 15′), there are 55 lines per column in G and 60 lines per column in F. There are thus some discrepancies in the line divisions among the tablets, making the exact number of lines in the composition impossible to calculate. Note that both King's copy of the reverse of tablet B and the photograph published on p. 406 are incorrectly aligned. King's copy indicates that B iii 18 is on the same line as iv 18′, but, as can be seen clearly in the photograph, a crack runs through the "7" of iii 18 to the bottom of the KA in iv 19′. The photograph also clearly presents the misalignment of the flake when attached to the tablet; the lines dividing the columns are not straight, those of the flake being at a slight angle to those of the tablet. Third, the combination of these two errors was compounded by leaving out a line on the edge. For these reasons, a new copy is given on p. 407 to show the correct alignment of lines.

The one Neo-Babylonian tablet, manuscript H, is a school exercise similar to that of the Neo-Babylonian tablet of the Sargon "Autobiography," text **2**. The obverses of both tablets contain exercises of lexical texts (manuscript H has Ḫḫ II), while on the reverse appear extracts of the literary texts. Note that the Sargon letter from Nippur (text **10**), of Old Babylonian date, likewise has a lexical text on its reverse. Further, the line division of manuscript H does not parallel that of the Neo-Assyrian library copies.

Orthography and Language

The texts written in Neo-Assyrian script exhibit typical orthography, with the exception that C employs only *šu* and never *šú*.

In morphology, the anaphoric pronouns display the following contrast: the -*š*- form is used for the accusative (e.g., *šâšunu*, lines 122–23), and the -*t*- form for the genitive (e.g., *šunūti*, lines 133ff.).[49] However, this distinction is not kept for the independent pronouns: *jāti*, line 83 but *kāša*, line 180. Other peculiarities of this composition are: the use of the *šūt* relative determinative for second singular 'you who' (lines 177 and 179) and of the indefinite impersonal pronoun *mimma* for the personal *mamman* (line 149). This composition exhibits the ba-

[49] For this contrast, see B. Groneberg, *Syntax, Morphologie und Stil der jungbabylonischen "Hymnischen" Literatur* (FAOS 14/1; Stuttgart, 1987) 114.

sic grammatical declension of nouns, with a few exceptions in manuscript G (e.g., line 8). Note, however, the many grammatical difficulties with the text as a whole elaborated in the philological notes.

The vocabulary of the manuscripts along with the order of the wording is virtually identical (see text score). There is an extra word in line 28 in manuscript B and in line 39 in manuscript G. A substitution of one lexeme for another can be seen in line 58: G has *ṣēru* for A's *sapannu*.

No evaluation can be made of the traits of the Neo-Babylonian tablet because of its fragmentary nature and because any exception may be due to the ineptitude of the student rather than to the peculiarities of the dialect.

Poetics

There is some evidence of sound patterning in this composition. Alliteration is shown in the use of /s/ words, *sapāḫu* . . . *sanāqu* as well as in phrases such as in line 65: *ina luṭê luput ina ṣillê* [*suḫul*].

Prosody of some sort seems indicated in a poetic line divided into two to four feet per line. The line ends in a trochee, shown by a shortening of the pronominal ending at the end of a line of verse: line 31, *pānūšun*; line 48, *šaparšun*.

The poetic structure is based on a tercet alternating with couplets (e.g., lines 1–3, 4–5; and 56–58, 59–60). Parallel couplets can be incremental (e.g., lines 32–33), synonymous (e.g., 80–81), or contrastive (e.g., 147–48). The language is terse, not given to abundant use of figures of speech or descriptions.

The structural device of repetition is applied monotonously. Verbatim repetition of phrases can be found in the consultation of the omens and in the description of Naram-Sin's defeat.[50] Even the scribe was so bored that he wrote "ditto" (KIMIN) in lines 86–87.

In general see the study by O. Gurney, "The Sultantepe Tablets IV: The Cuthean Legend of Naram-Sin," *AnSt* 5 (1955) 93–113; also *AnSt* 6 (1956) 163–64. More recent studies include R. Labat, *Les Religions du Proche-Orient asiatique* (Fayard/Denöel, 1970) 306–15; T. Longman, *Fictional Akkadian Royal Autobiography: A Generic and Comparative Study* (Winona Lake, Ind., 1991).

The treatment of this recension differs from the above treatments, in that it is given in transcription in a composite text as well as in a critical score of the manuscripts. The goal is to provide a clear view of the surface discourse structure of this literary composition, the most complete work in the corpus. The philological and textual notes will be attached to the composite text.

[50] For a discussion of mechanical repetition of formulas, see J. Cooper, "Gilgamesh Dreams of Enkidu: The Evolution and Dilution of Narrative," *Finkelstein Mem. Vol.*, 39–44; idem, "Symmetry and Repetition in Akkadian Narrative," *JAOS* 97 (1977) 508–12.

Composite Text and Translation

Notes on the Transcription

In order to appreciate the prosodic features of the composition, both phonetic and morphemic length are indicated, with certain exceptions. Morphemic length in both nominal plurals and verbal plurals is specified. Phonetic lengthening is indicated when followed by either enclitics or suffixes: the length of the genitive /i/, the final vowel /i/ in prepositions, the final vowels of pronouns

---

Transcription

1. [*ṭupšenna pitēma*] *narâ šitassi*
2. [*ša anāku Narām-Sîn*] *mār Šarru-kīn*
3. [*išṭurūma ēzibūšu ana*] *ūmē ṣâti*

4. [*šar Uruk*] *šadâ ēmid*
5. [*Enmerkar*] *šadâ ēmid*

Philological and Textual Notes

1. For this incipit, see the introduction to this chapter as well as C. B. F. Walker, *JCS* 33 (1981) 192ff., and references to similar statements quoted there; in particular note Gilg. I i 22–25:

[*šeʾīma*] GIŠ.*ṭupšenna ša e*[*rî*]	Seek the tablet-box of copper!
[. . .]*e ḫargallīšu ša sipa*[*rri*]	Lift it up by its bronze rings!
[*petēm*]*a* KÁ *ša niṣirtī*[*šu*]	Open the lock of its secrets!
[*amur*]*ma ṭuppi uqnî šitassi*	See and read out the lapis-lazuli tablet!

2–3. Another possibility would be to read the traces at the end as the word *mar-ṣa-ti*, similar to the statement in Gilg. I i 26: [*ša š*]*ū Gilgameš* DU.DU-*ku kalu marṣāti* 'that he, Gilgameš, went through all (types of) hardships'.

4–5. The phrase *šadâ*(*šu*) *emēdu* has been the subject of various studies. Landsberger (in *MAOG* 4 [1929] 320) stated that the phrase meant 'sich in seinem letzten Schlupfwinkel verkriechen'. The contemptuous tone suggested by Landsberger was used by Güterbock in his translation of the line 'er hat ins Gras beissen müssen' (ZA 42 [1934] 72). A thorough investigation by Weidner appeared in *AfO* 13 (1939–41) 233–34, where he reached the conclusion that

and pronominal suffixes, the subjunctive marker /u/, and the final vowel of final weak verbs. Other length marks indicate historical formations of the lexemes, whether or not it can be proved that the vowel in question was actually pronounced long.

Furthermore, morphophonemic writings are amended to their probable phonological shape. However, unless apparent and clearly intended in the surface discourse, assimilation and dissimilation are not assumed. Similarly, vowel elision and shortening of prepositions are not adopted if not explicit in the orthography.

Translation

Naram-Sin's Introduction

1. Open the tablet-box and read out the stela,
2. [which I, Naram-Sin], son of Sargon,
3. [have inscribed and left for] future days.

History of Enmerkar

4. [The king of Uruk] sought refuge in the mountain.
5. [Enmerkar] sought refuge in the mountain.

---

there was no negative aspect to this phrase. He translated it as 'er starb eines unnatürlichen Todes' and differentiated between (a) "er wurde gewaltsam beseitigt, ermordet" and (b) "er nahm ein unrühmliches Ende." For the most recent discussion of the semantics of this phrase, see Edzard (*Welt des Orients* 11 [1980] 156 and note 4) and Cogan (*JCS* 25 [1973] 99 n. 17), who mentions an "inner-Akkadian gloss" from the royal inscriptions of Aššurbanipal, *ēmedu šadâšu // illiku ana šīmti*, concerning the king of Arwad. Following Zimmern's suggestion, Edzard translates this phrase as: 'er landete an seinem (= dem ihm bestimmten) Berg (= Totenwelt)'.

In his investigation, Weidner noted that the phrase appears four times without the possessive suffix, but he did not think that including or omitting the suffix made any difference in the meaning of the phrase. However, in my opinion, omission of the possessive suffix may change the semantics of the phrase, in which case there may be no specific mountain. The references that contain the phrase without the suffix are the following: (1) Middle Assyrian Chronicle, VAT 10453+; Weidner, *AfO* 8 (1954–56) 384:8′: (the Assyrians went up to the mountains of Kirruria to save their lives, while the Arameans took away their gold,

6. [*inūmīšu Šamaš mum*]*a*ʾʾ*ir māti*
7. [. . . MU.MEŠ] *ina nasāḫi*
8. [. . . UD.M]EŠ *ina alāki*
9. [*Šamaš . . . ušan*]*ni milikša*

---

silver, and all their property) RN *šar Karduniaš* KUR-*a e-mi-id* 'Marduk-nadin-aḫḫe, king of Babylonia, disappeared forever' (see Tadmor, *JNES* 17 [1958] 133–34. Note that Tadmor states that this phrase has nothing to do with dying but means 'to disappear suddenly, to abscond for good'); (2) Assyrian King List #53 (A IV 3, B III 36, see *RlA* 6 111–12): 'Mutakkil-Nusku held the throne for "his tablet," KUR-*a e-mid*, then passed away'; (3) Treaty between Ḫattušili III, king of Hatti, and Bentešina, king of Amurru (KBo I 8:7): *enūma* RN *aba abīja* ḪUR.SAG *i-mi-id* 'when Šuppiluliuma, my grandfather, died (Muršili, my father, the son of Šuppiluliuma, sat on the royal throne)' (note the substitution of *ḫuršānu* for *šadû*); and (4) "Naram-Sin and the Enemy Hordes."

Weidner concluded from these examples that "es handelt sich um Angehörige des eigenen Volkes, hier wird man also am besten die Grundbedeutung 'eines unnatürlichen Todes sterben' einsetzen." In general, the evidence supports Weidner's conclusion, whether or not the dynasts were native ones. In particular, the literal translation of this expression, *šadâ emēdu* 'to take refuge in the mountain', is similar to that of the idioms *puzrāti, tubqāti emēdu*, and especially *šaḫāta emēdu*. Consequently, its euphemistic function is ironic and pejorative. Further, there is one caveat, that an "unnatural" death means a death without proper burial rights and not necessarily an unheroic, ignoble death.

The subject of the verbs in these two lines is either Sargon, Naram-Sin, or Enmerkar, all of whom are equally possible. Nothing is known of their deaths, but mountains appear in traditions about each of them. Enmerkar was chosen on a mountain called kur.šuba ("Lugalbanda II: Lugalbanda and Enmerkar," 296; "Enmerkar and the Lord of Aratta," 34). Enmerkar's father, Mes-kiağ-gašer, is noted for going down to the sea and ḫur-sag-šè ba-e_{11} 'coming out (from it) to the mountains' (Jacobsen, *Sumerian King List*, iii 6). Sargon's legendary connection with mountains is limited to *aḫ abīja irammi šadâ* 'my father's brother inhabits the highlands' (text **2**:3). Naram-Sin fought in certain mountainous regions and held sway over them.

5–8. The restoration of these lines depends on the Hittite version (cf. Güterbock, *ZA* 44 [1938] 50 Vs. I C′ 2′ff.), as already proposed by Gurney, *AnSt* 6 (1956) 163.

6. The subject of this sentence is either Enmerkar, as in the preceding sentence or two, or Šamaš, as I propose. The reason for selecting Šamaš is that Enmerkar was supposed to be the son of Utu (cf. "Enmerkar and the Lord of Aratta," line 214; and the discussions by S. Cohen in his dissertation on p. 29 n. 10; as well as C. Wilcke, *Lugalbandaepos*, 42ff.). Moreover, the beginning of

6. [At that time Šamaš was the com]mander of the land.
7. [... years] had elapsed,
8. [... days] had gone by,
9. [Šamaš chan]ged the decision concerning it (the land).

---

the second strophe of "Enmerkar and Ensuḫkešdanna," after the paean of praise to Uruk, begins with: u_4-ba u_4 en-na-àm gi_6 bára-ga-àm ᵈutu lugal-àm 'at that time the day was lord, the night was sovereign, Utu was king' (A. Berlin, *Enmerkar and Ensuḫkešdanna*, 38:14).

7–8. This expression is also found in the "Weidner Chronicle" (Grayson, *Chronicles*, 148:41): x *ūmē ina nasāḫi.*

9. The *milku* 'advice, instruction, order, decision (of a deity) commonly used of divine decisions' is directed towards various objects, in particular the king and the country. It is especially with countries that it is found in literary texts. For example:

> *rabûtum Anunnaki šāʾimū šimtim*
> *ušbū imlikū milikša mātam*
> ... the great Anunnaki, deciders of fate,
> sat (in council) and made their decision over it, the land ...
> (BRM 4 2 i 1–2; see Wilcke, *ZA* 67 [1977] 156 [OB "Etana"]; and Kinnier Wilson, *Etana*; 30).

> *enūma ilū imlikū milka ana mātāti*
> ... when the gods made their decision concerning the lands ...
> (Ugaritica 5 167:1; see Lambert-Millard, *Atra-ḫasīs*, 132).

> (Anzu with his talons rent the heavens)
> [... *m*]*āta kīma karpati milikša isp*[*uḫ*]
> ... the land like a pot, he scattered its counsel
> (Lambert-Millard, *Atra-ḫasīs*, 124 rev. 17).

In particular, the noun *milka* is found together with *šanû*/*šunnû* in this context:

> *milik mātim išanni*
> ... the mood of the country will change ...
> (YOS 10 31 vi 21 [OB ext.]).

> *ša Ištar ušannû milik ṭēmēšu*
> ... whose (Teumman's) mind Ištar had confused ...
> (Streck Asb. 112 v 23).

The subject of the sentence is unclear. It could be Ištar, Šamaš (Utu), or the land. For Utu in the Sumerian tradition, cf. uru-ki inim-inim-ma-bi ᵈutu ba-an-túm 'Utu took away the city's counsel' ("Curse of Agade," 70). According to Cooper (p. 238 n. 30), it has a specific legal connotation.

10. [. . .]*ma irkab*
11. [*Enmerkar išāl*] *ilāni rabûti*
12. [*Ištar Ilaba*] *Zababa Annunītum*
13. [*Šullat Ḫaniš Šamaš*] *qurādu*
14. [*ilsi mārē bārê*] *uma*ᵓᵓ*ir*
15. [7 *ana pān* 7] *puḫādī ilputū*
16. [*ukīn*] *guḫšê ellūti*
17. [*mārū bārê*] *kīam iqbûni*
18. . . . .
19. [. . . *t*]*urruqu zīma*
20. *u kīma* [. . .] *idâši*
21. [*ina*] *erṣeti* [. . .] *lipparqud pagarka*
22. *adī*[*na iqbûni*] *ilānu rabûtu*
23. *Enmerkar šal*[*amtašu* . . .] *dīna marṣa Šamaš išk*[*un*]
24. *dīnšu purussê ip*[*rusu*] *eṭemmēšu eṭem*[*me* . . .]

11–17. The order of the lines in this section is reversed in comparison to the order of the two later sections, lines 72–78 and 108–14:

Subject	Line Number		
a. Summoning the diviners	14	72	108
b. Bringing the offerings	15	73	109
c. Setting up the altars	16	74	110
d. Querying the gods	11–13	75–77	111–13
e. The answer	17ff.	78	114ff.

Although it is clear that either Enmerkar or Naram-Sin takes steps (a) and (d) and the diviners step (e), the performers of the actual ritual are not clear: cf. singular *ukīn* versus plural *ukīnnu* (line 110). For this reason, the hybrid form *alputu* appears in line 73. I interpret step (b) just as Labat does ('il consacra un mouton pour chacun des sept [dieux]'), seven lambs, one for each god, rather than 7 *ana pān* 7 = 7 + 7 = 14. In Gurney's first treatment of this text in 1955, he enumerated only six gods, but in 1956 he suggested seven gods in his notes in *AnSt* 6, 163. Those scholars who followed the earlier estimate of six gods had to relate the number of sacrifices to the number of haruspices, which were thus thought to be seven or fourteen.

15. The reading of the sign *x as either *a*[*l*] or *i*[*l*] is pivotal for understanding whether Naram-Sin or Enmerkar is the subject of these sentences. Gurney (*AnSt* 6, 163) stated the problem clearly, that although logically Enmerkar should be the subject, the apparent verbal forms, *al*[*-pu-ut*] (Sultantepe

10. [. . .] and rode.
11. [Enmerkar queried] the great gods:
12. [Ištar, Ilaba], Zababa, Annunītum,
13. [Šullat, Ḫaniš, and Šamaš], the hero.
14. [He summoned the diviners] and instructed (them).
15. They "touched" the lambs, [seven for seven].
16. [He set up] the holy reed altars.
17. [The diviners] spoke thus:
18. "[. . . .]
19. "[. . .] darkened/pale face.
20. "and like [. . .]. . . .
21. "[upon] the earth, . . . may your corpse lie(?)."
22. Scarcely had the great gods [finished speaking],
23. [. . .] Enmerkar['s cor]pse. A severe judgement Šamaš passed (upon him).
24. His judgement—the decision [that he decre]ed—(was that) his ghost, the ghosts of [. . .],

---

manuscript G) and *iqbûni*, would indicate a first-person involvement, disregarding the Kuyunjik obvious third-person plural [x]-*pu-tu* and the fact that the ventive does not need to indicate first-person dative. Despite this obstacle, Labat (*Les religions*) opted for third person. Furthermore, as Landsberger (H. Tadmor, B. Landsberger, and S. Parpola, "The Sin of Sargon and Sennacherib's Last Will," *SAAB* 3 [1989] 37) pointed out, the sign originally read *al* could just as well be the beginning of *i*[*l*]. This statement was negated by a footnote by Parpola (ibid., n. 19) stating that the proposed emendation is epigraphically impossible. When I collated the tablet, I found that the sign looks as copied and thus that both readings are possible.

18–21. The text of the omen is lost. It may have related to Enmerkar's sins, discussed in the preface to this section.

21. The first suggestion by Gurney (*AnSt* 5 [1955] 98) was to interpret ⸢*li*⸣-*tam-ḫaṣ* as an Ntn precative of *maḫāṣu*, and the second suggestion (*AnSt* 6 [1956] 163) was [*ē*] *tultā*[*bil*] *lipparqud pagarka* 'do nothing until the gods give you their orders'. However, the precative of the verb *naparqudu* has the form *lipparqid* rather than *lipparqud* and means 'to lie flat, to lie against' and does not take *pagru* or any accusative object.

23–27. As already pointed out by Gurney, the word order is unnatural, and Šamaš seems to be introduced without any evident grammatical construction. I have tried to improve the text by placing a finite verb *iškun* at the end of line 23, and interpreting lines 24ff. as a nominal sentence with *dīnšu* as subject and the *ša*-clause of line 27 as the nominal predicate. The reference to Šamaš I have taken as a vocative to ward off any evil effects of mentioning ghosts.

25. *eṭem kimtīšu eṭem pirʾīšu eṭem piriʾ pirʾīšu Šamaš qurādu*

26. *bēl elâti u šaplāti bēl Anunnaki bēl eṭemmē*

27. *ša mê dalḫūte išattû u mê zakûte lā išattû*
28. *ša igigallašu kakkašu ṣāba šuātu ikmû ikšudu inâru*

29. *ina narê ul išṭur ul ēzibamma pagrī u pūtī*
30. *šuma ul ušēṣīma ul aktarrabšu*

For the various meanings of *eṭemmu* 'soul, spirit, ghost', see J. Bottéro, "La Mythologie de la mort en Mésopotamie ancienne" (in *Death in Mesopotamia* [CRRAI 26; Mesopotamia 8; Copenhagen, 1980] 28ff.) and "Les Morts et l'au-delà dans les rituels en accadien contre l'action des 'revenants,'" (ZA 73 [1983] 153–203), and note the discussion (on p. 169 of "Les Morts") of confusion of the two signs UDUG and GIDIM that are also here in this manuscript.

28. Manuscript B has *i-na-ru* at the end of this line, for which there is insufficient room in the other manuscripts (C and G). It may have been added by mistake from the *ina narê* in the next line.

29–30. The problems in these two lines are: (1) the subjects, (2) the objects, (3) the parsing of the phrases, and (4) the meaning of the phrases.

(1) *The subjects.* It has been assumed that the subject of the first verb is Enmerkar and the subject of the last verb is Naram-Sin. Positive evidence is found in the Boghazköy version (text **21A** b 2′, 4′): the verb *šaṭāru* is in third person, *ul išṭuramma*; and the verb *karābu* is in first person, *ul akrubšuma*. Thus, the suggestion of Güterbock to read all the verbs as referring to Naram-Sin in the first person is not discussed in the following treatment. Likewise, the *iktarab* of manuscript G is probably a scribal mistake in face of manuscripts A and B, *aktarabšu*. However, the subject(s) of the verbs *ezēbu* and *šūṣû* are not obvious. There are four possibilities: (a) Enmerkar is the subject of both verbs, and the two sentences could be understood as: 'he did not write on a stela and did not leave (it) to me, even me, myself; he did not make a name for himself so that I could not bless him' (cf. Labat, *Les religions*, 310; and Longman, *Autobiography* [1991] 228, for other translations with Enmerkar as subject); (b) Enmerkar is the subject of *ezēbu* and Naram-Sin is the subject of *šūṣû*: 'he did not inscribe a stela and leave it to me // so that I had to act without the approval of the gods and could not bless him' (Gurney, *AnSt* 5, 110; CAD A/2 372b); (c) Naram-Sin is the subject of the verb *ezēbu*, and Enmerkar is the subject of *šūṣû*, with the resulting parallel sentences: 'On a stela he did not write so that I did not abandon my own pretensions; a name he did not proclaim so I could not bless him'; (d) Naram-Sin is the subject of both verbs, and the sentences are to be understood as: 'he did not write on a stela so I could not let go of myself,

25. the ghost(s) of his family, the ghost(s) of his offspring, the ghost(s) of his offspring's offspring; (praised be) Šamaš, the hero,
26. lord of the upper and netherworlds, lord of the Anunnaki, lord of the spirits of the dead,
27. (that) they will drink polluted water and not drink pure water.
28. He whose wisdom (and) whose weapons paralyzed, caught, and annihilated that army
29. on a stela he did not write (and) did not leave (it) to me, myself,
30. he did not make a name for himself so that I could not pray for him.

---

could not make a name for myself, and (thus) could not bless him'. All the above suggestions except (b) work on the basis of the present line division.

(2) *The objects.* There are two sets of objects, *pagrī u pūtī* in line 29 and the logogram MU in line 30. The first set apparently contains the first-person possessive suffix, and the only first person in the text is Naram-Sin. Gurney wanted to read the logogram MU as *anāku,* which is impossible (see CAD s.v.). The CAD reads the end of line 29 and the beginning of line 30 as one word, *pu-u-ti*-MU, which never occurs in any type of Akkadian text. There have been two other interpretations of the logogram in the early commentaries on this line: Zimmern (*ZA* 12 [1898] 319, 323) read the logogram as *šattu* and translated the sentence 'drum zog ich in eigener Person dazumal(?) nicht aus'; whereas Ebeling (AOTB[2] 1926, 231) read it the same way but translated it 'Ich selbst in eigner Person zog in dem Jahre (?) nicht aus'. On the other hand, Jensen (KB 6/I 292, 549) and King (STC 142) divide the logogram MU into its component parts, AŠ KUR, and read *ina māti* and translate the sentence: 'in mine own person from my land I went not forth'. Güterbock ignores the logogram in his translation (*ZA* 42 [1934] 67), probably on the basis of the omission of MU in C. However, the reliability of this manuscript can be shown to be uncertain, since the scribe also omitted the BU in line 36. Likewise, Labat in his translation ignores the logogram. The most probable meaning of the logogram MU and its most normal Akkadian equivalent is *šumu* 'name'. In this line, because of the noun *šumu,* one expects either the verb *šaṭāru* 'to write' in the sense of inscribing a tablet for future generations (see R. Ellis, *Foundation Deposits in Ancient Mesopotamia* [New Haven, 1968] 150–51) or the verb *zakāru* 'to invoke the name of the ghost' (see M. Bayliss, *Iraq* 35 [1973] 116–17). Either verb would make sense of this line in place of *šūṣû.*

(3) *The parsing of the phrases.* On the basis of the phrase *pagra u pūta šūṣû,* which occurs in line 93 and the OB parallel lines ii 14–15, all commentators want to parse this line into two verses, as though it reads:

ina narê ul išṭur ul ēzibamma
pagrī u pūtī ⟨⟨MU⟩⟩ *ul ušēṣima ul aktarabšu*

31. *ṣābu pagri iṣṣūr ḫurri amēlūta āribū pānūšun*
32. *ibnûšunūtīma ilānu rabûtu*
33. *ina qaqqar ibnû ilānu ālūšu*
34. *Tiʾāmatu ušēniqšunūti*
35. *šassūršunu Bēlet-ilī ubanni*

However, the lines are not written that way, and there are three manuscripts attesting to the correct line division. Consequently, one must ask whether the present lines contain two original idioms, *pagra u pūta ezēbu* and *šuma šūṣû*, with two objects, with the subject of the first phrase being Naram-Sin, and with the subject of the second phrase being Enmerkar, as in (1c) above.

(4) *The meaning of the phrases.* The author has employed the words *pagru* and *pūtu* separately and together many times in this text (lines 21, 29, 93, 165, and 178). He uses them in various idioms, and therefore we are not forced to fit line 29 to line 93. The previous meanings of *pagru u pūtu* (*pagru u ramanu*) are: (a) reflexive, 'moi-même' (see Labat, *Les religions*, 310); (b) 'in my own person, (to go forth in) one's own person', referring to his not accompanying his troops in person (see Güterbock, ZA 42 [1934] 68); (c) 'to withdraw oneself (from the struggle)' (see Gurney, *AnSt* 5 [1955] 110, who explains the phrase thus on the basis of line 174); (d) 'with body and forehead (held high in pride)' (see Tadmor, *Eretz-Israel* 5 [1958] 155); (e) 'record on a statue', referring to a message left on a statue (see Longman, *Autobiography* [1983] 307).

Because of the many problems the line exhibits, it must be concluded that some corruption occurred in the written tradition. Internal evidence seems to indicate that the original idioms were *narâm šaṭāru . . . ina . . . ezēbu* (cf. lines 151–53) and *pagram u pūtam šūṣû* (cf. line 93).

31. Again the word *pagru* occurs, and here it may be a later addition by the author of this recension, who liked using the word. The picture of these beautiful mountain people given in the succeeding lines is juxtaposed to this line, in which they are described as mixed creatures. In the introduction to chapter 10, I have compared this line to **21A** b 5–6: *[a]wīlūtum īrub ana panīšunu ana ḫurrī ālum ana panīšunu ul ālum qaqqaru ana panī*[*šunu*] *ul qaqqaru* 'Mankind scurried into caves before them. The city before them was not a city. The ground before them was not ground'. This would seem to reflect a better text, of which the Assyrian text is a corrupt descendant: *īrub* became *āribu*, *ḫurrī* became *iṣṣūr ḫurri*, and *pagru* was added to make sense out of nonsense.

Von Soden has suggested a different parsing and reading (ZA 50 [1952] 180 n. 2): *ṣābū Ḫu-ri* 'Churriter', *iṣṣur ḫurri amēlūti: āribu pānūšun* 'Steinhuhn-Menschen mit Rabengesichtern', with a play on the word *Ḫurri* (cf. AHw 390b). For descriptions of the subhuman barbarian, see Cooper, *Curse of Agade*, 30ff.

Creation of Naram-Sin's Opponents

31. A people with partridge bodies, a race with raven faces,
32. the great gods created them.
33. On the land which the gods created was their(!) city.
34. Tiamat suckled them.
35. Their progenitress, Bēlet-ilī, made (them) beautiful.

---

33. This line poses grammatical and semantic difficulties. Grammatically, the whole sentence is dependent on *qaqqar*, which must be understood as a noun in the construct with a subjunctive clause dependent on it, and *ālūšu*, a predicate nominative. Further, there does not seem to be any explanation for the third-person singular possessive suffix. It has been suggested that the singular refers back to the collective *ṣābu* or *ummānu* (see Zimmern, ZA 12, 323; Jensen KB 6/1 551).

Semantically, the meaning of the lexeme *ālu* is bothersome, since *ālu* 'city' is written elsewhere in this text with the logogram URU and in the nominative should be *ālšu*, at least in Old Babylonian (e.g., YOS 10 33:13). The form *ālūšu* might be an innovation created in analogy with *ilūšu* 'his god'. The alternative explanations of the writing *a-lu-šú* do not appear fitting in this context. Cf. perhaps *alû* = *pirḫu*, cited in AHw 206b, *alû* IV = *elû* II.

34. For Tiamat as a wetnurse, see Tallqvist, *Götterepitheta*, 471–72. Note that she is the wetnurse of Bēl in KAR 307:19. Cf. RN *šar ummān-manda tabnīt Tiʾāmti* (Streck Asb. 280:20).

35. For the word *šassūru*, see S. J. Lieberman, *Loanwords*, 473–74, no. 618, 'mother-goddess' and 529, no. 709, 'vagina'. This is a common epithet of Bēlet-ilī; see Tallqvist, *Götterepitheta*, 273ff.; and further, Lambert-Millard, *Atra-ḫasīs*, 56 I 189 et passim. The verb *banû* has been variously interpreted by translators and dictionaries: (1) 'blessed them in the womb' (Gurney, *AnSt* 5, 101); (2) '(après que) Bêlet-ili eut donné forme à leur embryon' (Labat, *Les religions*, 310); and (3) 'their mother DN has treated (them) kindly' (CAD B 93a sub *banû* B 'to be pleasant'). AHw follows the CAD division and puts this reference under *banû* II 'gut schön sein/werden'. The semantic range of the D stem of *banû* B, according to the CAD (note *banû* A only occurs in the D stem in EA), is: 'to beautify, adorn, improve, decorate, prepare carefully'. Since the enemy is described as *šūpû banûtu* 'resplendent with beauty', it seems most probable that Bēlet-ilī is endowing them with that beauty here in this line. The time sequence bothers Labat; translating 'in the womb' after the enemies have been suckled does not make much chronological sense. This is not a real difficulty, since *šassūru* can simply be understood in this line as the epithet of Bēlet-ilī. The problems with the chronological sequence and the true understanding of the meaning of the verb have already been discussed by Jensen (KB 6/1); he translates this line 'bildete sie ihr(e) Mutter(leib), die Herrin der Götter, schön'.

36. *ina qereb šadî irtebûma īteṭlūma irtašû minâti*

37. 7 *šarrānu atḫû šūpû banûtu*
38. 360,000 *ummānātūšunu*
39. *Anubanini abūšunu šarru ummašunu šarratu Melili*
40. *aḫūšunu rabû ālik pānīšunu Memanduḫ šumšu*
41. *šanû aḫūšunu Medudu šumšu*
42. *šalšu aḫūšunu* [. . .]*tapiš šumšu*
43. *rebû aḫūšunu Tartadada šumšu*
44. *ḫamšu aḫūšunu Baldaḫdaḫ šumšu*
45. *šeššu aḫūšunu Aḫudanadiḫ šumšu*
46. *sebû aḫūšunu Ḫurrakidû šumšu*

47. *šadî kaspi irkabūnimma*

---

36. See von Soden, "*utlellûm* 'sich erheben' und verwandte Bildungen" (ZA 50 [1952] 180). He describes our form as an SB invention of a new perfect with *i*-prefix and translates 'aufwuchsen'.

37. This line presents us with two types of problems, one logical and one grammatical. On the one hand, the opponents in this line are described as worthy antagonists of the great Naram-Sin, as if a family of Enkidus were being created. The expression *šūpû* is used to describe gods and occasionally kings (see AHw 1281a). In literary texts it is used of Gilgameš (Gilg. I ii 26) and Sargon (*Kramer AV*, 314 K.13684+:6, *Šarrukīn šu-p*[*u-ú*], as well as Rm. 618:5, *šu-pu-u*). It is used especially in relation to the beauty of the face. The grammatical problem concerns the use of the stative *šūpû*, rather than an adjective governing an abstract noun *banûtu*, which I have translated 'resplendent with beauty'.

In place of the six kings of text **21A**, this recension has seven. The number seven is a conventional number used of various groups of beings, human and divine, benevolent as well as malevolent.

39. For Anubanini, king of Lullubu, and his inscriptions found at Sar-i-Pūl-i-Zohāb, see Edzard, *AfO* 24 (1973) 73, although the date of his reign is uncertain. The Lullubu are mentioned in the list of 17 kings in coalition against Naram-Sin, **17** i 4′ (see note to line) and **18**:10′ (see ZA 44 [1938] 68). In the second millennium, the term Lullubu lost its specific ethnic and geographic identity and was extended to any barbaric mountaineer (note especially the occurrences in texts from Boghazköy; see H. Klengel, *MIO* 11 [1965] 357–58). It may be that the historical enemy as well as the literary enemy described in "Naram-Sin and the Enemy Hordes" are the Lullubu, with the proviso that their demographic situation is not that of the third millennium but of the second mil-

36. In the midst of the mountains, they grew up, reached man's estate, and attained full stature.
37. Seven kings, brothers, resplendent with beauty,
38. 360,000 were their troops.
39. Anubanini was their father, the king; their mother was the queen, Melili.
40. Their eldest brother, their leader, Memanduḫ was his name.
41. Their second brother, Medudu was his name.
42. Their third brother, [. . .]tapiš was his name.
43. Their fourth brother, Tartadada was his name.
44. Their fifth brother, Baldaḫdaḫ was his name.
45. Their sixth brother, Aḫudanadiḫ was his name.
46. Their seventh brother, Ḫurrakidu was his name.

Eruption of the Enemy Hordes

47. They were riding around the silver mountains, and

---

lennium. In other words, "Naram-Sin and the Enemy Hordes" has Anubanini and sons descending from the mountains of Anatolia towards the cities of the Anatolian plateau and then on towards the mountainous crescent surrounding the plains of the Near East, far away from their original eastern home in Iran around Suleimaniya. The direction of the raids seems to be from northwest to southeast: from Anatolia, Upper Mesopotamia (Subartu) as far north as the upper lakes of Lake Van and Lake Urmia, the eastern Zagros mountains (Gutium), Elam, and the countries surrounding the Persian Gulf (Dilmun, Makkan, and Meluḫḫa). If the raids begin in the Anatolian highlands, the proposed identification of the enemy as Lullubians is a difficulty. There are two factors that could have caused this situation: (a) the confusion of the coalition of the 17 kings, which included the kings of Anatolia through Elam (**17** i i′–21′, led by Gula-AN, king of Gutium; **18**:8′–6′; see ZA 44 [1938] 68ff.); and (b) the change in the historical demographic distribution during the third, second, and first millennia.

The MU.NI in manuscript G is probably incorrect and is placed here at the end of the line in analogy with the following lines.

40–46. The names themselves are the reduplicated type, which are typical of Old Akkadian period names. Their language has been termed by Landsberger "Proto-Tigridian" and by Gelb "Banana-language." In addition, the names may preserve some Hurrian influence, since they seem to rhyme with other known kings of the north and northeast: the reduplicated Duḫsusu of Mardaman, Rabsisi of Subartu, as well as names ending in *-aḫ*, such as Šulgi's famous opponent, Tabban-daraḫ of Simurrum.

47. It is true that KÙ.MEŠ in this text represents *ellūtu* (cf. lines 16, 74, 106, 107, 110, and 128) in relation to sacrifices, altars, and Ištar, meaning 'pure,

48. *rēdû iṣbassunūtīma imḫaṣū šaparšun*
49. *rēš sanāqīšunu ana Purušḫandar issanqūni*(!)
50. *Purušḫandar gimir*? [ ]*su ittaspaḫ*
51. *Puḫlû ittaspaḫ*
52. *Puranšû ittaspaḫ*
53. *lu samuḫ*(?) *nāš ḫuḫḫuḫ ḫaḫḫū*[*rim*(?)]
54. *luppudu narbû ummān-manda karā*[*šu*] *Šubat-En*[*lil*]

---

holy', but it never refers to secular terrestrial domains. Consequently, the translation 'the silver mountains' seems preferable to 'the shining mountains', since 'the silver mountains' functioned in the Old Akkadian period as the border land of the Old Akkadian realm. Sargon describes his empire as extending to the Cedar Forest and the Silver Mountains (ḫur-sag-kù-ga-šè [Sum.] :: KUR.KUR.KÙ [Akk.]; CBS 13972 v 30–31, vi 37–38; see *aK* 164–65:34, "Sargon C2"), while Naram-Sin delineates his border as extending to the Cedar Forest/Amanus, the Cedar Mountain, and the upper sea (UET 1 274 i 14ff. = *aK* 249:14–16, "Narāmsîn C 3"; UET 1 275 i 22ff. = *aK* 255:22–24, "Narāmsîn C 5").

Von Soden (AHw 944b G4) suggests that the phrase *šadâ rakābu* may be understood as 'ins Gebirge ausweichen'.

48. This line represents a turning point in the story: the provocation of the enemy. Does the word *ṣabātu* indicate that the peaceful mountaineers were attacked? The reaction of the mountaineers is stated in the phrase *imḫaṣū šaparšun*. This phrase has been studied by M. Gruber (*Aspects of Nonverbal Communication in the Ancient Near East* [Studia Pohl 12; Rome, 1980] 380), who understands it as a gesture of chagrin and not anger. Previously, it had been studied by A. L. Oppenheim (*Or* N.S. 17, 42), who thought that this gesture was one of either insult or sorrow and despair. Nevertheless, I must agree with Gurney that here it is an act of defiance (*AnSt* 5, 110), since as a result of their reaction, they begin their raiding expeditions. Another interpretation of this line has been offered by G. Komoróczy (*Acta Antiqua Academiae Scientiarum Hungaricae* 25 [1977] 60), who understands the gesture as one of defiance, of a call for military conscription. Last, T. Longman (*Autobiography* [1983] 307 n. 16) believes that here the idiom indicates frustration, based on the reference in the blessing of the prostitute Šamhat in SB Gilgameš vii iv 3 and MB Gilgameš UET VI 394:51. All these ad hoc interpretations demonstrate our ignorance of many aspects of the ancient culture of Mesopotamia. Gurney notes (*AnSt* 5, 110) that in the Iliad this gesture is a sign of any strong emotion, and such may also have been the case in Mesopotamia. It also existed in Sumerian (cf. "Enki and Ninmaḫ" 25 and "Lugale" 73). Regarding the Enki and Ninmaḫ citation ('Enki rose from his bed at the command of his mother Nammu, in Ḫalanku, his conference chamber, he [slapped] his thigh'), Jacobsen comments (*Harps*, 155): "A gesture expressive of decision, approximately: 'Let us get on with it!' "

48. A scout (tried to) intercept them, but they smote their thighs.
49. At the beginning of their approach, they proceeded against Purušḫanda.
50. Purušḫanda was completely scattered.
51. Puḫlu was scattered.
52. Puranshu was scattered.
53. Indeed, allied(?) was the bearer of . . . of rav[ens].
54. Weakened were the powers of the Manda hordes, the camps of Šubat-En[lil].

---

49. For previous references to Purušḫanda, see texts **9B** and **11**.

For the reading *ittaspaḫ* in this line and the following two lines, see Gurney, *AnSt* 6, 163. For *sapāḫu* in historiographic texts, see Glassner, *La chute d'Akkadé*, 61.

50. According to the traces, it is impossible to restore the line, since the possessive suffix *-su* should end an adverbial like *gipšussu* or *gitmalussu*, which do not fit the space available.

51–52. These cities are unknown.

53. The reading of this line is very uncertain. Gurney (*AnSt* 6, 163) suggests that this line and the beginning of the next may possibly enumerate a series of tribes. Longman (*Autobiography* [1983] 291) offers *lu-ṣa-a eli*(EGIR) *na-áš-ḫu-ḫu-uḫ-ḫa-ḫu* 'Should I go out after Našḫuḫuḫḫaḫu?' but the first person is not expected between lines 30 and 63, and the second word is rendered by the logogram UGU not EGIR. Since this text is replete with parallelisms and repetitions, perhaps we should understand this line by looking at the syntactical structure of line 54: a verb in first position followed by a nominal compound in second position. A verb that fits the context would be *samāḫu* 'to unite in alliance', but the writing *sà-a-muḫ* would be exceptional.

The remainder of the sentence could contain the subject of the sentence, such as a person, or an object, such as a toponym. Several known toponyms have similar names: Ḫaḫḫum/n in Anatolia (RGTC 1 68) and Ḫu-ḫu-un, Ḫu-ḫu-un-rí, and Ḫu-ḫu-un-si-ir-ḫa-ḫu-ir in the eastern highlands (RGTC 1 73). The signs can also be analyzed as a compound with *nāš* followed by an unknown word in construct *ḫu-ḫu-uḫ* plus a noun in the genitive *ḫa-ḫu*-[x-x-x]-⌈x⌉. For compounds with *nāš*, cf. **6**:51, **11**:26ff., and note that in the former the compounds are designations of types of people. The last word might be *ḫaḫḫuru* '(a bird of the raven/crow family)', a description of the enemies that would match line 31. Note that Longman left out the end of the line. Another possibility is to read *na-ás-ḫu* 'they were deported/eradicated', but no sense could then be made of the remainder of the line.

54. This pivotal line offers the basis for establishing the Ummān-manda as the antagonists of this composition. If, however, we read this line with the Ummān-manda as the direct object of the raid of the enemies, then we are rid of the perplexing Ummān-manda as the enemies of Naram-Sin. Ummān-manda

55. *u qereb Subarti kalûšunu it[taggišū(?)]*
56. *ispuḫūma tiamāti ana Gutium issan[qū]*
57. *ispuḫūma Gutium ana māt Elamti issan[qū]*
58. *ispuḫūma māt Elamti ana sapanni ikta[ldū]*
59. *iddūkūma ša nēberi iddû ana [. . .]*

60. *Dilmun Makanna Meluḫḫa qereb tâmtim mala bašû id[dūkū]*

61. 17 *šarrānu adi* 90 *līm ummānā[tīšunu]*
62. *ittīšunu ana rēṣūtīšunu it[talkūni]*

63. *[a]lsi redâ umaʾʾir*
64. *[luṭâ] ṣillâ ana q[ātīšu umalli]*
65. *ina luṭê luput ina ṣillê [suḫul]*
66. *[šumma dāmū ūṣûni] kī nâšīma amēlū šunu*
67. *[šumma dāmū la ūṣû]ni šēdū namtarū*
68. *[utuk]kū rābiṣū lemnūte šipir Enlil šunu*
69. *redû ṭēnšu utirramma*
70. *ina [luṭê] alput*
71. *ina ṣillê asḫulma dāmū ittaṣûni*

---

in this line may be a late corruption of the country Mardaman (Maridaban, RGTC 1 118 and 2 118), which is one of the countries that Sargon and Naram-Sin claim to have conquered and which appears in other Sargon and Naram-Sin legends: **7** i 16′, **16B**:34. Longman (*Autobiography* [1983] 291) offers *lul-pu-du lib-bu-ú ummān-man-da ka-[ra-aš-šu-nu] Šu-bat* ^{d}*En-[líl]* 'Should I have struck out into the midst of the host, whose camp is Šubat-Enlil?' but he does not explain the form *lulpudu*.

On the history and location of Šubat-Enlil, cf. D. Charpin, "Šubat-Enlil et le pays d'Apum," *MARI* 5 (1987) 129–40. The name of this city seems to be limited to the reign of Šamši-Adad I.

59. The phrase *ša nēberi* has been understood by Gurney and the CAD to refer to people rather than to places: 'the (people) of the crossing' (*AnSt* 5, 101) and 'ferryman' (CAD N/2 147, where this passage is the only nonlexical example). The enemy has now reached the shore ('flatlands') by the Persian Gulf, and they are fighting on or at the *nēberu* of the Gulf to reach the lands that surround it, Dilmun, Makkan, and Meluḫḫa. The people who are opposing them are referred to by the term *ša nēberi* 'the people who dwell in the area of the port'.

55. And in the midst of Subartu, they all [roamed].
56. They scattered the (army of the upper) seas, and reached Gutium.
57. They scattered (the army of) Gutium and reached Elam.
58. They scattered (the army of) Elam and reached the flatlands.
59. They killed those (who guarded) the crossing, casting (them) into [the sea(?)].
60. Dilmun, Makkan, Meluḫḫa in the midst of the (lower) sea, as many as they were, they slau[ghtered].
61. Seventeen kings, with [their] 90,000 troo[ps],
62. together with them, they had [march]ed to their aid.

Despatch of Scout

63. [I sum]moned an army scout and instructed (him).
64. [I handed over] to him a [stiletto and] a pin.
65. "Strike (them) with the stiletto! Prick (them) with the pin!
66. "[If blood comes out], they are men like us.
67. "[If blood does not come out], they are (evil) spirits, messengers of Death,
68. "[fie]nds, malevolent demons, creatures of Enlil."
69. The scout brought back his report:
70. "I struck (them) with the [stiletto];
71. "I pricked (them) with the pin and blood came out."

---

60. For the geographical identification of Dilmun, Makkan, and Meluḫḫa as the island of Bahrain, coastal Arabia and Makran, and the Indus Valley, see above, notes to **16B**:35 and **17** i 12. The phrase *mala bašû* also occurs in similar context in the "Sargon Geography" B rev. 5 (*AfO* 25, 63).

64. On the restoration of this line, see Gurney, *AnSt* 6, 163.

66–67. For the motif of the enemy's being made of flesh and blood, cf. **17** ii 17′.

68. The beginning of the TI sign in manuscript B seems to be certain, which means there were two traditions, one in which the enemy was supported by Tiamat (already mentioned in line 34) and another in which the enemy was supported by Enlil. On the other hand, the latter tradition, of Enlil being the enemy of Naram-Sin, is well known (e.g., the "Curse of Agade," lines 154–57) and may be the primary tradition. The tradition with Tiamat may be secondary, influenced by her appearance in line 34, as well as her creatures in "*Enūma eliš*," etc. On the other hand, the TI may be just a slightly miscopied ^{d}E[N].

72. *alsi mārē bārê uma*$^{\supset\supset}$*ir*
73. [7 *ana pān*] 7 *puḫādī alputu*
74. *ukīn guḫšê ellūti*
75. *ašālma* [. . .] *ilāni rabûti*
76. *Ištar* [*Ila*]*ba Zababa Annunītum*
77. *Šul*[*lat Ḫaniš*] *Šamaš qurādu*
78. *namzaq ilāni rabûti ana alākīja u zaqīqīja ul iddinamma*

79. *kīam aqbi ana libbīja umma lū anākūma*
80. *ajû nēšu bīri ibri*
81. *ajû barbaru iš*$^{\supset}$*al šā*$^{\supset}$*iltu*
82. *lullik kī mār ḫabbāti* [*ina*] *migir libbīja*
83. *u luddi ša ilimma jāti luṣbat*

---

78. This line is very difficult to read and understand. It must contain the negative response of the gods to Naram-Sin's query. The first word of this line, *nam*-[ ], should be compared with line 127, *namzaq ilī rabûti.* However, according to manuscript B, the comparison breaks down because there is no *rabûti.* The word is definitely in manuscript G, but there is a difficulty in the spacing: after *nam* there can only be one short sign before DINGIR!.MEŠ GAL.MEŠ. Thus, the question arises whether we are forced to restore *namzaq* in this line or are free to choose another word. Since the context of the gods' answer to Naram-Sin's query is the same, the restoration of *namzaq* seems correct, despite problems of spacing in G. On the meaning of *namzaqu* 'latch-hook', see E. Leichty, "Omens from Doorknobs," *JCS* 39 (1987) 191–92. Labat, in his translation, suggests 'Le veto des grands dieux m'interdit de marcher à ma perte'. This makes excellent sense, but unfortunately there is no such word as 'veto'. It should be mentioned that Šamaš holds the *uppu* of the Apsu and the *namzaqu* of Anu in the "Bīt-Mummu Prayer" (UVB 15 36:12) and opens the doors to the heavens as well as to the earth, as in the following lines from the "Šamaš Hymn":

> [. . .] x *gal sikkūr šamê mušpalkû dalāt dadmē*
> [. . .] x [*u*]*ppi sikkat namzaqi aškutta*
>
> . . . . the bolt of the heavens, who opens wide the doors of the inhabited world
> . . . . doorknob, latch-hook, and plaque (of the doorjamb) . . .
>
> (Lambert BWL 136:182–83; see A. Kilmer, *Finkelstein Mem. Vol.*, 130).

First Consultation of the Omens

72. I summoned the diviners and instructed (them).
73. I designated seven lambs, one lamb for each of the seven.
74. I set up pure reed altars.
75. I queried the great gods:
76. Ištar, Ilaba, Zababa, Annunītum,
77. Šullat, Ḫaniš, and Šamaš, the hero.
78. The "latch-hook" of the great gods did not give me permission for my going and my demonical onrush.

First Reaction of Naram-Sin and Its Aftermath

79. Thus I said to my heart (i.e., to myself), these were my words:
80. "What lion (ever) performed extispicy?
81. "What wolf (ever) consulted a dream-interpreter?
82. "I will go like a brigand according to my own inclination.
83. "And I will cast aside that (oracle) of the god(s); I will be in control of myself."

See also Lambert BWL 196, VAT 10349:5. If *namzaqu* is an obscure epithet of Šamaš, it would make good sense in this line, for then it would be Šamaš, the god of omens, who gives the decision of the gods. Futhermore, an elaborate *namzaqu* in bronze was manufactured for the temple of Šamaš (VAS 8 103:2; see F. Joannès, *RlA* 8 [1993] 107), possibly as a divine symbol.

The *namzaqu* may be the one held by Nedu/Petu, doorkeeper of the netherworld, who keeps the ghosts under lock and key by virtue of the power bestowed on him by Šamaš, who appears in the next line (see J. Scurlock, "KAR 267//BMS 53: A Ghostly Light on *bīt rimki*?" *JAOS* 108 [1988] 203–9).

The word *zaqīqu* has been variously interpreted but none of the interpretations fits as a parallel to the word *alāku*. An interesting insight into this line was offered by T. Longman (*Autobiography* [1991] 107 and 107–8 n. 30). He translates (p. 229): 'The "key" of the great gods did not allow me to go, even my *zaqīqu*' and comments (p. 107): "In the case of Naram-Sin the key does not function, thus preventing the *zaqīqu* (divine impulse)—the last recourse after divination—from entering. Thus, the gods instruct him to stay put." I have assumed a noun reflecting the action of the *zaqīqu*-demon or phantom.

The final problem in this line is the third-singular subject, if it is not a personified latch-hook. Who is the person who "did not give me. . . . "?

83. This line has posed problems: (1) the first word, *luddu*, has been translated as: (a) '*luddi*-weapon', as in lines 64, 65, and 70 (Gurney, *AnSt* 5, 103); (b) 'small cup, the reference being to some "black art"' (Gurney, *AnSt* 6, 164); (c) 'ein Baum mit essbaren Früchten' (AHw 561b); (d) 'mng. unkn.' (CAD L 238). All of these translators interpret the word *luddi* as a noun. It seems better to

84. *šattu maḫrītu ina kašādi*
85. 2 *šūši līm ummāni ušēṣīma ina libbīšunu ištēn balṭu ul itūra*
86. *šanītum šattu ina kašādi* 90 *līm* KIMIN(= *ummāni ušēṣīma ina libbīšunu ištēn balṭu ul itūra*)
87. *šaluštum šattu ina kašādi* 60 *līm* 7 *mē* KIMIN (= *ummāni ušēṣīma ina libbīšunu ištēn balṭu ul itūra*)

88. *esseḫu ennišu akkad āšuš uštāniḫ*
89. *kīam aqbi ana libbīja umma lū anākūma*
90. *ana palê mīna ēzib*
91. *anāku šarru la mušallimu mātīšu*
92. *u rēʾûm la mušallimu ummānīšu*
93. *kī luštakkanma pagrī u pūtī lušēṣi*
94. *šalummat nēši mūtu namtaru arurtu*
95. *namurratu ḫurbāšu ibissû nebrītu*
96. [*ḫušaḫ*]*ḫu diliptu mala bašû* [*itt*]*īšunu ittarda*
97. *elênuma ina pu*[*ḫri i*]*ššakin abūbu*
98. *šaplānu ina* [*erṣeti abū*]*bu baši*

---

understand it as a verb in first-person precative, from the verb *nadû* 'to cast aside', in parallel structure with *lullik* in the preceding line. Labat also takes *luddi* as a verb, 'faisant fi de dieu (?)', but it is not clear how he analyzes the verb.

(2) The next phrase, *ša* AN *ma ja a ti*, has been treated as: (a) *ša parzilli ja-a-ti* 'of iron, for myself' (Gurney, *AnSt* 5, 103); (b) *ša* ^{d}PA-*ia-a-ti*(B), *ša* ^{d}*Ma-ia-te* (G) 'belonging to the god Muati' (Gurney, *AnSt* 6, 164), as well as *ša* GN! (AHw 561b); (c) ^{d}MAŠ (DINGIR-*ma*) *ja-a-ti* 'I will seize the l. of Ninurta' (?) (CAD L 238).

The final solution given by A. Westenholz is that we have a bicolon line here: *luddi ša ilimma* 'I will cast aside that of god', *jāti luṣbat* 'I will be in control of myself' (see *Power and Propaganda*, 122 n. 31).

88. These verbs, *seḫû*, *ešû*, also appear in line 156 and in the OB recension. On the basis of the OB *a-ka-ad*, the word written *a-ka-la* has been read *a-ka-ad*(!) (see CAD K 35a sub *kâdu* B 'to be distressed(?)'). Note that these two references are the only citations of this verb. Therefore, we need to find another solution. Jensen offered *ekēlu* 'to be dark, to be gloomy' (KB 6/1 554). I suggest reading *a-ka-ad*! and taking it from *nakādu* with improper vocalization of *a* for *u*.

90. See discussion sub **20A** iii 13.

92. The student of the Neo-Babylonian manuscript H erred in this line and wrote *la ú-šal-*[. . .], a finite verb in place of the participle. Because the manuscript is so fragmentary, we do not know if it was an accidental error or an error that indicates that he had a different version in front of him.

84. When the first year arrived,
85. I sent out 120,000 troops, but none of them returned alive.
86. When the second year arrived, I sent out 90,000 troops, but none of them returned alive.
87. When the third year arrived, I sent out 60,700 troops, but none of them returned alive.

Second Reaction of Naram-Sin and the Intervention of Ea

88. I was bewildered, confused, sunk in gloom, desperate, and dejected.
89. Thus I said to my heart, these were my words:
90. "What have I left to the dynasty!?
91. "I am a king who does not keep his country safe
92. "and a shepherd who does not safeguard his people.
93. "How shall I ever continue to act so that I can get myself out (of this)!?"
94. Terror of lions, death, plague, twitching of limbs,
95. panic, chills, losses, famine,
96. [wan]t, sleeplessness, (and) whatever (evil) existed descended [with] them.
97. Above, in co[uncil,] the flood was decided.
98. Below, on the [earth], the fl[ood] came into being.

---

93. See discussion sub **20A** iii 15.

94–96. These lines do not appear in the OB recension in the description of the sack of the land of Akkade, and in the Boghazköy recension they appear in the description of the enemies (see above, notes to text **21A** b 10′–12′).

94. The word *nīši* should be understood in accordance with text **21A** b 10′, UR.MAḪ.[MEŠ], as well as *ni-e-ši* in manuscript G of this line.

The word *mu-ši* occurs in the more reliable manuscript B but not in the less reliable manuscript G and also is absent from the Boghazköy version; it makes little sense here. CAD M/2 293a indicates that this reference is "in difficult context." A. Westenholz suggests that it is probably a literal slip of the pen: . The empty wedges indicate the redundant dittography. Having written *-u-* of *mu-u-tu*, the scribe slipped back into *-ši* of *nēši* and repeated the signs from that point onward. For *arurtu*, see discussion in MSL 9 213ff.

96. For a discussion of *diliptu*, see MSL IX 85–86. In the break, Gurney (*AnSt* 5, 104) restores [*ana muḫḫī*]*šunu* 'upon them', but on the basis of text **21A** b 13′ (the plagues), *ittīšunu iṭrud* 'he (Ea) sent with them (the enemy hordes)', and the visible evidence of the cuneiform text, a better restoration is: (the plagues) [*itt*]*īšunu ittardâ* 'came down with them'.

97–98. For flood imagery, cf. OB recension of "Naram-Sin and the Enemy Hordes," **20A** col. iv.

99. *Ea bēl n[aqbi pāšu īpušma] iqabbi*
100. *izzakkara ana [ilāni aḫḫ]ēšu*
101. *ilānu rabûtu [mīna tēpu]šā*
102. *taqbânimma [abūba ad]ki*
103. *u šubšû ša* [. . .]*pa/di ta zur* [. . .]*a*
104. *zagmukku ša rebūti š[atti ina kašād]i*
105. *ina tēmēqi ša Ea* [. . .] *ša ilāni [rabûti]*
106. *niqê zagmukki ellūti [aqqi]*
107. *têrēti ellūti uš[te*ᵓ*]i*

108. *alsi mārē bārê u[ma*ᵓᵓ*]ir*
109. 7 *ana pān* 7 *puḫādī alp[u]t(u)*
110. *ukīn guḫšê el[lūt]i*
111. *ašālma ilāni rabûti*
112. *Ištar [Ilaba Zababa Annunī]tum*
113. *Šullat [Ḫaniš Šamaš qurād]u*
114. *mār[ū bārê kīam iqbû]ni*
115. *šu[mma . . . i]našši*
116. [. . .] *ibašši*
117. [. . . *i*]*mtaqtašši*
118. [. . . *dāmē*] *ušardâ qulmu*
119. [. . . *ina*] *dāmē iṭib[bu . . .*]

120. *ina libbīšunu* 12 *ṣābu ipparšūinni*

101–2. For the restoration of these lines, see Gurney, *AnSt* 6, 164.

106–7. There is a problem with the ordering of the events in chronological sequence. The following quotation gives the normal order: *lipit qāti ḫiniq immeri nīq niqî nēpešti bārûte* 'the ritual act, the killing of the sheep, the offering of the sacrifice, the performance of the extispicy' ("Maqlu" 7 125 and LKA 128:9). In these lines, Naram-Sin apparently brings an offering and asks for a performance of an extispicy, but in lines 108–14 he also brings offerings and asks for omens from them. Either there are two consultations of the omens in lines 106–7 and 108ff., or there is one consultation in lines 108ff. According to the first hypothesis, the first consultation is the regular New Year's sacrifice, and the second consultation takes places during the additional sacrifices brought at a later time and/or place. However, it seems more reasonable that the block of text

99. Ea, the lord of the d[eep, opened his mouth], saying,
100. Speaking to the [gods, his bro]thers:
101. "O great gods, [what have you do]ne?
102. "You spoke and I sum[moned a deluge].
103. "And the creation of . . . you. . . . "
104. When the New Year Festival of the fourth y[ear arri]ved,
105. with the fervent prayer which Ea [. . .] of the [great] gods,
106. I [sacr]ificed the holy sacrifices of the New Year Festival.
107. I sought the holy omens.

Second Consultation of the Omens

108. I summoned the diviners and instructed (them).
109. I designated seven lambs, one lamb for each.
110. I set up pure reed altars.
111. I queried the great gods:
112. Ištar, [Ilaba, Zababa, Annunītum,]
113. Šullat, [Ḫaniš, and Šamaš, the hero].
114. The [diviners spoke thus] to me:
115. "If [the liver(?) . . .] carries,
116. "And there exists [a hole(?)],
117. "And [. . .] it hangs down,
118. "[. . .] the battle-axe will make the [blood] flow,
119. "[. . .] they will drown in the blood [. . .]."

Capture of Enemy Soldiers

120. From their midst, twelve soldiers ran away from me.

---

concerning consultation of omens has been repeated verbatim from the previous occasion.

110–15. For the small fragment mentioned in the notes in *AnSt* 6, 164, see the copy in STT. This piece seems to be stuck on the main Sultantepe text in an inappropriate location at the beginning of the column.

115–17. The diviners' answer could be a quotation from the omen literature. The protasis would be lines 115–17, and the apodosis would be lines 118–19. For a summary of omens predicting death, see U. Jeyes, "Death and Divination in the Old Babylonian Period," *Death in Mesopotamia* (CRRAI 26; Mesopotamia 8; Copenhagen, 1980) 107–21.

118. For the use of the battle-axe, cf. **9E**:5, GIŠ.TUKUL.MEŠ URUDU *qul-mi-i*.

119. The reading for this line was already proposed by Jensen in KB 6/1 300:5.

121. *arkīšunu ardud aḫmuṭ urriḫ*
122. *ṣābe šâšunu akšussunūt[i]*
123. *ṣābe šâšunu utirraššu[nūti]*

124. *kīam aqbi ana libbīja [umma lū anākūma]*
125. *balu bīri šērēta u[mmudu(?)] ul ubba[l qātī(?)]*
126. *puḫāda ana muḫḫīšunu alpu[t]*
127. *namzaq ilāni rabûti gimilšunu [iqbi]*
128. *Dilbat elletu ištu šamê kīam issa[nqa]*
129. *ana Narām-Sîn mār Šarru-kīn*
130. *ezib zēr ḫalqātî lā tuḫallaq*
131. *ana arkât ūmē Enlil ana lemutti inaššâ rēssun*
132. *ana aggi libbi Enlil uqaʾʾû rēšu*
133. *āl ṣābe šunūti in[naqqar]*

---

125. The form of *šērētu* should probably be taken as a plural form of *šērtu* 'punishment', on the basis of analogy with *têrētu*, the plural form of *têrtu*. A different reading of this line leading to a converse interpretation of Naram-Sin's state of mind is offered by W. Sommerfeld: "Naram-Sin ist widerspenstig und hartnäckig: *balu bīri še-ri ta-*⌈*kal*!⌉-[*ti pānī*] *ul ubba*[*l*] 'Ohne (eine eindeutige Anweisung durch) Opferschau, "Fleisch" (und) "Magen" (= den wichtigsten Elementen der Eingeweideschau) werde ich keine Nachsicht üben.'" This attractive reading, however, seems to negate the contrast between the first and second divination requests and reactions. The first time, Naram-Sin does not take heed of the omen and proceeds against the enemy, while the second time, he listens to the oracular message and does not take any hostile action against the enemy—he has learned his lesson. In my opinion Naram-Sin's inner thoughts were more likely to have revolved around the advisability of projected actions than to have been concerned with mercy.

127. Note the unexpected form of *gimilšunu*. The normal form is *gimil* in the construct case and *gimill* +V+suffix with a possessive suffix.

128. For Ištar's manifestation to epic heroes in the guise of the Venus star, cf. Inanna as the Venus star appearing to the mortally ill Lugalbanda (Wilcke, *Das Lugalbandaepos*, 67). The form *issa*[*qra*] is unexpected in SB Akkadian, but there does not seem to be any alternative restoration.

130. The term *zēr ḫalqātî* may have many layers of meaning, more than just a double entendre. Literally it means 'a seed of (= member of) lost or missing ones'. On this basis von Soden translates 'Nomaden' (AHw 313b sub *ḫalqu* Adj. 3), while the CAD translates 'accursed, rebellious (as an invective referring to an ethnic group)' (CAD Z 87b). There are only four references to this expression, all SB (see AHw 1522 sub *zēru*). The two words *zēra* and *ḫalāqu*/*ḫulluqu* are found

121. I ran after them, I hurried, I hastened.
122. I overtook those soldiers.
123. I brought those soldiers back.

Third Reaction of Naram-Sin and the Intervention of Ištar

124. Thus I said to my heart, [these were my words]:
125. "Without omens, I will not bring myself to [impose] punishments."
126. I "touched" a lamb concerning them.
127. The "latch-hook" of the great gods, [commanded] mercy upon them.
128. Shining Venus from heaven approached me:
129. "To Naram-Sin son of Sargon,
130. "desist! Destroy not the brood of destruction!
131. "In future days, Enlil will summon them for evil.
132. "They will be at the disposal of the angry heart of Enlil.
133. "The city of those soldiers will be demolished.

---

in curses, which may be the reason the CAD chose the meaning 'accursed'. A similar-sounding word *zērmandu* 'vermin' also comes to mind. This term must be a pejorative one. Yet the employment of the factitive verbal stem *ḫulluqu* 'to destroy' in the same sentence affects the nuance of the noun. In order to capture this nuance, I have translated the line 'Do not destroy the brood of destruction'.

131. The two relevant nuances of the phrase *rēša našû*, 'to summon' and 'to honor', could be conveyed in this context: 'to summon them and to honor them as evil'.

132. The phrase *ana aggi libbi* is not a conflation of two phrases *ina uggat libbi* 'in the anger of the heart' and *libbu aggu* 'angry heart', since the adjective *aggu* may precede the noun it modifies. However, the verbal phrase is an inversion of *rēš libbi aggi ša Enlil uqaᵓᵓû*.

133–43. As has been repeatedly stated, there are grammatical problems in this section: the singularity of the noun and the plurality of the verb. In comparative omen literature, the 'city' often occurs as the subject matter of the extispicy. In such cases, as in this literary text, the word 'city' is extrapolated from its syntactical position and placed frontally at the beginning of the sentence, with or without a resumptive pronoun: *āla āšibūšu izzibūšu* 'the city, its inhabitants will abandon it' (Boissier DA 225:7); *ālam išātum ikkal* 'the city, fire will consume it' (YOS 10 31 xii 25–26). However, this syntactical order with a singular pronominal resumptive only occurs in line 144: *āla šâšu ālu nakru iṣabbassu*. In all other instances, the noun *ālu* seems to be used as a collective in the sense of 'the inhabitants of the city', and verbs seem to be third plural used impersonally. Further, there is a logical difficulty in identifying 'the city'. Is it identical to the city in line 33?

134. *iqammû ilammû šubāti*
135. *ālu dāmūšunu itabbakū*
136. *erṣetu išpikīša gišimmaru bilassa umaṭṭa*
137. *āl ṣābe šunūti imuttū*
138. *ālu itti [āli bītu] itti bīti inakkir*
139. *ab[u itti māre aḫu] itti aḫi*
140. *[eṭlu] itti eṭli rūʾua itti itbari*
141. *itti aḫāmeš kīnāti ul ītammû*
142. *nišū lā kīnāti šūḫuzāma šanâtim da pa ra qu*?

133–34. The term *ṣābē šunūti* may be either a genitive dependent on the nomen regens *ālu* or the accusative object of the verb. CAD Q 78a offers an interpretation based on the accusative: URU *ṣābē šunūti* [*i-na*]*-ru* (var. *in-*[. . .]) *iqammû ilammû* GIŠ (?).KU.MEŠ 'the city which kills these people, (the enemy's) weapons(?) will burn down (and) besiege'. However, such an interpretation with 'the city' as subject and 'that army' as object is impossible in the parallel sentence in line 137, where the verb is intransitive.

The form of the verb is difficult to analyze. The initial *in-*[. . .] is unexpected in SB for the verb *nâru*; it cannot reflect the OAkk. form *in-a-ru*. For the normal SB form, cf. GIŠ.TUKUL-*šú* ÉRIN *šuatu* . . . *i-na-ru* 'whose weapons annihilated that army' (line 28). Perhaps the two manuscripts differed in their choice of verb at this point. Manuscript A may have had *in-*[*na-qa-ar*] while G had [*i-na*]*-ru*, or both may have had *innaqqaru*.

134. For parallels to this picture of the burning and razing of the dwelling places of the lamented city, cf.:

> zag-è-ba gú-g[ìr] mu-ni-in-[gar-re-eš] uru giš.al-e bí-in-[ra-(ra)-aš]
> ki-gub-ba izi mu-ni-in-sum-mu-[uš] uru tuš-ba mu-u[n-x x x x x]
>
> They breached its buttresses; they hewed the city with axes;
> They set fire to its stations; they . . . the city's dwelling places.
> (Green, *Uruk Lament*, 5.13–14; *JAOS* 104 [1984] 274).
>
> ^{d}mullili é-mu šu ḫé-bí-in-bal giš.al-e ḫa-ba-ra
> sig-ta-di-mà izi ḫa-ba-ni-in-šub a úru-mu ḫu-mu-da-gul
>
> Verily, Enlil has turned inimical to my house, by the pickax verily it has been *torn up*.
> Upon him who comes from below verily he hurled fire—alas, my city verily has been destroyed
> (Kramer, *Lamentation over Ur*, 258–59).

135. For parallels to the flowing of blood, cf. ù-mu-un nam-lú-u$_{18}$ áb-gin$_7$ m[u-un-sur-sur-re-eš] níg-dím mu-un-z[i-(x)-r]e-eš 'they let the

134. "They will burn and besiege (its) dwelling places.
135. "The city—their blood will pour out.
136. "The earth will diminish its store, the date palm its yield.
137. "The city of those soldiers will die.
138. "City will fight with city, household with household,
139. "Father with son, brother with brother,
140. "Young man with young man, friend with neighbor.
141. "They will not speak truth with one another.
142. "People will be taught lies and. . . . aberrations.

---

blood of the people flow like that of a (sacrificial) cow; they tore out everything that had been built' (Green, *Uruk Lament*, 5.22).

136. For parallels to the disruption of the natural agricultural cycle, cf. *liš-šur eqlu išpikīšu* 'let the fields diminish their yield, (Let Nisaba stop up her breast)' (Lambert-Millard, *Atra-ḫasīs*, 72 II i 18; as well as pp. 108, 110 S iv 46, 56); *ša širʾi bilassu imṭīma* 'the yield of the furrow became scanty' (Cagni, *Erra*, I 135; as well as the references in the Sumerian city laments and the "Curse of Agade" collected by J. Cooper, *Curse of Agade*, 24–25).

138. The theme of the disruption of city and family life is common in the "Curse of Agade" (lines 215ff.), the "Lamentation over the Destruction of Ur" (231ff.), and other city laments, as well as in Akkadian literature ("Erra" IV 135ff.) and omen literature (cf. CAD A/1 384b bottom).

141. The inversion of the ethical standards is underlined in the following parallel:

> sag zi sag lul-la šu-bal ba-ni-ib-ak
> mèš mèš-e an-ta i-im-nú
> úš lú lul-e úš lú zi-da-ke$_4$ an-ta na-mu-un-DU
>
> Honest people were confounded with liars;
> Young men lay upon young men;
> The blood of liars ran upon the blood of honest men
> (Cooper, *Curse of Agade*, 190ff.).

For other Sumerian examples, see Cooper, *Curse of Agade*, 25; and for Akkadian examples, cf. "Dialogue of Pessimism," 76–78 (Lambert, *BWL*, 149).

142. The reconstruction of the second half of this line is difficult. The first signs *šá na tim* are usually understood as *šanâtim* 'strange, uncanny, revolting' (cf. Gurney's 'strange things' and Labat's 'des insanités'). Less likely readings are *ša naṭîm* 'what is proper' (cf. CAD s.v.) and in particular *la naṭâti šūḫuzu* '(he who) has learned unseemly things' ("Šurpu" II 64). However, the signs remaining to form the verb *di ra qu* or *di ra am ma* do not yield any obvious sense. If *ša naṭîm* were possible, the verb could have been restored ⟨*ud*⟩-*da-pa-ra-am-ma*! as a Dt passive from the root *dapāru* (*ṭapāru*) 'vertreiben, entfernen' (AHw

143. *ālu nakru šū iddukkū*
144. *āla šâšu ālu nakru iṣabbassu*
145. *ana* 1 [MA.NA K]Ù.BABBAR *sūtu uṭṭatu imaḫḫar*
146. *šarru dan*[*nu* . . .] . . . *ina māti ul ibši*
147. [⟨*ana*⟩ *ilāni*] *rabûti ana bibilti ūbilšunūti*
148. *qāti ana dâki ul ūbilšunūti*

149. *atta mannu lū iššakku u rubû lū mimma šanâma*
150. *ša ilānu inambûšu šarrūta ippuš*
151. *ṭupšenna ēpuška narâ ašṭurka*
152. *ina Kutî ina Emeslam*
153. *ina papāḫ Nergal ēzibakka*
154. *narâ annâ amurma*
155. *ša pī narê annâ šimēma*
156. *lā tessiḫḫu lā tenniššu*
157. *lā tapallaḫ lā tatarrur*
158. *išdāka lū kīnā*
159. *atta ina sūn sinništīka šipir lū teppuš*

1380a D). Some emendation to this line does not seem out of place, since manuscript G is replete with errors and omissions (cf. ⟨*ru*⟩ missing in *nak-ru* in line 144).

145. Cf. the better rate of exchange in "Curse of Agade," line 177: še diš gín-e bán sìla-àm 'one shekel's worth of grain was only one half quart'. The normal equivalence given in "Maništušu's Obelisk" is one shekel of silver to one gur.sag.gal of grain. For silver prices, see further Limet, *JESHO* 15 (1972) 31, table of prices.

147–48. Note the plural subject and the singular verb, which are discussed by Gurney (*AnSt* 5 [1955] 112–13), who suggests adding an ⟨*ana*⟩ but still prefers translating the sentence with the gods as the subject. On the other hand, Labat follows Gurney's suggestion, 'I brought them to the great gods as tribute' but translates, 'Je les ai laissés(?) aux grands dieux pour l'extermination(?)'. The object *bibiltu* is also unusual and rare, with only two other occurrences. The CAD B suggests the meaning 'decimation of the army', and von Soden, in his Ntrg. 1548a, 'Wegführung'. It does come from a prolific root *wabālu*, which has other nominal derivatives based on *babālu*, such as *babbilu*, *biblu*, etc., as well as those based on *abālu*, such as *biltu*. Interpreting this word as a synonym *biltu* 'tribute' would be appropriate, in light of the practice of the Old

143. "The city is a hostile one—they will be defeated.
144. "That city—an enemy city will seize it.
145. "For one [mina] of silver, (only) a seah of barley will be had."
146. There was no strong king in the land who [. . .].
147. I delivered them ⟨to⟩ the great gods for delivery(?).
148. I did not deliver them for my hand to kill.

Admonition to Future Ruler

149. You, whoever you are, be it governor or prince or anyone else,
150. whom the gods will call to perform kingship,
151. I made a tablet-box for you and inscribed a stela for you.
152. In Kutha, in the Emeslam,
153. in the cella of Nergal, I left (it) for you.
154. Read this stele!
155. Hearken unto the words of this stele!
156. Be not bewildered! Be not confused!
157. Be not afraid! Do not tremble!
158. Let your foundations be firm!
159. You, within the embrace of your wife, do your work!

Akkadian kings of bringing their captives in fetters to Enlil in Nippur. The remaining question is whether *bibiltu* should connote a gift or just the act of delivery. In the latter case, Naram-Sin would be emphasizing his role as a middleman, conveying a consignment. There is a play on the same root in this line as in line 130; in this line it is *abālu*, and in line 130 *ḫalāqu*.

A. Westenholz suggests that the passage must mean 'The great gods brought them to their downfall, but I did not lift my hand to kill them'. Thus he corrects *ūbilšunūti* to *ūbilū/ūblū-šunūti*. The meaning 'downfall' depends on the other two references to this lexeme, in the Mari letter (ARM 10 11 and KAR 423). However, there is a logical problem because the downfall of the enemy hordes has not yet occurred in the story.

153. For a discussion of the *papāḫu*, the cella of a temple, see D. Charpin (*Iraq* 45 [1983] 56–63) and W. von Soden (*Temple et Culte*, 137–38).

158–59. Note that Labat treats these lines as conditional: 'Si tu veux que tes bases soient stables, et, toi-même, faire l'amour sur le sein de ta femme, . . .' (*Les religions*, 314).

159ff. For a discussion of these lines, see Hoffner, *JCS* 23 (1970) 18ff. His first problem is the undeclined *ši-pir*, which he replaces with x x. However, the signs are clear on the tablets. Either the original written text had *šipir sinništi*

160. *durānīka tukkil*
161. *ḫirātīka mê mulli*
162. *pisannātīka šeʾaka kasapka bušēka makkūrka*
163. *ana āl dannūtīka šūrib*
164. *kakkēka rukusma tubqāti e*[*mid*]
165. *qarrādūtīka uṣur pūtka šullim*
166. *littaggiš mātka ē tūṣīšu*
167. *littidi būla ē tasniqšu*
168. *līkul šēr rīdû*[*tī*]*ka*
169. *lišaggiš li-tur-*[. . .]
170. *lū ašrāta lū san*[*qāta*]
171. *annû bēli apulšunūti*
172. *ana gullultīšunu rīb dumqi*

---

and the second word was omitted by chance in the course of recopying (it is only a small sign, SAL), or it is just ungrammatical.

164. For a parallel to this line, cf. *itammâ ana kakkēšu ummedā tubqāti* 'to his weapons he says, "stay in the racks!"' (Cagni, *Erra*, I 17). This parallel has already been mentioned by O. Gurney (*AnSt* 5, 113) and discussed by H. Hoffner, *JCS* 23 (1970) 19, who concludes that the phrase means 'to get yourself into a corner' and that Naram-Sin is telling the future king to hide. However, it is obvious that in both references it is the weapons that are to stand in the corner. Labat (*Les religions*, 314) takes the first half of the line to be a question and the second half of the line to be the answer: 'Ceins tes armes? Non, laisse-les à l'abri!' Landsberger (H. Tadmor, B. Landsberger, and S. Parpola, "The Sin of Sargon and Sennacherib's Last Will," *SAAB* 3 [1989] 44) suggests 'Gird yourself with weapons but go into hiding', in keeping with Gurney's secondary translation offered in his notes on this line (*AnSt* 5, 113).

167. The word *littiddi* comes from *nadû* I/3 and means 'to put animals out to pasture' (CAD N/1 79), as well as 'to cast down, abandon'; both meanings seem to be implied in this line. Cf. ùz-gi ^{d}En-líl-lá amaš-ta ba-ra-ra-aš . . . šilam tùr-bi-ta ba-ra-ra-aš . . . 'they (the Guti) drive the trusty goats of Enlil from the fold . . . they drive the cows from the pens . . . ' (Cooper, *Curse of Agade*, 164–65); šà-⌜tùm?⌝-ma dum-dam mu-ni-in-z[a] anše-udu im-mi-in-è 'in the pasture lands a tumultuous noise arose; the draft asses and sheep were driven away' (Green, *Uruk Lament*, 2.28). A. Westenholz suggests: 'Let him lose a cow; don't hold him accountable / don't check on him'.

168. For *rīdu*, cf. *rīdu* II, AHw 981b. Labat (*Les religions*, 314) offers 'S'il mange la chair de ton avenir', apparently restoring *rīdūtīka* here. Landsberger

160. Strengthen your walls!
161. Fill your moats with water!
162. Your chests, your grain, your money, your goods, your possessions,
163. bring into your stronghold!
164. Tie up your weapons and put (them) into the corners!
165. Guard your courage! Take heed of your own person!
166. Let him roam through your land! Go not out to him!
167. Let him scatter the cattle! Do not go near him!
168. Let him consume the flesh of your offspring!
169. Let him murder, (and) let him return (unharmed)!
170. (But) you be self-controlled, disciplined.
171. Answer them, "Here I am, sir"!
172. Requite their wickedness with kindness!

(H. Tadmor, B. Landsberger, S. Parpola, "Sin of Sargon," 44) suggests *rēdûtika* 'of your soldiers'.

169. The word *li-sag-gi-x* is listed as coming from the root *šagālu* (in AHw 1125b) with unclear meaning and read '(wer?) *li-šag-gi-lu*!' However, despite the traces the reading *-lu* is impossible, since the verbs in this section speak of the enemy in singular third person. Therefore, I propose the reading *li-šag-gi-iš* from a Gtn or I/3 form of the verb *šagāšu* 'to slay in battle, to murder, to slaughter'. The same opinion is now given by Landsberger (ibid.). Labat offers 'même s'il renouvelle (?) ses déprédations (?)', but it is uncertain how he reached this suggested reading.

170. The pair *ašru//sanqu* appear in the lexical section of *ašāru* A 'to muster, check controls' and not under *ašāru* B 'to be humble'. This line is not quoted under *ašru* adj. On the other hand, AHw 1488b has this reference under the adjective *ašru* 'mit gesenktem Kopf, demutig' and assumes an etymological relationship with *wašāru/ašāru* II, rather than with *ašāru* I (AHw 79a) 'ordnend überwachen, betreuen'. Note the interpretation of Landsberger (H. Tadmor, B. Landsberger, and S. Parpola, "Sin of Sargon," 44): "neither 'meek' nor 'humble'; *ašrāta* is not *wašrāta* but *ʾašrāta. ašāru, sanāqu, paqādu* = 'to check', in the sense of kontrollieren, 'be considerate and self-controlled.'" Following Landsberger, I argue that the pair *ašru//sanqu* cannot be translated as 'meek//humble' but must be translated 'disciplined//prudent//self-controlled'.

171. For the grammatical and semantic understanding of the phrase *annû bēli*, cf. Lambert BWL 323, and note his comment, "evidently the conventional answer of slaves."

173. *ana dumqi qīšāti u taṣbâti*
174. *ana maḫrīšunu etettiq*
175. *ṭupšarrē enqūte*
176. *liskurū narâka*
177. *šūt narēʾa tāmurūma*
178. *pūtka tušēṣû*
179. *šūt jāši taktarba arkû*
180. *liktarrabka kāša*

---

173. For *taṣbâtu*, see AHw 1337b, where the suggested etymology is offered: *ṣabû* IV (?) or *ṣabātu*(?). There von Soden gives the translation 'Wunscherfüllungen?' with two references only: this line in "Naram-Sin and the Enemy Hordes" and *ekal taṣbâti* in *ZDMG* 98 30:4. Landsberger (H. Tadmor, B. Landsberger, and S. Parpola, "Sin of Sargon," 44) proposes that *taṣbātu* could be a plural formation of *taṣibtu*, based on the verb *waṣābu* (Heb. *ysp*), which is an attractive suggestion.

174. There are two interpretations of this line: (1) taking the verb as a G vetitive in present tense, which is grammatically problematic: 'do not approach them in order to get favors . . . ' (Gurney, Labat); (2) taking the verb as Gtn imperative *etettiq* (suggestion, A. Westenholz). The latter interpretation makes better sense in the context.

173. And (their) kindness with gifts and supplementary presents(?)!
174. Always precede them (i.e., do more than they ask)!
175. Wise scribes,
176. let them declaim your inscription.
177. You who have read my inscription
178. and thus have gotten yourself out (of trouble),
179. you who have blessed me, may a future (ruler)
180. Bless you!

175ff. This conclusion reminds one of the "Idrimi Inscription": *mānaḫtīja ana ṭuppīja ašṭur lidaggal(ū)šunu u ana muḫḫīja liktanarrabū* 'My deed(s), I wrote upon my tablet; let them continually look upon them and upon me; may they continually invoke blessings" ("Idrimi," 103–4; see G. Oller, *JCS* 29 [1977] 167–68; J. M. Sasson, "On Idrimi and Šarruwa, the Scribe," *Studies on the Civilization and Culture of Nuzi and the Hurrians: In Honor of Ernest R. Lacheman on His Seventy-Fifty Birthday, April 29, 1981* [ed. M. A. Morrison and D. I. Owen; Winona Lake, Ind., 1981] 309–24; and Dietrich and Loretz, *UF* 13 [1981] 230).

Manuscripts

Neo-Assyrian: Nineveh

A	81-2-4,219	= CT XIII 44 (see photographs, p. 405)
B	K.5418a	= CT XIII 39–40 (see photographs and copy of rev., pp. 406–7)
C	K.5640	= CT XIII 41 (see photographs, p. 408)
D	K.8582	= Thompson, *Epic of Gilgamesh*, pl. 34 (see photograph, p. 408)
E	K.2021B, unpublished (see photograph and copy, p. 409)	
F	K.13328, unpublished (see photograph and copy, p. 409)	

Neo-Assyrian: Huzirina (Sultantepe)

G	S.U. 51/67A + 76 + 166 + 21923 = STT 30	

Neo-Babylonian: Kiš

H	Ash. 1924.2085	= OECT XI 103 (see photograph, p. 410)

1.	A i 1	[ ] NA.DÙ.A *ši-tas-si*
	B	[ ]
	C	[ ]
	D	[ ]
	E	[ ]
	F	[ ]
	G i 1	[ ]
	H	[ ]
2.	A i 2	[ ] DUMU ^{1}LUGAL.GI.NA
	B	[ ]
	C	[ ]
	D	[ ]
	E	[ ]
	F	[ ]
	G i 2	[ ]
	H	[ ]
3.	A i 3	[ ]*u_4-me ṣa-a-ti*
	B	[ ]
	C	[ ]
	D	[ ]
	E	[ ]
	F	[ ]
	G i 3	[*t*]*i*
	H	[ ]

4.	A i 4	[ ] KUR-*a e-mid*
	B	[ ]
	C	[ ]
	D	[ ]
	E	[ ]
	F	[ ]
	G i 4	[ ]-*mid*
	H	[ ]
5.	A i 5	[ ] KUR-*a e-mid*
	B	[ ]
	C	[ ]
	D	[ ]
	E	[ ]
	F	[ ]
	G i 5	[ ] *e-mid*
	H	[ ]
6.	A i 6	[*m*]*a-ʾ-ir ma-a-ti*
	B	[ ]
	C	[ ]
	D	[ ]
	E	[ ]
	F	[ ]
	G i 6	[*m*]*a-a-ti*
	H	[ ]
7.	A i 7	[ME]Š *ina*(AŠ) ZI-*ḫi*
	B	[ ]
	C	[ ]
	D	[ ]
	E	[ ]
	F	[ ]
	G i 7	[ ]-*sa-ḫi*
	H	[ ]
8.	A i 8	[M]EŠ *ina a-la-ki*
	B	[ ]
	C	[ ]
	D	[ ]
	E	[ ]
	F	[ ]
	G i 8	[ ]-*la-ku*
	H	[ ]

9.	A i 9	[ ]-*ni mi-lik-šá*
	B	[ ]
	C	[ ]
	D	[ ]
	E	[ ]
	F	[ ]
	G i 9	[*-li*]*k-šá*
	H	[ ]
10.	A i 10	[ ]-⸢x⸣-*ma ir-kab*
	B	[ ]
	C	[ ]
	D	[ ]
	E	[ ]
	F	[ ]
	G i 10	[ ]-*kab*
	H	[ ]
11.	A i 11	[ ] GAL.MEŠ
	B	[ ]
	C	[ ]
	D	[ ]
	E	[ ]
	F	[ ]
	G i 11	[ ] DINGIR.M[EŠ].MEŠ
	H	[ ]
12.	A i 12	[ ]-ba_4 ^{d}*A-nu-ni-tum*
	B	[ ]
	C	[ ]
	D	[ ]
	E	[ ]
	F	[ ]
	G i 12	[ ]^{d}*Za*-ba_4-ba_4 ^{d}[*-t*]*um*
	H	[ ]
13.	A i 13	[ ] *qu-ra-du*
	B	[ ]
	C	[ ]
	D	[ ]
	E	[ ]
	F	[ ]
	G i 13	[ ]
	H	[ ]

14.	A i 14	[ ] *ú-ma-ʾ-ir*
	B	[ ]
	C	[ ]
	D	[ ]
	E	[ ]
	F	[ ]
	G i 14	[ ] x x x (x) [ ]
	H	[ ]
15.	A i 15	[ ]-*pu-tu*
	B	[ ]
	C	[ ]
	D	[ ]
	E	[ ]
	F	[ ]
	G i 15	[ ] SILA$_4$ *x[ ]
	H	[ ]
16.	A i 16	[K]Ù?.MEŠ
	B	[ ]
	C	[ ]
	D	[ ]
	E	[ ]
	F	[ ]
	G i 16	[GUḪ]ŠU.MEŠ [ ]
	H	[ ]
17.	A i 17	[ ]-*ú-ni*
	B	[ ]
	C	[ ]
	D	[ ]
	E	[ ]
	F	[ ]
	G i 17	[ ] *ki-a-am iq-bu-u-*[x x]
	H	[ ]
18.	A i 18	[ ]-*kam*
	B	[ ]
	C	[ ]
	D	[ ]
	E	[ ]
	F	[ ]
	G i 18	[ ]-⸢x⸣-*šú ti riq* KUM/*qu u lid*(?)+x *lam*?[x (x)]
	H	[ ]

19.	A i 19	[ ]x
	B	[ ]
	C	[ ]
	D	[ ]
	E	[ ]
	F	[ ]
	G i 19	[*t*]*u-ru-qu zi-i-ma*
	H	[ ]
20.	A	[ ]
	B	[ ]
	C	[ ]
	D	[ ]
	E	[ ]
	F	[ ]
	G i 20	[x (x)] *ban* [*m*]*a*(?) *i-id/da-ši*
	H	[ ]
21.	A	[ ]
	B	[ ]
	C	[ ]
	D	[ ]
	E	[ ]
	F	[ ]
	G i 21	[x (x)] KI.TA [ ] ⸢x⸣ [*l*]*i*?-*par-qud pa-gar-ka*
	H	[ ]
22.	A	[ ]
	B	[ ]
	C i 1′	*a-di*![ ]
	D	[ ]
	E	[ ]
	F	[ ]
	G i 22	*a-di* [ ].MEŠ GAL.MEŠ
	H	[ ]
23.	A	[ ]
	B	[ ]
	C i 2′	*En-me-kár* LÚ.Ú[Š-*šú*]
	D	[ ]
	E	[ ]
	F	[ ]
	G i 23	*En-me-kár* [ ] *di-na mar-ṣa* ^{d}UTU GAR-[*un*]
	H	[ ]

24.	A	[ ]
	B	[ ]
	C i 3′	di-en-šu EŠ.BAR [ ]
	D	[ ]
	E	[ ]
	F	[ ]
	G i 24	di-en-šú EŠ.⸢BAR x x⸣ [x] ⸢x⸣ GIDIM-šú GIDIM.GI[DIM (x)]
	H	[ ]
25.	A	[ ]
	B	[ ]
	C i 4′	UDUG NUNUZ-šu UDUG NUNUZ [ ]
	D	[ ]
	E	[ ]
	F	[ ]
	G i 25	GIDIM IM.RI.[A]-šú ⸢GIDIM⸣ NUN[UZ]-šú GIDIM NUNUZ NUNUZ-šú ^{d}UTU q[u-ra-du]
	H	[ ]
26.	A	[ ]
	B	[ ]
	C i 5′	EN(?) AN.TA.MEŠ ù KI.TA.MEŠ *EN(?) ^{d*}E-*ni-[ ]
	D	[ ]
	E	[ ]
	F	[ ]
	G i 26	EN AN.TA.MEŠ u KI.TA.MEŠ EN ^{d}A-nun-na-ki EN e-⸢ṭím-me⸣
	H	[ ]
27.	A	[ ]
	B	[ ]
	C i 6′	šá A.MEŠ dal-ḫu-te NAG u A.MEŠ za-ku-te N[U]
	D	[ ]
	E	[ ]
	F	[ ]
	G i 27	šá A.MEŠ dal-ḫu-te N[AG u A].MEŠ za-[ku-t]e NU NAG.MEŠ
	H	[ ]
28.	A	[ ]
	B i 1′	[šá igi]-⸢gál-la-šú⸣ [GIŠ.TUKUL-šú ÉRIN] ⸢šu-a-tu ik-mu-ú⸣ // ik-šu-du i-na-ru
	C i 7′	šá igi-gál-la-šu SIPA-šu ÉRIN šu-a-tu ik-mu-u ik-[šu-du]
	D	[ ]
	E	[ ]
	F	[ ]
	G i 28	šá igi-gál-la-šú GIŠ.TUKUL-šú É[RIN] šú-a-tu i[k]-mu-u ik-[šu-du]
	H	[ ]

29.	A	[ ]
	B i 2′	*ina* NA.DÙ.A *ul* SAR *ul* TAG$_4$-*am-ma pag-ri u pu-u-ti*
	C i 8′	*ina* NA$_4$.NA.DÙ.A *ul* SAR *ul* TAG$_4$-*am-ma pag-r*[*i* . . .]
	D	[ ]
	E	[ ]
	F	[ ]
	G i 29	*ina* NA.DÙ.A *ul* SAR *ul* TAG$_4$-*am-ma* ⸢*pag*⸣-*ri u* [*pu*]-*ti*
	H	[ ]
30.	A	[ ]
	B i 3′	MU *ul ú-še-ṣi-ma ul ak-ta-rab-šú*
	C i 9′	*ul ú-še-ṣi-ma ul ak-*[ ]
	D	[ ]
	E	[ ]
	F	[ ]
	G i 30	MU *u*[*l*] *ú-še-ṣi-ma ul ik-tar-rab-š*[*ú*]
	H	[ ]
31.	A	[ ]
	B i 4′	ÉRIN.MEŠ *pag-ri iṣ-ṣur ḫur-ri a-me-lu-ti* // *a-ri-bu pa-nu-šú-un*
	C i 10′	ÉRIN.MEŠ *pag-ri* MUŠEN *ḫur-ri a-me-lu-ta* [ ]
	D	[ ]
	E	[ ]
	F	[ ]
	G i 31	ÉRIN.MEŠ *pag-ri* MUŠEN *ḫur-*[*ri a-me-lu-*]*ta a-ri-bu pa-*[ ]
	H	[ ]
32.	A	[ ]
	B i 5′	*ib-nu-šú-nu-ti-ma* DINGIR.MEŠ GAL.MEŠ
	C i 11′	*ib-nu-šu-nu-ti-ma* DINGIR.[ ]
	D	[ ]
	E	[ ]
	F	[ ]
	G i 32	*ib-nu-šu-nu-ti-ma* DINGIR.MEŠ GAL.MEŠ
	H	[ ]
33.	A	[ ]
	B i 6′	*ina qaq-qar ib-nu-ú* DINGIR.MEŠ *a-lu-šú*
	C i 12′	*ina qaq-qar ib-nu-ú* DINGIR.M[EŠ]
	D	[ ]
	E	[ ]
	F	[ ]
	G i 33	*ina qaq-qar ib-nu-ú* DINGIR.MEŠ *a-lu-šú-*[*nu*?]
	H	[ ]

34.	A	[ ]
	B i 7′	*Ti-a-ma-tu ú-še-niq-šú-nu-ti*
	C i 13′	*Ti-a-ma-tu* [ ]
	D	[ ]
	E	[ ]
	F	[ ]
	G i 34	*Ti-a-ma-tu ú-še-niq-šú-nu-ti*
	H	[ ]
35.	A	[ ]
	B i 8′	*šà-sur-šú-nu* ^{d}*Be-let-ì-lí ú-ban-ni*
	C i 14′	[*šà*]*-sur-šu-nu* ^{d}*Be-let-*[ ]
	D	[ ]
	E	[ ]
	F	[ ]
	G i 35	*šà-sur-šú-nu* ^{d}*Be-let-ì-lí ú-ban-ni*
	H	[ ]
36.	A	[ ]
	B i 9′	⸢*ina qé-reb*⸣ KUR-*i ir-ti-bu-ma i-te-iṭ-lu-ma* // *ir-ta-šú-u mi-na-ti*
	C i 15′	*ina qé-reb* KUR-*i ir-te-u-ma i-te*?[ ]
	D	[ ]
	E i 1′	[*-e*]*ṭ-lu-ma* // [ ]*-na-ti*
	F	[ ]
	G i 36	*ina qé-reb* KUR-*i ir-te-u-ma i-te-eṭ-lu-ta-ma ir-ta-šú-u mi-na-*[*a-t*]*e*
	H	[ ]
37.	A	[ ]
	B i 10′	[x] LUGAL.MEŠ-*ni at-ḫu-ú šu-pu-u ba-nu-tu*
	C i 16′	7 LUGAL.MEŠ *at-ḫu-ú* [ ]
	D	[ ]
	E i 2′	[ ] *ba-nu-tu*
	F	[ ]
	G i 37	7 LUGAL.MEŠ *at-ḫu-u šu-pu-u ba-nu-*[*t*]*u*
	H	[ ]
38.	A	[ ]
	B i 11′	[ ]A.AN *um-ma-na-tu-šú-nu*
	C i 17′	6-LIM.A.AN *u*[*m*]
	D	[ ]
	E i 3′	[ ]*-tu-šú-nu*
	F	[ ]
	G i 38	6-LIM.A.AN *um-ma-na-tú-šú-nu*
	H	[ ]

39.	A	[ ]
	B i 12′	[ ] AD-*šú-nu* LUGAL AMA-*šú-nu* // [*šar*]-*ra-tu* ^{SAL}*Me-li-li*
	C i 18′	*Anu-ba-ni-ni* AD-*šu-nu* LUGAL A[MA]
	D	[ ]
	E i 4′	[ ]-*tu* ^{SAL}*Me-li-li*
	F	[ ]
	G i 39	*Anu-ba-ni-ni* AD-*šú-nu* LUGAL ⌜AMA⌝-*šú-nu* *ša*[*r-r*]*a-tú* ^{SAL}*Me-li-lim* MU.NI
	H	[ ]
40.	A	[ ]
	B i 13′	[ ] ⌜*a-lik*⌝ *pa-ni-šú-nu* ^{1}*Me-ma-an-duḫ* MU.NI
	C i 19′	ŠEŠ-*šu-nu* GAL-*ú* *a-lik* [ ]
	D	[ ]
	E i 5′	[ ]-*duḫ* MU.NI
	F	[ ]
	G i 40	ŠEŠ-*šú-nu* GAL-*u* *a-lik* IGI-*šú-nu* ^{1}*Me-ma-an-daḫ* ⌜MU⌝.NI
	H	[ ]
41.	A	[ ]
	B i 14′	[ ]^{1}*Me-du-du* MU.NI
	C i 20′	2-*ú* ŠEŠ [ ]
	D	[ ]
	E i 6′	[ ] MU.NI
	F	[ ]
	G i 41	2-*ú* ŠEŠ-*šú-nu* ^{1}*Mi-du-du* MU.NI
	H	[ ]
42.	A	[ ]
	B i 15′	[ ]-*paḫ* MU.NI
	C i 21′	3-*šu* ŠEŠ [ ]
	D	[ ]
	E i 7′	[M]U.NI
	F	[ ]
	G i 42	[3]-*šú* ŠEŠ-*šú-nu* [^{1}x]-⌜*ta-piš*⌝ [M]U.NI
	H	[ ]
43.	A	[ ]
	B i 16′	[*d*]*a-da* MU.NI
	C i 22′	4-*ú* [ ]
	D	[ ]
	E i 8′	[ ]NI
	F	[ ]
	G i 43	[4]-*ú* ŠEŠ-*šú-nu* ^{1}*Tar-ta-da-da* [M]U.NI
	H	[ ]

44.	A	[ ]
	B i 17′	[ ]-*daḫ* MU.NI
	C i 23′	5-*šu* [ ]
	D	[ ]
	E	[ ]
	F	[ ]
	G i 44	[5]-*šú* ŠEŠ-*šú-nu* ^{1}*Bal-daḫ-daḫ* ⸢MU.NI⸣
	H	[ ]
45.	A	[ ]
	B i 18′	[ ]x MU.NI
	C i 24′	6 [ ]
	D	[ ]
	E	[ ]
	F	[ ]
	G i 45	[6]-*šú* ŠEŠ-*šú-nu* ^{1}*A-ḫu-da-na-di-iḫ* MU.NI
	H	[ ]
46.	A	[(end of column)]
	B i 19′	[M]U.NI (end of column)
	C	[(probably also end of column)]
	D	[ ]
	E	(possibly end of column but note difference in length of col. ii in B and in E)
	F	[ ]
	G i 46	[7]-*ú* ŠEŠ-*šú-nu* ^{1}*Ḫur-ra!-ki-du-u* MU.N[I]
47.	A ii 1	KUR.MEŠ [ ]
	B	[ ]
	C	[ ]
	D	[ ]
	E	[ ]
	F	[ ]
	G i 47	[KU]R.MEŠ KÙ.MEŠ *ir-ka-bu-nim-ma*
	H	[ ]
48.	A ii 2	*ri-du-ú* [ ]
	B	[ ]
	C	[ ]
	D	[ ]
	E	[ ]
	F	[ ]
	G i 48	[*r*]*i-du-u iṣ-bat-su-nu-ti-m*[*a i*]*m-ḫa-ṣu šá-par-*⸢*šú-un*⸣
	H	[ ]

49.	A ii 3	*ri-eš sa-na-q*[*í*] // *is-sa-*[ ]
	B	[ ]
	C	[ ]
	D	[ ]
	E	[ ]
	F	[ ]
	G i 49	[*r*]*i-eš sa-na-qí-šu-nu a-na* U[R]U.[*P*]*u-ru-uš-ḫa-an-dar is-sa-qu-*[(x)]*-ni*
	H	[ ]
50.	A ii 4	URU.*Pu-ru-uš-*⸢*ḫa-an-dar gi-mir*(?)⸣ [ ]
	B	[ ]
	C	[ ]
	D	[ ]
	E	[ ]
	F	[ ]
	G i 50	[UR]U.*Pu-ru-uš-ḫa-an-dar gi-*⸢x⸣-[x]*-su it-tas-paḫ*
	H	[ ]
51.	A ii 5	URU.*Pu-uḫ-lu-ú* [ ]
	B	[ ]
	C	[ ]
	D	[ ]
	E	[ ]
	F	[ ]
	G i 51	[UR]U.*Pú-ḫu-lu-u it-tas-paḫ*
	H	[ ]
52.	A ii 6	URU.*Pu-ra-an-šu-ú* [ ]
	B	[ ]
	C	[ ]
	D	[ ]
	E	[ ]
	F	[ ]
	G i 52	[UR]U.*Pú-ra-an-šu-u it-tas-paḫ*
	H	[ ]
53.	A ii 7	*lu-za-a* UGU *na-áš ḫu ḫu uḫ ḫa ḫu* [ ]
	B	[ ]
	C	[ ]
	D	[ ]
	E	[ ]
	F	[ ]
	G i 53	[*lu*]*-za-a* UGU *na-áš ḫu ḫu uḫ ḫa ḫu* [ ] x
	H	[ ]

54.	A ii 8	*lup-pu-du nar-bu-ú* ÉRIN-*man-da ka-*[ ] // *šu-bat* ^{d}*E*[*n-líl*]
	B	[ ]
	C	[ ]
	D	[ ]
	E	[ ]
	F	[ ]
	G i 54	[x]-*pu-du nar-bu-u* ÉRIN-*man-*[*da*] *ka-ra-*[ ] ^{d}*E*[*n-líl*]
	H	[ ]
55.	A ii 9	*u qé-reb Su-bar-ti* DÙ-*šú-nu it-*[ ]
	B	[ ]
	C	[ ]
	D	[ ]
	E	[ ]
	F i 1′	*ù* [ ]
	G i 55	[x *q*]*é-reb Su-bar-du-u* DÙ-*šú-n*[*u*]
	H	[ ]
56.	A ii 10	*is-pu-ḫu-ma ti-a-ma-ti ana*(DIŠ) *Gu-ti-um is-sa-*[ ]
	B	[ ]
	C	[ ]
	D	[ ]
	E	[ ]
	F i 2′	*is-pu-ḫu-ma ti-*[ ]
	G ii 1	[*i*]*s-sa-an-*[*qu*]
	H	[ ]
57.	A ii 11	*is-pu-ḫu-ma Gu-ti-um ana* KUR.NIM.MA.KI *is-sa-*[ ]
	B	[ ]
	C	[ ]
	D	[ ]
	E	[ ]
	F i 3′	*is-pu-ḫu-ma* KUR.*Gu-*[ ]
	G ii 2	[K]I *is-s*[*a*]
	H	[ ]
58.	A ii 12	*is-pu-ḫu-ma* KUR.NIM.MA.KI *ana sa-pan-ni ik-*[ ]
	B	[ ]
	C	[ ]
	D	[ ]
	E	[ ]
	F i 4′	*is-pu-ḫu-ma* KUR.NIM.[ ]
	G ii 3	⸢*is-pu*⸣-*ḫ*[*u* *ana ṣe-*]*ri ik-t*[*a*-x]
	H	[ ]

59.	A ii 13	*id-du-ku šá ni-bi-ri* ŠUB-*ú a-*[ ]
	B	[ ]
	C	[ ]
	D	[ ]
	E	[ ]
	F i 5′	*id-du-ku šá ni-*[ ]
	G ii 4	*id-du-ku ša*(?) [*ni*]-*bi-ri* ŠUB-*ú ana a-*[ ]
	H	[ ]
60.	A ii 14	*Dilmun*.KI *Má-gan-na Me-luḫ-ḫa qé-reb* [ ] // *ma-la ba-šu-ú id-*[ ]
	B	[ ]
	C	[ ]
	D	[ ]
	E	[ ]
	F i 6′	*Dilmun*.KI ⸢*Má*⸣-*gan-n*[*a*]
	G ii 5	*Dilmun*.KI *Má-g*[*an-n*]*a Me-luḫ-*[*ḫ*]*a qé-reb Tam-tim ma-*[. . .]
	H	[ ]
61.	A ii 15	17 LUGAL.MEŠ *adi*(EN) 90 LIM *um-ma-*[ ]
	B	[ ]
	C	[ ]
	D	[ ]
	E	[ ]
	F	[ ]
	G ii 6	17 LUGAL.MEŠ *adi*(EN) 90 LIM *um-ma-na-*[ ]
	H	[ ]
62.	A ii 16	*it-ti-šú-nu ana ri-ṣu-ti-šú-nu it-*[ ]
	B	[ ]
	C	[ ]
	D	[ ]
	E	[ ]
	F	[ ]
	G ii 7	KI-*šú-nu ana ri-ṣu-*⸢*ti*⸣-*šú-nu it-*[ ]
	H	[ ]
63.	A ii 17	[ ]-*da-a ú-ma-*[ ]
	B	[ ]
	C	[ ]
	D	[ ]
	E	[ ]
	F	[ ]
	G ii 8a	[*a*]*l-si ri-da-*[*a*] ⸢*ú*⸣-*ma-ʾ-ir*
	H	[ ]

64.	A ii 18	[ ] *ṣil-la-a a-na q*[*a-*]
	B	[ ]
	C	[ ]
	D	[ ]
	E	[ ]
	F	[ ]
	G ii 8b	// [ ]
	H	[ ]
65.	A ii 19	[ ]*-ut ina ṣil-li-e* [ ]
	B	[ ]
	C	[ ]
	D	[ ]
	E	[ ]
	F	[ ]
	G ii 9	*ina lu-*[*d*]*i-e lu-pu-ut ina ṣi*[*l-*]
	H	[ ]
66.	A ii 20	[*k*]*i-i na-ši-ma* [ ]
	B	[ ]
	C	[ ]
	D	[ ]
	E	[ ]
	F	[ ]
	G ii 10	[*šum*]*-ma* [ÚŠ.MEŠ *ú-ṣu-ni k*]*i na-ši-ma* LÚ.MEŠ-*šú-nu*
	H	[ ]
67.	A	[ ]
	B	[ ]
	C	[ ]
	D	[ ]
	E	[ ]
	F	[ ]
	G ii 11	[ ]*-ni še-e-du* NAM.TAR
	H	[ ]
68.	A	[ ]
	B ii 1′	[ ]*ki* ⌈*ra-bi*⌉*-ṣu lem-nu-te ši-*⌈*pir* ^{d}⌉[ ]
	C	[ ]
	D	[ ]
	E	[ ]
	F	[ ]
	G ii 12	[*l*]*em-nu-te ši-pir* ^{d}*En-líl šú-nu*
	H	[ ]

69.	A	[ ]
	B ii 2′	*re-du-ú ṭè-en-šú ú-tir-*[ ]
	C	[ ]
	D	[ ]
	E	[ ]
	F	[ ]
	G ii 13	[ ]*-en-šu ú-tir-ram-ma*
	H	[ ]
70.	A	[ ]
	B ii 3′	*ina* [*lu-di*]*-e al-p*[*u-ut*]
	C	[ ]
	D	[ ]
	E	[ ]
	F	[ ]
	G ii 14	[ ] *al-pu-ut*
	H	[ ]
71.	A	[ ]
	B ii 4′	*ina* [*ṣil-li*]-⸢*e*⸣ *ás-ḫul-ma da-me it-ta-ṣ*[*u-ni*]
	C	[ ]
	D	[ ]
	E	[ ]
	F	[ ]
	G ii 15	[ ]*-e ás-ḫul-ma* ÚŠ *it-ta-ṣu-ni*
	H	[ ]
72.	A	[ ]
	B ii 5′	⸢*al-si*⸣ DUMU.MEŠ LÚ.ḪAL.MEŠ *ú-ma-ʾ-*[*ir*]
	C	[ ]
	D	[ ]
	E	[ ]
	F	[ ]
	G ii 16	[ ] DUMU.MEŠ LÚ.ḪAL *ú-ma-ʾ-ir*
	H	[ ]
73.	A	[ ]
	B ii 6′	[x x x (x)] 7 UDU.SILA$_4$ *al-pu-*t*[*u*]
	C	[ ]
	D	[ ]
	E	[ ]
	F	[ ]
	G ii 17	[x x -*a*]*n* 7 UDU.SILA$_4$ *al-pu-ut*
	H	[ ]

74.	A	[ ]
	B ii 7′	[ ] X.MEŠ KÙ.MEŠ
	C	[ ]
	D	[ ]
	E	[ ]
	F	[ ]
	G ii 18	[*ú-ki*]*n-nu* GI.GUḪŠU.MEŠ KÙ.MEŠ
	H	[ ]
75.	A	[ ]
	B ii 8′	*a-šal-m*[*a*] DINGIR.MEŠ GAL.MEŠ
	C	[ ]
	D	[ ]
	E	[ ]
	F	[ ]
	G ii 19	[ ] DINGIR.MEŠ GAL.MEŠ
	H	[ ]
76.	A	[ ]
	B ii 9′	^{d}*Iš-tar* [*Ìl-a-ba*$_4$] ^{d}*Za-ba*$_4$*-ba*$_4$ ^{d}*A-nu-ni-tum*
	C	[ ]
	D	[ ]
	E	[ ]
	F	[ ]
	G ii 20	[^{d}]*Iš-*[*tar Ìl-a-*]*ba*$_4$ ^{d}*Za-ba*$_4$*-ba*$_4$ ^{d}*A-nu-ni-tum*
	H	[ ]
77.	A	[ ]
	B ii 10′	^{d}P[A] ^{d}UTU *qu-ra-du*
	C	[ ]
	D	[ ]
	E	[ ]
	F	[ ]
	G ii 21	[^{d}]PA x x [ ] ^{d}UTU *qu-ra-du*
	H	[ ]
78.	A	[ ]
	B ii 11′	*nam-*[*za-aq*] DINGIR.MEŠ *ana a-la-ki-ja* // [*-i*]*a ul i-di-na-am-ma*
	C	[ ]
	D	[ ]
	E	[ ]
	F	[ ]
	G ii 22	*nam*(?) x DINGIR.MEŠ GAL.MEŠ *ana a-la-ki-iá u za-qí-qí-iá ul i-di-na-am-ma*
	H	[ ]

79.	A	[ ]
	B ii 12′	*ki-*[*a*]*-am aq-bi ana* ŠÀ-*bi-ja* // *um-ma lu-u a-na-ku-ma*
	C	[ ]
	D	[ ]
	E	[ ]
	F	[ ]
	G ii 23	*ki-a-am aq-bi ana* ŠÀ-*bi-iá um-ma lu-u ana-ku-ma*
	H	[ ]
80.	A	[ ]
	B ii 13′	*a-a-ú* UR.[MAḪ *bi-r*]*a ib-ri*
	C	[ ]
	D	[ ]
	E	[ ]
	F	[ ]
	G ii 24	*a-a-ú* UR.MAḪ *bi-ri ib-ri*
	H	[ ]
81.	A	[ ]
	B ii 14′	*a-a-ú* UR.BAR.[RA *iš-al*] *šá-il-tu*
	C	[ ]
	D	[ ]
	E	[ ]
	F	[ ]
	G ii 25	⌈*a-a-ú* UR⌉.BAR.RA *i*[*š*]*-al šá-il-tú*
	H	[ ]
82.	A	[ ]
	B ii 15′	*lul-lik ki-i* DUMU *ḫab-*⌈*ba-ti ina me-gir*⌉ ŠÀ-*bi-ja*
	C	[ ]
	D	[ ]
	E	[ ]
	F	[ ]
	G ii 26	[*lul*]*-lik ki-ma* DUMU *ḫab-ba-t*[*i ina*] *me-gir* ŠÀ-*ja*
	H	[ ]
83.	A	[ ]
	B ii 16′	*ù lu-ud-di šá* DINGIR-⌈*ma*⌉ *ja-a-ti lu-uṣ-bat*
	C	[ ]
	D	[ ]
	E ii 1′	*ù* [ ]
	F	[ ]
	G ii 27	*u* ⌈*lu*⌉*-ud-di* [x] DINGIR-*ma ja-t*[*e* x (x) x]*-uṣ-bat*
	H	[ ]

84.	A	[ ]
	B ii 17′	MU.AN.NA *maḫ-ri-tu ina ka-šá-di*
	C	[ ]
	D	[ ]
	E ii 2′	MU.[ ]
	F	[ ]
	G ii 28	⸢MU.AN.NA⸣ *maḫ-ri-tú ina* [*k*]*a-š*[*á*]*-di*
	H	[ ]
85.	A	[ ]
	B ii 18′	2-UŠ LIM ÉRIN *ú-še-ṣi-ma ina* ŠÀ-šu-nu // 1-*en* TI NU GUR.RA
	C	[ ]
	D	[ ]
	E ii 3′	2-UŠ [ ]// 1-*en* [ ]
	F	[ ]
	G ii 29	2!-UŠ LIM ÉRIN-*ni ú-*[*še*]*-ṣi-ma ina* ŠÀ-*šú-nu* 1-⸢*en*⸣ ⸢TI⸣ [. . .]
	H	[ ]
86.	A	[ ]
	B ii 19′	2-*tum* MU.AN.NA *ina* KUR-*di* 90 LIM KIMIN
	C	[ ]
	D	[ ]
	E ii 4′	2-*tum* MU.[ ]
	F	[ ]
	G ii 30	2-*tu* MU.AN.NA *ina* KUR-*di* 90 LIM KI[MIN]
	H	[ ]
87.	A	[ ]
	B ii 20′	3-*tum* MU.AN.NA *ina* KUR-*di* 60 LIM 7 ME KIMIN
	C	[ ]
	D	[ ]
	E ii 5′	3-*tum* MU.[ ]
	F	[ ]
	G ii 31	3-*tu* MU.AN.NA *ina* KUR-*di* [60] LIM 7 ME KIMIN
	H	[ ]
88.	A	[ ]
	B ii 21′	*es-si-ḫu en-ni-šú a-ka-la // a-šú-uš uš-ta-ni-iḫ*
	C	[ ]
	D	[ ]
	E ii 6′	*es-si-*[ ] // *a-šú-*[ ]
	F	[ ]
	G ii 32	*es-si-ḫu en-ni-šú a-ka-la a-šú-uš uš-ta-ni-iḫ*
	H	[ ]

89.	A	[ ]
	B ii 22′	*ki-a-am aq-bi a-na* ŠÀ-*bi-ja um-ma lu-u a-na-ku-ma*
	C	[ ]
	D	[ ]
	E ii 7′	*ki-a-am* [ ] // *um-ma* [ ]
	F	[ ]
	G ii 33	*ki-a-*[*am aq*]*-bi ana* ŠÀ-*bi um-ma l*[*u*]*-u ana-ku-ma*
	H 1′–2′	⸢*ki-a-am*⸣ *a*[*q*]; *a-na-ku-ma*
90.	A	[ ]
	B ii 23′	*a-na pa-li-e mi-na-a e-zib*
	C	[ ]
	D	[ ]
	E ii 8′	*a-na pa-li-*[ ]
	F	[ ]
	G ii 34	[ ]*-li-e me-na-a e-*[x]
	H 2′	[ ]
91.	A	[ ]
	B ii 24′	*a-na-ku* LUGAL *la mu-šal-li-mu* KUR-*šú* (end of column)
	C	[ ]
	D	[ ]
	E ii 9′	*a-na-ku* LUGA[L]
	F	[ ]
	G ii 35	*ana-ku* LUGAL *la mu-šal-li-mu* [ ]
	H 3′	*a-na-ku* LU[GAL]
92.	A	[ ]
	B iii 1	*ù ri-é-um la mu-šal-li-mu um-ma-ni-šú*
	C	[ ]
	D	[ ]
	E ii 10′	*ù ri-é-*[ ]
	F	[ ]
	G ii 36	*u ri-é-um la mu-šal-li-mu* [ ]
	H 3′–4′	[ ] *la ú-šal-*[ ]
93.	A	[ ]
	B iii 2	*ki lu-uš-tak-kan-ma pag-ri u pu-ti lu-še-ṣi*
	C	[ ]
	D	[ ]
	E ii 11′	*ki lu-*⸢*uš-tak*⸣*-*[ ]
	F	[ ]
	G ii 37	*ki lu-uš-tak-kan-ma pag-r*[*i*] *u p*[*u*]
	H 4′–5′	[ ] *pag-ri u p*[*u*]

94.	A	[ ]
	B iii 3	*šá-lum-mat ni-ši mu-ši mu-u-tu nam-tar a-ru-ur-tú*
	C	[ ]
	D	[ ]
	E	(probably end of col. ii)
	F	[ ]
	G ii 38	*šá-lum-mat ni-e-ši mu-u-tu* [ ]
	H 6′	*šá-lum*^{um}[ ]
95.	A	[ ]
	B iii 4	*na-mur-ra-tu ḫur-ba-šú ì-bí-su-u ni-ib-ri-tu*
	C	[ ]
	D	[ ]
	E	[ ]
	F	[ ]
	G ii 39	[x x x (x)]-*tú ḫur-ba-šú* [ ]
	H 7′	*na-mur-*[ ]
96.	A	[ ]
	B iii 5	[x x x]-*ḫu di-lip-tu ma-la ba-šu-u* // [*t*]*i-šú-nu it-tar-da*
	C	[ ]
	D	[ ]
	E	[ ]
	F	[ ]
	G ii 40	[x x x *ḫ*]*u di-lip-tú ma-*[ ]
	H	[ ]
97.	A	[ ]
	B iii 6	[ ] *šá-kin a-bu-bu*
	C	[ ]
	D	[ ]
	E	[ ]
	F	[ ]
	G ii 41	*e-li-nu-ma ina* UK[KIN?]
	H	[ ]
98.	A	[ ]
	B iii 7	[ ] *bu ba-ši*
	C	[ ]
	D	[ ]
	E	[ ]
	F	[ ]
	G ii 42	*šap-la-a-nu ina* [ ]
	H	[ ]

99.	A	[ ]
	B iii 8	^{d}[*i-*]*qab-bi*
	C	[ ]
	D	[ ]
	E	[ ]
	F	[ ]
	G ii 43	^{d}*Ea*(DIŠ) EN K[A?]
	H	[ ]
100.	A	[ ]
	B iii 9	*i-zak-*[ ]*-e-šú*
	C	[ ]
	D	[ ]
	E	[ ]
	F	[ ]
	G ii 44	MU-*ra a-na* [ ]
	H	[ ]
101.	A	[ ]
	B iii 10	DINGIR.MEŠ G[AL.MEŠ] *šá*
	C	[ ]
	D	[ ]
	E	[ ]
	F	[ ]
	G ii 45	DINGIR.MEŠ GAL.M[EŠ]
	H	[ ]
102.	A	[ ]
	B iii 11	*taq-ba-nim-ma* [*k*]*i*
	C	[ ]
	D	[ ]
	E	[ ]
	F	[ ]
	G ii 46	*taq-ba-nim-*[ ]
	H	[ ]
103.	A	[ ]
	B iii 12	*ù šub-šu-ú* [*d*]*i*(?) // *ta zur* [ ] *a*
	C	[ ]
	D	[ ]
	E	[ ]
	F	[ ]
	G ii 47	[*ù*] *šub-šu-u šá* [ ]
	H	[ ]

104.	A	[ ]
	B iii 13	ZAG.MUK *šá* 4-*ti* M[U *d*]*i*
	C	[ ]
	D	[ ]
	E	[ ]
	F	[ ]
	G ii 48	[ZA]G.MUK *šá* 4-*t*[*i*]
	H	[ ]
105.	A	[ ]
	B iii 64	*ina te-me-qí šá* ^{d}*É-a* [ ] *a* // *šá* DINGIR.MEŠ[ME]Š
B	C	[ ]
	D	[ ]
	E	[ ]
	F	[ ]
	G ii 49	*ina* [*te*]-*me-qí šá* ^{d}[ ]
	H	[ ]
106.	A	[ ]
	B iii 15	SISKUR.SISKUR ZAG.MUK KÙ.MEŠ [ ]⸢x⸣
	C	[ ]
	D	[ ]
	E	[ ]
	F	[ ]
	G ii 50	SISKUR.SISKUR Z[AG]
	H	[ ]
107.	A	[ ]
	B iii 16	*te-ri-e-te* KÙ.MEŠ *uš*-[x x]-⸢*i*⸣
	C	[ ]
	D	[ ]
	E	[ ]
	F	[ ]
	G ii 51	*te*-⸢*ri*⸣-[ ]
	H	[ ]
108.	A	[ ]
	B iii 17	*al-si* DUMU.MEŠ LÚ.ḪAL.MEŠ *ú*-[*ma*-ʾ-*i*]*r*
	C	[ ]
	D	[ ]
	E	[ ]
	F	[ ]
	G ii 52	[ ]
	H	[ ]

109.	A	[ ]
	B iii 18	7 *a-na pa-an* 7 UDU.SILA$_4$ *al-p*[*u-t*]*u*
	C	[ ]
	D	[ ]
	E	[ ]
	F	[ ]
	G ii 53	[ ]
	H	[ ]
110.	A	[ ]
	B iii 19	*ú-kin* GI.GUḪŠU.MEŠ K[Ù.ME]Š
	C	[ ]
	D	[ ]
	E	[ ]
	F	[ ]
	G iii 1	*ú-kin-nu* [ ]
	H	[ ]
111.	A	[ ]
	B iii 20	*a-šal-ma* [x x] DINGIR.MEŠ G[AL.ME]Š
	C	[ ]
	D	[ ]
	E	[ ]
	F	[ ]
	G iii 2	*a-šal-ma* [ ]
	H	[ ]
112.	A	[ ]
	B iii 21	^{d}*Iš-tar* [-*t*]*um*
	C	[ ]
	D	[ ]
	E	[ ]
	F	[ ]
	G iii 3	^{d}*Iš*-[ ]
	H	[ ]
113.	A	[ ]
	B iii 22	^{d}PA[-*d*]*u*
	C	[ ]
	D	[ ]
	E	[ ]
	F	[ ]
	G iii 4	^{d}[ ]
	H	[ ]

114.	A	[	]
	B iii 23	DUMU [	]-*ni*
	C	[	]
	D	[	]
	E	[	]
	F	[	]
	G iii 5	DUMU [	]
	H	[	]
115.	A	[	]
	B iii 24	*šu*[*m-ma*	]MEŠ
	C	[	]
	D 1′	[	] *na-áš-š*[*i* (x)]
	E	[	]
	F	[	]
	G iii 6	*šu*[*m-ma*	]
	H	[	]
116.	A	[	]
	B iii 25	[	*š*]*i*(?)
	C	[	]
	D 2′	[	]*i-ba-áš-ši*[(x)]
	E	[	]
	F	[	]
	G iii 7	[	]
	H	[	]
117.	A	[	]
	B	[	]
	C	[	]
	D 3′	[	*i*]*m-tak-ta-áš-ši* [(x)]
	E	[	]
	F	[	]
	G iii 8	[	]
	H	[	]
118.	A	[	]
	B	[	]
	C	[	]
	D 4′	[	] *ú-šar-da-a qul-mu* [(x)]
	E	[	]
	F	[	]
	G iii 9	[	]
	H	[	]

119.	A	[ ]
	B	[ ]
	C	[ ]
	D 5′	[*i*]*na da-me i-ṭib-*[x (x)]
	E	[ ]
	F	[ ]
	G iii 10	[*qu*]*l-m*[*u*]
	H	[ ]
120.	A	[ ]
	B	[ ]
	C	[ ]
	D 6′	*ina* ŠÀ-*bi-šú-nu* 12 LÚ.ÉRIN.MEŠ *ip-par-šu-in-n*[*i*]
	E	[ ]
	F	[ ]
	G iii 11	[ ] *ip-par-*[ ]
	H	[ ]
121.	A	[ ]
	B	[ ]
	C	[ ]
	D 7′	[(?)] EGIR-*šú-nu ar-du-ud aḫ-muṭ ur-ri-iḫ* [(x)]
	E	[ ]
	F	[ ]
	G iii 12	[*a*]*r-du-*⟨*ud*⟩ *aḫ-*[ ]
	H	[ ]
122.	A	[ ]
	B	[ ]
	C	[ ]
	D 8′	ÉRIN.MEŠ *šá-šú-nu ak-šu-su-nu-t*[*i*]
	E	[ ]
	F	[ ]
	G iii 13	[x x] *šá-šú-nu ak*?*-šu-us-su-*[ ]
	H	[ ]
123.	A iii 1′	⸢ÉRIN.MEŠ⸣[ ]
	B	[ ]
	C	[ ]
	D 9′	[ÉR]IN.MEŠ *šá-šú-nu ú-tir-ra*[*š*]*-š*[*ú-nu-ti*]
	E	[ ]
	F	[ ]
	G iii 14	ÉRIN.MEŠ *šá-šú-nu ú-tir-raš-šú-*[ ]
	H	[ ]

124.	A iii 2′	*ki-a-am aq-*[ ]
	B	[ ]
	C	[ ]
	D 10′	[*k*]*i-a-am aq-bi ana* ŠÀ-*bi-j*[*a*]
	E	[ ]
	F	[ ]
	G iii 15	*ki-a-am aq-bi ana* ŠÀ-*ja* ⸢*um*⸣-[ ]
	H	[ ]
125.	A iii 3′	*ba-lu bi-*[ ] // *ul ub-b*[*a*]
	B	[ ]
	C	[ ]
	D	[ ]
	E	[ ]
	F	[ ]
	G iii 16	*ba-lu bi-ri še-ri-ta ú-*[ ]
	H	[ ]
126.	A iii 4′	UDU.SILA$_4$ *a-na* UGU-*šú-nu* [ ]
	B	[ ]
	C	[ ]
	D	[ ]
	E	[ ]
	F	[ ]
	G iii 17	UDU.SILA$_4$ *ana* UGU-*ḫi-šú-nu* ⸢*al*⸣-*pu-*[*ut-*(*ma*)]
	H	[ ]
127.	A iii 5′	*nam-za-aq* DINGIR.MEŠ GAL.MEŠ g[*i*]
	B	[ ]
	C	[ ]
	D	[ ]
	E	[ ]
	F	[ ]
	G iii 18	*nam-za-aq* DINGIR.MEŠ GAL.MEŠ g[*i*]*-mil-šú-nu* [x x (x)]
	H	[ ]
128.	A iii 6′	MUL.*Dil-bat* KÙ-*tum iš-tu* AN-*e* [ ]
	B	[ ]
	C	[ ]
	D	[ ]
	E	[ ]
	F	[ ]
	G iii 19	MUL.*Dil-bat* KÙ-*tu iš-t*[*u* AN-]*e ki-a-am is-sa-*[ ]
	H	[ ]

129.	A iii 7′	*a-na* ^{1}*Na-ram-*^{d}30*-mi* DUMU [ ]
	B	[ ]
	C	[ ]
	D	[ ]
	E	[ ]
	F	[ ]
	G iii 20	*a-na* ^{1}*Na-ram-*^{d}30 DUMU L[UGAL?].GI.NA *e-zib*
	H	[ ]
130.	A iii 8′	*e-zib* NUMUN *ḫal-qá-ti-i la* [ ]
	B	[ ]
	C	[ ]
	D	[ ]
	E	[ ]
	F	[ ]
	G iii 21	NUMUN *ḫal-qá-ti-i la tu-ḫal-laq*
	H	[ ]
131.	A iii 9′	*ana ár-kat* u_4*-me* ^{d}*En-líl ana* ḪUL*-ti i-na-á*[*š*]
	B	[ ]
	C	[ ]
	D	[ ]
	E	[ ]
	F	[ ]
	G iii 22	*a-na ár-kat* u_4*-me* ^{d}BE *a-na* ḪUL*-tim i-na-áš-šá ri-su-un*
	H	[ ]
132.	A iii 10′	*ana ag-gi* ŠÀ*-bi* ^{d}*En-líl ú-qa-a* [ ]
	B	[ ]
	C	[ ]
	D	[ ]
	E	[ ]
	F	[ ]
	G iii 23	*a-na ag-gi* ŠÀ ^{d}BE *ú-qa-ʾ-u ri-e-šú*
	H	[ ]
133.	A iii 11a′	URU ÉRIN.MEŠ *šu-nu-ti in-*[ ]
	B	[ ]
	C	[ ]
	D	[ ]
	E	[ ]
	F	[ ]
	G iii 24	URU ÉRIN.MEŠ *šu-nu-ti* [x (x)]-⸢x⸣-*ru*
	H	[ ]

134. A iii 11b′ // *i-qam-mu-ú i-lam-mu-u* [ ]
B [ ]
C [ ]
D [ ]
E [ ]
F [ ]
G iii 25 *i-qam-mu-u i-lam-mu-u* [K]I.DÚR.MEŠ
H [ ]

135. A iii 12a′ URU *da-mu-šú-nu i-tab-ba-ku*
B [ ]
C [ ]
D [ ]
E [ ]
F [ ]
G iii 26 URU *da-mu-šú-nu i-tab-*[*ba*]*-ku*
H [ ]

136. A iii 12′ KI-*tu iš-*[ ] // GIŠ.GIŠIMMAR *bi-lat-sa* [ ]
B [ ]
C [ ]
D [ ]
E [ ]
F [ ]
G iii 27 KI-t*um iš-pi-ki-šá* [*b*]*i-lat-sa ú-maṭ-ṭa*
H [ ]

137. A iii 13′ URU ÉRIN.MEŠ *šú-nu-ti i-m*[*ut-tu* (?)]
B [ ]
C [ ]
D [ ]
E [ ]
F [ ]
G iii 28 URU ÉRIN.MEŠ *šu-n*[*u-ti i*]*-mut-tu*
H [ ]

138. A iii 14′ URU ⸢KI URU É ⸣ KI É ⸢*i*⸣-[ ]
B [ ]
C (beginning of col. iv?)
D [ ]
E [ ]
F [ ]
G iii 29 URU KI [ ] *i-nak-kir*
H [ ]

139.	A iii 15′	*a*-[*bu*]
	B	[ ]
	C iv 1a′	AD K[I]
	D	[ ]
	E	[ ]
	F	[ ]
	G iii 30	AD [ŠE]Š KI ŠEŠ
	H	[ ]
140.	A	[ ]
	B	[ ]
	C iv 1b′	[ ]
	D	[ ]
	E	[ ]
	F	[ ]
	G iii 31	[x] KI GURUŠ *ru-*u_8*-a* KI *it-ba-ri*
	H	[ ]
141.	A	[ ]
	B	[ ]
	C iv 2′	*it-t*[*i*]
	D	[ ]
	E	[ ]
	F	[ ]
	G iii 32	[x x] *a-ḫa-meš* [*k*]*i-na-a-ti ul i-ta-mu-u*
	H	[ ]
142.	A	[ ]
	B	[ ]
	C iv 3′	UN.MEŠ *la* [ ]
	D	[ ]
	E	[ ]
	F	[ ]
	G iii 33	[x].MEŠ *la ki?-na-a-ti šu-ḫu-za-ma šá na tim ma di* (or:*da pa*) *ra qu*(or:*am ma*)
	H	[ ]
143.	A	[ ]
	B	[ ]
	C iv 4′	URU *nak*-[ ]
	D	[ ]
	E	[ ]
	F	[ ]
	G iii 34	[x (x)] *nak-r*[*u*] *šu-ú i-duk-ku*
	H	[ ]

144.	A	[ ]
	B iv 1′	[ ] ⸢x⸣ [ ]
	C iv 5′	URU *šá-a-*[ ]
	D	[ ]
	E	[ ]
	F	[ ]
	G iii 35	[*š*]*á-a-šú* [U]RU *nak-*⟨*ru*⟩ *i-ṣab-ba-su*
	H	[ ]
145.	A	[ ]
	B iv 2′	[ ] *i-m*[*aḫ*]
	C iv 6′	*a-na* 1 [ ]
	D	[ ]
	E	[ ]
	F	[ ]
	G iii 36	[ ]GIŠ!.BÁN.ŠE.BAR *i-maḫ-ḫar*
	H	[ ]
146.	A	[ ]
	B iv 3′	[ ] *ul lu* [ ]
	C iv 7′	LUGAL *dan-*[ ]
	D	[ ]
	E	[ ]
	F	[ ]
	G iii 37	[ ] *iḫ šú* x *šu-u i-na* KUR *ul ib-ši*
	H	[ ]
147.	A	[ ]
	B iv 4′	[*bi*]*l-ti ú*[ ]
	C iv 8′	DINGIR.MEŠ [ ]
	D	[ ]
	E	[ ]
	F	[ ]
	G iii 38	[x].MEŠ GAL.MEŠ *a-*[*n*]*a bi-bíl-ti ú-bil-šú-nu-ti*
	H	[ ]
148.	A	[ ]
	B iv 5′	[ ]*-*⸢*a*⸣*-ki ul* [*ú-b*]*il-šú-nu-ti*
	C iv 9′	*qa-t*[*i*]
	D	[ ]
	E	[ ]
	F	[ ]
	G iii 39	[*qa*]*-ti a-na da-a-*[*k*]*i ú-bil-šú-nu-ti*
	H	[ ]

149.	A	[ ]
	B iv 6′	[L]Ú.PA.TE.SI [*u* NUN *l*]*u mim-ma šá-na-ma*
	C iv 10′	*at-ta* [ ]
	D	[ ]
	E	[ ]
	F	[ ]
	G iii 40	[x (x)] *man-nu lu-u* LÚ.PA.TE.[S]I *u* NUN *lu-u mìm-ma šá-na-ma*
	H	[ ]
150.	A	[ ]
	B iv 7′	[x x] *i-nam-b*[*u*-(x)-*šú* LU]GAL-*ta* DÙ-*uš*
	C iv 11′	*ša* DINGIR *i*-[ ]
	D	[ ]
	E	[ ]
	F	[ ]
	G iii 41	[x DING]IR *i-nam-bu-šú-ma* ⸢LUGAL⸣-*ta* DÙ-*uš*
	H	[ ]
151.	A	[ ]
	B iv 8′	[x x *n*]*a e-pu-u*⸢*š-ka* N⸣A.DÙ.A *áš-ṭur-ka*
	C iv 12′	*ṭup-šin*-[ ]
	D	[ ]
	E	[ ]
	F	[ ]
	G iii 42	[*ṭup*]-*šin-na e-pu-uš-k*[*a* NA.DÙ].A *áš-ṭur-ka*
	H	[ ]
152.	A	[ ]
	B iv 9′	[x x]DU$_8$.A.KI *ina* É.MES.LAM
	C iv 13′	*i-na* GÚ[ ]
	D	[ ]
	E	[ ]
	F	[ ]
	G iii 43	[ ].⸢DU$_8$.A.KI⸣ [ ]MES.LAM
	H	[ ]
153.	A	[ ]
	B iv 10′	[x *p*]*a-paḫ* ^{d}U.GUR *e-zi-bak-ka*
	C iv 14′	*i-na pa-paḫ* [ ]
	D	[ ]
	E	[ ]
	F	[ ]
	G iii 44	[ ]-*zi-bak-ka*
	H	[ ]

154.	A	[ ]
	B iv 11′	NA$_4$.NA.DÙ.A *an-na-a a-mur-ma*
	C iv 15′	NA$_4$.NA.DÙ.A *an-na-a* [ ]
	D	[ ]
	E	[ ]
	F	[ ]
	G iv 1	[x x x *a*]*n-na-a a-mur-ma*
	H	[ ]
155.	A	[ ]
	B iv 12′	*šá pi-i* NA$_4$.NA.DÙ.A *an-na-a ši-me-ma*
	C iv 16′	*šá pi-i* NA$_4$.NA.DÙ.A *an-na-a* [ ]
	D	[ ]
	E	[ ]
	F	[ ]
	G iv 2	[x x x N]A$_4$.NA.DÙ.A *an-na-a ši-mi-ma*
	H	[ ]
156.	A	[ ]
	B iv 13′	*la te-si-iḫ-ḫu la te-en-niš-šú*
	C iv 17′	*la te-ís-si-iḫ-ḫu la te-*[ ]
	D	[ ]
	E	[ ]
	F	[ ]
	G iv 3	[x x x *-ḫ*]*u la te-en-niš-šu*
	H	[ ]
157.	A	[ ]
	B iv 14′	*la ta-pal-laḫ la ta-tar-ru-ur*
	C iv 18′	*la ta-pal-la-aḫ la ta-*[ ]
	D	[ ]
	E	[ ]
	F	[ ]
	G iv 4	[x x x x]*-aḫ la ta-tar-ru-ur*
	H	[ ]
158.	A	[ ]
	B iv 15′	*iš-da-a-ka lu-u ki-na*
	C iv 19′	*iš-da-ka* [ ]
	D	[ ]
	E	[ ]
	F	[ ]
	G iv 5	[x x]*-ka lu-u ki-na*
	H	[ ]

159.	A	[ ]
	B iv 16′	*at-ta ina su-un* SAL-*ka ši-pir lu* DÙ-*uš*
	C iv 20′	⌜x⌝ [ ]
	D	[ ]
	E	[ ]
	F	[ ]
	G iv 6	[x (x)] *i-na su-un* SAL-*ka ši-pir lu-u* DÙ-*uš*
	H	[ ]
160.	A	[ ]
	B iv 17′	BÀD.MEŠ-*ka tuk-kil*!
	C	[ ]
	D	[ ]
	E	[ ]
	F	[ ]
	G iv 7	[x].MEŠ-*ka tuk*-⌜*kil*⌝
	H	[ ]
161.	A	[ ]
	B iv 18′	*ḫi-ra-ti-ka* A.MEŠ *mul-li*
	C	[ ]
	D	[ ]
	E	[ ]
	F	[ ]
	G iv 8	[x-*r*]*a-tu-ka* A.MEŠ ⌜*mul-li*⌝
	H	[ ]
162.	A	[ ]
	B iv 19′	*pi-sa-an-na-ti-ka* ŠE.AM-*ka* KÙ.BABBAR-*ka* // NÍG.ŠU-*ka* NÍG.GA-*ka*
	C	[ ]
	D	[ ]
	E	[ ]
	F	[ ]
	G iv 9	[*pi*]-*sa-an-ti-ka* ŠE.AM-*ka* KÙ.BABBAR-*ka* NÍG].ŠU-*ka*
	H	[ ]
163.	A	[ ]
	B iv 20′	[x x x x x]-*nu-ti-ka šu-rib*
	C	[ ]
	D	[ ]
	E	[ ]
	F	[ ]
	G iv 10	[NÍG].GA-*ka ana* URU [x x *t*]*i-ka šu-r*[*ib*]
	H	[ ]

164.	A	[ ]
	B iv 21′	[x x x x x *k*]*u-us-ma túb-qa-a-ti e-mid*
	C	[ ]
	D	[ ]
	E	[ ]
	F	[ ]
	G iv 11	[GIŠ].TUKUL.MEŠ-*ka ru-ku-us-ma túb-qa-a-ti um-*[*mid*]
	H	[ ]
165.	A	[ ]
	B iv 22′	[x x x x x] *ú-ṣur pu-ut-ka šul-lim*
	C	[ ]
	D	[ ]
	E	[ ]
	F	[ ]
	G iv 12	*qar-ra-du-ti-ka ú-ṣur pu-ut-ka* [ ]
	H	[ ]
166.	A	[ ]
	B iv 23′	[x x x x x] ⸢x⸣ *e tu-ṣi-šú*
	C	[ ]
	D	[ ]
	E	[ ]
	F	[ ]
	G iv 13	*lit-tag-gis* KUR-*ka e tu-*[ ]
	H	[ ]
167.	A	[ ]
	B iv 24′	[x x x x x *l*]*a e ta-as-niq-šú*
	C	[ ]
	D	[ ]
	E	[ ]
	F	[ ]
	G iv 14	*li-it-ti-di bu-la e ta-*[ ]
	H	[ ]
168.	A	[ ]
	B iv 25′	[ ]-*ka*
	C	[ ]
	D	[ ]
	E	[ ]
	F	[ ]
	G iv 15	*li-kul* UZU *ri-du* [ ]
	H	[ ]

169.	A	[	]
	B	[	]
	C	[	]
	D	[	]
	E	[	]
	F	[	]
	G iv 16	*li-šag-gi-iš*! *li-tur-*[x x (x)]	
	H	[	]
170.	A	[	]
	B	[	]
	C	[	]
	D	[	]
	E	[	]
	F	[	]
	G iv 17	*lu áš-ra-ta lu-u sa-an-*[x x]	
	H	[	]
171.	A	[	]
	B	[	]
	C	[	]
	D	[	]
	E	[	]
	F	[	]
	G iv 18	*an-nu-u be-lí a-pul-šu-nu-ti*	
	H	[	]
172.	A	[	]
	B	[	]
	C	[	]
	D	[	]
	E	[	]
	F	[	]
	G iv 19	*ana gul-lul-ti-šú-nu ri-ib dum-qí*	
	H	[	]
173.	A	[	]
	B	[	]
	C	[	]
	D	[	]
	E	[	]
	F	[	]
	G iv 20	*ana dum-qí qí-šá-a-ti u ta-aṣ-ba-ti*	
	H	[	]

174.	A iv 1′	[ ]-⌜*iq*⌝
	B	[ ]
	C	[ ]
	D	[ ]
	E	[ ]
	F	[ ]
	G iv 21	*ana maḫ-ri-šú-nu e-te-it-ti-iq*
	H	[ ]
175.	A iv 2′	[*q*]*u-ti*
	B	[ ]
	C	[ ]
	D	[ ]
	E	[ ]
	F	[ ]
	G iv 22a	LÚ.DUB.SAR *en-qu-te*
	H	[ ]
176.	A iv 3′	[ ].A-*ka*
	B	[ ]
	C	[ ]
	D	[ ]
	E	[ ]
	F	[ ]
	G iv 22b	*lis-ku-ru* NA.DÙ.A-*ka*
	H	[ ]
177.	A iv 4′	[ ]-*mu-ru-ma*
	B	[ ]
	C	[ ]
	D	[ ]
	E	[ ]
	F	[ ]
	G iv 23a	*šu-ut* NA$_4$.NA.DÙ.A-*e-a ta-mu-ru-ma*
	H	[ ]
178.	A iv 5′	[ ]-*ṣu-u*
	B	[ ]
	C	[ ]
	D	[ ]
	E	[ ]
	F	[ ]
	G iv 23b	*pu-ut-ka tu-še-ṣu-u*
	H	[ ]

179.	A iv 6′	[*a*]*r-ku-u*	
	B	[	]
	C	[	]
	D	[	]
	E	[	]
	F	[	]
	G iv 24a	*šu-ut ja-ši* ⸢*tak-tar-ba*⸣ *ar-ku-u*	
	H	[	]
180.	A iv 7′	[*k*]*a-a-šá*	
	B	[	]
	C	[	]
	D	[	]
	E	[	]
	F	[	]
	G iv 24b	*lik-ta-rab-ka ka-a-šá*	
	H	[	]

Colophon

	A	[*ekal* ^{1}AN.ŠÁR].DÙA
		[*šar kiššati šar māt*] AN.ŠÁR.KI

Indexes

Adad-nirari I 179
Amar-Enlila 244–45
Amar-girida 225, 227–28, 245
Amenophis III 120
Ammi-ṣaduqa 269, 278–79
Anubanini 250, 294–95, 310–11
Anu-šar-ilāni 282, 292–93
Aqqi 40–41
Arnuwanda 105
Ašduni-erim 241, 259
Aššurbanipal 37, 263, 296, 301
Atra-ḫasīs 253

Banana 258, 260–61, 265
Bēl-ēṭir 263
Bentišina 302

Didnu-nomads 84–85, 150
Duḫsusu 311

Enḫeduanna 78, 226
Enmerkar 264, 266, 280, 284–85, 294–95, 300–302, 304–6, 308
Erridu-pizir 238, 249

Gilgameš 101, 264, 310
Gula-AN 222, 246, 248–49, 254–55, 311
Gungunum 85

Hammurapi 182, 204, 219, 248, 273
Hanikuili 292–93
Ḫattušili I 250
Ḫattušili III 302

Idrimi 18, 331
Ìl-a-ba$_4$-AN.DÙL-šu 148, 150–51
Ilu-šumma 178
Ipḫur-Kiš(i) 222, 224–30, 234–37, 253
Ipiq-Ištar 199, 211
Ir-Enlila 244–45

KÙ-Aya 269

Lipiš-iāum 236
Lipit-ili 234
Lugal-Anne 222, 224, 226–27, 244–45
Lugalbanda 264–66, 322
Lugalnizu 245
Lugalzagesi 51

Maništušu 1, 3, 240
Manum 244–45
Mengi 246, 254–55
Mes-kiag-gašer 302
Muttakkil-Nusku 302

Nabi-Ulmaš 236
Nabonidus 2
Nebuchadnezzar 297
Nur-Dagan (Nur-Daggal) 57–58, 94, 102–3, 106–7, 120–27, 134–35

Puzur-Ulmaš 246, 256–57

Qurdi-Nergal 297

Rabsisi 311
Rib-Addi 58
Rim-Sin 203, 205
Rimuš 1
Riš-Adad 174, 244–45
Riš-Zababa 246, 256–57

Samsu-iluna 142, 194, 205, 211, 234
Sennacherib 37
Sin-iddinam 212

Ṣummirat-Ištar 234–35, 242–43

Šamši-Adad I 2, 47, 175, 234, 314
Šar-kali-šarri 179
Šulgi 43, 237, 311
Šuppiluliuma I 282–83, 302
Šu-Sin 34, 85
Šutruk-Naḫḫunte 2

Tabban-daraḫ 311
Takil-ilissu 191
Tušratta 120

Ur-gigira 240
Ur-nigina 240
Ur-Zababa 51–53
Uta-napištim 70
Uta-rapaštim 57–59, 68–70

Yaḫdun-Lim 261
Yasmaḫ-Adad 2

Index of Divine Names

Adad/(Ḫ)addum 99, 182, 261, 274–75, 292–93
Annunītum 143–45, 150–51, 174, 180–81, 189–90, 222, 238, 240–41, 292–94, 304–5, 316–17, 320–21
Anu(m) 198–99, 238, 240–41, 292–93, 316
Anunna 82
Anzû 182–83
Aššur 109, 179, 200, 292–93

Bēlet-ilī 294–95, 308–9

Dagan 226
Damkina 211

Enbilulu 292–93
Enki/Ea 211, 260–61, 264, 280, 286–87, 294–95, 319–21
Enlil 103, 109, 152, 174, 182–85, 189, 220, 230, 238–41, 260–61, 264, 294–95, 314–15, 322–23, 327
Erra 12, 97, 178, 184, 189–201

Gula 242–43, 253

Haniš, (Šullat and) 83, 151, 222, 242–43, 252–53, 258–59, 292–94, 304–5, 316–17, 320–21
Hepat 292–93
Huwawa (Humbaba) 78, 101, 182

Igigi 198–99
Ilaba 150–51, 174–75, 180–83, 222, 226, 230, 238–43, 258–61, 292–94, 304–5, 316–17, 320–21
Inanna 264
Irnina 78, 82–83, 136, 174
Ištar ix, 34–35, 40–41, 69, 78, 82–83, 87, 108–9, 119, 136–39, 150–51, 164, 167, 180, 182–83, 189–90, 194–96, 222, 234–35, 238, 240–43, 252–53, 258–59, 294–95, 303–5, 311, 316–17, 320–23
Ištarān 43
Ištar-kakkabi 204, 218–19

Laz 189–90, 198–99
Lugal-Marada 234

Marduk 68, 184, 274
Muati 317

Nabû 184
Nedu/Petu 317
Nergal 7, 58, 96–97, 184, 189, 260–61, 294, 326–37
Ninegal 292–93
Ninkar(ak) 229, 234–35, 253
NIN.KIŠ.UNU 195
Ninurta 58, 318
Nisaba 261

Sibittu 178

Šakkan 96–97
Šamaš 48–49, 96, 100–101, 150–51, 203, 210–11, 214–15, 222, 242–43, 260–61, 280, 286–87, 294, 302–5, 316–17
Ši-labba(t) 174, 180–81
Šullat and Ḫaniš 150–51, 222, 242–43, 252–53, 258–59, 294, 304–5, 316–17, 320–21
Šušinak 179

Tiamat 7, 68, 294–95, 308–9, 315

Ūmšum 150, 222, 242–43, 258–59
Ūmumšû 150, 242–43
Uttu 151

Zababa 89, 102–3, 116–17, 126–27, 150–51, 174, 180–81, 222, 294, 297, 304–5, 316–17, 320–21

Index of Geographical and Topographical Names

Adab 245
Alalakh 105, 174
Amanus 75, 82–83, 254–55, 312
Amurru 74–75, 78, 86–87, 105, 248, 250–51, 302
Apiak 222, 232–33, 240–41
Apišal 173–74, 184–87, 244–45
Apum 248, 250–53
Aranzaḫ 83
Ararrû 248, 250–51
Aratta 83, 248, 250–51, 266
Armanum 174, 248, 252–53
Arwad 301
Assur 102, 134
Azupīrānu 38–39

Babylon 51, 53
BÀD.AN.KI 42–43
Boghazköy 105

Carchemiš 74–75, 105
Cedar Forest 78, 94, 100–101, 254–55, 312
Cuthah (Kutha) 7, 189–90, 222, 232–33, 236–37, 240–41, 294, 326–37

Dêr 42–43, 248, 250–51
Dilbat 37, 222, 232–33, 240–41
Dilmun 40, 42–43, 294, 311, 314–15
Diyala 80, 223

Ebarbar 204–5, 212
Ebla 174, 248
Egypt 105
Ekur 152, 221–23
Elam 94, 248, 250–53, 311, 314–15
Emar 105
(E)meslam 190, 198–99, 294, 326–27
Esabad 234–35, 242–43, 253
Ešnunna 2, 80, 189, 223–24, 255, 266, 275
Eulmaš 2, 137–39
Euphrates 38–39, 83, 88–89, 238, 240–41

Giritab 222, 232–33, 240–41
Gišgi 248
Gutium 222, 246, 248–49, 274, 311, 314–15

Ḫaḫḫum 248, 250–51
Ḫamšā 252–53
Ḫana 249
Ḫaššum 67, 252
Ḫattuša (Boghazköy) 9, 11, 105–7, 119, 205, 263, 265, 281, 287, 310, 319

Ibrat 222, 232–33, 240–41
Irnina 238, 240–41
Isin 245

Jebel Ḥamrīn 81, 244

Kakm(i)um 248–50
Kaniš 103, 110–11, 222, 248, 250–51
Kaššu 250–51
Kazallu 43–44, 71, 222, 232–33, 240–41
Kimaš 81
Kiš(i) 51, 114–15, 222–30, 232–35, 240–43, 297

Lagaš 245
Larsa 12, 190, 203–5, 207, 212–13, 259
Lebanon 75
Lullubu 237, 248, 250–51, 310–11

Makkan 244–45, 251, 294, 311, 314–15
Malgium 191, 199, 211, 233, 274–75
Mardaman (Maldaman) 78, 84–85, 87, 244–45, 311, 314
Marḫaši 69, 241, 244–45, 248, 250–51
Mari 2, 11–12, 66, 174, 204, 231–32, 234, 244–45, 255, 266, 327
Meluḫḫa 248, 250–51, 294, 311, 314–15
Mitanni 105

Nagu 246, 254–55
NaGURzam 74
Nawar (Namar) 86, 174, 244–45, 254
Nineveh (Kuyunjik) 12, 37, 263, 296, 305
Nippur 1, 9, 12, 51, 94, 141, 143, 221, 223, 244–45, 298, 327

Purušḫanda 57–58, 94, 102–3, 112–13, 118–19, 150–51, 294, 313

Simurrum 38, 59, 70–71, 90–91, 237, 242–43, 311

Sippar 3, 222, 232–33, 240–41, 250, 268–69
Subartu 74–75, 78, 88, 311
Sultantepe 11, 263, 297
Susa 2

Šubat-Enlil 312–13
Šuruppak 245, 251
Šušarra 70

Tell el-Amarna 9, 102, 104
Tell Harmal 12, 79, 83
Tigris 198, 238, 240–41
Tiwa 222, 232–35, 240–43
Tukriš 251
Turukkû 248, 250–51
Ugarit 105–6
Ugar-Sin 234–35, 242–43
Umma 174, 244–45
Ummān-Manda 264–66, 312–13
Ummānu 266
Ur 11–12, 141, 148–49, 212, 222, 224, 226–27, 245
Uruk (Warka) 9, 51, 212, 222–29, 232–33, 240–41, 244–45, 266
Urum (Wurumu) 222, 232–35, 240–43
Utûm 70

Zubi 82–83

Index of Literary Texts

Agušaya 26, 63, 65–66, 101, 207
Anzu 69, 210
Atra-ḫasīs 115, 196–97, 210, 216–17, 268–69, 274, 303, 325

Cow of Sin 213

Descent of Ištar 215
Descent to the Netherworld, A Babylonian 207, 217
Dialogue of Pessimism 325

Enki and Ninmaḫ 312
Enmerkar and Ensuḫkešdanna 52, 303
Enmerkar and the Lord of Aratta 83, 302
Enūma eliš 68, 193, 315
Erra 63, 113, 178, 325, 328
Etana 200, 213, 303

Fable of the Fox 185

Gilgameš 7, 20, 26, 70, 78, 90, 99–101, 105, 109, 182, 205–6, 208, 210, 214, 287, 300, 310, 312
Gilgameš and Huwawa A 101

Hymn to Adad 207
Hymn to Bēlet-ilī 176, 196–98
Hymn to Ištar (RA 22) 192, 197
Hymn to Nanaya 206, 210–14
Hymn to Sin and Išum 205

In-nin-šà-gur$_4$-ra 69, 78, 82, 182

Lamentation over Ur 324–25
Letter of Gilgameš 18, 142
Lugalbanda Epic I 83, 322
Lugalbanda Epic II 302
Lugal-e 63, 69, 312

Man and His God 201, 217
Marduk "Autobiography" 17

Nergal and Ereškigal 215

Sargon Geography 43, 127, 315
Siege of Uruk 22

Šulgi "Autobiography" 17

Tukulti-Ninurta Epic 63, 100, 200

Uruk Lament 324–25, 328

Zimri-Lim Epic 182

Index of Words Discussed

ababdû 152
abālu 326–37
AB.BA.URU 154
ADDIR 162
aggu 323
A.GIGRÍ 158
aguḫḫu 218
akāšu 183
alaktu 112
alāku/atalluku 34, 123, 176–77, 197, 317
alālu 65–66
ālilu 65–66, 108, 127
ālu 309, 323
anzalīlu 164
apluḫtu 68
apu 252
arītu 275
(*w*)*arû* 95, 101, 111, 114
arurtu 319
ašarēdu 57, 59, 111,
ašru 329
aštalû/eštalû 87, 164

bâʾu 183
BAḪAR$_x$ 157
BALA 228–29, 272
balag-di 165, 236
banû 176, 309
banûtu 309–10
bašmu 182, 198
bazāʾu 129
bēl marṣātim 98–99
bibiltu 326–27
buʾʾû 109–10
b(/p)uzzuʾ(/ḫ)u 129

dajjānu 154
dâku 125
damāmu 112–13
dapāru/duppuru 218, 325–26
dāpinu 101
dāṣātu 117
dekû 125
diliptu 319

eʾēlu 122
ebēbu 66
ebēṭu 46
eddam qarnīn 177, 181
eddetu 120–21
ēdiku 161
ellūtu 311–12
emēdu 229, 300–302
emqam birkim 69
ēnetu 38
EN.NU.UN È 161
EN.NU.UN TIR 161
erûtu 66
ešgallu 212
ešû 272, 318
etēqu 330
eṭemmu 306
ezēbu 306–8

ga-an-dúr 162
GAM 120
gamāru 255
gana 95
GA.RAŠ 158
garāšu 227
gerru 118, 128
gerû 118, 128
giḫlu 286
gimillu 322
ginâʾu 157
GÌR.NITÁ 240
girru 107, 128
gudapsû 152

ḫabātu 69, 210
ḫabibu 165
ḫalāqu 322–23, 327
ḫallallāniš 255
ḫapāru 123
ḫarrānu 111–13
ḫarû 258, 265, 275
ḫelû 215
ḫepēru 123
ḫubūru 275–76
ḫubutu 122
ḪÚL 160
ḫuluqqû 283
ḫuppû 162
ḫurru 265, 308
ḪUR.SAG *ga-ap-šu* 110, 119–20
ḫuršānu 302

idru 110–111
ì-du$_8$ 166
idu 239–40
ikū 124
illatu 240
il mātim 174, 179–80, 221
ina kīma 95
inbu 129
īnu 234
inūma 231, 234, 239
inūmīšūma 231, 233–34, 239
irnittam kašādu 82
išti 177, 186, 191
itangušu 287
ittadu 120

kalû 121
kanāšu 83, 106, 110, 125
kartappu 160
kasāsu 72
kaṣāṣu 73
kazû 167
ki 206–7, 209
kīdu 72
KI.LAM 278–79
kililu 119
kirru 118
kirû 118
kisal-luḫ 166
kisû 199
kiṣru 122
kiṣṣaru 122
kiṣṣu 199
KIŠIB.DU$_8$ 155
kiššatu 115, 127, 252
kiššu 116
KÙ.MEŠ 311–12
kuliltu 119
KUN.GÁL 162
kurusissu 73
KU$_6$.UR 156

līšu 129
LÚ.A.AB.BA 156
LÚ.A.IGI.DU$_8$ 162
LÚ.AN.TI.BAL 163
LÚ.A.TAR.LÁ.LÁ 163
LÚ.EGIR.MEŠ 152
LUGAL.KALAG.GA 38
lú.géšpu 164
lú.gi-di-da 165

LÚ.GI$_6$.DU.DU 154
LÚ.GIŠ.KAK 167
lú.idim 155
lú.i-lu 165
LÚ.KAR 156
LÚ.KAS$_4$.E 160
lú.ka-tar-ri-a 164
LÚ.LIRUM 159–60, 163
lú.má-gíd-da 158
lumaḫḫu 152
LÚ.PA.PA 164–65
LÚ.SAG.BA 154

mā 95, 98
*mâ*ʾ*u* 114–15
madādu 261
mādidu 161
maḫāru 61, 100
maḫāṣu 165, 305, 312
maḫḫû 165
māḫiṣu 167
mālikū 154
mannu 126
marṣātu 300
marû 167
mātu 127
meḫû 114–15
mēlû 121
milku 303
mīlu 121
mīru 67, 84, 86
mummu 201
murdinnu 120–21
musarriru 91
*mūṣā*ʾ*um* 215
muṣarriḫtum 235–36
mušēṣû 241
mušmellilu 166
mutu 63, 240
mūtu 63

*na*ʾ*ādu* 65
nabalkutu 239
nadû 124, 318, 328
nagāšu 125, 287
naḫallu 85–86
nâḫu 278
nakādu 272, 318
nakāru 239
nakāšu 183
nalbašu 68
namāšu 106–7, 131
namkūru 89
NAM.LAGAR 152
namzaqu 316–17
naparqudu 305
napluḫtu 68
NAR *a-ú* 162–63
narû 16–20, 142, 264, 266, 284, 294, 296
nâru/nêru 324
nāš kussêm 153
nāš šu-ši-ip-pi-im 153
našû 129, 226–27, 323
nāš za-ap-pi-im 153
nēberu 314–15
nēšu 286, 319
*nēšu nā*ʾ*iru* 182
nimru 100

padû 90
pagra u pūta šūṣû 273–74, 306–8
pagru 308
pālil urḫim 177, 180–81
papāḫu 327
parakku 111
parzillu 68
pasāḫu 129
pasāsu 85
pašāḫu 129
pašīšu 240
pemtu/pentu/pettu 178
puluḫtu 68
purīdu 136
puṣṣudu 41
pūtu 87

qablam qabû 109–10
qablam rakāsu 109–10
qadû 46
qallu 122
qanû 92
qaqqaru 309
qātam abālu 66, 88
qerītu 118
qištu 122, 252
qurādu 195

*râ*ʾ*u* 114
rābiṣu 125, 194, 240
radādu 255
rapaštum 70
rapāšu 124
râšu 194–95, 255
*re*ʾ*û* 130
redû 130
rēša našû 323
rēšīššu 125
riāšu 187
rīdu 328
*rū*ʾ*u* 195

SAL.an-dùl 155
sanāqu 299, 329
sapāḫu 299, 313
sapannu 299
seḫû 318
siparru 198
siraš 282–83
SUKKAL/*šukkallu/sukkallu* 57, 64, 102, 154, 174, 184–85
sullulu 234

*ṣabā*ʾ*um* 237
ṣabātu 169, 285
ṣāripu 158
ṣēra rapādu 45
ṣēru 160, 270, 299
ṣuppā(n) 121

ša A.KU$_5$.DA 156–57
ša A.LÁ 154
ša É.PAP 155
ša GI.GÍD 164
ša INIM.MA.BI 153
ša manzaztim 153
ša UR.GI$_7$ 162
šadâ rakābu 312
šadâ(šu) emēdu 229, 300–302
*šaddû*ʾ*a* 68
šagāšu 329
šakānu 274
šakkanakku 240
šalbubu 177, 184
šalummatu 99, 286
šamaišam 210
šamšu 203, 206, 214
šandabakku 160
šanû/šunnû 303
šapra maḫāṣu 312
šapû 82, 217
šar tamḫāri 9, 58, 105
šarrum dannum 38
šāru 115
šarūru 35
šassūru 309
*še*ʾ*û* 192, 227
šêpu 82
šērtu 322

šerṭu 73
šētu 46
šiddu 87
šikaru 120
šinšeret 82
šipram šapārum 185
šipru 113, 185
šitʾāru 192
šu-ḫa-ḫád-da 156
ŠU.KAL.DÙ 159
šulputu 275
šumam zakārum 116, 307
šummu 193
šupālāššu 125
šūpû 310
šurḫullu 63
šurrû 63
šūru 109, 117
šūṣû 193, 273–74, 306–8
šu-tag 163
šūt GA 157
šūt GI.PISAN *nusḫu* 155
šūt kitî 68–69
šūt NÍG.KUD 158
šutarruḫu 61
šūtatû 62, 84

târu 63
tarû 111, 129
tēbibtu 66
têlišam 83, 253
telîtu 253
têrtu 185, 322
tešê 255
tiʾāmtum 42
tuša 70

ṭeḫû 124
ṭēmu 63, 275–77
ṭūdu 177–78

udû 116
UGULA.DAG.GI$_4$.A 154
ulpānu 129
ūmšum 229, 242
unnedukku 142, 148
urdu 121
urḫu 106, 112
ūru 117
uzibu 178
uzzum 100

warādu 116
warḫum 112
watû 70
wildu 208
wutturu 269, 271–72

zamāru 27
zaqīqu 145, 317
zâzu 117
zēr ḫalqāti 322–23
zummu 286
zūzu 117

General Index

alliteration 26, 61, 191, 299
archaism 26–27, 61
asseveration 37
assonance 26, 61, 191, 269
audience 23, 33, 59, 223, 267, 296
autobiography 18, 33, 296
  fictional Akkadian royal 19
  poetic 17
  pseudo 17, 19
  simulated 18

broken writing 66, 199

chiasm 27, 81
chronicles 3, 130–31, 173
  "Chronicle of Early Kings" 42, 71–72, 99
  "Weidner Chronicle" 52, 111, 142, 264, 274, 303
couplet 28, 61, 95, 299

dialogue 6, 58, 78, 94, 104, 174, 190
didacticism 19–20, 23
direct speech 191–92
discourse 24
  space 24
  time 24, 33, 296

Emesal 54
enjambement 231, 247
epic 17, 20
  heroic 20, 264
  historical 17
event 23, 33
existent 33

flood imagery 275–77, 319
folklore 2, 21–23

folktale 2, 21–22
folktale motif 2

genre 16–21

hero 264, 267
heroism 59
historicity 23, 173
homoeoteleuton 26, 29, 37
hymno-epic "dialect" elements 25–26, 61, 95, 107, 176–77, 191, 247, 283

iron 67–68

kinship, fratriarchal 39

legend 3, 21–24
locative adverbial postposition 27, 177, 228
lyric 20

metaphor 27–28
meter 25, 28
mimation 61, 191, 206
monologue 6, 94, 203–4
myth 20, 21–22

narrative element 23–24
narrative mode 20, 24, 246
narrative poetry 6
narrative statement 24
narrative voice 23
  first-person 19–20, 33–34, 223, 231, 246, 259, 267, 296
  second-person 203
  third-person 6, 78, 94, 203, 223–24, 231
narrator 23, 33, 58, 78, 104, 174, 223, 296

narû-literature 16–21, 266
nunation 35

omen literature 3–4, 57, 69, 71–72, 98, 131, 173, 179, 272, 295-96, 321, 323, 325
orality 6

panegyric poetry 6, 203
parallelism 29, 37, 61, 107, 268, 276, 283, 299
plene writing 26, 95, 106, 176, 205, 233, 239, 283
prophecy 17
prose 6, 231
prosody 27–28, 176–77, 299

quatrain 28–29, 207

reading out 24
repetition 29, 61, 81, 207, 247, 268, 299
rhetorical question 36–37, 204
rhyme 26, 269
rhythm 25, 28
ring composition 27, 191, 268

sandhi-writing 66, 183
stanza 29, 37, 95 207, 247
stich 28, 61
story element 23
story space 24
story time 24, 33, 296

tercet 28, 207, 299
terminative adverbial postposition 27, 95, 177, 184, 191, 206, 215, 228, 283
trochee 26, 299

Plates

Text 1

MLC 641

Text 2

i ii

B: K. 4470

Text 2

A: K. 3401+ Sm. 2118

C: K. 7249

Text 2

D: BM 47449 Obverse

D: BM 47449 Reverse

Text 5

VAT 17166

Text 6

i ii

AO 6702 Obverse

Text 6

iv iii

AO 6702 Reverse

Text 7

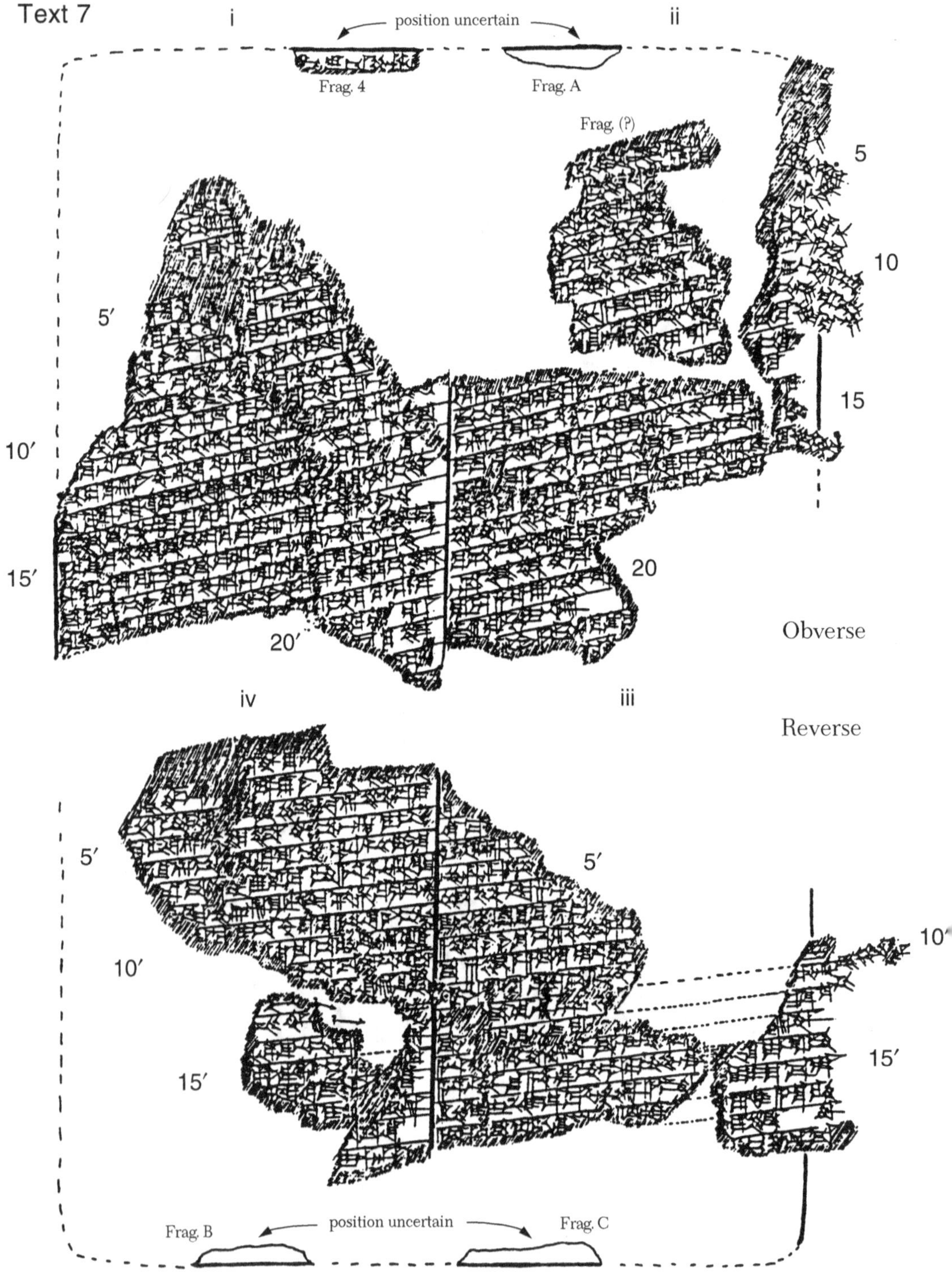

IM 52684A + 52684B + 52305 + fragments
reassembled on the basis of the copy by J. J. A. van Dijk, TIM IX 48

Text 8

Obverse

Reverse

8A: UM 29-13-688

Text 8

Obverse

Edge

Reverse

Side

8B: St. Étienne 150

Text 8B

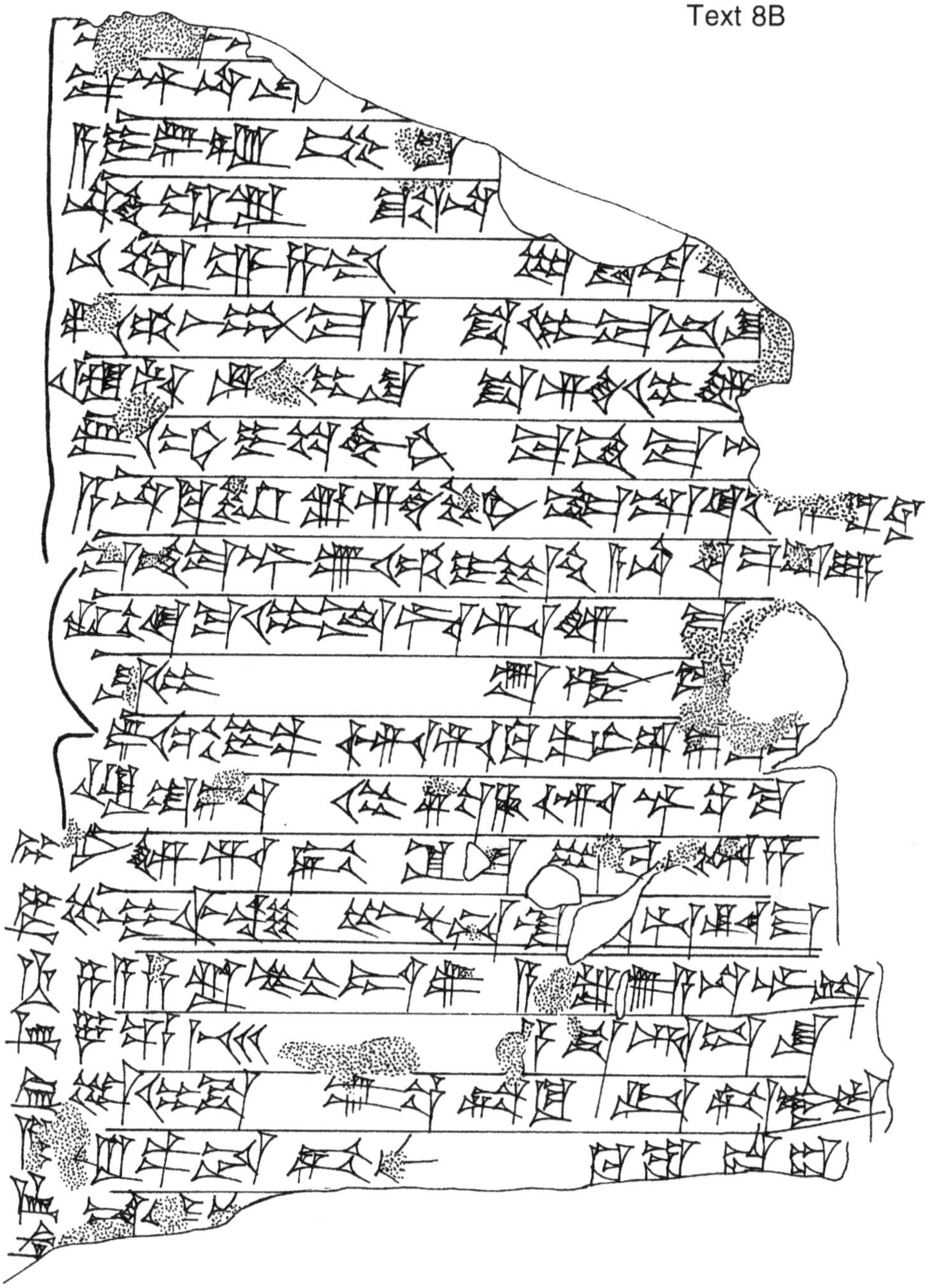

8B: St. Étienne 150
(copy by A. Millard)

Text 9D

VAT 10290

Text 10

Obverse

CBS 15217

Text 12

ii

i

BM 139965

iii

vi v iv

Text 13

BM 120003 Obverse

Edge

Text 13

BM 120003 Reverse

Text 14

L. 74.225 side a

Text 14

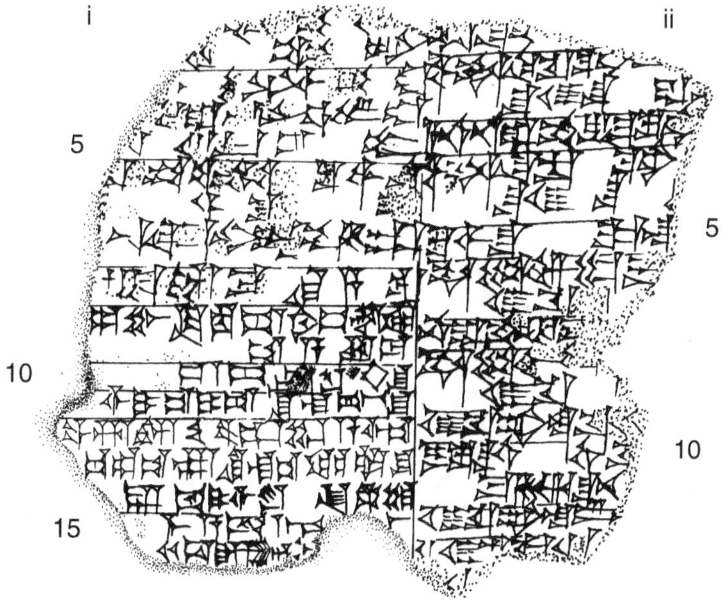

L. 74.225 side a

Text 14

iii iv

L. 74.225 side b

iii iv **Text 14**

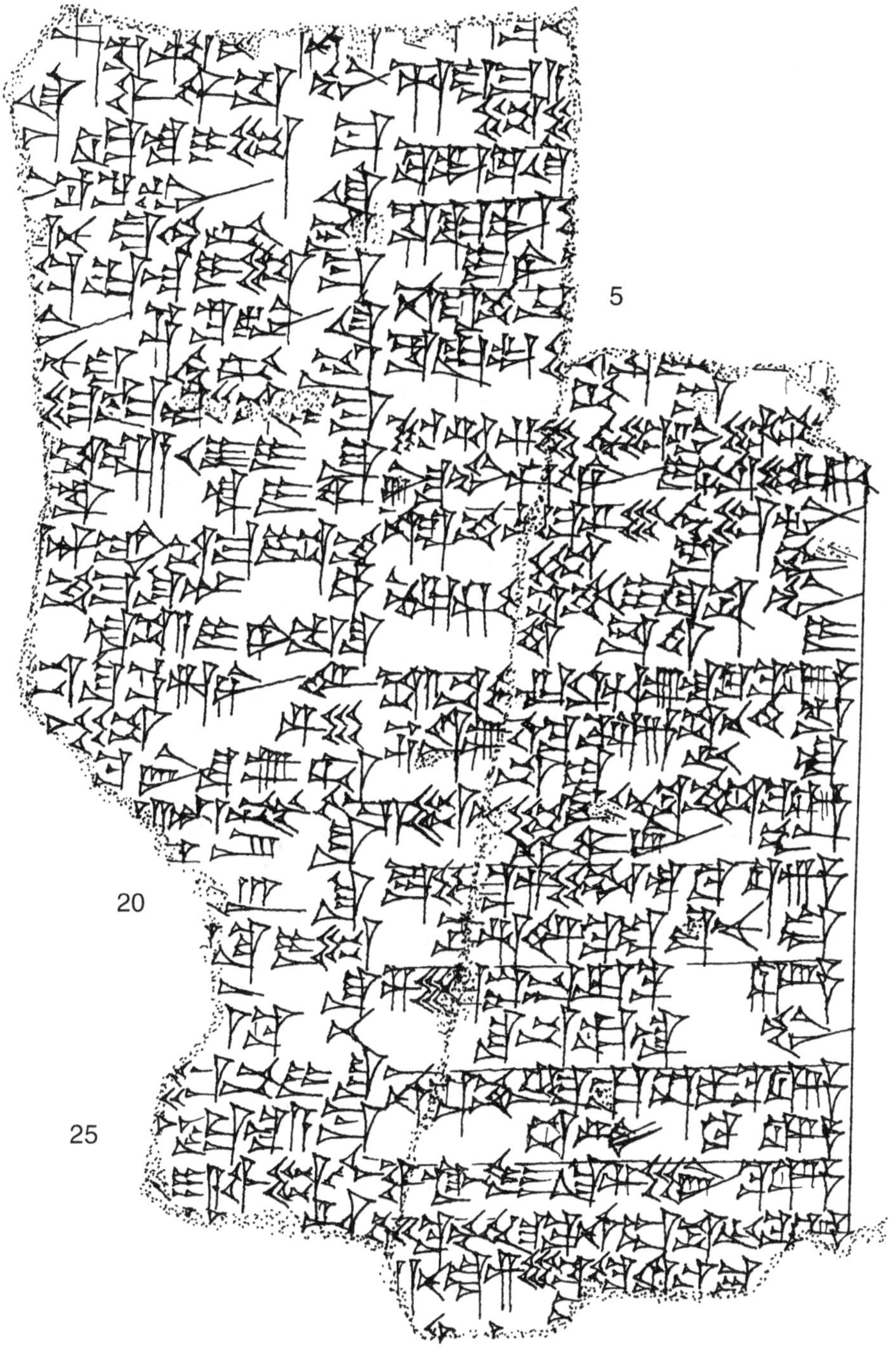

L. 74.225 side b

Text 14

v vi

L. 74.225 side c

Text 14

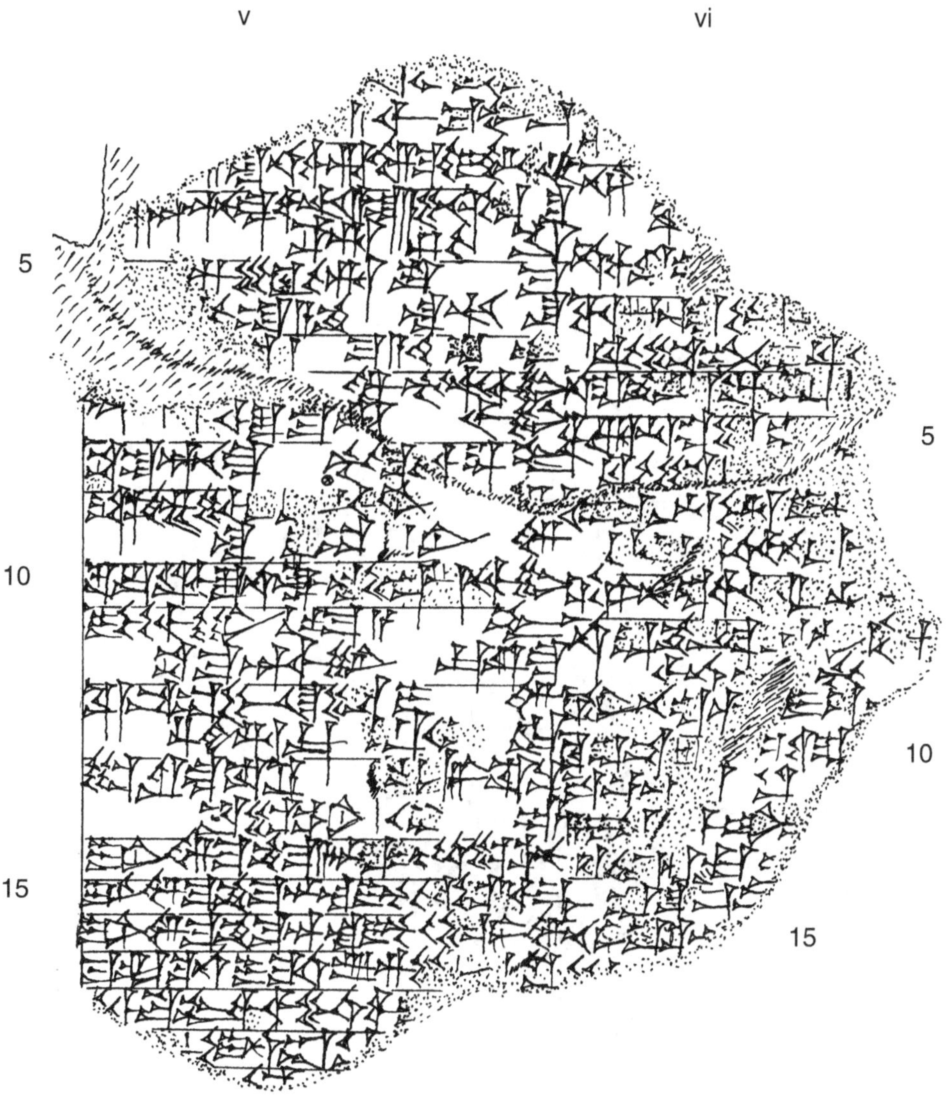

L. 74.225 side c

Text 14

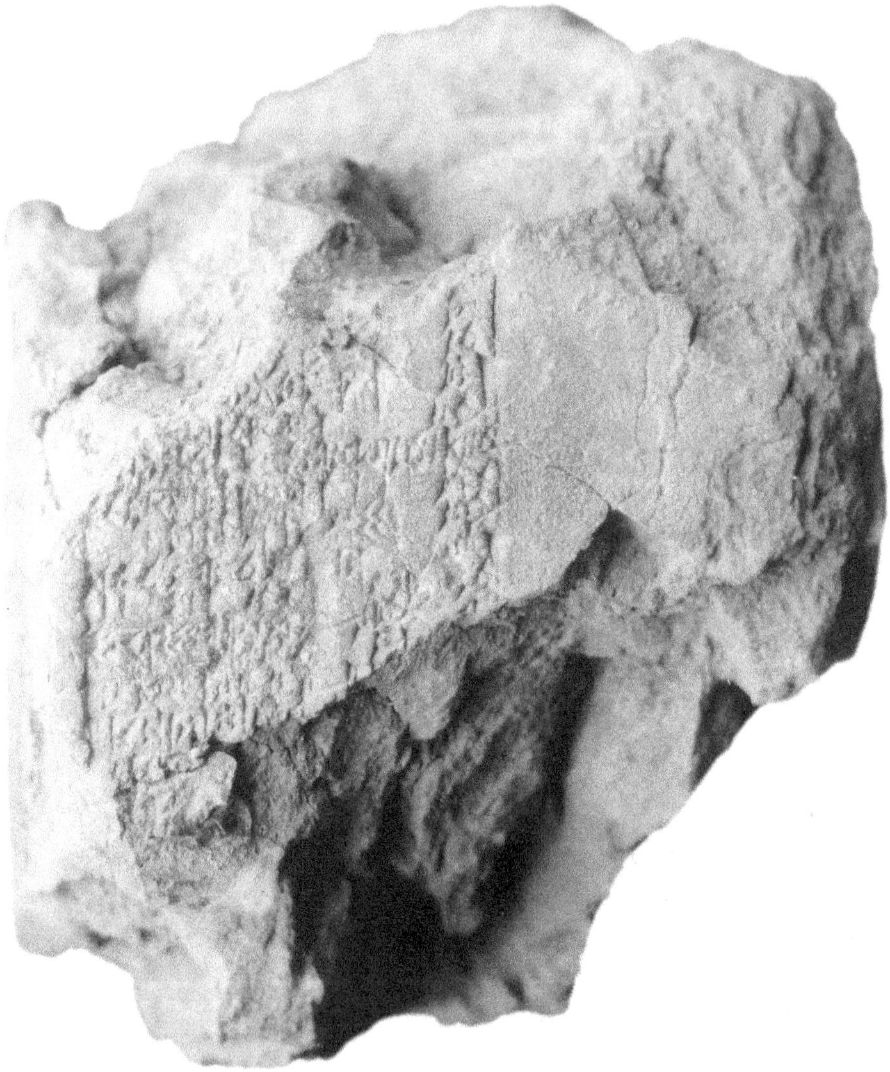

L. 74.225 side d

Text 14

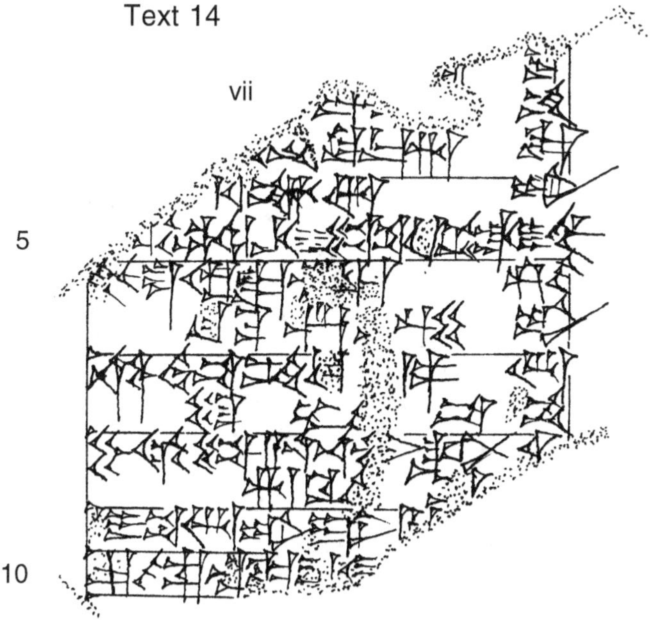

L. 74.225 side d

L. 74.225 fragments

Text 15

TA 1931, 729

Obverse

Reverse

Side

Text 15

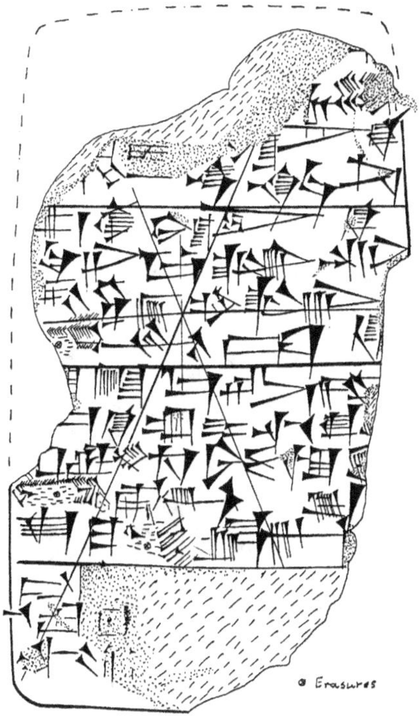

TA 1931, 729

Obverse

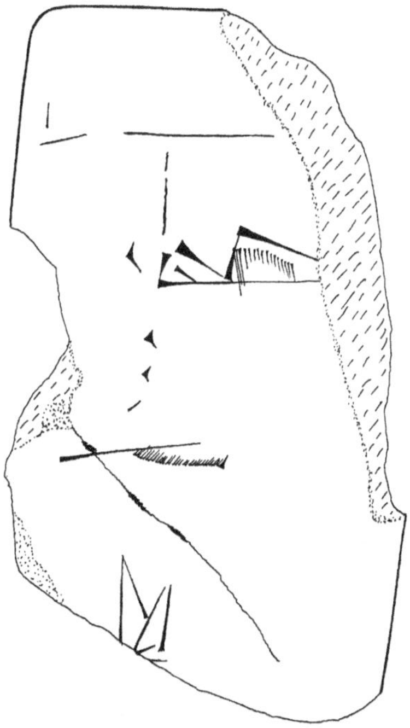

Reverse
(copies by A. Westenholz)

Side

Text 16A

A 1252 Obverse

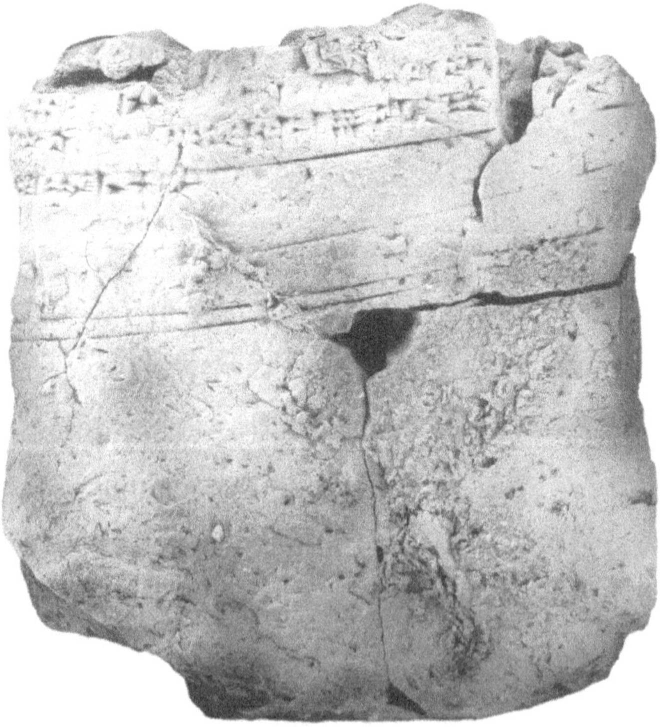

Reverse

Text 19

Obverse

Right Edge

Reverse

VAT 7832a

Text 20A

MLC 1364

ii iii

Obverse

v iv

Reverse

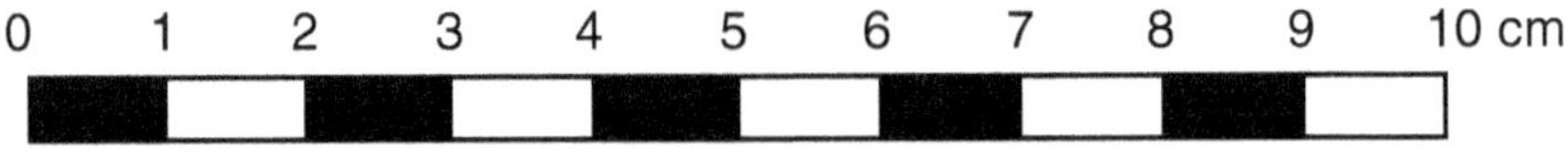

Text 22

i ii

A: 81-2-4, 219

Obverse

iii

iv

Reverse

Text 22

i ii

B: K. 5418a

Obverse

iv iii

Reverse

Text 22

B: K. 5418a

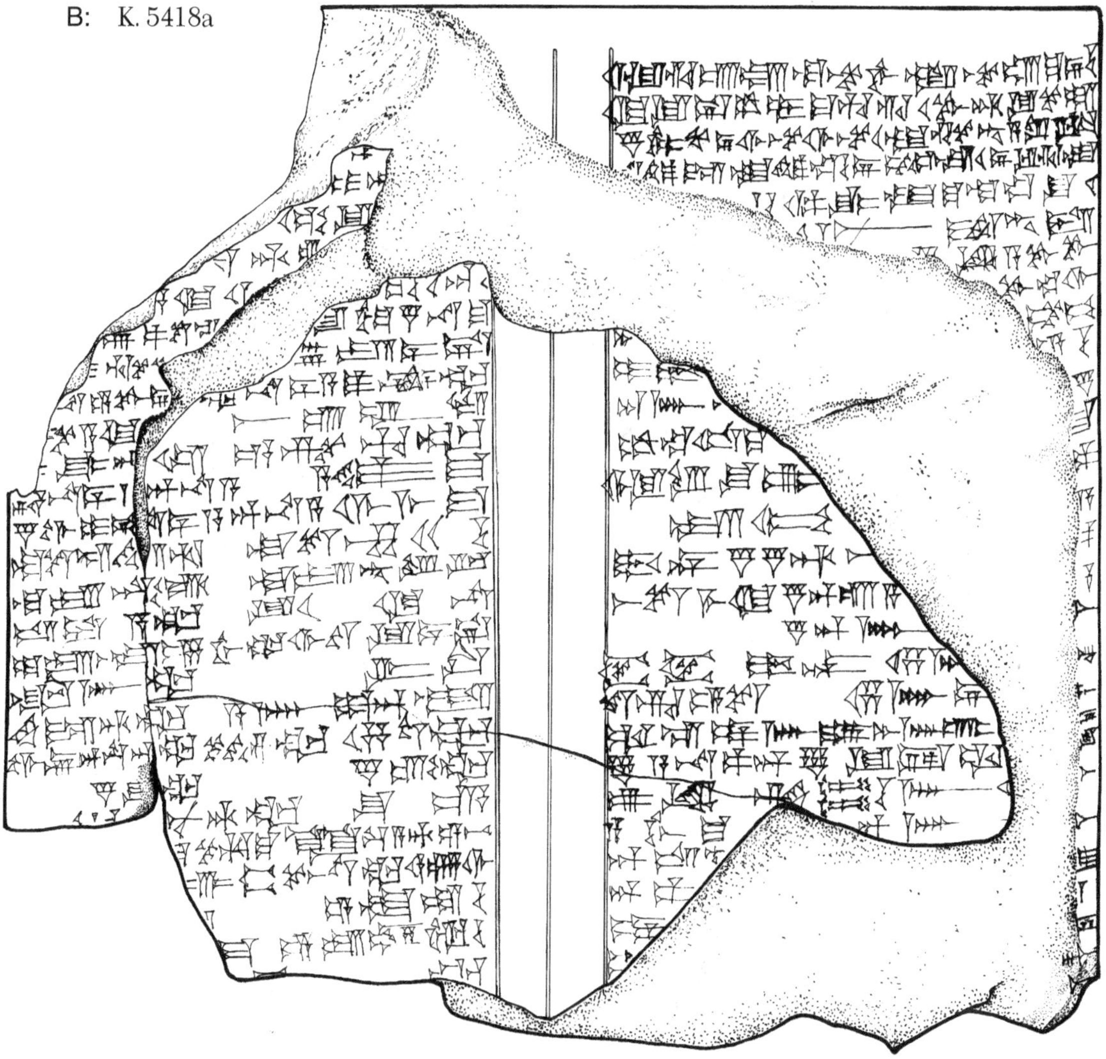

Reverse

Text 22

C: K. 5640

i

Obverse

iv

Reverse

D: K. 8582

Text 22

E: K. 2021B

i ii

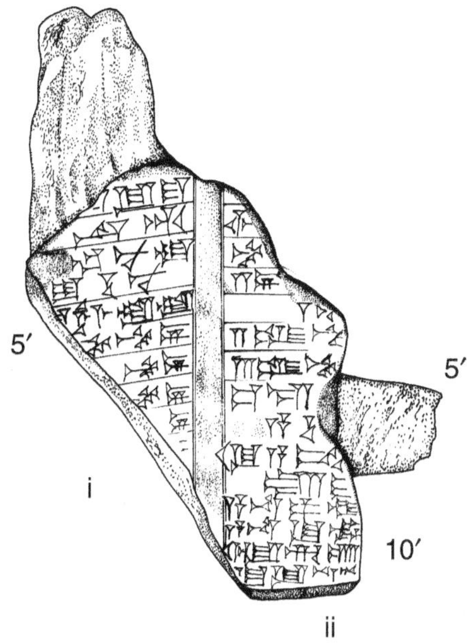

F: K. 13328

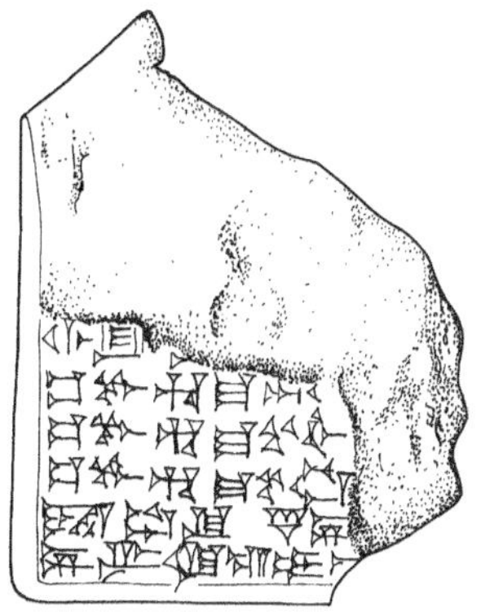

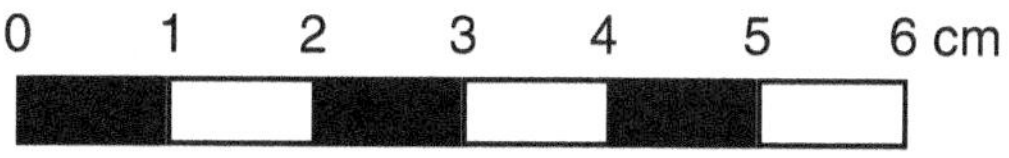

Text 22

H: Ash. 1924.2085

www.ingramcontent.com/pod-product-compliance
Lightning Source LLC
Chambersburg PA
CBHW051358070526
44584CB00023B/3210
9781575063119